D'ANNUNZIO

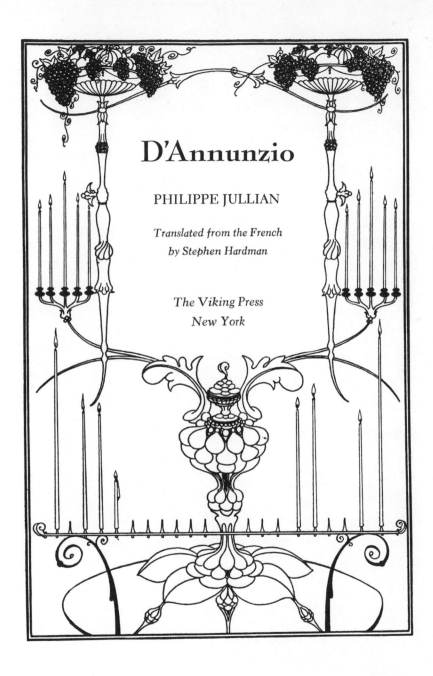

D'Annunzio

PHILIPPE JULLIAN

*Translated from the French
by Stephen Hardman*

The Viking Press
New York

Originally published as *D'Annunzio*
© 1971 by Librairie Arthème Fayard, Paris
Translation Copyright © 1972 by Pall Mall Press

All rights reserved

Published in 1973 by The Viking Press, Inc.
625 Madison Avenue, New York, N.Y. 10022

SBN 670-25603-x

Library of Congress catalog card number: 72-78981

Printed in U.S.A. by The Book Press

To Nancy Mitford

Acknowledgements

D'Annunzio wrote more than ten thousand letters, most of them carefully preserved by his correspondents; he was frequently photographed and his books have been published in a variety of editions, many of them illustrated and very rare. Many persons who knew him are still alive and have vivid memories of this man, who dazzled some and antagonized others. He is constantly mentioned in the memoirs of his contemporaries. I therefore wish to express my gratitude both to collectors of d'Annunzian mementoes and to those in Italy and in France who have been kind enough to talk to me about their memories of the poet.

I must express my deep gratitude to Her Majesty Queen Maria José, a great admirer of the poet, who in two long conversations described to me her visit to the Vittoriale and defined the political position of the Comandante.

I was most warmly received at the Vittoriale degli Italiani by its director, Professor Mariano, and his assistants, who placed their archives at my disposal and allowed me to visit the most secret rooms of that dwelling.

In Rome, Professor Mario Praz offered me much advice, gave me access to the archives of the Primoli Collection and allowed me to reproduce some unpublished photographs. Signor Ferdinando Gerra, a commentator of d'Annunzio's works, gave me the benefit of his erudition and allowed me access to his collections. Count Borromeo d'Adda described a visit to the Vittoriale with his mother, as did Baron Rafaello de Banfield. In Florence, Count Tancredi talked to me about d'Annunzio, whom he had known as a student, and Baron Rappizardi gave me access to his precious collections.

In Turin, Signor Aldo Caputto allowed me to consult documents on his grandfather, Sommaruga, the poet's first publisher, and Signor Mirandola to refer to his most interesting study on Proust and d'Annunzio. The director of the college at Prato kindly arranged for me to be shown round the place where the poet was educated and to see the books which had belonged to him.

The late Violet Trefusis provided me with the hospitality of her villa at Bellosguardo throughout the period of my researches in Italy and introduced me to some Florentine friends of the poet.

In London, Lady Moera Blake lent me some documents on her grandmother, the Marchesa Casati; Mr. Raymond Mortimer gave me details of English works on d'Annunzio.

In France, I must first of all thank MM. Guy Tosi and Pierre de Montera, the leading specialists on d'Annunzio. M. Tosi, in addition to offering much advice, made available to me books that would otherwise have been unobtainable and gave me permission to quote his studies on d'Annunzio's relations with Anna de Noailles, Anatole France and Romain Rolland. M. de Montera has guided my researches into the poetic works and French friendships of d'Annunzio.

M. André Malraux, in the course of a conversation, clarified certain aspects of d'Annunzio in a most striking fashion and recalled his meeting with the poet as a young man.

Mme. Simone described to me the man whom she knew well, with the verve and depth of judgement characteristic of her memoirs, and provided me with some unpublished anecdotes. The late Miss Nathalie Barney talked to me of the less attractive side of the legend. M. Benoist-Méchin read to me and commented upon his unpublished recollections of a visit to the Vittoriale. The former Mme. Hubin spoke to me at length in the house that d'Annunzio helped her to choose, near Chantilly, and showed me the photographs which she took of the poet in England and in Venice. The late Don Antonio de Gandarillas recalled visits to the Vittoriale and spoke to me of his two friends, the Marchesa Casati and the Duchess de Gramont. Princess Bibesco recalled d'Annunzio's rather unsuccessful encounters with her, under the aegis of Montesquiou, when she was a young married woman. A granddaughter of Ernesta Stern talked to me about her extraordinary grandmother. Mr. Aubry, of New York, who had been in d'Annunzio's squadron, spoke to me of his memories of the poet during the war. M. Paul Lorenz described his recollections of Ida Rubinstein and of a curious encounter with the poet. Signor

Spadolini, the celebrated dancer, told me of the time when he stayed at the Vittoriale as a young man. M. Jean Chuzeville, the eminent translator, has helped me to place d'Annunzio in relation to the other Italian writers of the same generation. Mme. Fourgette talked to me about the d'Annunzio she knew as a young girl in the southwest of France.

The author was fortunate enough to obtain a number of unpublished documents. The most important of these were the Journal and the letters of Miss Romaine Brooks. Mme. Albert Henraux allowed me to refer to the unpublished Journal of her husband, a great admirer of Eleonora Duse, and M. Bréal, the ambassador, provided me with information and documents concerning his aunt, Mme. Romain Rolland.

A number of persons have asked me, for family reasons, not to quote the source of the information which they have so kindly given me, and not to mention certain episodes in the emotional life of the poet. There were so many other such episodes in the life of d'Annunzio that I willingly bowed to this request.

I am especially grateful to Mme. Hélène de Wendel, whose commentaries on the numerous passages from the *Libro segreto* which have been used in this book clarified certain mysterious aspects of the life of the poet.

Mme. Tristan Vieljeux has made a very careful study of d'Annunzio's handwriting, which also reveals some unexpected aspects of his character. The Italian Institute in Paris kindly lent me several works otherwise unobtainable in France.

The publisher and myself wish to thank the firm of Mondadori of Milan and the publishing houses of Calmann-Lévy and Pierre Seghers of Paris for their permission to quote numerous passages from the works of d'Annunzio; Doubleday & Co., Inc. for permission to quote from *L'Innocent*, *Il Fuoco*, and *Gioconda*; David Higham Associates, Ltd., for permission to quote from *Noble Essences* by Osbert Sitwell.

We would also like to thank Mr. Stephen Hardman for the care and effort which he has put into translating this biography.

Contents

List of Illustrations

xiii

Introduction

The end of the last century produced a number of remarkable beings whose extravagances, while reminiscent of Romanticism, proved even more bizarre, for they belonged to a generation which proclaimed itself 'decadent'. Affectations hitherto unparalleled, a cult of Beauty and a partiality for those who exemplified Beauty, an unbelievable seriousness, a preposterous fantasy and an impudence that was sometimes heroic—all these are qualities which the subjects of the author's previous studies, Montesquiou, Wilde and Sarah Bernhardt, possessed in common with the subject of the present book. Yet Gabriele d'Annunzio alone succeeded in living his wildest dreams: ugly, he was irresistible; a petty bourgeois, he became a prince; a worldly aesthete, he was a hero and dictator. This he achieved because of his prodigious vitality, certainly, but also because, absolutely sure of his own genius and quite untrammelled by scruples or by a sense of humour, he embodied the myth of the closing nineteenth century, the Nietzschean superman with the heroism and the crudity inherent in that concept. D'Annunzio may be less attractive to us than Montesquiou or Wilde, whom it was possible to mock while retaining a certain sympathy for them; his genius did indeed sometimes reveal itself in ways which nowadays seem laughable, but which it would be unjust to scorn. E. M. Forster, probably as far removed from d'Annunzio as a writer could be, recognized him as a true hero and a true poet, but also pronounced him a 'cad'. This life of d'Annunzio will take into consideration both the legend of the 'poet and hero' and the reputation that earned him the epithet 'cad'. A reputation is rather like a work written in collaboration between an individual and his *milieu;* each makes a contribution and the result is rarely the truth. If the reputation is a bad one, the individual blames his collaborator, the public. D'Annunzio's reputation was execrable. The audacities of his youth aroused indignation and the political aberrations of his old age provoked contempt. But a reputation is part of the man and must be taken into account in any faithful portrait. The author has therefore called attention both to calumnies and to justified accusations, while striving to avoid excusing one by the other. And then, there is a French saying: 'Truth on the other side of the Alps, untruth on this side.' However close to France the Italy of sixty years ago might be, the rules of life there were very different from those north of the Alps. To avoid moralizing, the author has consequently referred frequently to the brilliant book by Barzini, *The Italians,* for an explanation of certain aspects of behaviour that might astonish the non-Italian reader.

Similarly, in studying a literary achievement that has suffered much at the hands of time and the greatest beauties of which can be appreciated only by Italians, it would be futile to emphasize the borrowings and the failures. Rather than a series of pastiches, as his enemies have described it, the work of d'Annunzio was the emanation of his time, above all of the Decadent movement which occupied the latter years of the nineteenth century, and which he prolonged until the eve of the last war.

For the Italians of today, d'Annunzio was too closely connected with Fascism. They prefer not to speak of him. His lyricism is outmoded, his sense of splendour odious to a literature of the Left. Some say that he was mad, a theory which graphology does not contradict. If so, he was a madman who thought he was d'Annunzio, to parody Cocteau's *mot* concerning Victor Hugo. Those who take an interest in him, as Professor Praz has pointed out, seek out the shadows and the mystery, turning their backs on what they consider to be plaster glories. Indeed, this is precisely what the author would have done, had he not discovered that sometimes these glories were of marble and in a fine Baroque style.

Prosperous modern Italy, where leisure-hours are occupied by cars and television, has no place for heroic example or reckless love-affairs. It is extraordinary that the walls of the Capitol carry not a single plaque commemorating a famous speech by d'Annunzio, that the majority of the great cities, including Milan, should have renamed their former Piazza Gabriele d'Annunzio, and that in Rome only an alley leading up to the Pincio still bears his name. This unique example of a country being ashamed of one of its greatest writers is a clear reflection of the mediocrity of Christian Democracy. For other Europeans, moreover, d'Annunzio's patriotism and his abhorrence of the Germans have, over the years, come to be regarded as parochial chauvinism. The tendency is thus to look on him as an excellent tenor who sang only bad operas. Those who knew d'Annunzio say that his conversation displayed a prodigiously lyrical invention. It therefore seemed to the author that an abundant use of quotations would help to set the tone of an existence that was always excessively literary.

D'Annunzio was the first writer to exalt the two myths of sun and speed. The aeroplane and the automobile occupied an immensely important place both in his life and in his work. He adored horses, dogs and the sea, at a time when most writers shut themselves up in their rooms. In his tastes, and also in his scandalous love-affairs and his heroic enterprises, only Lord Byron can be compared with him. But Byron was handsome, of high birth, and nothing about him suggests effort, while d'Annunzio's life was a succession of perilous leaps which succeeded, but only just. And then, Byron died young. Our poet, mindful of his legend, did his utmost to avoid reaching old age.

Which was the true d'Annunzio, behind so many roles so brilliantly performed—the aesthete, the aviator, the magician, the lover and the demagogue? Professor Praz has probably discovered the truth in recalling that the poet came from a primitive district, the Abruzzi. To d'Annunzio, Florence no less than Paris was a fascinating foreign city which had to be conquered: 'Culturally he was a parvenu, like a barbarian borne onto the throne of Byzantium who immediately covers himself with jewellery.' Professor Praz adds: 'This barbarian was also a decadent; he lacked that temperate zone of culture which we call humanity.'

The Barbarian-Poet's residence, the Vittoriale, is a mausoleum filled with the spoils of an entire lifetime. No less than the poet's works and the witness of those who knew him, this monument, both revealing and disconcerting, explains the motive principles of a career which the reader will find either absurd or sublime, according to whether or not he takes as his standpoint the mediocrity of the present time. D'Annunzio, the slightly ridiculous hero of a Europe weary of heroism, seems to have lived again in recent years, in the person of Yukio Mishima, whose suicide was a condemnation of a Japan that has become materialist. How strong a resemblance there is between the great oriental writer, who with his militia aimed to give back to his country an outmoded honour, and the man who at Fiume confronted the democracies: the same narcissism (though the Japanese, unlike the Italian, was certainly a very handsome man), evident in photographs which suggest museum postcards, like deliciously tortured St. Sebastians, and the images of the fetishist, but in which the hero wears boots and rides a motor-cycle; the same Nietzschean attitude, the same pederastic tendency repressed in cruel affairs with women, the same fecundity. These two men, both disciples of beauty and courage, separated by half a century, were disturbing reincarnations of the breed that was thought to have vanished a hundred years ago—the great Romantics.

D'ANNUNZIO

1

The Hope
of Pescara

In the middle of the nineteenth century Italy had experienced
some years of exaltation. The conspiracies, uprisings and battles
of the three Romantic decades had borne fruit: the Austrians had
been driven out; the dynasties, tyrannical in varying degress, had
been swept aside, and the Church had been given cause for alarm.
The capture of Rome in 1871 crowned half a century of effort.
The red shirt of Garibaldi, the frock-coat of Cavour and the
plume of Victor Emmanuel became, in the popular imagination,
inseparable from a sublime and familiar myth that had furnished
a host of heroes and thinkers. Glories such as these inspired Italians with the desire, now that they had become a single country,
to become a very great nation. The Risorgimento had been one
of the most soul-stirring movements in history. Its actors had gone
to their deaths singing, like the heroes of the operas which they
loved so deeply. They destroyed the wicked and acclaimed the
liberators to melodies from *Il Trovatore* and *Rigoletto*. Until the
moment of unification, the love of fatherland was almost wholly
undisturbed by politics, despite the differences between the king

3

and Garibaldi, and there was no shadow cast by gratitude to a foreign power, for the help given by Napoleon III to the beleaguered Pius IX effaced the memory of Solferino and his support of Piedmont against Austria.

As soon as peace was established, parties made their appearance and engaged in the struggle for influence. The Right, after imposing the House of Savoy on Italy, retained power, while the Left grouped itself round Garibaldi. The Right, composed of landowners and industrialists of the North, was intellectual, upright and liberal. The Left strove to combine the ideal of 1848 with the practice of commerce. Thus, the fall of the Right after the elections of March 1876 seemed, according to Benedetto Croce, 'a proof of moral weakness in the Italian people'. In the first decade of the new kingdom it was seen that the ideal of the Risorgimento was far removed from the reality, that, despite her glory, Italy was only a second-rank power, that political Rome was nothing by comparison with religious Rome and that the Italians, after having held the attention of Europe for three or four decades, had no longer any great contribution to make to humanity.

The politicians had none of the prestige that the liberators had enjoyed. Montecitorio, the seat of the Chamber of Deputies, rapidly became the principal centre of intrigues in the kingdom. The same failure was encountered abroad: Bismarck humoured the Italians only to annoy the Holy See, without offering them anything except an alliance with the Austria they hated; later, he tricked them out of Tunisia, which he presented to France. Apart from William II, no sovereign would agree to visit the king of Italy in his new capital, in order to avoid antagonizing the Church. But this did not mean that the new state was regarded with favour by those countries in the process of becoming democracies. The franchise was still restricted, public education was totally neglected in the South and, in spite of arbitrary confiscations, the priests, who could be considered 'obscurantists', retained almost as much importance as in Spain. Yet there was no class struggle; this began only at the very end of the century, with the spread of industrialization. In a still paternalist society, the struggle for influence was fought between two groups whose way of life was largely the same: the clericals and the Freemasons (the latter played quite an important part in ministerial activity). The ministers who followed one another in quick succession wisely adopted the advice of Victor Emmanuel: 'No one should be refused a cigar or a cross of knighthood.'

Italy thus seemed condemned to remain a vast museum, the sanctuary of a Church that despised its government, and so poor that every year nearly half a million inhabitants had to emigrate. In order to cut a *bella figura*, it was necessary to fall back on memories. Throughout the peninsula a craze for erecting monuments manifested itself: swaggering bronzes and marble allegories in which the sculptors returned to the gesticulation of the Baroque. In their historical tableaux painters imitated the colour and movement of opera. Italy had its equivalent of Alma-Tadema and Millais as a consolation for no longer having a Raphael. These painters were masters of their craft, and their works, to be found in the forgotten rooms of museums, should be seen if one is to obtain an idea both of the illusions and of the realities of Italian life between 1870 and 1890; on the one hand, canvases of grandiose inspiration, usually military in theme, and on the other, scenes of popular life. Artists such as Favretto in Venice and Morelli in Naples embellished the sordid with all the picturesque adornment that attracted tourists; often, cultivated Italians saw their compatriots through the eyes of those English ladies who strolled along with Baedekers in their hands. This theatrical art overshadowed the delightful school of the Tuscan Intimists (*Macchiauoli*), who had a close affinity with the French Impressionists.

The same constraints were evident in *belles-lettres*. The moral and patriotic romanticism of the Risorgimento was beginning to pall. The novel had for long been monopolized by feeble imitators of Manzoni, the stage by imitators of Sardou. National history was the domain of foreigners—John Addington Symonds, Taine, Mommsen and Burckhardt. Only the young Carducci, whose poems recalled those of the French *Parnassiens*, rose above the

general mediocrity. This eminently patriotic poet, at first a Garibaldian and then a monarchist, was no less bound by frontiers
than were the superficial writers who imitated Heinrich Heine;
the influence of Baudelaire came only later. The best novelists,
such as Verga, who imitated the French realists, used a provincial
Italian that smacked of the soil, by contrast with the more official
and insipid writers who, guided by the ideal of unification, tried
to impose the Tuscan style. Above all, there was no major intellectual centre in a society still divided by the memory of the old
states, more concerned with local quarrels than with general ideas,
except when some chimerical glory was at stake.

Fortunately, music reassured Italy of her genius. Every town
had its opera house; the tenors and sopranos were the only Italians
known abroad. Cultivated Italians, perplexed and bored, felt that
they were living through an interval in the too brightly lit hall of
a decrepit opera house where illusion was no longer possible.
What a disappointment after the sublime act of the Risorgimento! The words of Garibaldi remained engraved in people's
memories side by side with the most famous arias; the king, nicknamed the *galantuomo*, was also a figure in the repertory. The
traitors had been supplied by the reactionaries and even by the
Church; in those exalting and now bygone times, even the vanquished had an awe-inspiring heroine: the beautiful queen of
Naples who for several months, in besieged Gaeta, stood by the
soldiers who went to their deaths for a second-rate cause. Thus,
amid the disappointment that followed victory, the phrase of
Heinrich Heine seemed almost as appropriate as it had been in
the time of the oppressors: 'Music, the sole hope of enslaved
Italy'.

THE ABRUZZI

The former kingdom of the Neapolitan Bourbons, bound to ser-
vile traditions and to a Catholicism whose superstitions stifled
almost all Christian sentiment, was to remain a denial of Italian
unity even up to the present day. The administrators, generally

from the North, considered the South, the *Mezzogiorno*, a kind
of Africa, difficult to colonize and condemned to poverty and
paganism. The land belonged to feudal families each branch of
which bore two or three princely titles and who resided in Naples,
mourning for the days of Bourbon splendour. The impecunious
bourgeoisie provided the Church with a great many priests, lived
in miserable towns and sought escape from boredom in politics.
The clergy, hardly less poor, clung to customs of greater interest
to the ethnologist than to the economist. The fishermen and
sailors represented the most active element of a population whose
way of life had changed little since antiquity. The secret societies
occupied a position of great importance, for they brought hope to
this stagnant world, the chance of success to enterprising young
men, and a complicity in feuds of vengeance which still displayed
a tribal violence. With unification, all who wanted to survive
headed for the north; the 'barbarous South' invaded Lombardy
and Tuscany (the same phenomenon is taking place today among
the working class). Lawyers, teachers and mere adventurers were
anxious to abandon a patriarchal régime for a bourgeois régime;
the career of the young d'Annunzio was to provide a dazzling
example of this exodus of the ambitious.

Of all the provinces of the old Neapolitan kingdom, the
Abruzzi remained the least accessible to the benefits of unification. Mountain chains dominated by the Gran Sasso isolated this
province from the Roman states and the agriculturally rich Neapolitan regions. Its only link with the rest of the world was by the
low and sandy Adriatic coast, which gave access to a Venice in
decline, a wild Albania and a poverty-stricken Greece. As a result
of these contacts, the population of the coastal region was of
fairly mixed blood; on the other hand, no exotic element tainted
the customs of the hinterland and the folklore of the Abruzzi
remained one of the most original in Europe. On the first Thurs-
day in May, the snake festival was celebrated at Coculla; the
festival of San Pantaleone at Miglianico attracted the hernia
sufferers of the province. For the procession of the Madonna of
Casalbordino, an indigent population covered itself with spangles

and carried multi-coloured statues, each village vociferously lauding the glory of its saint. The most famous painting of Italy around the year 1880, *The Vow* by Michetti (a native of Pescara fifteen years older than d'Annunzio, on whom he was to have a great influence), depicts a tribe of villagers who, in reparation for a crime, are seen licking the floor of the church as they crawl towards the miraculous statue. From time to time a religious visionary would traverse the countryside predicting the end of the world, accompanied by ragged peasants who had burned their homes to follow him; the last of these visionaries, kept in confinement, was still alive when d'Annunzio was born. At the gates of the town of Pescara a druid-like creature practised prophecy in a cottage shaded by an oak-tree, 'a veritable sorcerer's cave with its crude Christian idols of clay'. This bone-setter cured herds, but his wife was an abortionist. In the mountain areas superstitions became more fanatical; villages would cut one another's throats for a silver saint; when the bearer of a miraculous statue had his hand crushed by the idol, he severed the hand and offered it to the saint. There were men resembling fakirs, 'half-naked *zingari* who travel across the countryside on red asses'; the blind Mugio, who sang folk-myths and accompanied himself on the clarinet; the 'Caterpillar', an old woman who found lost objects; forgotten hermits in abandoned monasteries, visionary nuns. These holy persons were surrounded by maimed beggars with repulsive deformities, simple of mind or feigning simpleness. One might almost be in India, judging by d'Annunzio's descriptions of the courts with which these miracle-workers surrounded themselves. Gabriele's childhood was certainly strongly marked by this primitive environment and its poetry. Every Christmas the shepherds would come down from the mountains to Naples and Rome to play the pipes in front of the cribs; they would return with their sacks full of money. These *zampognari* (known further north as *pifferai*) would then appear in the streets of Pescara and play their shepherds' tunes on the public squares.

The Abruzzi is the region of Italy least rich in works of art; it has only a few Romanesque abbeys and Baroque fortresses. The

Renaissance did not reach these towns: in their narrow streets no monument to a pope, a tyrant, or a saint is to be found; they had produced no great men, nor had they been able to hold great men for long. At the time of unification, Pescara, beside the river of the same name, was a small town of five to six thousand inhabitants, with a partly silted-up harbour whose only picturesque feature was provided by the multi-coloured sails, triangular on the fishing-boats and rectangular, splashed with red and orange, on the *paronzelle*, heavy barges that moved slowly along the coast. There was a pontoon-bridge, a breakwater, on a promontory a half-ruined fortress that had resisted the assault of the Turks in 1566, and, in the suburbs, barracks that stood three-quarters empty, the old prisons for galley-slaves; the straight streets lined with low houses soon led to the olive-plantations or the *laguna*; seedy-looking inns were dotted here and there over the marshland. A few kilometres away, surrounded by tracts of pine forest, lies the only healthy part of the coast, the beautiful beach of Castellammare, where one can go in the evening to watch the fishermen raising the huge nets called *trabacco* at the end of the wooden jetties. Ortona, the neighbouring town, can pride itself in having a larger citadel and Guardiagrele, situated inland, a Gothic church. The Maiella (the 'mother mountain') towers above the countryside; it is reached along rocky valleys from which wolves are said to emerge in winter. In a region too wild to induce Frederick II to stay there, no monuments are to be found like those left by the German emperors at Lucera and Manfredonia.

In the second half of the nineteenth century the people of Pescara led a sleepy existence (since the last war the town has become an important industrial centre). Sometimes a touring company came to perform opera or comedy. The theatre was a disused hospital. The curtain, the work of a local artist, bore a representation of Pescara surrounded by allegories. There were boxes where the ladies displayed their outmoded costumes. The men in the pit sat on benches borrowed from the school or even from the church. When an actress rose a little above the ordinary, the town lost its head, as happened in the case of Violetta Kutufà, the heroine of one of d'Annunzio's best stories. In the theatre, every Shrove Tuesday, a masked ball was held at which the disreputable elements in the town stirred the curiosity of the respectable inhabitants.

The women, dressed in black, met in church, the men at the café. People opened their houses only for great family occasions; everyone tried to conceal the mediocrity of an existence for which consolation was sought in aristocratic pretensions. All those who used the title 'Don', the mark of notability, in front of their names acted the part of lords, but very few became *commendatore* or even *cavaliere*, for the seat of power lay too far away. 'During the solemn repose of Lent, the inhabitants of Pescara indulged the modest pleasures of scandalmongering and calumny', d'Annunzio was to write. One of the hotbeds of gossip was the Casino, a sort of club where the notables mingled with their parasites (the system of clients established by ancient Rome still existed in the kingdom of Naples). Then there were the professional busybodies: the laundry-women, nurses, poor relations, nuns and alms-collectors who went from house to house peddling news. D'Annunzio was to recall Rosa Catena, a former prostitute who had become a hired mourner, and the garrulous women who prattled about the affairs of others as they hung up their washing at their windows. This was a world belonging to the comedies of Goldoni, but one shaken by bloody dramas when, from beneath the humbug on the surface, the savagery of the race re-emerged.

RAPAGNETTA D'ANNUNZIO

In a house a little taller than the others, with balconies on the first floor and shops occupying the ground floor, a house rather reminiscent of the Casa Bonaparte in Ajaccio, there lived a family which, in the years following the departure of the Bourbons, would have led the same drowsy existence as the other leading families of Pescara, if the father had not attracted attention by his political ambition and his scandalous love-affairs. Just like the *galantuomo* king whom he resembled—large moustache, wavy hair, the broad shoulders of a stevedore and the belly of a debauched monk—Don Francesco Paolo, not content with running after whores, installed them in a lodge which he owned at the gates of the town. If local reports are to be trusted, Don Francesco Paolo used to take bread from the mouths of his legitimate children to feed his bastards and, even worse, as soon as his bastard daughters became nubile, abused them. Even if one allows for an element of calumny in such accusations, Don Francesco Paolo's appetites were of a somewhat monstrous nature, judging by the portrait left by his son in *Il Trionfo della Morte*: 'Fat, florid and powerfully built, this man seemed to emit through every part of his body an inexhaustible warmth of carnal vitality. His very large jaws, his thick-lipped, imperious mouth filled by his vigorous breathing, his restless, rather equivocal eyes, his large, throbbing nose dotted with freckles, every feature of his face bore the stamp of violence and harshness. [. . .] Flesh, this brutal thing, full of veins, nerves, tendons, glands and bones, full of instincts and needs, the flesh that sweats and stinks—this brutal thing which is flesh thrived in him with a kind of impudence.'

He was also smooth-tongued, with a verve and lack of scruples that were as effective in politics as in love. This *brio* cloaked the intrigues of a life that would otherwise have been merely sordid. In his book Barzini reminds us that, for the Italians, 'everything must be made to sparkle, a simple meal, an ordinary transaction, a dreary speech, a cowardly capitulation must be embellished and ennobled with euphemisms, adornments and pathos'. Don Francesco Paolo d'Annunzio carried his head as high as his apparently noble name permitted him, though he had been entitled to that name only since adolescence. In fact, the father of our hero, born Rapagnetta, had been adopted by a bachelor uncle on his mother's side, a certain d'Annunzio who was known as a shipowner, for he possessed a few large boats. This undistinguished name of Rapagnetta was from time to time to be hurled at the poet by his enemies, when he annoyed them with his aristocratic postures. Having at one time been mayor of Pescara and then a provincial councillor, Don Francesco Paolo was in a good position to have the unmelodious 'Rapagnetta' removed from all official documents; moreover, not satisfied with the too common *cavaliere*, he styled himself *commendatore*, though he had never received the decoration which would have entitled him to use that designation.

Naturally, the wife of such a man was a saint. Luisa de Benedictis, known by all the town as Donna Luisetta, came from a better background than her husband. Through her, Gabriele was able to enter into contact with the provincial minor nobility and to make the acquaintance of persons more refined than the Rapagnettas or even the d'Annunzios: 'The other family connection I cherished greatly, especially that of the Onofrii with whom I had a greater affinity, who possessed the beautiful dishes of Francescantonio Grue and claimed title to the fief of Paganica and to the works of art preserved in the ducal town, in particular the stupendous Greek marble unearthed in the ruins of the temple of Hercules—possibly the statue of the naiad named Vera' (*Libro segreto*). A Francesco de Benedictis was a pupil of Guido Reni. The family residence of the Benedictis at Ortona, 'which was like a monastery and a fortress', perhaps assumed an exaggerated majesty in the writer's memory. It was, however, more imposing than the d'Annunzio house, whose sole magnificence consisted of frescoes depicting the story of Ulysses which had been daubed a generation previously.

Small, pretty, resigned as befitted a Christian wife, Donna Luisetta gave all her love to her children: a son who emigrated as a young man to the United States, three daughters (one did not marry for lack of a dowry, the other two made ordinary marriages) and, finally, the son born on 12 March 1863 who received the Christian names of Gabriele, Michele, Raffaele and Ugo—no less than three archangels to watch over the newcomer: 'He [Gabriele's father] uttered my name, only my name . . . "Gabriele". It was from him that I received the name "*pien d'annunzio*" [i.e. "full of signs"]. When I was born I was almost gagged to death; indeed, I was unable to cry. I would not have been able to draw the first breath of life if prompt and expert hands had not broken the knots and severed this extinguishing cord. During the first years of childhood I wore round my neck, wrapped in a piece of silk, this strange ligature which my family's ancient superstition considered propitious' (*Libro segreto*). 'You were born in March and on a Friday. Who knows what great things you will do!' declared his mother when, not without difficulty, the infant was taken from her breast. Later, Gabriele took pleasure in relating how he was born in the middle of the Adriatic on one of the ships belonging to his family. For the purposes of legend, a tempest was better than the vast, barely furnished house with shutters nearly always closed, where he took his first steps.

Small, but vigorous and exceptionally precocious, the child was pampered by a household of women—his nurse, his sisters and his grandmother; to send him to sleep his grandmother told him stories 'while through his closed eyelids his dream among the flowers followed a joyous dance of light and resplendent phantoms'. There were also two aunts, two old maids who lived on the upper floor and divided their time between devotion and gluttony. There was a mysterious uncle who played the violin and ended by killing himself in a room which thereafter was a forbidden place; the women crossed themselves whenever his name was mentioned and went in fear of his ghost. The entire household lived in close familiarity with the irrational—stories of miracles, cures worked by bone-setters, charms given by sorceresses. In addition to his frightful cord, the child wore scapularies, medals blessed by some convent sibyl and, of course, the coral branch as protection against the evil eye. He believed that a goblin called Mazzamoriello hid in the woodshed and watched all his movements, if only to help him to find things he had lost. In short, he was plunged into what sociologists call the prelogical mentality; all his life d'Annunzio was to believe in portents, visiting fortune-tellers, even devoting himself to magic and cultivating countless little superstitions. His Catholic education was to be merely a poetic veneer, a rhetoric superimposed on this pagan foundation.

Religion certainly gave a rhythm to the daily life of the little town, as the church bells summoned people to masses, benedictions and funerals; at each season of the year ceremonies were held in which the parishes tried to excel one another in brilliance, with processions that led to squabbles between different districts. Inculcated with Church Latin at an early age, d'Annunzio was often to use this language to emphasize the ridiculous or sordid aspect of certain episodes. With a taste for sacrilege that was aroused by his first erotic experiences, he was to recall the moments of physical contact in crowded churches, the secret meetings in deserted churches—but never the slightest religious respect. The contrariness and perverseness of the young Gabriele show that, impervious to the morality of Catholicism, he acquired his contempt for the conventions of a ridiculous society and for all delicacy of feeling in these early years. Born into a race that lived apart from civilization, d'Annunzio gloried in belonging to a primitive world which he was to endow with heroic dimensions in his drama *La Figlia di Iorio*. The dedication of this play reads: 'To all my dead, to all my race by sea and mountain, this poem of an ancient blood is dedicated.' He was to describe the type characteristic of the Abruzzi thus: 'A vigorous profile, of a radiant olive hue, the pure Greek lines of the nose and chin standing out against the Latin fullness of the face.' This was a masculine beauty in which the women had little share; d'Annunzio saw the peasant women as 'almost dwarfs, with snub noses and flattened lips, Kaffir women with white skins'. The ladies of society, flabby and pallid behind their closed shutters, were regarded no more favourably. The most elegant, Teodolinda, looked like 'a young monkey with a powdered face and a red fringe'. Only the daughter of a mason, 'la Ciccarina', radiated a beauty 'above the fashion'. To these two Gabriele addressed his first declarations of love.

A CHILD PRODIGY

'When your nurse offered you her right breast, you demanded the left one simply to annoy her.' This was a habit of which Donna Luisetta was to remind the son whom she had nicknamed the *Lupetto della Maiella* ('the wolf-cub of the Maiella'). Gabriele's contrariness was thus quick to manifest itself, and the women who surrounded the child were reluctant to provoke him, for he would immediately throw a dreadful fit of temper; they preferred to give in to the caprices of this lively but delicate boy. His intelligence soon astounded the two old maids charged with teaching him the alphabet, Ermenegilda and Adele Del Gado. These aged and pretentious ladies were horrified to find themselves portrayed in one of the most cruel stories which the little world of Pescara inspired in the young writer. Their empty nonsense certainly lacked the element of the fantastic which he found in the tales of the peasants who came with their meagre rents, as it lacked the comic attraction of the gossips who came hawking petty scandals, inflated out of all proportion, and frightful stories of abortions, cut-throat friars and depraved priests. The tales written by the young d'Annunzio reveal a grotesque quality in the manner of Gogol, for the world in which he was brought up bore a certain resemblance to that of the Russian provinces. There, too, a thin veneer of civilization had been laid over a base of superstition and pettiness. But in d'Annunzio pity is to be observed only in a few sentimental episodes, and during the war. His provincial world is totally devoid of generosity. He remembered it with the scorn of one who has made his way and who looks back towards his native land only to make fun of his compatriots. On the other hand, he was to retain an immense tenderness for the beauty spots and the plant-life of the Abruzzi.

Don Francesco Paolo, whose vanity was gratified by his son's rapid progress, soon entrusted him to two teachers of a much higher intellectual level than the Del Gado ladies, and who were also not slow to spread the news of Gabriele's extraordinary intelligence around the town. These diocesan priests possessed a solid classical culture; they set their pupil to work learning Latin, and before long Gabriele was translating the most difficult authors and able to memorize entire poems without difficulty. This clerical education left d'Annunzio with a gift for a liturgical style; traces of a sacred and even visionary eloquence are to be found in his most pagan works. Italy is the land of child prodigies, for there the first manifestations of talent are generally respected instead of being regarded as mere childish tricks; the examples of Raphael and Rossini spring immediately to mind.

Gabriele's prestige in Pescara was soon considerable. Yet he was by no means one of those puny creatures with tiny heads who are generally typical of precociousness. He spent his holidays scuffling with other boys and riding his Sardinian horse, Aquilina, but above all he loved to go out to sea with the fishermen. In his old age he was able to recapture the freshness of those first vertiginous moments. As he lay in a fishing-boat, stretched out on the wet nets amid the smell of salt and seaweed, the revelation of the sea came upon him. On the beach he experienced a sense of possession, his young body rolling in the burning sand and then offered in ecstasy to the sun. In later years, whenever he returned to his native Abruzzi, he would immediately jump into a boat to rediscover these wondrous sensations. In the first notebook, in 1882, beside a sketch of a *felucca*, he described the colours of the sails and added these words: '*Siamo in Oriente. Delirio del sole.*' ('We are in the East. Delirium of the sun.') His memories, precise yet exalted, indicate an extreme sharpness of the senses. His ear perceived and distinguished the lightest sounds; his sight, which was to deteriorate quite rapidly, remained sensitive to the slightest gradations of colour. Prodigiously endowed to enjoy the world as d'Annunzio was, the ecstasy into which he was plunged by a rare perfume or hue was no aesthetic pose, but a profound satisfaction of the senses that enabled him to derive as intense a relish from works of art as from physical pleasures.

Almost as much as going out to sea, d'Annunzio loved to frequent the dilapidated lodge at the gates of the town, surrounded by a terrace ornamented with terracotta busts, in a garden invaded by a wild profusion of vines, with fig-trees and tall cypresses—the Villa del Fuoco where his father installed his successive mistresses. It was here that Gabriele used to bury his face in clusters of lilies and became so familiar with the lizards and the birds that he felt able to call them his brothers, as St. Francis of Assisi had done. Each time that he came back to Pescara, he recaptured

these early sensations so vividly that he believed he had penetrated the secret of matter.

This young Pan soon began to look at girls with the same eye
and fell in love long before what is called the age of reason,
which, moreover, he was never to reach. At the age of seven,
Gabriele quite lost his head over a very pretty little girl with
long blonde hair, a doll-like creature particularly precious in this
land of dark hair and swarthy skins, who was constantly being
titivated by her mother, the Marchesa Pomàrici di Castrovalese.
The girl's first name, Teodolinda, taken from Tasso's *Gerusalemme
Liberata*, added to the glamour of the loved one. Gabriele, timid
in this first experience of love, asked a cousin to make his feelings
known. Linda blushed, the marchesa shrieked and thereafter
came alone to the d'Annunzio house. Throughout his life d'Annunzio was drawn towards the aristocracy and, as a bourgeois of
Pescara, dreamed of high society and of those sonorous and
legendary names that are to be found at every stage of Italian
history. If the poet was touched by the decline of grandeur, by
the dilapidated palaces and the precarious beauties that still inhabited them, the ambitious climber imagined himself adorned
with all the prestige that attracted him to elegant mistresses.
Teodolinda is only worth mentioning because she was the first
of the *Mill'e tre*, a list in which princesses and countesses were
to prove even more numerous than peasant women.

By the age of ten, Gabriele was thus a celebrated figure in
Pescara. This slender, nervous boy with frizzy hair and grey eyes,
who laughed and handed out insults with equal readiness and was
welcome in everyone's house, seized upon the absurdities of people and made fun of the family dramas which he divined. He was
always ready to take his comrades on expeditions from which they
returned with clothes torn and knees bleeding. At the same time,
his sensibility was such that no one dared to maltreat an animal in
his presence. Everyone congratulated Don Francesco Paolo on his
offspring—Gabriele's teachers, the citizens of Pescara and the
fishermen of the town; already it was predicted that one day the
d'Annunzio house would be decorated with a plaque bearing

immortal inscriptions, like the houses of Rossini and Alfieri. The father, filled with pride at having given the town such a son, decided that it would be sufficient glory for Pescara to have been his birth-place, and that the education of such a phoenix should no longer be entrusted to a province whose inhabitants spoke a dialect. After consulting Gabriele's teachers, the *commendatore* resolved to send his son to an excellent college in Tuscany, where the purest Italian was spoken.

2

The
Enfant sublime

AT COLLEGE

In the autumn of 1872 Don Francesco Paolo, Donna Luisetta and
little Gabriele went to Florence to visit an old friend, the retired
Colonel Coccolini, who had commanded the garrison of Pescara
in the time of the Bourbons. The purpose of the visit was to find
a college of a high scholastic standard which charged low fees.
The colonel recommended the college at Prato founded during
the Renaissance by Cardinal Cicogna and known as the Cicognini
College, with a stork (*cicogna*) as its emblem. This was not the
most elegant college in Italy, but it was quite the best; it was
organized by Jesuits with priests occupying the senior positions,
but the staff also included lay teachers, mostly positivists or anti-
clericals who had fought with Garibaldi. The vast, severe Baroque
building had icy galleries, staircases of grey stone decorated with
black busts and a narrow courtyard between two wings which
opened onto a dismal garden. But discipline there was more hu-
mane than in those wealthy English schools situated in vast
grounds and where children were martyred, especially if they were

19

intelligent. The institution was the only living glory of a small town which owed its fame to its cathedral.

This church, which played an important part in the artistic development of the college boy, contains behind its Romanesque façade, streaked with white and green marble, some of the most outstanding works of the early Renaissance: a chapel decorated by Filippo Lippi and another by a painter reminiscent of Paolo Uccello, a statue of the Madonna by Benedetto da Maiano, a famous bronze candelabrum by a pupil of Donatello, and a pulpit carved in marble by Rossellino; the cathedral's most precious relic, the Virgin's Girdle, is kept behind bronze grilles ornamented with seraphs and birds. The statue by Niccolò Pisano above the reliquary stands against an Annunciation by Agnolo Gaddi. To enter the cathedral one passes beneath a blue and white tympanum modelled by Andrea della Robbia. But the most famous work, situated at the south corner of the building, is the round pulpit carved by Donatello with a circle of seraphs and protected from the weather by a sort of umbrella of white marble. Along one side of the cathedral stands a small cloister of green marble with white mouldings. The names of the artists who contributed to the edifice were to reappear constantly in d'Annunzio's writings; their works inspired a kind of aesthetic patriotism in this child who had grown up far from any centre of artistic activity.

There was nothing to recall Pescara in this city, with its narrow streets huddled together and here and there a forbidding palace; but its severity is always mitigated by some graceful detail, such as the little bronze Bacchus in front of the town hall. Beside a fortress built by the Ghibellines stand a church designed by Sangallo, a ravishing neo-Classical theatre and some statues to great local figures which bear witness to the concern which the *Pratesi* have always felt for their city. Beyond the fortifications of pink brick lies a rich and graceful countryside that serves as a garden for a number of villas, of which the most celebrated is Poggio a Caiano, built for Lorenzo the Magnificent and later decorated by Pontormo and other Mannerists.

The middle class of Prato, which over the centuries had enriched itself in the wool trade, no more resembled that of Pescara than the proud Tuscan city resembled the little Adriatic town. The new pupil was coming to a part of Italy as far removed from his native province as Malta is from Oxford. At first, his shepherd's head, his provincial expressions and his accent earned him the gibes of his comrades and the reprimands of his teachers, but the military uniform gave him a more orderly appearance and his highly sensitive ear enabled Gabriele to assimilate every nuance of Tuscan speech. His father wisely forbade him to return home for two years, so that he should not fall back into bad habits. Gabriele quickly asserted himself with his masters no less than with his fellow-pupils. The photograph of the class in which he started shows him to have been smaller than his comrades, with an angelic expression on his little cat-like face, in which there is also a hint of mischief. Hardly had a master turned his back than the angel was transformed into a devil; his teachers, however, were soon undeceived. Already very good at Latin, he took readily to Greek, learnt French without difficulty and also the rudiments of English; history fascinated him. Only mathematics always remained foreign to him. One of his teachers was divided between admiration and fear, for Gabriele read Byron's *Cain, Paradise Lost* and even Darwin. 'When God is mentioned,' said this excellent man to his superior, 'd'Annunzio bursts out laughing and says that he does not want to believe in a Supreme Being who could create man only to see him suffer.' And yet, at about this same time, when he visited the church of Santa Maria della Vita in Bologna, the great terracotta *Deposition* produced such a vivid impression on Gabriele that he was able to recall his feelings clearly some sixty years later: 'I glimpsed, in the shadow of a kind of grotto, a strangely painful agitation. It seemed that I was struck by a wind of agony, a storm-cloud of disaster, a laceration of grievous passion. It was the presence of Christ being revealed to me, just as the presence of death had been revealed to me' (*Libro segreto*). Then the thundering of the organ lifted his emotion to its climax and revealed to the adolescent d'Annunzio the thing which was to count so much more than faith in his life—music. 'I had become an instrument in the hands of the invisible musician. It was as if, for the first time, Palestrina was creating through me his sublime motet *Peccantem me quotidie* . . . At that moment I was born to music, I had my nativity in the infinity of music, I had in music my nativity and my destiny . . .'

While his fellow-pupils fell asleep over their Latin translations, Gabriele remained awake late into the evening, seeking in Horace and Virgil the inspiration for the Latin verses that would earn him the compliments of those masters whom his bad behaviour irritated most. The oil-lamp which remained lit so late on his desk is still preserved in the little museum at the college. Gabriele was not allowed to go alone into the vast library for fear that an infallible instinct might lead him to the unexpurgated editions of Catullus and Tibullus. He immersed himself in Petrarch and Dante instead of translating Livy, who was too easy and too moral. At the age of fifteen, his head was already filled with poems and rare words, and he had accumulated a prodigious store of images and rhythms. For a whole year he carried on him a complete edition of Ariosto in two small volumes. But the prodigy who juggled with spondees and dactyls also established his supremacy among his fellow-pupils, by his southern verve, by the audacity and the ingenuity of his mischievous pranks. Among his comrades he was known as '*subilloso*' ('the rebel') and '*burraschino*' ('the stormy one').

In his third year at college, Gabriele began to seek friendship rather than mere comradeship. One of his friends, Dario Biondi, who looked like Bonaparte, shared all his enthusiasms. Like Gabriele, 'the companion with the eyes without lashes' worshipped Alexander and Napoleon. The two boys learnt by heart Napoleon's proclamations to the Grand Army and devoured all the books that they could find about the man who had started from circumstances no less humble than Gabriele's and from no less distant a province. Some letters have been discovered which he wrote to another friend, a short time after this phase of historical fervour had passed: 'Yes, it is pleasant to have a close friend with whom to exchange a little chit-chat amid the tremendous boredom of college, especially if the friend is not ugly and can, unconsciously, take the place of a sweetheart.' G. Gatti, the Italian biographer of d'Annunzio, says that, if the young Gabriele, in writing to his friend, used expressions which he was to use in writing to a girl the following year, this was only because he sought from that friend the same kind of moral support which a boy expects from his sweetheart. Even in the midst of passionate affairs d'Annunzio was always to retain a nostalgic regard for friendship and a youthfulness of spirit that was later to enable him to enjoy the comradeship of young airmen during the war. This primitive despised women and reserved his noble sentiments for men.

More important than these college friendships was the meeting in Milan, in 1879, with Cesare Fontana, who was some ten years older than d'Annunzio and had a great influence on his reading. Here is the first letter to this amiable aesthete, who quickly vanished from d'Annunzio's life, written in a style that must have been strongly influenced by Byron's *Manfred:* 'I am sixteen . . . I have in the depth of my heart an immoderate desire for knowledge and glory, which often overwhelms me with a dark and tormenting melancholy and makes me weep: I can suffer no yoke . . . an ardent lover of the New Art and of beautiful women, highly individual in my tastes, enthusiastic to the point of folly, a frantic poet and an indefatigable narrator of dreams.' The letters to his father are equally exalted; Don Francesco Paolo could exhibit these patriotic missives with pride: 'Oh! how shall I be able to recompense you? . . . Even if one day I could lay at your feet the immortal laurel of the poet, even if one day I could let you hear the applause of all Italy . . . Oh! if I had genius, the genius that flashes like lightning, illuminating the earth, and wrings cries of admiration and tears of emotion . . .'

THE CHERUB UNCHAINED

In the Mediterranean countries boys look on themselves as men at a very early age and speak of women with cynicism. The careful watch that was kept over girls represented a challenge to the bold; to steal a kiss was a victory that gave a boy prestige among his comrades. While sharing his romantic dreams with two or three close friends, Gabriele was just as much at ease with the most disreputable elements in the college. He loved the company of boys even more exotic than himself, a Cuban and two Italians from Tunisia whom he called Sidi and Ali; these semi-Negroes with their precocious imaginations inspired in him a yearning for Africa. They had already had some singular experiences: what might Gabriele do to astound them? His temerity earned him the detention-cell on more than one occasion. One day, a Father who had not despaired of leading this exceptional pupil along the straight and narrow path asked him to serve Mass to mortify his pride, and on the following Sunday, to the amazement of the teaching staff, the child gave all the responses in Greek. But can one speak of a 'child' when confronted with evidence of a much more scandalous precociousness? At the age of twelve, when the sewing-sister was trying a shirt on him, Gabriele guided her hand towards his private parts. There followed loud threats of dismissal, but the little monster knew well that the college would never allow its most brilliant pupil to go to a rival establishment.

A blind eye was also turned whenever he disappeared to meet his art teacher, who was restoring Filippo Lippi's fresco, *The Feast of Herod*, in the cathedral. The rather morbid grace of Lucrezia Buti, who four hundred years earlier had posed for Salome, may have excited the child—at least, so he tells us in a chapter of reminiscences entitled *Il secondo amante di Lucrezia Buti* ('The second lover of Lucrezia Buti'). The scabrous life of the painter of Prato must surely have seemed exemplary to the boy from Pescara. After becoming a monk at the age of fifteen, Filippo Lippi pursued an adventurous existence until his capture by the Saracens. After being released by the Saracens, he became a monk again and was appointed chaplain to a convent, which he decorated with frescoes. He seduced a beautiful nun, the blonde Lucrezia, who gave birth to Filippino, the son who was to continue his father's artistic manner. Cosimo de' Medici admired the painter and arranged matters: the monk was able to marry the nun, whose cat-like face is recognizable in his Madonnas. But Filippo, incapable of behaving himself for long, was poisoned by a jealous husband.

Whether the young d'Annunzio was in fact excited by the idea of the ravished nun or not, it was certainly from these frescoes that he acquired the aesthetic sensitivity which enabled him to re-create poetically the paintings of the great artists. In Tuscany also, where the names made famous by Dante and Machiavelli were those of palaces and villas passed constantly by the boy from the undistinguished province, everything around him spoke of glory; and so Gabriele invented imaginary memories for himself, a sort of spiritual family which he laid like polished marble over the rock of the Abruzzi. But the audacity of the urchin from Pescara quickly penetrated Tuscan urbanity whenever the college-boys passed a pretty girl on a walk; on more than one occasion the modesty of the ladies of Prato was startled by the compliments thrown out by d'Annunzio and his band. When they went on a walk into the country, always in single file, Gabriele would manage to slip away to meet on some hidden path a girl who, not surprisingly, resembled Lippi's Salome: 'I liked her because she had elegant long legs like the Salome of Fra Filippo Lippi . . . and a mouth so fleshy and so red that one wondered where in that pale face she found so much blood.' Gabriele made the girl bite into a bunch of cherries and she thought he was mad. Her name was Emilia Corsani, but d'Annunzio called her Gorella Gheri; he had probably seen her in the college visiting-room when she came to visit her brother.

When Gabriele was allowed to spend his holidays in Pescara, he regaled his comrades with stories of his good fortune. He saw Linda (Teodolinda, the daughter of the marchesa) and stole a kiss from 'la Ciccarina', the stonemason's daughter. Much later, he confided to his secretary that at the age of fourteen, 'with a kind of horrified intoxication and a spirit of bold perdition', he had discovered that 'one could bite a woman's mouth like some dainty morsel and that there was another, secret mouth to plunder'. But d'Annunzio had forgotten the name of a harvesting girl who, biting into a bunch of grapes like a bacchante, allowed him to find her mouth through the crushed fruit. At times, puberty brought the adolescent boy to a state verging on madness. At the age of sixteen, Gabriele had his first woman, a prostitute, in Florence where he had gone to visit the museums with his class in the charge of a master. After managing to escape from the rest, he left his watch with a pawnbroker and then gave a large tip to a coachman, asking to be taken to the best address. This episode was to be repeated many times in the course of d'Annunzio's insatiable life. The girl was charming and came from a family of musicians; she even wanted to give him an old violin. There was nothing sordid in this first venture—which resembles a page from Casanova—at least, as remembered by d'Annunzio.

His first 'love story' also had Florence as its setting; Gabriele spent his Easter holidays there to soak himself in the Tuscan style. The heroine of this story was Clemenza, the daughter of Colonel Coccolini, the family friend acting in loco parentis; Gabriele preferred to call the girl 'Clemàtide' or 'Malinconia'. He always used to rename the women he loved, as if to mark their initiation into the d'Annunzian religion, just as novices lose their identity on the day when they consecrate themselves to God. Clemenza deserved the nickname of Malinconia ('Melancholy'); though normally of a teasing disposition, she was subject to dreamy moods. She was sixteen and Gabriele fourteen; their youth reassured the parents, who let the 'children' go on walks together. The boy haunted the museums, where the masterpieces stirred both his patriotism and his sensuality; the Titians and Bronzinos fired him with love for the beautiful bodies which were still beyond his reach. One morning in April, Gabriele took Clemenza to the Etruscan Museum; the attendant was dozing between the showcases full of red vases decorated with grimacing black men. When they came to a bronze chimera with open jaws and claws extended, the boy, as if to brave the monster, pushed his fist into the creature's mouth with such force that his hand was bleeding when he pulled it out. 'Did the mouth burn you?' asked Clemenza, drawing close to him. 'It seemed to me as if she was naked, suddenly quite naked and burning. If the Chimera breathed flame from its jaws, she breathed *caeci Cupidinis ignes* from her swollen and sour nostrils . . . That seductive flesh bit into me more than the bristling metal had done. There, in that deserted museum room, I felt the first deep turmoil of the juvenile lover, the first lyrical tumult of the obscure forces re- leased by puberty. "Let me feel if yours burns . . ." ' After this kiss the young faun threw himself at Clemenza's bosom, where his hands wandered without arousing a protest. The poet was often to think of 'that hour of the Chimera': 'Suddenly I felt myself capable of bearing with equal courage the maximum of pleasure and the maximum of knowledge . . . *volontà voluttà*' (*Le Faville del Maglio*).

At the college two years later, Gabriele, by this time a cele- brated figure, fell truly and deeply in love with the daughter of one of the masters. Tito Zucconi, dazzled by his pupil's intel- ligence and charm, frequently invited him to a small villa which he owned near Florence. Giselda Zucconi had 'mysterious eyes deep as the sea'. This young girl, whom Gabriele liked to call Elda, was a little older than himself and also wrote poems. But, more important than her own efforts, she was the inspiration for some very beautiful love-poems that were dedicated to her in the first edition of *Canto novo* (1881); in later editions the dedication was omitted. Some two hundred and fifty letters to Giselda have been discovered which contain much material that was re-used in the poems, for it was always to be d'Annunzio's practice to enrich his writings with the lines inspired in him by passion. Life was constantly to arouse in him emotions which he enshrined in perfectly expressed form in a poem or story, rather like a conqueror who embellishes his armour with jewels taken from his hostages. Giselda, whom he respected and whose fiancé he was considered to be, suffered much, for she was the first to know the sad satisfaction of finding expressed, here and there in the poet's writings, the joys and hopes which she had shared and inspired.

FIRST TRIUMPH

The verses addressed to Giselda were by no means the schoolboy's first attempts. At the age of sixteen, he had written an ode in thirteen strophes for the birthday of King Umberto; if the sentiments are banal in their fervour, the prosody, on the other hand, is already extremely skilful, reflecting the happy influence of the only true poet whom Italy could claim at this time—Giosuè Carducci. The inspiration of this great writer was a blend of heroism (he had been the poet of the Risorgimento) and Baudelairean melancholy. His impeccable and varied technique sometimes endowed his works with a rhetorical tone reminiscent of Victor Hugo. Gabriele had happened to buy the *Odi barbare* at a bookshop in Bologna; he immediately made them his model, wrote delirious letters to Carducci and received advice from him. The patriotic ode and the love-poems addressed to various young girls, among them the little Marchesa Pomàrici and the devourer of cherries, were passed around the college. While the masters showed reticence in their admiration of the poems because of the subject-matter, Gabriele's comrades committed to memory the verses that expressed all their own dreams. In a country other than Italy a schoolboy-poet would have been afraid of inviting the jeers of his comrades and the reprimands of his teachers, but at Prato, where glory and beauty were cherished, d'Annunzio aroused a fervour that was to accompany him almost to the end of his career. The reaction of his family was similar: never has a poet been less cursed by his own. Italy had need of genius and Don Francesco Paolo had need of prestige; and so the mayor of Pescara had his son's works printed—a fine gesture for a man harassed by creditors.

At the end of 1879 the collection *Primo vere* ('Early Spring') appeared, with a dedication betokening the assiduous pupil: *Meis musis et paucis amicis* ('to my muses and few friends'). D'Annunzio warned his friend Fontana what he would find in this collection: 'It's not much—rosy flashes of youth, ecstasies filled with tremors and senseless words, moments of fever and intoxication . . . Therein is all my burning soul: an exuberance of feelings poured forth in hymns, in sweet elegies, in dazzling images, in strange sounds convulsed and languorous—but do not look for the spark of genius, like thunder and lightning, that strikes and enthralls: that genius I do not have, the spark is lacking in me.' M. P. de Montera, who quotes this letter, adds: 'The only sin of modesty ever committed by the poet.'

The success of this work by an unknown poet, published at the author's expense by a provincial printer-publisher, was immediate, thanks to a long article by Italy's best-known critic, Chiarini, who in the *Fanfulla della Domenica* hailed the birth of a genius. D'Annunzio's teachers, forgetting the consternation caused by the poem about girls bathing, applauded the glory which he had brought to the college; his father had the drawing-room at Pescara painted in fresco with the titles of his favourite poems surrounded by flowered borders. Six months later a second edition appeared, on this occasion from a well-known publisher; certain pieces judged to be licentious were suppressed, including the following poem which, nevertheless, possesses the grace of Botticelli's allegories or of the mythological scenes of Piero di Cosimo:

'And you, Glycera, fled along the shore of the lake, your ebony hair given to the breeze, your swelling bosom heaving beneath the light silk of your bodice. In your haste you revealed your shining flesh in all its whiteness, and as you ran your rounded loins quivered in provocative ripples. I followed you through the tall reeds, and my heart was beating with desire . . . With trembling agitation I laid you on the water-lilies and kissed you with convulsed lips, crying: "You are mine! . . . You are mine! . . ." And beneath my embraces, like a viper, you writhed and groaned

. . .' The daring pieces were replaced by very free translations of classical poems and by rustic idylls inspired by Gabriele's native province; to one of his masters he wrote: 'When I was at home I used to spend hours in the countryside, lying on my stomach among the tall grass and the flowers, under the great sun of the Abruzzi, my eyes half-closed, imagining I was a conscious atom sucked into vast whirlpools, into the irresistible currents of universal matter. These were ecstasies: at times it seemed that I had myself become the fertilizing humus.'

The magazine which had first made mention of d'Annunzio asked him for a few stories, but these were ignored by the critics. Their silence was intolerable to the impatient genius, who sent a report of his death to the *Gazzetta della Domenica*—an appropriately romantic death, caused by falling from a runaway horse! Telegrams arrived in Pescara from every part of Italy and the neglected stories were eulogized in the obituary notices.

HAPPY INFLUENCES

In June 1880, d'Annunzio left the college whose most illustrious pupil he had become. He stayed for twelve days in Florence with Elda Zucconi, to whom he considered himself engaged; the girl's father, dazzled by the boy's youthful glory, was ready to give his blessing. During this stay Gabriele was constantly in the company of Enrico Nencioni, a rather poor minor poet. Among this colony of Ruskinian aesthetes, a number of Italians had belatedly become Pre-Raphaelites; Nencioni's room was decorated with reproductions of Rossetti and Burne-Jones and with the scenes of antiquity painted by Alma-Tadema, who always remained one of d'Annunzio's favourite artists. The young Nencioni and the schoolboy had already exchanged letters, in which Gabriele described himself as the Alcibiades of 'this new Socrates'. Nencioni, one of the first Italian Decadents, wrote a *Treatise on Baroque* in which he announced the coming of 'a sinister new art'. His poems sang of Semiramis and Sappho. The memory of this rather strange person has survived not through his own works, no longer read, but in the early poems of his young admirer. With Nencioni's help, Gabriele read Tennyson's long poem *Maud*, Keats's *La Belle Dame sans Merci* and the *Laus Veneris* of Swinburne, whose cruel extravagances were to influence a number of d'Annunzio's poems. At the same time, he began to identify himself with the character of Ariel, feeling it his mission to change reality into 'something rich and strange'. It is probable that, during this stay in Florence, d'Annunzio for the first time made the acquaintance of one of those beautiful and eccentric Anglo-Saxon ladies whose artistic and social prestige still fascinated him fifty years later.

The child prodigy then returned to his native province, where he received a welcome which consoled him for having left both his fiancée and his aesthete friend. His mother, his sisters, the old aunts who now never left their rooms, the servants who were never paid and the poor tenant-farmers, all greeted him with tears in their eyes. Don Francesco Paolo walked arm in arm with his son round the town, and the smiles of the girls whom they passed promised a delicious holiday. Gabriele had an opportunity to explore the lower depths glimpsed in his childhood—the street where the brothels stood with flowers at their windows, but where heaps of rubbish were piled up in the middle of the road, and the smugglers' inns. He met ladies who came from Rome to spend the summer in modest villas, many of them unappreciated, romantic persons who a little later were to provide him with subjects for two or three stories.

However, the eighteen-year-old poet was not the only glory of Pescara. At Francavilla another native of the Abruzzi, the painter Michetti, had installed his studio. Michetti needed a great deal of space in which to paint his canvases, which recall the operas of Mascagni in their combination of precise detail and melodramatic sentiment; Italian lyricism often seeks a compromise with reality. Michetti was the great painter of *verismo*, the literary school that derived from the French realists, but he refined the most sordid scenes and most bizarre customs, as in his famous *The Vow* for which d'Annunzio was to provide the literary counterpart in the *Trionfo della Morte*. The artist was a much more serious and even reticent person than one would imagine from his canvases, which display the fluency of a painter of opera scenery. Michetti was fifteen years older than d'Annunzio, whom he treated as a younger brother and whom he invited to Francavilla. Gabriele was glad to leave a house where the women were always crying and which his father's conduct had given a bad reputation. At the studio he met the musician Paolo Tosti (composer of the *Serenade*) and two or three youths who dreamed of attaining glory with pen or paint-brush. Michetti, older than the rest and more sober-minded, guided the enthusiasms of his juniors; he opened Gabriele's eyes to the ancient world that surrounded them; they visited the fairs and places of pilgrimage, went swimming and riding, and spent the evenings discussing philosophy or politics. This summer of 1881 brought a breath of fresh air into Gabriele's hitherto bookish culture. Having absorbed what Michetti had to teach him, he completed the manuscript of *Terra vergine* ('Virgin Land'), a collection of stories, before the end of the holiday, which lasted until the feast of All Saints. Gabriele then had to leave for Rome to register in the faculty of law. Life with Michetti had been so good that he had no desire to return to Florence to see Elda. The situation would have been difficult in any case, for d'Annunzio's parents were firmly opposed to a marriage that would have done nothing to gratify their vanity nor to fill their half-empty purses. Instead Gabriele wrote Elda some beautiful letters . . .

A GREAT MAN FROM THE PROVINCES IN ROME

One might have guessed that Gabriele's first visit to the capital was not, in fact, to register in the law faculty; he would never have followed a course of study after having endured seven years of college with such impatience; he wished only to be a poet and for the time being, in order to earn a living, a journalist. Almost as soon as he arrived, the young man, armed with the success of the *Primo vere* collection and with the recommendations of

Michetti, went to the offices of the two reviews on which artistic, literary and political opinion depended. The first, the *Capitan Fracassa*, more fashionable, imitated the Parisian *Gil Blas*; the other, the *Cronaca Bizantina*, was more *avant-garde*, its very title savouring of decadence.

The editor of the *Cronaca*, Sommaruga, a Balzacian character who loved literature almost as much as money, had a genius for publicity and a flair for business. An impresario as much as a publisher, Sommaruga liked to launch young talents; it was he who had sent the painter de Nittis to Paris, one of those gestures in which it is difficult to distinguish between the motives of the speculator and the patron. His *Cronaca Bizantina*, the first number of which appeared in June 1881, was elegantly presented with a headpiece inspired by the Ravenna mosaics. Carducci was the real driving-force behind this review, which aspired to become the artistic organ of the 'Third Rome'. Cesare Fontana was one of the first contributors, with some mediocre verse. Each number of the *Cronaca* provoked controversy and even duels—an excellent form of advertisement that soon brought an extraordinarily large circulation of twelve thousand copies. The offices, accommodated in the Ruspoli palace on Via Due Macelli, near the Piazza di Spagna, became one of the liveliest places in Rome. Sommaruga also owned a publishing-house. His first discovery was a Florentine lady who signed herself 'Contessa Lara', a real *femme fatale* who eventually was murdered by a jealous admirer. But the Olympian Carducci towered above everyone and, until the arrival of d'Annunzio, the young authors seemed quite insipid by contrast. When Gabriele appeared on the scene, he had not a single rival among his generation.

Angelo Sommaruga, who always gave a warm welcome to anyone in whom he scented success, opened his arms to the newcomer and introduced him into his literary coterie, where he immediately became an object of adoration. The publisher, following the example of Chateaubriand, never failed to re-enact the scene of the *'enfant sublime'* with this Victor Hugo of the Abruzzi, each time he presented Gabriele to a celebrity. He had been truly touched by 'this slip of a boy with frizzy hair who always gave his name in a woman's voice'. According to the publisher's memoirs, d'Annunzio at once became 'the object of unbelievable favour and a cult. He was so affable and so modest, and bore the weight of his budding glory with such grace, that all flocked to him as if drawn by a sudden feeling of friendship.' Sommaruga immediately agreed to publish the stories which the young author had written at Pescara; he promised a luxury edition for the forthcoming collection of verse, from which d'Annunzio showed him the poems inspired by Elda (Lalla). Before tracing the newcomer's rapid success in Roman society, it may be worthwhile to examine briefly these poems which were to be published the following year with illustrations by Michetti, and which were to justify the celebrity of the prodigy from Pescara. The faun who, in the early poems, pursued young girls along streams had become the Great Pan himself. The new poems, in their vigorous and uninhibited paganism, might have been composed by Pierre Louÿs; they sang of

> . . . Il mare, il sole, gli alberi,
> i frutti, una chioma, l'amore,
> la giovinezza fiamma del mondo,
>
> e le squillanti risa feminee
> come i cristalli, e i rosei vertici
> d'un seno, ed i gesti leggiadri,
> ed una musica di parole . . .

('The sea, the sun, the trees,
  Fruits, a head of hair, love,
  Youth, the flame of the world,

  And the ringing laughter of women
  Like glass, and the rosy tips
  Of a breast, and the graceful gestures,
  And a music of words.')
('Canto dell'Ospite' from the collection Canto novo.)

Never has a poet found greater happiness in being young and alive. In all sincerity d'Annunzio could ask himself: 'Am I not a god?', so fully did he participate in the joy of creation, giving new colour to the most overworked themes. One believes in his nymphs and dryads. The whole of the *Canto novo* is full of the only god that he ever worshipped (after himself)—the sun. D'Annunzio was the first to revive the cult of what was to become the great myth of our century. He loved to brown his body on the sand, to bathe and ride bareback over burning beaches, passing for a madman at a time when people wore gaiters at the seaside. Later, we shall see the poet elevating the other myth of our time—speed. These poems written at the age of nineteen are like a storehouse of fruit, the reserve from which he was to draw all the delicious images that are to be found throughout his works. No one was better able than d'Annunzio to convey the freshness of the pomegranate and the moistness of the fig. Similarly, his nymphs are creatures of flesh, the loves of his forest-land belong to the animal world. Persons of delicate feelings were rather shocked by the light which the poems shed on the appetites of their highly romantic young author. Yet even the most niggling critics could not help admiring unreservedly the expertise of the prosody, the diversity of the metres often resuscitated from Latin poetry. Young people were conquered by the poet who sought 'a new spasm' and who evoked 'the torture of art'. The ladies appreciated the harpsichords and the sedan-chairs skilfully placed between these lively images.

The great Carducci himself had agreed to correct the proofs. The two poets met by chance in the ante-room of Sommaruga's office: 'He [Carducci] resembled those Etruscans with thin legs and bulging stomach seen crouching on the lids of burial urns. The acridity of the already poisoned blood coloured his cheeks and inflamed his ears. Often, with a brusque movement, he would raise his chin as if to face some invisible mob . . . He continued to look at me without saying a word . . . Nature had endowed me with a simple grace which reassured him. He smiled at last and exclaimed jovially: "Thàlatta! Thàlatta!" This was a

cry from one of my Asclepiadean strophes.' Secretly the young
d'Annunzio promised himself that he would never come to
resemble this provincial intellectual. The success of *Canto novo*
was immense: 'Everyone sought me, praised me, proclaimed me a
god; the women in particular were moved.' The time had come
to cast off the skimpy black suit with shiny elbows and the poet's
bow-tie, and to leave the skimping *pensione*. Yet the image of the
'accursed poet', thin, with burning eyes and bushy hair, might
still serve to touch sensitive hearts and to preserve the confidence
of the *avant-garde*: for a little while longer d'Annunzio, whom
the journalist Scarfoglio called 'the Bonaparte of Italian letters',
behaved 'like a coquette who calculates her timidity and her
shyness'.

3

Rome

THE BOHEMIAN WORLD

D'Annunzio's career in Rome was indeed an Italian campaign crowned by a marriage with one of the most eligible women in the city. Yet not all doors were opened easily to 'the Bonaparte of Italian letters' and it was several months before the poet felt socially acceptable. Between the unkempt raw genius and the refined aesthete, there was a period when Gabriele played the part of the bumpkin in his Sunday best. The life he led during these first six or eight months of his stay in Rome was in some respects, even after the success of the *Canto novo*, that of any sensible young man. He lived in a modest room but in a respectable district, on Via Borgognona, between the Corso and the Piazza di Spagna, a convenient place from which to stroll in the gardens and along the avenues. The view of Rome from the steps of Santa Trinità dei Monti enchanted him and he was to give an admirable description of these first impressions in a novel which he wrote five years later, *Il Piacere*: 'Rome appeared, all pearly gray, spread out before him, its lines a little blurred like a faded picture, under a Claude Lorrain sky, sprinkled with ethereal clouds, their noble grouping lending to the clear spaces between an indescribable delicacy, as flowers lend a new grace to the verdure which surrounds them. On the distant heights the gray deepened gradually to amethyst. Long trailing vapours slid through the cypresses of the Monte Mario like waving locks through a comb of bronze. Close by, the pines of the Monte Pincio spread their sun-gilded canopies. Below, on the piazza, the obelisk of Pius VI looked like a pillar of agate. Under this rich autumnal light everything took on a sumptuous air.' (From the translation by Georgina Harding.)

Gabriele wrote long letters to his family; he even embarked on several study courses and still believed himself in love with the girl whom he persisted in calling his fiancée, despite Don Francesco Paolo's determination not to see his phoenix married to the daughter of a teacher. The letters which Elda received at first were more or less similar to the one that follows, which could almost be sung to a melody of Donizetti: 'Mia divina, mia bella, mia buona, mia santa . . . Volevo la tua lettera, l'ho trovata, l'ho baciata, l'ho aperta tremando . . . Reprimi questo fuoco che ti ucciderà, e ucciderà me con te, o unica mia, unico mio sospiro! Tuo sempre sempre sempre sempre sempre tuo tuo tuo Gabriele tuo tuo.' ('My divine, my beautiful, my good, my holy one . . . I wanted your letter and I found it, I kissed it, I opened it shaking . . . Quench this fire which will kill you and will kill me with you, my only one, my only sigh! Always . . . your Gabriele . . .') But two years later, after long periods of silence, the tune had changed: 'Addio, mia buona, mia santa, mia bella bambina pallida e sofferente. Addio, addio, addio. Sono stanco e convulso.' ('Goodbye, my good, my holy, my beautiful pale and suffering child. Goodbye . . . I am weary and distressed.') The 'fiancée' whom he had not gone to see even once in Florence withdrew into the shadows with her grief. Another victim, this time a woman of quality, was to succeed Giselda. But before tracing the conquest of Maria di Gallese, in the course of which d'Annunzio moved into circles that were beginning to embellish the capital with a certain brilliance after the torpor of the papal régime, our Bonaparte must be seen in the much less important social group which had accorded him such a warm welcome.

Although a few writers in this literary *milieu* were managing to make a great deal of noise, Rome was not lifted out of her apathy. The leading intellectuals of the North or even of Naples never counted for much in the capital. They could, however, lead an extremely pleasant existence there at little expense and, by forming a mutual admiration society, believe themselves famous. This little world was dominated by two great journalists: Sommaruga, whom we have already met, and Scarfoglio, the editor of the *Corriere di Roma,* another Balzacian figure; Scarfoglio's wife, Matilde Serao, a novelist of talent, sentimental and a demagogue, also bore a certain resemblance to the author of *La Comédie humaine,* but showed a greater affinity with George Sand (she had already had some successful novels published, in a colourful style and devoted to the life of the poor people of Naples). At first captivated by d'Annunzio, whom they invited to contribute to their newspaper, Scarfoglio and his wife were soon disillusioned; but, in spite of a number of violent ruptures, they allowed the young man, whom they regarded as charming but irresponsible, to live more or less at their expense. In May 1882 the poet went with Scarfoglio to Sardinia, at that time a veritable expedition. Although they were accorded a triumphal welcome— no one ever bothered to go to Sardinia—the two friends were forced, three weeks later, to leave the island incognito: after reading the articles which they had sent to the *Corriere di Roma,* all the husbands on the island were ready to stone them to death.

Scarfoglio's first cause for disappointment was to see d'Annunzio, in November of that same year, return from Pescara a different man; he was no longer 'the affected, timid provincial poet', or even 'the ancient ephebe with his mass of curls, large sea-green eyes and almond eyelids'; nor was he yet the dandy and *condottiere,* but rather 'a small young man, slender, with a thin voice and locks of brown hair sleek with fragrant pomades and floating gently over a forehead as smooth and rosy as that of a cherub in a procession. He has the hairless, velvety cheeks of a chaste young girl. He speaks little, but he speaks in the same way that he dresses: fastidiously and graciously, with a feminine refinement, with the artificiality of those who look at themselves and listen to themselves with a certain self-satisfaction . . .'

What did Gabriele live on? How did he manage to find the money for such elegance? People were already beginning to ask the questions that were to haunt the poet throughout his career, and which on more than one occasion were to give rise to malicious gossip. His correspondence with Sommaruga shows that beneath the free and easy manner there was hidden a certain ruthlessness; the young man discussed percentages with authority. D'Annunzio was, in fact, an excellent businessman, but always spent three times as much as he earned. Sommaruga paid advances without needing too much prompting; with his genius for *combinazioni*, he was able to obtain a certain amount of credit for the poet from the suppliers whom his protégé was to mention in his articles. Florists, shirtmakers, shoemakers and confectioners saw their products praised lyrically from time to time in articles signed with preposterous and often aristocratic pseudonyms. Usually d'Annunzio signed himself 'Il duca Minimo', an allusion to Prince Massimo who was famous for his love-affairs; but he was also the 'Marchese di Colonia', 'Happemouche', 'Vere de Vere', 'Puck' and 'Svelt'. Sometimes, like his Parisian counterpart, Jean Lorrain, he used women's names such as 'Mab' or 'Lila Bisquit'. These articles showed a keen curiosity about all the latest trends —English habits and French fashions. D'Annunzio wrote about exhibitions, lauding Rosa Bonheur and Alma-Tadema. He used fashionable words side by side with sacred words to gratify his taste for sacrilege: the Piazza di Spagna thus became *Divina tepidaria cattolica della flirtation*. For the *Cronaca Bizantina* he wrote a poem on horse-racing entitled *Turf* and signed 'Mario de' Fiori'. In the poem he noted the names and the postures of the women in the stands; though he had observed them only from the public enclosure, he was confident that these beauties would wonder how they might make the acquaintance of this agreeable young poet.

He was now beginning to arouse a curiosity which was soon to satisfy his inordinate craving for high society. Even the Italian language did not seem to have superlatives ecstatic enough to praise the elegance of a duchess or a princess in d'Annunzio's articles. All his life he retained a passion for frills and flounces, describing a woman's costume with the precision of a dressmaker. His habit of adorning the most trivial fripperies with his lyricism was certainly one of the reasons for his success with women. What woman would not feel herself to be understood by a lover who could remember all the hats she had worn since their first meeting and who would help her to choose materials? However, d'Annunzio had not yet reached that stage. The novice saw the princesses, the English ladies and the Viennese baronesses at the Pincio reclining in their victorias, at the opera, at charity sales and at the races. At this very same time, Wilde in London and Paul Bourget in Paris were also fascinated by a magnificent but closed world, a world that Balzac had endowed with a chimerical prestige.

But Rome was much less accessible to talent than Paris or even London; d'Annunzio had to be content with seeing friends until he could gain acceptance by Society. These were indeed charming friends, judging by this account (by d'Annunzio) of an evening at the apartment of the musician Tosti: 'Oh that unforgettable year 1883! Paolo Tosti was the life and soul of a small group of artists which had its own tables in a special corner of the Caffè di Roma and was based in a house on Via de' Prefetti, in a mysterious apartment full of dark corridors and hiding-places from which the unrestrained laughter of a woman could often be heard by any one of us who happened to pass by unexpectedly . . . The rather narrow drawing-room had as its main decoration Michetti's sketch of the *Corpus Domini* . . . What delightful afternoons and even more delightful evenings in that room! When he was in the mood, Paolo Tosti would make music for hours on end without tiring, forgetting himself as he sat at the piano, sometimes improvising with a truly remarkable verve and felicity of inspiration. We lay on divans or on the floor, immersed in that kind of spiritual intoxication which is induced by music in a quiet, secluded place . . . During that year a frequent guest at our festivities was Mary Tescher, a most beautiful creature with the voice of a nightingale. She sang the songs of Schubert with such sweet passion and such exquisite art that Paolo Tosti would sometimes break off his accompaniment in a flush of enthusiasm and would start making wild gestures without saying a word. She was so nimble and supple, nearly always covered with black lace and moulded in a jersey splashed with iridescent jet; as she sang she swayed gently with the rhythm and, as she did so, she looked like a great flower.' The famous painting by Balestrieri entitled *Beethoven* might almost be an exact representation of those evenings.

Sometimes the group went to have lunch in an *osteria* outside the city walls, amid countryside that was still just as Chateaubriand and Keats had seen it. In the evening they would go down the steps of the Ripetta, which were shortly to be demolished; there, in a barge, surrounded by barrels, they bought genuine Marsala from a Sicilian. On the way back they passed the Borghese palace, which 'in the moonlight looks like a great silver harpsichord'. This wing of the palace accommodated the Circolo della Caccia, the Turf Club of Rome, and d'Annunzio gazed in wonder at the gentlemen who came out of the building, invested with the twofold prestige of an historic name and an English tailor. When a certain lady asked d'Annunzio to write on an album what he would most like to be, he replied: 'A Roman prince.'

THE *MONDO NERO*

Readers of Zola's novel *Rome* imagined palaces with closed shutters, solemn and lugubrious meetings of decrepit cardinals, princesses hidden under their mantillas, intriguing priests and antiquated diplomats, the last pillars of 'obscurantism' sighing at the thought of the encyclical *Rerum novarum*. In Zola's bizarre work, poison would put an end to sinister machinations, and love could be associated only with death, as in the extraordinary and truly d'Annunzian scene which shows the whole of Rome filing past the intertwined corpses of the young prince and his cousin. The great 'black' families—the Orsini, the Colonna, the Aldobrandini, the Altieri, the Borghese, the del Drago—were certainly more magnificent than the ruined family described by Zola; but, just as in their galleries the pontifical throne was turned to the wall, so these princes turned their backs on the new Italy. A number of marriages with rich Anglo-Saxon ladies brought a breath of fresh air into some palaces—the princesses Colonna, Massimo and Doria were English, the princesses Viccovaro and Bracciano American. This social world, which had so many features in common with that of the Faubourg Saint-Germain, except its culture, was from time to time shaken by terrible scandals. There was much talk about two sisters-in-law, the Duchess Sforza-Cesarini and Mimi Santa Croce; Matilde Serao called the first an 'African beauty' and the second the '*contessa fatale*'. The most exclusive *salon* was that of the Princess Pallavicini, 'a madonna of Raphael'; the only 'black' houses accessible to writers and artists were those of the Marchesa del Grillo and Count Primoli. The marchesa had been the great tragedienne Adelaïda Ristori, at one time the rival of Rachel; the count, the favourite nephew of Princess Mathilde of France, was the ambassador of *le tout Paris* in Rome. A descendant of Lucien Bonaparte, he belonged essentially to the *nerissimo* clan, although as a rich bachelor he frequented various social circles; he was one of the first friends, or rather one of the first patrons, that d'Annunzio found in elegant society.

At Primoli's gatherings it was possible to meet actresses and writers, but not the *gente nuove*, the architects of the new Italy who had come mostly from the North. D'Annunzio never felt anything but contempt for this new class that had emerged from the reunification: 'These men who, from afar, had appeared like flames in the heroic sky of their unemancipated country, these same men now became "dirty charcoal only good for drawing an obscene figure or a dirty word on walls", to use the atrocious image of an indignant orator. They, too, were intent on selling, bartering, legislating and setting traps.'

The court was no more brilliant than that of Louis-Philippe had been, for it was necessary to invite the *gente nuove* and resign oneself to the scorn of the *mondo nero*. Nevertheless, Queen Margherita, wife of King Umberto, of the house of Savoy-Genoa, stood out in this court; a magnificent woman, who loved to cover herself with jewellery, she took an interest in literature and music, which was unusual in her family. On the fringe of the court there was gradually established a circle of opportunist-politicians who speculated on the Garibaldian idea of the Third Rome as the capital of a triumphant Italy. Thus around the year 1880, built on the gardens of the old villas, streets of pretentious houses began to appear, but the houses found few occupants and were soon dilapidated. The *mondo nero* also involved itself in business affairs: Mgr. de Merode bought an entire district behind the Quirinale, and Prince Ludovisi built what is today the Via Vittorio Veneto; but in 1891 the Borghese, badly advised, went resoundingly bankrupt and their villa and collections became the property of the State. In a novel in which he speaks as an aristocrat as much as an aesthete, d'Annunzio was to deplore the decline of the Roman patriciate and the disfigurement of the city: 'The magnificent families which had been founded, regenerated and strengthened by nepotism and civil war, were degrading themselves one after the other, slithering in the new mire, sinking into it and disappearing. The vast wealth accumulated over centuries of happy rapine and Maecenean splendour was now exposed to the hazards of the Stock Exchange . . . It seemed that over Rome a storm of barbarism was blowing which threatened to snatch from her that radiant crown of princely villas unparalleled in human memory or in poetry.' Between 1885 and 1895, Rome changed its aspect and became an international capital, losing in the process not a little of her charm, without gaining much in the way of political prestige.

COSMOPOLIS

Cosmopolis is the title of one of the best novels (published in 1891) of Paul Bourget, who visited the new Rome, the capital of the kingdom, the city which, having failed to become a political centre (the important newspapers were those of Milan and Naples), a financial centre or an artistic centre (the Rome Opera was one of the least good in Italy), had established itself as the social capital of Europe: eighty years before Fellini, Rome was the city of *la dolce vita*. Café society can be seen taking shape in the pages of Bourget's novel, which portrays a Venetian lady of intrigue, a Viennese banker, a Polish count, a French novelist, an American painter, and a ruined prince representing the *mondo nero* where duels put an end to adulteries, where heiresses were the object of fierce rivalries, and where the treasures of an illustrious family were sold by auction. *Cosmopolis* was dedicated to Count Primoli.

It is worth pausing to study the dwelling of this delightful man, a small, excessively restored *palazzo* beside the Tiber, not far from the Piazza Navona, for d'Annunzio here found the inspiration for most of the decorative ideas which he was to put into practice once he had gained sufficient means to live according to his deserts: on the painted beams, moral or poetic quotations; large *cassoni* (Renaissance-style chests) and armchairs, hangings of Genoa velvet and pictures by the early masters side by side with modern casts and paintings, heavy upholstered furniture and a profusion of green plants; on the staircase, a collection of ancient sculptures. Count Primoli was a man of imposing appearance, with a white beard that created a fine effect when he dressed himself as a doge or a Renaissance prince: then he really looked like a portrait by Titian. 'Gégé', as he was known in the drawing-rooms, was a truly charming person, curious to know all the latest news and a great gossip. Edmond de Goncourt was often to echo him, for the count included among his friends both *académiciens* and young men like Abel Hermant and later Proust. His library, bequeathed to the city of Rome, is that of a remarkably well-read man. In addition to his social and literary activities,

Count Primoli was a talented photographer. The hundreds of photographs preserved in the Primoli Foundation give a very exact idea of the Rome of d'Annunzio. In addition to portraits of society women, Gégé photographed scenes of a picturesque aspect of Rome that was soon to vanish, and also some curious 'visions of antiquity' reminiscent of the photographs taken by a German baron which made the reputation of Taormina. The Primoli palace was the first to which d'Annunzio gained access. It seems that the young poet and the Maecenas were bound by some kind of complicity, for d'Annunzio sent Count Primoli a copy of his *Intermezzo* with this dedication: 'To the guardian of the hidden treasures.' Perhaps this is an allusion to two ladies, mother and daughter, who were intimate friends of the count and lived in the austere Altemps palace next to the Primoli residence. Primoli's *salons*, where Bourget met the characters of his *Cosmopolis*, were also to be opened to Henry James, who was to find there his models for Daisy Miller and Princess Casamassima.

The grand old man of Rome at this time was not the Pope but the Abbé Liszt, who lived in the Villa d'Este; from time to time his tall figure, crowned with a white mane, could be seen in a church or among the ruins. D'Annunzio met him at the home of a sculptor friend, Moïse Ezekiel, whose studio was situated in the Baths of Caracalla. Glory, women and a wonderful physique— all of which the old man had possessed—represented everything of which the young d'Annunzio dreamed. His enthusiasm charmed the maestro, who invited him to Tivoli, where he played, specially for d'Annunzio, Bach's *Variations on a Ground Bass* and all the themes from the *Dante Symphony*: 'The precursor of all new music, a unique friend, an incomparable lover, the features of a lion'; then, in his recollection of an evening which he perhaps embellished somewhat, the poet added this comment by an English lady: 'What a pity to put such a handsome man in front of a piano.' In a novel of which he himself was to be the hero, the young d'Annunzio described another, imaginary meeting with Liszt: 'The abbé raised his thin, bony body, which seemed gripped in a coat of mail; holding himself thus erect, he uncovered his head to address his silent prayer to the god of the Tempests. The wind ruffled his long, thick hair, that leonine mane from which so many flashes and quivers had moved women and crowds. His magnetic eyes were raised to the clouds, while the unspoken words that sketched themselves on his long thin lips spread a mystic air over that face, rough with lines and enormous warts.'

D'Annunzio's society columns referred in familiar terms to all the stars of *Cosmopolis*, most of them from the *mondo nero*, and even the queen herself, seen one evening applauding *Lohengrin*: 'This royal eternal feminine.' On the Corso, one carnival day, d'Annunzio observed in the loggia of the Tittoni palace 'the beautiful androgynous head of Signora X appearing among her besiegers, while the strange Japanese coiffure of Signora Duse stood out against the flowered curtains as if against an embroidered screen'. This Signora X, a very pretty woman who moved in Bohemian circles, was attempting to enter journalism; she was the young d'Annunzio's first mistress of vaguely fashionable pretensions. It was in the course of this liaison that the St. Sebastian myth, which was to acquire such importance in the poet's life, made its first appearance. Gabriele liked to compare his body, bruised by the kisses of his mistress, with the body of St. Sebastian: one evening, to make the analogy more striking, he took her into a secluded lane near the Pincio, removed his clothes and pressed his body against a tree, allowing the moon to illuminate his voluptuous wounds.

MARRIAGE

Some careers are rather like raids in which booty is seized indiscriminately, whether it is real or sham, merely because it glitters; moreover, the booty sometimes proves too heavy. To a certain extent this was true of Gabriele d'Annunzio's too ambitious marriage; any ordinary social climber might have spent the rest of his life regretting such a burdensome success. In the case of d'Annunzio, however, only his reputation and, on occasion, his self-esteem suffered. On the other hand, the reputation of the woman on whom he had brought unhappiness possibly gained a little more than it deserved. As will be seen later, of all the poet's 'victims', his wife was to be the only one who had the last word.

In the spring of 1883, Gabriele was invited by the Duchess di Gallese to a gathering at the Altemps palace (now a seminary), an imposing Renaissance building with high latticed windows, a dark porch opening onto a colonnaded courtyard and a loggia over-looking the entire district, from the Farnese palace to the Piazza Navona. Although the gallery of the palace was famous for its frescoes by Albani, and although the name of Gallese was an illustrious one, the invitation would not have dazzled a Roman already in the social swim. In fact, palace, title and fortune had come to the duke by one of those master-strokes the very thought of which thrilled the young d'Annunzio. Twenty-five years earlier, a non-commissioned officer from Normandy, who was in the army sent by Napoleon III to protect the Papal States, was billeted with his company in the outbuildings of the Altemps palace. From her rooms the recently widowed Princess Altemps spent her leisure-hours watching the soldiers, whose red trousers brightened up the courtyard. One of them in particular, a strapping fellow with a fine blond moustache, attracted her attention and soon the non-commissioned officer, Jules Hardouin, was promoted from the stable to the bedchamber, where he made himself so indispensable that the princess decided to hold him by more sacred bonds. But, since she had no desire to become Mme. Hardouin, the widow persuaded Pius IX to allow her husband to assume the title of Duke of Gallese, which had been borne by the Altemps family.

Their happiness was short-lived. Shortly after her marriage the duchess died and the new duke, determined to become part of Roman society, remarried; his second wife was Donna Natalia Lezzani, the daughter of a marquis. The young duchess preferred to shine at the Quirinale rather than live the withdrawn life of the *mondo nero*, and she accepted the post of lady-in-waiting to the queen, much to the chagrin of her *nerissimo* husband. The birth of three children did nothing to unite this household. The duke transferred all his hopes of social success to his daughter,

Donna Maria, a blonde with a slender figure and a dazzling complexion, assets which, combined with a handsome dowry, should have enabled her to marry a Ruspoli or an Aldobrandini. Alas, the duchess thought that it would be amusing to invite a little journalist-rhymester to one of her evenings, an invitation which the vanity of the young upstart found irresistible. A narrow lane separated the Altemps palace and the Primoli palace. The two ladies doted on Gégé, who photographed them in their hunting costumes and ball dresses. The mother had the vivacious elegance which Boldini was beginning to give to his portraits; as for the daughter, everyone agreed that she was a 'Pre-Raphaelite' beauty. The meeting with d'Annunzio could only have taken place at the count's *salons*. It has been said that the duchess was the first to prove susceptible to Gabriele's charm and that her daughter thought him ridiculous, only allowing herself to be wooed in order to sting the jealousy of a cousin. All that can be known for sure is that the poet always regarded his mother-in-law with a respect sometimes mingled with fear; many years later the duchess described her son-in-law as 'a painted woman'.

The young girl was soon caught in her own snare: she agreed to secret meetings and was lost. D'Annunzio, who had never met girls from high society, saw in Donna Maria one of those heroines of English novels who serve tea under pink lamp-shades—and, moreover, the lamp-shades belonged to one of the most celebrated salons in Rome! He did not pause to observe the complex character of the young girl, which combined the touchiness of those who do not feel quite at home in their social class with the impulses of a lively sensuality. Impetuous and romantic, Maria threw herself into an adventure that promised to take her away from her dismal palace and the family obsessed with its social world. Arranging rendezvous in deserted gardens with the help of a governess no less romantic than her pupil, slipping love-letters to each other as they left a concert, Gabriele and Maria experienced all the emotions of Romeo and Juliet, whose ages were barely less than their own. His vanity far outstripping his discretion, d'Annunzio confided in twenty or more persons, but this was not enough. The whole of Rome must know of his happiness and so, in the *Cronaca Bizantina*, he had a sonnet published with the title *Peccato di Maggio* ('Sin of May'); the poem told of a blonde virgin who resembled the portraits of Alma-Tadema and of the gift that she made to the poet.

The family in Pescara were kept informed of events, while the family in Rome pretended not to know anything; but, though the duchess tried to delay the catastrophe, it was not possible to delay the arrival of the child conceived in the 'sin of May'. To force the girl's hand, the seducer decided to abduct her; who, after such a scandal, would want to have anything to do with her? His position as a journalist enabled d'Annunzio to play an amusing but quite unwarranted trick on his future mother-in-law. Under the signature 'Bull-Calf' there appeared an account of a meeting at the Capitol, over which the Duchess di Gallese presided with 'the serenity of a dogaressa under her mantle of raised velvet'; the meeting had been called to decide on the appropriate protocol and gift with which the ladies of Roman society would greet the arrival in Rome of a Bavarian princess, who had just married the Duke of Savoy-Genoa. Confident that the princess would be occupied at the Quirinale the whole of the following day, d'Annunzio chose this opportunity to abduct Donna Maria. The lovers took the train to Florence, but a policeman in the duke's pay followed them; when they arrived at Florence station they were met by the chief commissioner himself, who ensured that Donna Maria returned to her parents under close guard.

The ensuing scandal was enormous, but the glory that redounded to its originator did not leave his pride altogether undamaged. Jealous journalists seized on the opportunity to point out how much this nonentity from the Abruzzi would benefit from the whole business; d'Annunzio's friend Scarfoglio sneered rather cruelly at the snobbery of his protégé; insults were bandied to and fro in verse and in prose; more or less scurrilous lampoons were secretly circulated; challenges to duels were almost exchanged. The poet assumed a high and mighty tone and addressed a sonnet of vengeance to *tutta la gran canaglia dei moralisti* ('all the great rabble of moralists'). Donna Maria, shut up in the Altemps palace, suffered some terrible scenes with the duke, whom she resisted with quiet stubbornness. The duchess, guilty of having introduced the wolf into the fold, received her share of insults; but she remained secretly in touch with Gabriele, for, after all, even such a husband would be better than no husband at all. Eventually the duke told the two women: 'Let her marry him then! Without guests, without presents, in a small chapel, and let me hear no more of it!' And so the marriage took place. But at least a prelate was found to marry the daughter of a duke. Hidden behind a pillar, the duchess watched the ceremony, and left without kissing her daughter. Gabriele's friends, Sommaruga, Scarfoglio and Michetti, did their best to create a jovial atmosphere.

The d'Annunzio family had wisely remained in Pescara, and that same evening the couple set off to join them. They lived at first in a small villa beside the sea and then in the Villa del Fuoco, objects of curiosity throughout the neighbourhood. What a prize had Gabriele brought back with him! Pescara gaped as the blonde figure of Donna Maria passed along the beach, her fair complexion protected by veils and a parasol, on the arm of her husband who wore an impeccable white suit, pointed shoes, gloves and a straw hat. The gossips of the town said that the couple's 'nest' was furnished with fabrics from England, that the young wife gave her husband tea, that most aristocratic of beverages, and that she also made nosegays and played the piano. The villa, for so long soiled by the love-affairs of Don Francesco Paolo, thus became a sanctuary of elegance. The poet, like Bourget's heroes, savoured the *lunghe ore di tè* and thought himself infinitely refined.

Donna Luisetta quickly gained the confidence of the young girl, who did not feel herself completely ruined. Moreover, during the first months of their marriage her husband never left her for an instant and she enjoyed what she herself described as 'an intoxicating happiness'. Later, Donna Maria realized that this was 'a purely physical happiness, for, even in my intoxication, something was missing; I felt no contact, no communion, between his soul and mine'. The young wife found herself rather in the position of a European who had married an Arab. At first blinded by pleasure, fascinated by the incessant serenade of love with which her husband charmed her, and proud to be the inspiration of a genius, she accepted the mediocrity of her new condition, the petty and even barbarous customs, the poverty and the violence of the tribe. But, as soon as she found herself alone, the enchantment dissolved and she realized that she had made a terrible blunder. This marriage was much more than a misalliance: Donna Maria found herself bound to someone of another race, for whom only physical suffering counted and who saw mental suffering merely as a theme for literary exploitation, a man for whom women were objects of pleasure and animals for breeding—above all, a man who easily descended into vulgarity as soon as he was not in circles where he had to play the gentleman, a man very much at ease in bad company: 'Before me, he had only had cheap women', the disillusioned sweetheart was later to say. Since Donna Maria had not brought her husband the means with which to play the gentleman, she soon found herself reduced to the status of a semi-servant, like the other wives of the Abruzzi, receiving sufficient recompense in the form of 'an intoxicating night' from time to time.

But this is looking ahead. When a son, Mario, was born six months after their marriage, Gabriele was delighted. His friends thought that he was going to have a great but sober career, like Victor Hugo, that his wife would domesticate him and that gradually, as the scandal was forgotten, the prestige of the Gallese family would help to make the 'enfant sublime' an official poet, the successor to Carducci. The publication of a new collection of verse, however, demolished such fantasies once and for all and placed d'Annunzio among the ranks of poètes maudits or damned poets.

4

Pleasure

THE DECADENT

The collection *Intermezzo di rime*, printed on pink paper and published by Sommaruga in July 1883, during the poet's honeymoon, confirmed what was already a bad reputation. In these poems d'Annunzio appeared as the flaunter of vice and, what is even worse in Italy, of sacrilege—a formidable example of the Decadence that was already raging in Paris. The motto taken from the Apocalypse gave the collection a vaguely Satanistic invocation: *In fronte ejus nomen scriptum: Mysterium.* ('On her forehead a name was written: a Mystery'.) The poems were as deplorable from the literary as from the moral point of view. A few titles will give an idea of their tone: *The Blood of the Virgins, The Thirteenth Labour;* twelve sonnets each devoted to a famous adulterer, including one called *Godoleva* which is almost obscene. The following lines from *Four Nude Studies* are enough to explain the scandal which the volume provoked:

'Beautiful breasts with your flowery points, you on which my weary head falls at dawn when, in the supreme prostration of pleasure, I stiffen and lose my strength;

'Feline haunches in whose furrows my musician's fingers rise rhythmically as on the strings of a lyre'.

53

This specimen of *fin-de-siècle* eroticism recalls the boldest pages of Albert Samain; Maupassant also served as a model. The following lines go even further in their frank allusion to a specific pleasure: 'O sinuous, moist and burning mouth, where my desire is intensified when I am sunk in deep oblivion, and which relentlessly sucks my life. O great head of hair strewn over my knees during the sweet act. O cold hand which spreads a shiver and feels me shivering.'

Women had been warned: the poet, who was beginning to look on himself as a god, loved above all to offer himself lazily for oral homage. He recognized his weakness in verse: 'My barbarous and vigorous youth is slain in the arms of women'; and also in prose, in a letter to Sommaruga (24 June 1884): 'The *Intermezzo* is the product of an illness, of a feebleness of mind, of a momentary decadence. The reasons for *Intermezzo* are to be found in my way of life at that false period. The *Intermezzo* is not a pornographic book; it is a human document; it is a manifestation of an unhealthy art . . . Now I am renewed and fortified . . .' (probably by marriage).

The words 'barbarous' and 'decadence', inseparable from this period, reveal the poet's inward contradictions and the absurdities which have too often prevented his work being taken seriously. They also indicate a certain lucidity, which in this 'barbarian' sometimes compensated for his complete lack of a sense of humour.

While the critics launched their assault and creditors became threatening, the announcement of the marriage had tempted imprudent usurers, who enabled the barbarian and decadent to play the paterfamilias in a delectable little house, under the fond eye of his family. In this serene atmosphere he wrote some very pretty love-poems for his wife and some realist stories for his publisher.

Here is yet another contradiction: if *Le Novelle della Pescara* outdo even the French Naturalist school in their treatment of the sordid, the poems in the collection *Isaotta Guttadauro ed altre poesie* are permeated with a Pre-Raphaelite sweetness. The volume of verse, the third, appeared in January 1886 in a luxurious edition with numerous illustrations by artists influenced by Burne-Jones. The most skilful, Aristide Sartorio, was always to remain strongly influenced by d'Annunzio; this charming young man was a protégé, though an ungrateful one, of Count Primoli, who had photographed him in some Greek scenes. The limited edition, which was rapidly exhausted, had been financed by Prince Sciarra. The dedication to Donna Maria printed in this first edition was omitted in the augmented edition of 1890 (retitled *L'Isotteo–La Chimera*). The cover of the book, decorated with the motto of the Guttadauro family—'A shower of gold for the thirsty'—made jealous men smile, for the duke was less willing than ever to lavish his money on the young couple. D'Annunzio imitated barcaroles and ballads with a genuine grace, sprinkling them with archaic words and with echoes of Petrarch and Boccaccio. The beautiful women whose praises he sang wear extravagant costumes in the manner of Pisanello, scatter roses like the nymphs of Botticelli and, with their retinue of pages and musicians, seem to belong to the processions painted by Benozzo Gozzoli. If the poet's sources were pictorial as much as literary, his poems are in no sense dusty theatrical masquerades and the flowers are much fresher than those of rhetoric. With his gift for adaptation, d'Annunzio must have imagined himself as Petrarch, as Politian lauding a mistress of Lorenzo the Magnificent, or as a humanist at the court of Sigismondo Malatesta. When these poems are deprived of their music by translation, they call to mind a collection by Jean Lorrain entitled *La Forêt bleue*, abounding with Mélusines and *Demoiselles Élues*. A comparison of the images reveals the same atmosphere of eroticism and legend—hennins and serpents, pages and swans living happily together in the moonlight or in the depths of the forest.

Under the influence of his young wife and the cups of tea which she brought him, d'Annunzio had seen Florence through the blue spectacles of an English lady—but a lady who would not flinch from the realities of life, for, inevitably, all these delicate images serve ultimately to exalt physical love. To prepare the public for a form of writing so alien to Italy, d'Annunzio invented, probably with the help of Nencioni, an English poet by the name of 'Adolphus Hanaford' whom he pretended to quote in brilliantly fabricated 'translations' in an enthusiastic critical article:

> O Viviana May de Penuele
> Gelida virgo prerafaelita . . .

(the 'Pre-Raphaelite virgin' holds out a lily to Dante-Gabriele). The public, however, received the *Isaotta Guttadauro* poems rather coolly; some, hungry for scandal, were disappointed at not finding the same subjects as those treated in the *Intermezzo di rime*, while others pointed to the imitations and ignored the beauties. One sonnet, for example, paraphrased this line of Victor Hugo in *Les Contemplations*: '*Car le mot, c'est le Verbe, et le Verbe, c'est Dieu.*' Italy, too young a nation to appreciate such decadent graces, expected something different from a great poet, something for which d'Annunzio was to make it wait for another five or six years. The critics sneered and Gabriele was infuriated when a burlesque of his poems appeared with the title *Risaotto al Pomidauro* ('Tomato Risotto'). Only a small group of artists who had been shocked by the *Intermezzo di rime* showed enthusiasm. Among the latter were Adolfo de Bosis, a great Roman lawyer, and Angelo Conti, a young Venetian art critic. De Bosis, a passionate admirer of Shelley, and Conti, a whole-hearted disciple of Walter Pater, were to complete the education which d'Annunzio had begun with Nencioni and thus help the poet to become one of the greatest figures of the Aesthetic Movement.

Shortly afterwards, Sommaruga published a collection of stories, *Il Libro delle Vergini* ('The Book of the Virgins'). In d'Annunzio's own words, the virgins of the title 'went to church from the brothel'. To the publisher, who had not read these bitter provincial tales, three naked women, rather badly drawn, therefore seemed a suitable illustration for the cover of the book. D'Annunzio assumed a high moral tone, demanding a public apology and a decent cover. It was on this occasion that he wrote the letter to Sommaruga quoted earlier in which he referred to *Intermezzo di rime*. Clearly, he now wished to embark upon a respectable period. Sommaruga, who had compromised him, disappeared from his life and founded other reviews—*The Nabab* and then *Le Forche Caudine*, in which 'he adopted American publicity methods to sell the products of a romanticism gone bad', in the words of his rival Scarfoglio.

RETURN TO REALITIES

The happiness of the husband and wife ('lovers' would be nearer the truth) lasted for about a year, but the pressures of the outside world were such that the couple would sooner or later have to leave their retreat. In Pescara, Don Francesco Paolo's creditors were threatening to sell the villa; in any case, where could the money be found to make the house comfortable? It was delightful in summer but damp in winter. When Michetti returned to Rome, Pescara once more became an intellectual desert; the 'exquisite hour' of drinking tea could seem decidedly long and Gabriele yearned for the evenings with Tosti, the chit-chat at the Caffè Greco and the adulation which his presence aroused. Might he not be forgotten if he remained too long out of the public eye? This man who genuinely loved solitude had an insatiable need to shine in society, in any kind of society, provided that it included pretty women and a few men of wit. At the same time, in Rome the Duchess di Gallese was anxious that the young couple should come to her: it was vital that this undesirable son-in-law should become rich and famous as quickly as possible and thereby make his detractors jealous. One of her cousins, Prince Sciarra, who had been in love with Donna Maria, owned the *Corriere di Roma*; he was persuaded to offer Gabriele commissions for literary and social features that were better paid than his first essays in journalism. It was also important to find a publisher other than Sommaruga, who dealt in scandal and was always on the verge of bankruptcy. But the essential thing was to return to the civilized world.

The couple settled in a modest apartment on Via delle Quattro Fontane, not far from the Quirinale. Donna Maria was pregnant again. As soon as he found himself back in Rome, the husband reverted to the habits of his youth, leaving his wife to argue with upholsterers and to cope with the problems of a petty-bourgeois household for which she was quite unprepared. In this respect, Gabriele was little different from most Italian husbands, who spend much of their time away from the home; however, unlike other Italian husbands, who are excellent fathers, he did not remain with his wife for her confinement, but stayed as far as possible from her at this time when he found her fretful and unattractive. (Oscar Wilde also turned his back on a wife disfigured by pregnancy.) While the birth of the love-child had redounded to the glory of the young father, the births of his other two sons—Veniero, named after a doge of Venice, and Gabriele, named after the greatest man in Italy—were hardly noticed by the head of the family. Donna Maria, separated from her own social sphere and having no wish to be visited on the sly and for motives of charity, found herself ill at ease in her husband's world. She had hardly a friend apart from Matilde Serao and Primoli.

Shortly after their return from Pescara, Donna Maria found a love-letter in one of her husband's jackets. The world of Shakespeare's *Romeo and Juliet* now made way for that of George Ohnet's *Le Maître de forges:* with as much tenacity of purpose as the proud heroine of Ohnet's play, who had also been trapped in a misalliance, and for the honour of the Gallese from whom she was so tenuously descended, Donna Maria resolved to suffer in silence—even better, to continue to brave opinion by remaining faithful to the man who was deceiving her. One evening, at the Opera, Gabriele left the box of Prince Sciarra, who had invited the couple, to visit another box occupied by Olga Ossani, who wrote under the name of Febea. When the prince pointed out the couple to Donna Maria, she replied: 'Febea is so beautiful that if I were a man I would do the same.' This Febea was the 'Signora X' of the 'androgynous head', the admirer of the 'St. Sebastian' at the Pincio, the poet's first vaguely 'fashionable' mistress, whose acquaintance he had quickly renewed as soon as he arrived back in Rome. D'Annunzio called her 'Helen the Silent': this very beautiful woman, slightly eccentric and very much on the fringe of Society, became a duchess, Elena Muti, in his novel *Il Piacere*.

But this liaison was of little importance. What was important was the novel, the fruit of his Roman experience, which d'Annunzio had just begun. Nothing was to distract him in the creation of a masterpiece—neither the scenes of a mistress nor the tears of a wife and the cries of his children. Nor did he wish to spend his time on the daily routine of newspaper columns; he was no longer interested in writing about hats, princesses and royal carriages for *La Tribuna*, or offering recipes for intellectual elegance in the *Cronaca Bizantina*, which had also recently been bought by Prince Sciarra. A few months after returning from Pescara, d'Annunzio wrote to the prince announcing his intention of leaving Rome: he could only work in solitude. His salary was increased and he remained in Rome. This moderate rise in income resulted in a frenzy of immoderate spending; when he arrived home, his arms were laden with *objets d'art* or silk shirts. Instead of sharing his joy in these pretty things, his wife buried her reddened nose in her knitting and reminded him that they owed their one and only servant three months' wages. If such scenes had been observed by witnesses, they might have disarmed the malice of jealous persons; but the couple's pride and their determination to cut a *bella figura* in public prevented the truth from being suspected. However, the rumour soon passed round Rome that if Prince Sciarra paid his reporter so well, it was not so much for his talent as for his complaisance. Scarfoglio repeated the gossip and d'Annunzio challenged him to a duel. Fortunately for the honour of his wife, d'Annunzio had a literary reason for quarrelling with Scarfoglio: the easily offended husband had just learnt that Scarfoglio was the author of the parody of *Isaotta Guttadauro*. The duel was fought with swords in the *campagna*, on 20 November 1886; d'Annunzio was wounded in the arm. Shortly afterwards, the poet resumed friendly relations with the Scarfoglio household. This was not the first duel: in the previous year, on 30 September, d'Annunzio had fought a duel against a certain Carlo Magnico, who had published some offensive remarks. Gabriele was wounded in the head and his face was covered with blood; the poet had saved his honour but lost his hair: so much ferric chloride was poured on his scalp to stop the bleeding that the fuzzy shepherd's mop rapidly made way for a distinguished baldness.

During this same season a book on Roman society by Count Vassili was published in which the French public found the poet's name mentioned for the first time: 'Among the young people, Gabriele d'Annunzio is esteemed for his vigour and the youthfulness of his ideas, but he is affected, tortuous and often obscure' (the book was the result of the collaboration between a come-down Radziwill and Juliette Adam, the republican Egeria). In a book on Parisian society published two years earlier, the same authors had written in almost the same terms of the man who one day was to become a great friend of d'Annunzio's, Robert de Montesquiou, the supreme example of the 'aesthete' as portrayed in Huysmans' novel À rebours, published in 1884. With his wealth of vocabulary, the sole wealth that d'Annunzio possessed, and a will untrammelled either by feelings of delicacy or by a sense of duty towards anyone but himself, the scandalous and impecunious poet, the provincial who had made a bad marriage (or too good a marriage, which comes to the same thing), succeeded in breathing into the exquisite and macabre puppet described by Huysmans his own savage taste for pleasure and his own turbulent imagination—in other words, the very life which was lacking both in Montesquiou and in his literary projections, Des Esseintes and Dorian Gray.

IL PIACERE

Barbara Leoni, whom some biographers have called d'Annunzio's 'greatest love', and whose relationship with him is described later on, influenced the famous novel Il Piacere ("The Child of Pleas-

ure') to a much lesser extent than the poems of *La Chimera*, for
the novel was certainly conceived before their meeting in the
spring of 1887. In the novel, two women occupy the attentions of
Andrea Sperelli, a sublimated d'Annunzio: Elena Muti, Duchess
of Scerni, and Maria Feres. For the first, sensual and enigmatic,
Barbara Leoni provided only her voluptuous disposition and a
few impressions remembered from walks in the gardens of Rome.
The duchess owed her intelligence and her mystery to the journalist Olga Ossani, while the costumes were taken straight from *La
Vie parisienne*, to which d'Annunzio continued to subscribe all
his life and which was at this time the arbiter of elegance in
dress and interior decoration. The gentle Maria Feres obviously
owed much to Donna Maria. There are also countless echoes
from d'Annunzio's society columns, those ravishing women
glimpsed at the races and photographed by Primoli: 'The Duchess Grazzioli, fair as a rose, who seems to belong to one of Kate
Greenaway's keepsakes', and the Countess of Santifioro: 'Behind
the veil, the almost sorrowful face of the Venus of Cyprus . . .'
Such women, and their male counterparts, served as models for
the minor characters; Prince Odescalchi, with his tawny beard
and the physique of Hercules, was the Prince Secinara of the
novel. When a novelist desires to enter a world which does not
easily open its doors, all he can do is to shine in imaginary salons.
Balzac had set an example. Andrea Sperelli is a d'Annunzio descended from Gonzagas and Estes rather than the Rapagnettas,
from a long line of artistic and corrupt lords who all 'were intent
on making their life a work of art'.

The novel itself is a work of art composed with the utmost care,
engraved with marvellous detail, encrusted with unforgettable
phrases and some purple passages. D'Annunzio made his intentions clear in describing the work of his hero: 'For the execution
of his art, he chose by preference the most difficult, exact, and
incorruptible vehicles—verse and engraving; and he aimed at ad-
hering strictly to, and reviving, the traditional Italian methods, by
going back to the poets of the *stil novo* and the painters who were
precursors of the Renaissance.' 'His *Story of the Hermaphrodite*

imitated in its structure Poliziano's *Story of Orpheus* and contained lines of extraordinary delicacy, power and melody, particularly in the choruses of hybrid monsters—the Centaurs, Sirens and Sphinxes. His new tragedy, *La Simona*, of moderate length, possessed a most singular charm. Written and rhymed though it was, on the ancient Tuscan rules, it might have been conceived by an English poet of Elizabeth's time, after a story from the *Decameron*, and it breathed something of the strange and delicious charm of certain of the minor dramas of Shakespeare.' (From the translation by Georgina Harding.)

A man is never better served than by himself! But Sperelli was primarily an engraver rather than a writer. At the time of the novel's publication, the art dealers on the Via del Babuino were offering for sale an etching signed 'Andrea Sperelli' which showed Barbara Leoni, naked on a counterpane embroidered with the signs of the Zodiac (an important part of the furnishings of the hero's bedroom), and teasing a greyhound. Fashionable Rome attributed the etching to the author of the novel and recognized his mistress. In fact, the etching had been done by Sartorio, following d'Annunzio's directions.

The plot of the novel is simple. Sperelli and Elena Muti meet at a great dinner and immediately fall wildly in love, for Elena has 'the mouth of the Medusa of Leonardo, that human flower of the soul rendered divine by the fire of passion and the anguish of death.' (Georgina Harding's translation.) These monsters of elegance meet again at an auction, among other panthers of the same kind. Elena makes Andrea buy a watch in the shape of a death's-head. They see each other again at a ball. The duchess falls ill, Sperelli goes to see her and she gives herself to him in her overheated bedroom, which smells of chloroform. Their happiness is immeasurable. 'Admirably fashioned in body and in mind for the practice of the highest and rarest pleasures, both pursued relentlessly the Absolute, the Supreme, the Inaccessible.' They go for walks through Rome and then Elena leaves mysteriously. At the races, Sperelli devotes his attentions to the haughty Donna Ippolita Albinoco. Gravely wounded in a duel with this lady's lover, the seducer goes to convalesce with a female cousin in a villa on the Adriatic. A Sienese friend, Maria Feres, arrives for a stay with her young daughter: 'The refined features had that subtle expression of suffering and lassitude which lends the human charm to the Virgins of the Florentine *tondi* of the time of Cosimo. A soft and tender shadow, the fusion of two diaphanous tints—violet and blue, lay under her eyes, which had the leonine irises of the brown-haired angels.' (Georgina Harding's translation.) The contrast with the duchess is as great morally as physically. Virtuous and unhappily married, Maria Feres defends herself despairingly, rather like the Présidente de Tourvel besieged by Valmont in *Les Liaisons dangereuses*. Her diary records the progress of passion: walks through gardens, magnificent rides on horseback through the pine-trees, musical evenings. They part, however, without anything final having taken place. Sperelli returns to Rome and to his facile affairs. He meets Elena Muti, who no longer wishes to be his, for she has just sold herself to a rich and corrupt Englishman, Lord Mount-Edgecumb. He is smitten with jealousy and despair. When Maria Feres returns, Sperelli resolves to hasten her downfall, but he is caught in his own snare and falls truly in love with Maria. Alas, obsessed with the redoubtable duchess at the very moment when Maria finally gives herself to him, Sperelli utters Elena's name. Her dishonour thus crowned with treachery, Maria departs. The novel ends with the despair and solitude of Sperelli, who finds himself once more among the society monsters encountered at the beginning of the book and learns that the duchess has a new lover.

Il Piacere is an excellent novel which can be read at a single sitting, though some minutely detailed descriptions can be skipped. Like Huysmans, Wilde and, a little later, Elémir Bourges, d'Annunzio was a born interior decorator: how he indulges his love of Genoa velvet and Casteldurante majolica! The auction (there was also to be an auction in Paul Bourget's *Cosmopolis*) is one of the best chapters of the book. The writing is most dated when the language of the soul is employed. Maria Feres abuses such language in the same way as the Présidente de Tourvel abuses religious expressions in *Les Liaisons dangereuses*. For the French reader the translator wisely suppressed those parts of the book that would have called to mind the then famous works of Péladan, passages of mystical eroticism and even some rather scabrous lines in the description of the supper with the *demimondaines*.

The whole novel does seem to bear out d'Annunzio's own words: 'I am the mythical composite of all fruits, of all secret gardens—a bee that plundered freely from French flower-beds.' In more than one passage of the novel d'Annunzio plagiarized *L'Éducation sentimentale*; he also borrowed from a story by Jean Lorrain in which the heroine, like Elena Muti, describes too explicitly the pleasure that she experiences in dancing. The description of the dinner and the meeting with Elena, in the very first pages of the book, might almost come from a novel by Alphonse Daudet—*L'Immortel*, for example; the description of the cutlery is pure Goncourt; the teas under lamp-shades and the frequent use of English expressions recall the novels of Paul Bourget. The scene at the races calls to mind a similar episode in *Nana*. These Parisian frills were skilfully superimposed on a solid Roman architecture. By a highly effective contrast, the open-air cure in the Baroque villa where Scarlatti is played charmed those ladies who were rather disconcerted by the raciness of certain pages, though these passages were usually toned down in the translations. The crude pleasantries of Sperelli might appear shocking if one did not remember that this hero is above all laws, even those of decorum. His laugh is the laugh of Boccaccio. In this contempt for the proprieties, coupled with a contempt for women, *Il Piacere* is a work in the main stream of the Aesthetic Movement; it has its Nietzschean aspects, but it is almost certain that d'Annunzio did not read Nietzsche until two or three years after writing this novel (and then in a French translation).

One of the chief reasons for the success of *Il Piacere* when it appeared in translation (*L'Enfant de volupté* in French, *The Child of Pleasure* in English) was the fact that it coincided with the beginnings of *art nouveau*. Certain descriptions bear an exact resemblance to the paintings that were now appearing in English magazines: 'She wore a dress of a curious indefinable dull rusty red, one of those so-called aesthetic colours one meets with in the pictures of the Early Masters or of Dante Gabriel Rossetti. It was arranged in a multitude of straight regular folds beginning immediately under the arms, and was confined at the waist by a wide blue-green ribbon, of the pale tinge of a faded turquoise, that fell in a great knot at her side.' (From the translation by Georgina Harding.) The description of Maria's hair suggests the blurred, sinuous lines of a drawing by Gallé; also reminiscent of Gallé is the sinister orchid which, in the first chapter, decorates the marchesa's table.

Il Piacere was thus regarded as a lesson in artistic and social refinement, an invitation to live above laws, splendidly and dangerously. The lesson was to bear fruit some fifteen years later, when 'd'Annunzian' ladies roamed across Europe leaving a trail of scandals and tuberoses in their wake, loving pleasure even to the point of being prepared to perish in its pursuit, if they could not at the last minute find some English milord to subsidize their whims. These creatures were to gather round the novelist when at last he became as grand a figure as his hero, when, like Sperelli, he could say to himself each time he met a woman: 'She wants me! She wants me!' D'Annunzio's ability to identify himself with the great lord and aesthete of his invention played a large part in the successes of the Don Juan of Pescara.

As soon as it appeared, in 1889, *Il Piacere* enjoyed an enormous success, in spite of hostile critics (described by the author as 'the asinine chorus of journalists'), but for reasons in which a love of scandal played a larger part than artistic judgement. The same was true, three-quarters of a century later, in the case of *La Dolce Vita. Il Piacere* is a *roman-à-clef* full of extremely bold scenes, published at a time when Italian literature was producing works of the most nauseating mawkishness, such as *Cuore* by De Amicis. Despite the critics, *Il Piacere* enabled the Italians to see that they at last possessed a writer of international class. Four years later, the French were amazed to discover in *L'Enfant de volupté* the themes of the Decadence and the dandyism of Paul Bourget, treated with a passion which no French writer of the time could emulate. (Translations of d'Annunzio's books were not made until much later in England, where the reactions were much less enthusiastic.) The French public was also gratified to read the wonderful descriptions of Rome, of all Italian cities the one dearest to the French, who left Florence to the English and Venice to the Germans. The novel became an indispensable supplement to Baedeker, for it described the city from the English cemetery to the Zuccari palace, near Santa Trinità dei Monti; Sperelli would pass through the doorway of this palace, carved with the jaws of a monster, to reach his Renaissance bachelor apartment. D'Annunzio was to return, always with success, to the idea of linking the plot of a novel with a city, thereby enhancing his story with the prestige of famous monuments of architecture: Venice served as the background for *Il Fuoco*, Mantua and Volterra for *Forse che sì forse che no*. In an article entitled *Roma Amor*, published in 1906, d'Annunzio said that Rome was the principal theme of his novel; he explained his characters' relationships with the city, and the only debt which he admitted was the *Roman Elegies* of Goethe. The characters themselves are less interesting than the places where they live, the objects that they love, the music to which they listen. The finest lines in *La Chimera* recall some of the delicious moments that d'Annunzio experienced so frequently in the Rome of 1885:

> *Odor di rose, forse da i giardini*
> *chiusi del Re, venìa confusamente;*
> *e splendea ne la fredda ora, imminente,*
> *la Luna, su'l palazzo Barberini.*

> *Mormorvan con voci roche e lente*
> *le fontane invisibile tra i pini:*
> *or sì or no li stocchi adamantini*
> *oltre i rami balzavan di repente.*

('A perfume of roses, perhaps from the closed gardens of the king, hovered vaguely; and at that cold hour, high in the sky, the moon shone on the Barberini palace.

'With their slow, hoarse voices, the fountains murmured, invisible among the pines; from time to time daggers of diamonds would suddenly dance above the branches.')

('Donna F' from the collection *La Chimera.*)

5

Mondo cane

BARBARELLA

In 1890 Gabriele published a collection of poems entitled *L'Isotteo—La Chimera*, in which the poems of the *Isaotta Guttadauro* volume were revised and a number of new poems were added. The excitement of a new liaison had revived d'Annunzio's poetic inspiration, which had been threatened by the mediocrity of family life and the harassing cares of journalism. The memory of the beautiful Barbara Leoni is inseparable from the best of the poems in *La Chimera*, evoking as they do meetings in the gardens and the old districts of Rome.

These memories were also recorded in *Il Piacere*. Possibly because his own literary personality was too tarnished, d'Annunzio had created a double of himself, a sublime artist, Andrea Sperelli, a combination of Des Esseintes and Don Juan, torn between a frenzy for female conquests and the disgust that follows. Sperelli, as we have seen, was an engraver rather than a man of letters; above all, he was a man of the world. Both poems and novel exalted 'the struggle of a monstrous aesthetico-aphrodisiac chimera against the palpitating phantom of life in the soul of a man.' The aphrodisiac element was distinctly inferior to the aesthetic element. Of course, the poems of *La Chimera* hark back to the vo-

68

luptuous themes of the *Intermezzo di rime*; they parade all the monsters from the menagerie of the Decadence—Gorgons, Mandragoras, Medusas, succubae and hermaphrodites. Yet these fashionable myths do not prevent the reader from believing in the agony of their insatiable hero. The poem *A Andrea Sperelli* contains the most beautiful flashes of late Romanticism; one can almost imagine Gustave Moreau's Sphinx speaking:

> *Io guardo in me. Le tenebre ch'esplora*
> *il mio sguardo profondo, internamente,*
> *m'attraggan più d'ogni più bella aurora.*
>
> *Che è l'aurora? Che è mai l'ardente*
> *spira de li astri, il mar blando e feroce?*
> *Io guardo in me con le pupille intente.*
>
> *Sola io contemplo, sola e senza voce,*
> *un mar che non ha fondo e non ha lido.*
> *O tu che soffri, il tuo soffrire è atroce.*

('I gaze into myself. The shadows within me explored by my deep gaze draw me more than the most beautiful dawn. What is the dawn? What is the burning spiral of the stars, the calm and raging sea? I gaze into myself with pupils rapt. Alone, I contemplate, alone and without voice, a bottomless and shoreless sea. O you who suffer, your suffering is cruel.')

The woman who inspired these poems looked like the *fin-de-siècle* sphinxes of the kind that Khnopff was beginning to paint in Brussels. She was a Roman from the Trastevere and had the figure of a goddess, with enormous eyes and wavy hair. The poet had met her on 2 April 1887, in a small concert-room on Via Margutta. Her dazzling beauty, though she was modestly dressed, entranced d'Annunzio, who made enquiries about her. She was the daughter of a lower-middle-class family and was married to a Bolognese count. Gabriele went to consult a fortune-teller and asked her for a talisman with which to win the love of the countess, an aspiration soon to be fulfilled. Immediately renamed

'Barbarella', the countess became the woman cherished as an object of art, the woman so dear to the aesthetes; this was in no sense contrary to d'Annunzio's conception of woman as an object of pleasure. The poet saw in Barbarella the embodiment of his literary ideal. He described her perfections in many poems and, a little later, in a novel which he devoted to the history of this liaison, Il Trionfo della Morte: 'The narrowness of the hips gave her the appearance of an adolescent. The sterile belly had kept its virginal purity. The bosom was small and firm, as if carved in a delicate alabaster, with violet-pink points on the extraordinarily erectile breasts. The whole of the posterior part of the body, from the nape of the neck to the knees, resembled an ephebe: this was one of the fragments of the ideal human type which nature sometimes throws among the multitude of mediocre casts with which the race is perpetuated. But the most precious feature of this body, in Giorgio's eyes, was the colouring. The skin had an indescribable colour, very rare and quite different from the usual colouring of dark women.'

This passage from Il Trionfo della Morte had been foreshadowed by dozens of letters which make monotonous reading. The best that the letters contained was used in the poems of La Chimera. One often observes a certain ambiguity that seems strange in a man apparently so passionately fond of women, but perhaps d'Annunzio was merely following a fashion: 'I kiss your sad mouth, like the mouth of a young god—Antinous has your pure but sad mouth, voluptuous but with a strange bitterness, passionate but cruel.' A later poem also emphasizes this ambiguity: 'She too resembled obscurely the ambiguous being, the prodigious myth, which Leonardo loved in his mind. She was the ideal Hermaphrodite, she was the dreamed-of Androgyne. Her look aroused an indefinable disquiet.' Other poems show to what extent d'Annunzio's eroticism was sensitive to fashion: 'When, for the first time, she offered herself to me with a mighty cry (my spirit trembles still), a great bunch of lilies, a pure emblem, breathed forth a pure incense beside the couch.' Lilies appear again in another poem: 'Tall and solitary, my soul sees them shine in the shadow at that moment when, dying, it plunges once more into pleasure.'

The idea of death, which was to grow into an obsession, also appears in these letters. Woman, as an object of art, would be even more artistic without the always slightly vulgar attribute of life: 'I dream that I see you white on a divan, like a corpse . . . I suck the blood from your heart. In the words of Goncourt, I felt the need to die a little.' This was not a pose, but a state of mind. Other letters reveal a partiality for flesh remarkable in one who signed himself 'Ariel': 'Kiss my eyes slowly; caress my lashes with your soft, moist tongue, in the way you know so well.' Many of these letters are unprintable, for in them the poet dwelt lyrically on the delights of oral intercourse, a pleasure which he cherished above all others. When she found herself far from her beloved, Barbara would reply on this same theme with a vividly descriptive nostalgia. Then, as with one of his first sweethearts, d'Annunzio would from time to time resort to the language of opera: '*Addio! Addio! Amami! Amami! Tutti i moti del animo tuo tutti tutti i tuoi pensieri e i sogni per me. Tutti . . . tutti . . . tutti . . .*'

The critics had given *Il Piacere* a cool reception, for this novel was in advance of the fashion which they were following. During the past ten years, in an Italy that had turned to Realism and had made Zola its model, a whole generation of novelists had adopted the label *veristi*; nowadays it would be more accurate to call them 'regionalists', for their studies of manners were provincial rather than social. The best of them, Verga, a Sicilian who wrote the well-known *Don Gesualdo* among many other novels, had anticipated the naturalism of Zola's Médan school. After the publication of his prose tales, the critics who had placed d'Annunzio in this category were as angry as their French colleagues had been when Huysmans, the author of *Les Sœurs Vatard*, published *À rebours*. As soon as he had exhausted the aesthetic seam, d'Annunzio, who did not mind what label he was given and, though highly susceptible to influence in matters of form, always followed his own inclinations, returned to realism and said goodbye to the lamp-shades and the orchids. He now went back for long periods to Pescara (where he had written *Il Piacere*) to plunge into another novel. There were other reasons for this return to the land: the love of a simple woman, to whom life in Rome prevented him from devoting his attention, and the disgust with which that life had filled him—the pettiness, the financial difficulties of married life, the jealous colleagues.

The love of Barbara Leoni brought the poet back to an existence that was more frugal, if not more sensible. The history of this liaison is revealed in all its detail by the letters already quoted, by the poems which she inspired in *La Chimera* and in the *Elegie romane*, and by the novel *Trionfo della Morte*, the supreme record of their relationship. Barbara had been married, or rather sold, to Count Leoni, a Bolognese so brutal that the young wife was unable to bear more than a week of marriage, and returned to her parents to live in a shabby and possibly even a somewhat lewd environment. Barbara was modesty itself, a nice girl rather embarrassed by her goddess-like appearance. At the Bach concert where d'Annunzio had met her, she had been conspicuous, with 'her barbarian queen's head', in the simple room among the eccentrics, some 'Buddhists', the others 'Pre-Raphaelites', who had come to listen to such unfashionable music. She had gone there as a spirit in distress might go to a spiritualist seance. She lived frugally with her family, who spied on her, exasperated at seeing such beauty unproductive. This situation soon began to vex Gabriele. During the four years of their liaison, the jealousy of the poet and the erotic demands of his mistress led the lovers, stage by stage, to the brink of a crime which, fortunately, was committed only in the final chapter of *Trionfo della Morte*. Whenever she was obliged to return to her brutal husband, d'Annunzio would implore her to spare his feelings: 'Spare me the sight of your bruises, my heart would break at the sight of your flesh battered by those hands. Horrible! Horrible!' The description of Barbara's charms quoted above explains how such an attachment was formed in spite of the distance separating the position of La Leoni and the social aspirations of her lover. During the periods of tenderness, the poet assured his friends that he had at last found a sister. D'Annunzio was also to bestow the title of sister on his wife and on many other women throughout his life, a title as sacrosanct as that of cardinal. The 'sisters' were the pillars of the d'Annunzian church. In moments of crisis, he would reproach Barbara for the plebeian side of her character and for her stupidity; he would have been more justified if he had accused her of naïveté.

In the year that he met Barbara, the year during which he practically abandoned his wife and home, which he now found far too gloomy, d'Annunzio began to discover Italy. His friend de Bosis, as generous as he was cultured, invited him to join a cruise to Venice on a small yacht named *Lady Clara* in homage to Shelley. The sailors chosen by the poet for their sonorous names were few and inexperienced. After sailing along the Adriatic coast for two weeks, they drifted too far from land and lost their bearings; *Lady Clara* made a pitiful entrance into the lagoon, towed by a military patrol-boat. When they had anchored near a beach, the crew carried ashore a multi-coloured tent, carpets, copper salvers, champagne buckets full of sparkling wines, and all kinds of exotic luxuries which to the poet seemed the marks of high living, but which gave the inhabitants of the shore the impression that a travelling circus had arrived to give a performance. Alas, there was not a single woman on board! Barbara rejoined her lover in Rimini and then, escaping once again from her family, managed to come to Venice for forty-eight hours, which the couple spent in the Danieli hotel without leaving their room. This was one of their moments of extreme passion, like the 'great week of love' which the pair had spent at the beginning of their liaison in a small hotel in Albano—an experience begun, so great was Gabriele's impatience, in the crawling suburban train that served the outskirts of Rome. Venice fascinated d'Annunzio, who stayed there, leaving Barbarella to return alone to Rome and Donna Maria to give birth to a son who was named Veniero, after a doge, to celebrate his father's mystical marriage with *La Serenissima*. During that season Venice inspired the poet to write *Prologo d'una allegoria dell'autunno*.

From the very beginning of this liaison, d'Annunzio rediscovered the poetic verve of his early months of marriage; the four years that the affair lasted were remarkably productive. One of his finest collections of verse, *Elegie romane*, published in 1892 and permeated with the figure of Barbarella, commemorates the various episodes of this relationship from the first meeting to the final abandonment; it is the lyrical counterpart of the novel *Trionfo della Morte*, which presents the realistic version of the lovers' passion. The outline of the novel can be found in the love-letters, as can the inspiration for the poems, which become more affecting when love begins to weigh heavily. The poem devoted to the break-up of the affair is the most beautiful:

> *Dunque nell' alta selva, che udisti cantar su'l mio capo,*
> *sepellirai tu, senza pianto, il tuo grande amore?*
>
> *Intenderò io dunque nel dolce silenzio, che amammo,*
> *la verità crudele . . .*
>
> *Pure, io non altro feci che amarti, che amarti; non altro*
> *feci che amarti sempre! Io non ti feci male.*
>
> *Vano ogni sforzo. Un freddo suggel mi chiudeva la bocca.*

('In this tall forest which you heard sing above my head
Will you then bury your great love, without a tear?
And in the sweet silence that we loved
Shall I then hear the cruel truth? . . .
Yet all I did was love you, love you; all I did was
Love you always! I did not hurt you.
All effort was vain. An icy seal closed my mouth.')
('Villa Chigi' from the collection *Elegie romane*.)

The poems on the fountains, the Villa Medici and the Villa d'Este are also very fine; they have the sonority of certain of

Liszt's works which were similarly inspired by the Eternal City. Unfortunately each rendezvous in these gardens put the young woman in a difficult situation. Weary of being watched by her parents and her husband, she took refuge with a sister in Milan, whereupon the poet became wild with jealousy. Was his mistress to be sold once more to some rich admirer? By a strange paradox, d'Annunzio at this point wrote her some appalling letters; however, finding Rome without Barbara unbearable, he returned to Pescara for a long stay with his friend Michetti.

IL TRIONFO DELLA MORTE

The whole story of d'Annunzio and the 'Trasteverina' is related in *Trionfo della Morte* ('The Triumph of Death'), but in an excessively sombre manner: the plot even contains a crime of passion, as well as a large number of revolting descriptions. Never did d'Annunzio so thoroughly indulge his taste for the morbid. This novel is a *danse macabre* of the kind painted in charnel-houses: intestines protrude from under dresses and bones clatter. At the beginning of the novel, Giorgio and Ippolita witness a suicide; from that moment onwards, death stands between them, even during the frantic week of love at Albano. The hero has to go away to arrange the affairs of his family, whose situation has been jeopardized by a ghastly father. In the house at Pescara, haunted by childhood memories in the form of senile aunts, he finds the weapons of an uncle who killed himself. To escape the phantom of suicide, he sends for Ippolita and installs her in a hermitage amid glorious countryside. But this idyllic existence is disturbed by the repulsive squalor and disease rife among the local population. In his long description of the pilgrimage—reminiscent of both Huysmans and Zola, the fair on the church terrace and the beggars' camp—d'Annunzio invites the reader to a festival of human depravity. These horrors give the copulation of the lovers a sinister atmosphere. The hero 'bore in the depths of his substance the germs inherited from his father. He, a thinking and feeling being, had in his flesh the fatal heredity of this brute being. In him instinct became passion and sensuality assumed morbid forms.' Erotic crises alternate with paroxysms of disgust. Luckily, a piano is brought onto the scene to draw the lovers together again. Through music, 'a mysterious faculty drew them together, made them mingle and dissolve in one another, rendered them alike in body and soul, and united them into a single being. A mysterious faculty separated them, estranged them, drove them back into solitude, fixed a great gulf between them, planted in their souls a desperate and mortal longing.' (From the translation by Georgina Harding.) Like all lovers in the aesthetic period, they experienced a paroxysm in listening to the prelude of *Tristan und Isolde*: '. . . love's breathless longing for death rang out with unexampled vehemence . . . insatiable desire rose to the frenzy of destruction.' There follows a long analysis of Wagner's drama, to prove that death is the only solution to their too violent love. Finally, after one last spasm of voluptuous pleasure, Giorgio leads Ippolita to the edge of a cliff; she no longer wants to die, but he drags her with him and they fall into the sea, locked in each other's arms.

This novel, the action of which takes place in the middle of the summer, reeks of sweat and filth. Yet it would be unfair to d'Annunzio not to recognize the insights which it contains, with its long meditations on death. Illusory or not, this communication with the world beyond transformed the writer's view of everyday life, leading him to despise the uninitiated and to indulge in every sort of extravagance in order to explore all the possibilities of an existence which it seemed futile to confine within the limits of the rational.

RETURN TO THE LAND

Two years earlier, d'Annunzio, disgusted with Rome, had written the letter (6 April 1886) to Prince Sciarra which had earned him an increase in salary. That he should have decided to remain in the city is no reason to doubt the sincerity of these lines: 'Rome has defeated me. I have, by temperament and by instinct, a *need of the superfluous.* My aesthetic education draws me irresistibly to the desire and the purchase of beautiful things. I could easily have lived in a modest house, . . . drunk tea from a cheap cup, blown my nose with handkerchiefs costing two *lire* a half-dozen . . . Instead, inevitably, I wanted divans, precious fabrics, Persian carpets, Japanese plates, bronzes, ivories, trinkets, all those useless and beautiful things for which I have a deep and ruinous passion. And also, I was anxious that Maria, born in a lordly house, should not live in surroundings too different from those to which she had been accustomed. But I have done what I was in no position to do. Rome has defeated me. I shall go back to my homeland.' D'Annunzio did not go to his parents' house, where things were going from bad to worse. The portrait of Don Francesco Paolo in *Il Trionfo della Morte* concentrates on the degeneracy of this man who, though a braggart and a libertine, was certainly intelligent and had given his son a good education. No *verista* had ever written a page as cruel as this. A part of this passage has already been quoted in the first chapter. As the years passed, the son saw his father without pity: 'The flesh which becomes deformed and infected, which is covered with calluses, wrinkles, pimples, warts and hair . . . This extension of latent brutishness seemed to have taken place gradually . . .' 'In the corners of the eyes, on the temples, this man had a cluster of wrinkles, and beneath each eye a swelling, a sort of violet pouch . . . the short neck, swollen, red and apoplectic. The moustaches and hair showed traces of dye.'

D'Annunzio's experience of this family decline, of a father who degenerated into a monster and ruined his family for the sake of cheap girls, reinforced his interest in Dostoevsky, and he could find in his own life a parallel with the world of the Karamazovs. The Villa del Fuoco had to be sold and the house mortgaged. Donna Luisetta now spent more and more of her time in church, the aunts wallowed in their sweetmeats and their rosaries, the daughter who had married badly was filling the house with her brood of children, and nothing was heard of the brother who had gone to seek his fortune in America (he ended in poverty after having been a piano-teacher, too proud to ask his illustrious younger brother for anything). The stables were empty, the garden a jungle. In June 1893 Don Francesco Paolo died suddenly, but Gabriele did not go to Pescara until several weeks after the funeral; the son who was himself so improvident tried to set his mother's affairs in order, arranging for the house to be bought back from the creditors with what remained of her dowry. He even had to defend the poor woman against the cupidity of cousins in Chieti and challenged the head of this family to a duel, but his challenge was spurned. The whole of Pescara sided with Donna Luisetta: her own misfortunes and the glory of her son suggested that she would soon become a sort of local saint.

The curiosity of the little town, which only recently had seen him happily walking arm in arm with Donna Maria, began to exasperate d'Annunzio. He therefore settled himself in Michetti's new home, a Baroque monastery on the edge of Francavilla's pine-groves, overlooking the sea. In the chapel which he had converted into a studio, Michetti, who had adopted a highly bizarre way of life, sketched vast canvases which he never finished. In the partly furnished refectory his woman companion served meals of uncertain quality. The poet had a huge room from which he could see the shore through the olive-trees and which he adorned with a few articles of splendour; here, and in the little cloister where leadwort grew, he wrote a large part of *Il Piacere* and later another novel, *L'Innocente*. From Rome came musician and artist friends, but no writers, for d'Annunzio found the mediocrity of his fellow-authors wildly irksome. Here, in a more romantic setting, he was able to indulge once more in the conversations and the reveries which he had shared with Michetti at the age of eighteen; they would also set off on expeditions through the mountains. This was a period of continence to which d'Annunzio attributed the erotic exaltation of his novels: 'In a cruelly hot summer I had been compelled by events to retire to the Abruzzi, to seek refuge in the hospitable house of a friend . . . I had sent the first of my *Romanzi della Rosa* to the printer . . . When I brought him . . . one of the first copies, he asked me to leave him time to read it so that he could give me his frank opinion. I returned a few days later. He opened the volume, seemed to illuminate it with his huge smile, sniffed the pages and said: "The smell of sperm." He had divined the cause of my erotic agitation.' (*Libro segreto.*)

D'Annunzio returned, shortly followed by Barbarella, to spend the summer of 1889 near Pescara. He had rented a country cottage some dozen miles from the town; the cottage boasted a few architectural features in the form of three stone arches and some paving-stones. The little hermitage of San Vito, nestling among orange-trees below a cluster of yews, calls to mind the ruins in which the old artists loved to place their paintings of the Nativity. In this paradise, soon to be poisoned with jealousy, and with his mistress at his side, d'Annunzio set about writing the cruel story of their liaison. One of the commonest manifestations of his sadism was a persistent treachery in his writings, carried out right beside the loved one whose indiscretions and physical defects he would reveal with such self-satisfaction, as if he were making her pay for the physical substance of which she was draining him and the time which she consumed.

When he found it necessary to work twelve hours a day, however, women were banished; Barbarella did not go with him when he returned to spend several months at Francavilla in 1891. It was at Francavilla that he completed *L'Innocente*. Barbarella received some melancholy love-letters which said between the lines: Adore me but above all do not disturb me. D'Annunzio was a highly conscientious writer for whom morality existed only in relationship to his work; like all great virtuosi, he worked with enormous energy and protected his peace of mind with a colossal egotism. His picaresque life, so full of treachery and despair, bluff and heroism, which did more for his legend than his finest poems, seemed to him of little value set beside his art. In this respect, d'Annunzio resembled Cellini or Caravaggio, who led lives of scandal and even crime, but were integrity itself in their art. In this connection, it could be said that the work of d'Annunzio reveals the Mannerist elegance of the former, with his finely chiselled figures and his *cabochons*, and the Baroque dramatization of the latter, who thrived on popular and low-life scenes. D'Annunzio-Cellini was responsible for the poems and *Il Piacere*, d'Annunzio-Caravaggio for the *Novelle della Pescara* and *L'Innocente*.

MONDO CANE

Around 1960 an Italian film of this title lyrically described scenes of cruelty taken from everyday life (though largely from exotic environments), both in the animal world and among human groups on the fringe of our society. The world of d'Annunzio the realist was a *mondo cane* both comic and primitive, the ridiculous world of Pescara and the savage world of the Abruzzi. He needed to immerse himself once more in that world to regain his strength. The first short stories, *Terra vergine* (1880, 1882), which he described as 'physiological studies', are permeated with the provincial atmosphere of the *veristi*. *The Bell-ringer*, with its lyrical realism, is reminiscent of Zola's *La Faute de l'abbé Mouret*, but *The Sister-in-law*, which is set in a Chekhovian world, is much more disturbing and heralds the great novels: an aristocratic atmosphere, temptations of incest, guilty hands meeting in the hair of a small girl. Other stories followed in various magazines and were published in the *Libro delle Vergini*; they were republished in 1902 under the title *Novelle della Pescara*, together with other stories, the most striking of which are *I Violenti* ('The Violent Ones') and *San Pantaleone*. The influence which the *veristi* novelists could claim to have exerted on these stories came not so much from Zola as from Maupassant and Flaubert; thus, the story *Vergine Anna* is a pastiche of *Un cœur simple* both in subject and in style. Generations of critics—d'Annunzio has always exasperated academic critics—have emphasized the links between the Abruzzi of d'Annunzio and the Normandy of Maupassant. The narrative methods of the two writers are the same; their characters, equally lacking in intellectual and spiritual depth, are exactly the opposite of the characters Chekhov was beginning to create. With his artist's eye, d'Annunzio fashioned the décor of his stories in the style of Michetti, Favretto and the early works of Boldini, but the lyricism is always discernible beneath the realism.

It must be admitted that Pescara seems less vulgar than Maupassant's Honfleur, because poorer and more passionate. The puppets which d'Annunzio re-created from his childhood memories possess something of the gaiety of Goldoni, though this does not prevent them from quickly sinking into degradation. Only two or three beautiful girls found mercy with the ruthless d'Annunzio; even the good ladies who taught him to write became monsters in his stories—one a nymphomaniac, the other a hysterical neurotic. With a curious gusto sometimes spoilt by a banal touch of pity, d'Annunzio describes brutal scenes, revolting infirmities and degrading superstitions. The quality of his tales derives from a feeling for situations which foreshadows his dramatic writings: the Neapolitan duke disappearing in his palace burned down by the Garibaldians, with a too well loved manservant in his arms, and the funeral vigil where incest is born between a young priest and his sister-in-law could provide a Visconti and a Pasolini with some ideal material for films; while *The Duchess of Amalfi*, which recounts the arrival of a theatrical company in Pescara and the havoc wrought by the ageing actress among the local notables, would be a perfect subject for De Sica!

If the stories are read one after the other, they become rather monotonous. The protagonists, described from the same viewpoint of burlesque, eventually come to resemble one another: they are all scrofulous invalids and alcoholics. The women are mostly idiots or whores. The comedy is a humourless buffoonery. Humour requires self-analysis on the part of the writer, and the faculty for looking at oneself with detachment is very rare in Mediterranean countries. Basically, the comedy in these tales is like that provided by monkeys: a guffaw followed by disgust. In the *Trionfo della Morte*, the descriptions of the peasants exhausted with fever and squalor and the pilgrimage of cripples provoke revulsion without inspiring the slightest pity. This is a subhuman world, like that of Swift's *Yahoos:* 'A thousand hands were stretched towards the altar in savage frenzy. Women dragged themselves along on their knees, sobbing, tearing their hair, beating their foreheads on the stone floor, writhing in convulsions. Several of them slowly approached the altar on all fours, supporting the whole weight of their bodies on their elbows and the balls of their bare feet. They crawled like reptiles, arching their bodies and progressing in a series of slight propulsions, their horny yellow heels and projecting ankle-bones appearing from under their petticoats. From time to time, the hands seconded the efforts of the elbows or trembled round the mouths that kissed the dust, near the tongue which traced in the dust the sign of the cross, with saliva mixed with blood.' (From the translation by Georgina Harding.) Another passage describing beggars running after the lovers' car is a masterpiece worthy of Flaubert.

As d'Annunzio observed the decline of his family, everything at Pescara spoke of death; under the scorching sun, the little town seemed ready to fall like a rotten fruit. With fewer sordid details and much more humour, the stories which Pirandello was to devote a little later to his native Sicily reflect the despair of this *Mezzogiorno* abandoned both by God and by the government.

Although the action of *L'Innocente* does not take place at Pescara, the novel was written there and the sinister atmosphere of the town pervades this tale of adultery, the heroine of which bears a disturbing resemblance to Donna Maria. Although the framework of the story is borrowed partly from a tale by Maupassant called *La Confession*, the influence of Tolstoy appears for the first time and is openly admitted, for the brother of the hero, a sort of rustic Christ, reads *War and Peace;* this brother indulges in tedious sermonizing, as does a peasant who is just as fond of fantasies as the peasants in *Resurrection.* If the jealousy felt by the hero had already been analysed in *Anna Karenina,* the idea of causing the death of a baby of doubtful origin is typically d'Annunzian; Tolstoy would have brought up the child of shame with even greater care than his own offspring. But d'Annunzio had probably himself experienced the temptation to rid himself of an unwanted child. This story certainly owes much to the conjugal life of its author. A libertine husband is no more than a brother to his wife. The wife of the novel shows even greater self-abnegation and adoration than Donna Maria. At the beginning of the book she is ill, and her convalescence brings about a reconciliation; at one moment the husband is stirred by the idea of incest, for this wife has become his 'sister'. In the works of d'Annunzio a curious form of eroticism often develops at the bedside of the sick. However, the husband returns to his mistress. A few months later, he is puzzled by his wife's coquettish manner; his first doubts are kindled when he discovers in her writing-desk a novel by a fashionable writer with a dedication to her. The couple then go into the country to purge themselves of the noxious air of Rome; there they meet Frederico, the Tolstoyan brother. The presence of an Englishwoman and the delightful comings and goings of two little girls give the drama a poetic decorum. In the spring, among the lilacs, the husband, Tullio, takes his wife to a summerhouse where they indulge in reminiscences of their early married life. But on the following day a fainting fit reveals that the young woman is pregnant. Tullio fears that he will go mad with jealousy; he feels 'atrocious agonies, abject joys, immodest surrenders, tears more bitter than any poison, sudden frenzies that drove him to the brink of madness, violent descents into the abyss of lust . . . all the miseries and ignominies of carnal passion exacerbated by jealousy'. The seducer is a caricature of d'Annunzio himself and his methods: 'He had talked of the ideal, of a mystical alliance, at the very moment when his hands were busy discovering other mysteries; he had combined snatches of platonic eloquence with a delicate act of possession.'

The wife admits that she wanted to die in order to spare her husband this grief, for he is her only love (d'Annunzio thereby preserves his self-esteem). Tullio falls at his wife's knees 'in an instinctive need to assume the same attitude as this creature who was suffering and causing me to suffer', though this does not prevent him from raping her in a fit of jealousy the next day. Then the baby is born and the husband directs all his hatred against the child. The baby is a sickly creature and one day, when the rest of the household has gone to church to say a novena for the infant, Tullio holds it up to the open window and the icy air. The child dies. While the despairing family keeps watch over the little corpse, Tullio tries to confess, but his words are taken for the incoherent mumblings of grief; the novel is the confession which he writes one year later.

Giovanni Episcopo, a shorter tale of more concentrated depravity which d'Annunzio wrote in Rome during the winter of 1890–1, was influenced by Dostoevsky, whose story *The Eternal Husband* had just been published in a French translation by Eugène Melchior de Vogüé. But d'Annunzio's story is devoid of the slightest hint of charity and shows utter contempt for heroes who are from the very lowest orders, procurers and drunkards, a riff-raff with pretensions. In the course of his adventures d'Annunzio had come to know the inhabitants of the dwellings erected overhastily by speculators on the grounds of the old villas, in those gloomy villages on the outskirts of Rome. Some photos taken by Count Primoli show these disreputable creatures taking the sun along the ancient walls covered with torn posters, strolling in public gardens in worn frock-coats and battered top hats. Until the beginning of this century Italy remained a very poor country where those who had no taste for work lived by their wits. The most important thing was to preserve appearances; whoever failed to do so, even if he was an upright man like the hero of *Giovanni Episcopo*, descended much lower than the rabble. This tale of masochism is thus comic rather than sad, written as it is without a trace of compassion. In the *mondo cane* of the Roman petty bourgeoisie, the portraits of the procuress and the jovial commercial traveller are admirable. D'Annunzio must have become acquainted with this world as soon as he first arrived in Rome, when he had stayed in seedy boarding-houses. The rabble, with all the opportunities for delectable adventures that it offers, has always amused the Don Juans. In such circles the poet also found a number of naïve persons who were dazzled by his glibness of tongue, but who, when their patience was exhausted, turned into ruthless creditors—the waiter at the Caffè Greco, for instance, from whom d'Annunzio obtained loans, not realizing that one day the bailiffs would be at his heels.

A VARIETY OF TROUBLES

The *mondo cane* was a world seen through the jaundiced eyes of a man forced to struggle with life, but sufficiently gifted to derive artistic advantage from even the worst experiences. Yet the disappointments, even when overcome with a brave face, left their mark, as did ambitions that were too easily gratified and finally led nowhere—his marriage, for example, or the success of a book of verse. When real troubles presented themselves, the egotist was overwhelmed. Rather strangely, d'Annunzio took some time to learn how to deal with bailiffs, those nasty creatures whom he had to ward off by showing them a new contract, or who made it necessary to take flight if they became too numerous. To announce his arrival at Francavilla in March 1891, he wrote to a friend: 'I left the house full of bailiffs and set off feeling ill, desperate, without strength, in a sinister dawn which stirred the fever in my blood.'

The poet had contracted this recurring fever in a *mondo cane* of a different kind—the army. In October 1889 d'Annunzio was summoned to Rome and declared fit to perform military service, an unforeseen catastrophe. In despair he wrote to a friend: 'Can you imagine Ariel a corporal? . . . Eighteen months in barracks? Certain suicide.' On his first day in barracks he wrote to Barbarella: 'Today I have been thrust amid brutality . . . Today I have had a terrible vision of the life that awaits me. I shall no longer be a man, but a brute among brutes, like my horse.' One of the utterances of Andrea Sperelli that had most angered public opinion was an allusion to the soldiers who had died at Dogali (the rout which put an end to the first Italian expedition in Ethiopia): 'For four hundred brutes who died brutally!' mur-

murs Sperelli when his carriage is forced to slow down by a crowd of demonstrators. Yet patriotism, so often a sublimated form of vanity, inspired d'Annunzio in 1888 to write a series of articles on the Italian navy and the need to enlarge it (published in a single volume entitled *L'Armata d'Italia*), and in 1887 an 'Ode to the soldiers who died in Africa'. Indeed, the aesthete could not help sharing the humiliation of his compatriots after the failure of an expedition that should have brought the new kingdom both glory and a colony. It was a woman who stirred this patriotic impulse in Gabriele: Olga Ossani, alias 'Febea', who was taking tea with a group of poets, reproached her friends for squandering their talents in aesthetic discussions instead of lauding their country. Thereupon d'Annunzio scribbled a few stanzas and read them aloud under the pink lamp-shade, rather as Rouget de Lisle had sung *La Marseillaise* at the home of the mayor of Strasbourg. The poet had thus launched a few noble appeals to his countrymen, and had offered advice to the naval minister with all the authority attaching to his own maritime origins; but actually being in barracks was quite a different matter.

The man who was to glorify the army and cheerfully send so many young soldiers to their deaths wrote to his mistress: 'I have had a bath, after five days of living among garbage, a bath that seemed an unutterable joy . . . My worst enemy could not have imagined a more cruel and inhuman torment for me.' D'Annunzio certainly wanted to be a hero, and one day he was to become one, but a washed and perfumed hero and not just another piece of cannon fodder with dirty feet. Eventually, headquarters were informed of the identity of the reluctant 'volunteer' and things were arranged; the poet soon became a corporal in a smart regiment, the Novara Lancers, with a most becoming uniform copiously trimmed with braid. The corporal was able to choose a fine horse. A year later, after numerous sick leaves, he caught a fever during manoeuvres in the marshes of Romagna, and the future hero was restored to civilian life for thirty years.

D'Annunzio returned to civilian life, but not to married life, for Donna Maria was demanding a legal separation; an unfortunate incident had recently transformed an already strained relationship into a formal rupture. Donna Maria had fallen from a window in circumstances over which biographers have shown as much reticence as they have in connection with another mysterious fall which, thirty-three years later, was to endanger d'Annunzio's own life. Why had Donna Maria attempted to commit suicide on 6 June 1890? Was it in despair at having been rebuffed by her father to whom she had turned, penniless, for charity? Had her husband subjected her to some dreadful but not altogether unjustified scene of jealousy? Nothing is known for certain. There were rumours about a liaison with the journalist Morello and it is quite probable that the Abruzzian, as sensitive as an Arab where his honour was concerned, completely forgot his role of 'gentleman'. Luckily the young woman was only slightly hurt; her husband went to live on Via Gregoriana, in the bachelor rooms where he arranged his meetings with Barbara Leoni, opposite the Zuccari palace which he had made the residence of his brilliant double, Andrea Sperelli. Having officially regained his liberty, Gabriele once more became full of attentions towards his wife who, as a result of the separation, now received financial support from her family. Donna Maria was certainly not the innocent victim burnt by contact with the Poet-God; the girl who, at the age of eighteen, had had the character to throw herself into an adventure of this kind must have been very different in temperament from the true 'victims'; but, since she was a 'perfect lady', her complaints were discreet and her methods of revenge secret. In reading the portrait of the husband in *L'Innocente*, one might well wonder if d'Annunzio, a rather Nietzschean cuckold, was not seeking to reassure himself, to make himself appear a very hard person, when in fact he was merely crude:

'The admitted superiority of my intelligence partly excuses the disorders of my life, for I have often explained to my wife the theory which, proclaiming me superior to the mass of men, places me above all morality. The certitude of not being judged by her as a man like any other relieves my conscience of the weight of my errors . . . I was convinced of being not only an elect spirit,

but a rare spirit, and I believe that the rarity of my sensations en-
nobles my every act.' When this novel was published, a very
limited first edition was printed *ad personam* and, although the
first page bore a dedication to his reigning mistress, Donna
Anguissola Gravina Cruyllas di Ramacca, his wife received her
copy, with a dedication to herself; whether this was an oversight,
an insult or an act of vengeance it is difficult to say. At all events,
as mentioned above, the dedication to Donna Maria in *Isaotta
Guttadauro* had been omitted in the new edition, revised and entitled *L'Isotteo–La Chimera*.

As if shattered by his wife's attempted suicide, grieved at
neglecting Barbarella, and ashamed at having created vile and
even criminal characters in his novels, d'Annunzio now sought to
refresh his inspiration with a sentiment new to him, though one
fashionable at this period. Goodness was, indeed, in vogue around
the year 1890—the universal love preached by the Russians, the
compassion of Verlaine, the naïveté of Maeterlinck. Wilde also
experienced this same temptation, but, since he really had a heart
of gold, the tales that he wrote under the influence of this
fashion are a delight to read. The same cannot be said of a story
entitled *St. Laino the Navigator*, an imitation of Wilde and of
Schwob's *The King in the Golden Mask*, nor of the 'human'
poems published in the collection *Poema paradisiaco* in 1893 and
written in an attempt to forget the sordid aspects of existence (the
best poems in the collection are not those composed in this
sentimental vein). There are verses for his mother and his nurse:
'Perhaps I would again weep wholesome tears, perhaps from the
depths within me some ancient and sacred affection would again
rise up.' He writes tenderly of the fate of Barbarella, whom he was
about to abandon. He, too, was unhappy, but his inspiration was
in need of renewal: 'I was beginning to pay for my grief, my
disorderly life, my excesses. I was beginning to suffer as intensely
as I had enjoyed.' Other poems, more accomplished and more
fashionable, recall the atmosphere of Georges Rodenbach's *Bruges
la Morte*, with a touch of necrophilia: 'She will go to my bed as to
a tomb.' One is also reminded of Albert Samain: 'The hands of

the women whom we met once, both in a dream and in life.'
The poem *Consolazione* is reminiscent of *Soirs moroses* by Catulle
Mendès. The most famous poem in this collection, *La Passeggiata*
('The Walk'), which Italians still recite readily, was written for
the woman who was to dissipate all d'Annunzio's good intentions
and drag him into a Neapolitan-style *mondo cane*:

> Voi che passate, voi siete l'Eccelsa.
> E passate così, per vie terrene!
> Chi osa? Chi vi prende? Chi vi tiene?
> Siete come una spada senza l'elsa,
> pura e lucente, e non brandita mai.

('You who pass, you are the Most High. And you pass thus,
along earthly paths! Who dares? Who takes you? Who holds
you? You are like a sword without hilt, pure and shining, never
brandished.')

6

From Vesuvius
to Parnassus

NAPLES

In August 1891, d'Annunzio and Michetti decided to visit Sicily
and, on the way, to spend a few days in Naples with their friend
Scarfoglio, who was now editor of the *Corriere di Napoli*. Naples,
whose picturesqueness and rich, dilapidated buildings attracted
so many tourists, held no appeal for the poet. What could he
learn from a city which was simply a vast, grotesque and syphilitic
Pescara? Naples was no more a part of Europe than was the
Abruzzi. The aristocracy concealed its poverty in palaces that contained few works of art. D'Annunzio was irritated to find himself
immediately the object of popular curiosity and lionized by
literary circles. He had come merely to read the manuscript of
L'Innocente to the Scarfoglios; the reading took three evenings
of enthusiastic listening, at the end of which Scarfoglio decided
to publish the novel in serial form in his newspaper.

D'Annunzio was then due to leave, but on the day following
his arrival he had seen a woman who had made a great impression

on him, an impression immortalized in *La Passeggiata*. Then, either by chance or through some helpful friends, he found himself once again in the presence of the unknown woman and decided to stay another week in the city; in fact, he was to remain there for two and a half years. These were the bitterest years of his life, for the unbalanced character of his new mistress was to lead to troubles of every kind—a black period brightened by pink cravats. As soon as he had resolved to prolong his stay indefinitely, d'Annunzio had a large summer wardrobe sent from Rome: four frock-coats, a vicuña jacket, trousers of a gaudy check pattern and a 'very light grey knick-knack'. Like the sinister Queen of Spades of the fortune-tellers, which she rather resembled, this tall, dark woman with the figure of an Amazon, eyes that were too large and perpetually ringed, and thick black hair streaked with red, brought unhappiness and provided inspiration of only the most sombre kind; a woman quite different in breeding from Donna Maria and quite different in heart from Barbara Leoni.

The Countess Maria Anguissola Gravina Cruyllas di Ramacca, a Sicilian and the wife of a Neapolitan count, Anguissola di San Damiano, fulfilled all the romantic promise which a reading of her visiting-card suggested. Unhappily married, of course, to a regular officer, a gentleman and a rather dull fellow, she had already had affairs and found herself the object of the attentions of the future king. The little Savoyard Prince of Naples resided in the Bourbon palace, although his presence could not console the Neapolitans for having lost their own kings.

D'Annunzio, impressed by the aristocratic prestige of the countess, after his liaison with the girl from the Trastevere, did not pause to consider what lay behind such an appearance: a fortune in jeopardy, a hysterical temperament, a susceptibility to jealousy bordering on madness, an indiscretion that was impervious to scandal—in short, the worst possible mistress for a writer.

The conquest of La Gravina was not easy, for this woman, even more haughty than she was loose in morals, knew how to make a man dance to her tune; and so, when Barbara came to see Gabriele in October, she was still fairly well received. The lovers rediscovered some of the sweetness of their relationship as they walked through the outskirts of Naples, to the Carthusian monastery of San Martino and in the park of Capodimonte. These were hours tinged with melancholy which were to inspire some beautiful poems. But jealous persons said that d'Annunzio was also sleeping with Scarfoglio's mistress, a common woman, very dark, whom the poet nicknamed 'La Moricicca' ('the Moorish woman'). 'What have I become to you during these five years?' wrote Barbarella to her lover. Her question was answered in a fine poem, *Nella Certosa di San Martino*, in which the poet invites 'Life' to see in his eyes and in the eyes of his companion (*negli occhi nostri*) the bonds that unite them. But a little later a poem that appeared in the *Corriere* under the title *Nel bosco* (*Capodimonte*) reawakened Barbara's anxiety. On this occasion the poet's eyes had been drawn, despite the presence of Barbara beside him, to a shadowy figure which they had passed in a lane. Yet in November of this same year the lovers went to Albano to spend the anniversary of the famous 'week of love'. When Barbara came back to Naples in February, however, she found in her lover's jacket a letter (possibly left there deliberately) from La Gravina which removed all possible doubt about the relations between the countess and the poet; she returned at once to Rome.

In April 1892 *L'Innocente* was published with a dedication to the countess to announce to the world that a new reign had begun. Nevertheless, the correspondence with Barbara Leoni continued for a time. D'Annunzio, who never knew how to break off a relationship (some see this as a sign of a kind heart), entangled himself in grandiose lies: 'And even if all the women of Don Giovanni's dreams were to pass through my bed, you would have reason to be happy, for they would all truly, truly, leave me with a longing and a fierce desire for you.' Then came the break, accompanied by a prudent request: 'Goodbye; I would be very grateful if you would return me my letters instead of burning them . . . I shall read and re-read them so that I shall remember always . . . until I die.' Some of these letters, it will be recalled, were frankly obscene; others, written under the influence of jealousy, the letters of a madman. Barbara only sold the letters after the poet's death, to extricate herself from poverty.

DRAMAS

So that she might devote herself wholly to her happiness, the countess left her home and went to live with her lover in a wing of a palace belonging to some cousins at Resina, nowadays a frightful suburb of Naples, but at that time planted with beautiful gardens from which there was a view of Ischia. They were wildly happy—at least from time to time. In the intervals, d'Annunzio wrote articles for the *Corriere,* and dallied in cafés with literary persons whom he thought second-rate or in salons which the countess thought second-rate (she was afraid of the opportunities for gallantry which such occasions offered). The most interesting of these salons was held by a Russian woman, Madame Polotsov, a devoted spiritualist who modelled herself vaguely on Madame Blavatsky. Here were to be found German homosexuals who were colonizing Capri, artistic English ladies, enthusiastic university teachers and those vibrant, faded beauties who, having sunk in the social scale, are always drawn towards celebrities. In this travesty of a salon the poet allowed himself to indulge all his eccentricities and to accept the most extravagant compliments; then, in moments of lucidity, he would recognize the poor quality of the incense and his whole life would seem a ghastly muddle. Creditors from Rome found their way to Naples, from Pescara came cries of distress, and then the husband arrived on the scene.

First of all the count demanded satisfaction in a duel, in which the seducer suffered a scratch. His honour thus safeguarded, the count then insisted on a legal separation and, in order to obtain the best conditions, brought an action for adultery against the countess and her accomplice. All this seemed a great joke to d'Annunzio, until the terrible day in July 1893 when he found himself in the law courts with the countess, mingling with a mob of common crooks, while hidden behind veils, ladies stared through lorgnettes. The tribunal was embarrassed by their elegance: the countess all in white, d'Annunzio in morning-coat. With some difficulty their advocate established that there had been extenuating circumstances (one wonders what they were); nevertheless, the accused were sentenced to five months in prison, which meant the separation, the opprobrium and the horror of Neapolitan prisons. Luckily, on the occasion of some political event, an amnesty was proclaimed for minor offences and the lovers were able to resume their scandalous life, which became more and more scandalous but less and less brilliant. The feckless countess became pregnant and soon a daughter, called Renata, was added to the little family that had followed its mother. Renata was to be the only one of his children to whom d'Annunzio was even slightly attentive. After this daughter, there was a boy, Dante Gabriele. Finding it impossible to write amid the hurly-burly of a brood of Neapolitan urchins, d'Annunzio went more and more often into the city; when he returned late, he found his mistress waiting for him at the top of the steps with a loaded revolver in her hand, which she fired on more than one occasion, chipping the stuccoed walls of the rooms. La Gravina accused the man 'for whom she had sacrificed everything' of being responsible both for her poverty and for her dishonour, and would shriek and start battles that usually ended on a divan. Living with this demented creature, the poet began to fear for his own sanity. As in many a cheap melodrama, there was a reconciliation over the cradle, when their little daughter nearly died of croup. D'Annunzio, who had so cold-bloodedly described the death-agony of an infant in *L'Innocente*, proved the most affectionate of nurses.

At the time of the publication of *L'Innocente*, which aroused passionate controversy, the author found himself reduced to the most humiliating expedients to squeeze a little money from his creditors. In his desperation he contemplated the idea of joining with Madame Polotsov in founding a spiritualist centre. At the same time, while tradespeople were having the furniture seized from the villa at Resina, the countess's parents offered to help her provided that she left her lover, but she preferred poverty. It must be admitted, this Neapolitan poverty retained a certain panache; Gabriele and the countess were forced to resort to moonlight flits, but only to move into a different palace; they still possessed a carriage and servants. Later, when such things could be seen in an amusing light, d'Annunzio was to speak of *splendida miseria*. The worst aspect of this period in the poet's life was the intellectual isolation. It is true that Naples boasted one of Italy's most eminent minds, the historian Benedetto Croce, but the latter was always insensible to d'Annunzio's charm. Fortunately, d'Annunzio now made two discoveries: Nietzsche and Wagner. A friend, an excellent pianist, helped him to endure his absurd existence by playing and explaining to him *The Ring* and *Tristan und Isolde*. The example of Wagner, the repetition of themes from one work to another, certainly broadened the poet's view of his art, while Nietzsche justified his view of himself. *Zarathustra* became an alibi, replaced Des Esseintes, gave his pride a purpose and encouraged his horror of democracy. (D'Annunzio, it will be recalled, read Nietzsche in a French translation.)

Influenced by Nietzsche and by what he had learnt of the Neapolitan aristocracy, which had withdrawn into itself since the departure of the Bourbons, d'Annunzio had wanted to write a new novel, but in this period of instability it was easier to make plans than to settle down to work; he thought of writing a *Vita di Gesù* and a novel entitled *La Madonna di Pompèi*; he also informed a friend that he was contemplating a novel with incest as its theme, '*La Sorella*, a frightful purple novel set against the grand and mystical background of Rome. I shall have the courage to explore the psychology of incest with the most extreme intensity.' But the novel turned out to be merely a short story, a very strange one, situated in one of those half-abandoned country houses whose atmosphere he was so well able to convey; as in *L'Innocente*, the presence of a small girl introduces an element of innocence which gives an extra savour to the sin.

In order to finish *Trionfo della Morte*, d'Annunzio left Naples and took the countess and her brats to his own province, where he rented a villa at Francavilla and furnished it in theatrical style.

Maria Gravina had a Japanese room and the drawing-room was Renaissance, a first modest attempt at the kind of interior decoration in which d'Annunzio was so strikingly to indulge. These draperies, a few suits and some trinkets for the countess absorbed the advances which he had received for *Trionfo della Morte*. There was no longer any question of staying with Michetti, who had become a quite outlandish character; the artist had built a sort of tower without windows beside the sea where he shut himself up, not to paint, but to invent his own particular kind of bicycle and his own photographic processes. As for the poet's other old friends, they had all been more or less in love with Barbara Leoni and found the countess unbearable.

LE VERGINI DELLE ROCCE

One of the reasons for the move to Francavilla had been political ambition. Always impatient to try himself in new fields, d'Annunzio stood as a candidate for the constituency of Chieti. In spite of the hostility of the Church to a candidate who had been found guilty of adultery, things were going well until the rival party learnt that he had advised the countess to procure an abortion and that Maria Gravina possessed letters to this effect. The countess threatened her lover that she would hand over the letters to the authorities unless he came back to her. Although the electors had been persuaded to swallow the fact of adultery, they would certainly not have felt the same about abortion. From whom was d'Annunzio to seek advice? It was Donna Maria who saved her husband with a stratagem from the world of comic opera. D'Annunzio returned to his mistress with a very handsome valet, who quickly charmed the Neapolitan chambermaid and, with the help of a few gold pieces in case his charm should not have sufficed, easily persuaded the girl to steal the letters from her lady's writing-desk. The plan succeeded and enabled d'Annunzio to be elected by a large majority in September 1897, on an Extreme Right platform, despite professions of faith inspired by Tolstoy.

Parliament was an admirable pretext for leaving the countess in her villa and d'Annunzio, whom the French academician Melchior de Vogüé was to call 'the Representative for Beauty', went to Rome, there acquiring a delightful *pied-à-terre* in the harness-room of the Borghese palace, which he rapidly arranged in oriental style, like an artist's studio. The Bohemian life was resumed, interrupted for a short time by political preoccupations which did not, however, prevent him from writing to an unknown acquaintance: 'Oh! a whitewashed room, a huge pine table, ten reams of virgin paper, twenty litres of ink, fifty boxes of pens and, for several miles around, not a soul, not a voice, not a sound, not a single human being.'

The lawyer de Bosis, responsible for winding up the affairs of the bankrupt Prince Borghese, who had been ruined in property speculations, had offered d'Annunzio this very agreeable accommodation. He had taken an apartment in the palace as the editorial office of a review which he had just founded, *Il Convito*, elegantly printed on the best paper and which emulated the literary and artistic qualities of its foreign models, the British *Yellow Book* and the German *Pan*. For *Il Convito*, d'Annunzio rapidly completed *Le Vergini delle Rocce* ('The Virgins of the Rocks'), which he had at first intended to call *Le Tre Principesse* ('The Three Princesses'), but this title seemed too reminiscent of Maeterlinck. The book brings to life the fantastic atmosphere of a mansion inhabited by an aristocratic family that has withdrawn from the world, living its exalted dreams by ceremoniously maintaining appearances, and is one of the finest achievements of Symbolism, earning a place by the side of Rodenbach's *Bruges la Morte* and even Villiers de l'Isle-Adam's *Axel*. It has all the grotesque melancholy of *Götterdämmerung*: an old mad princess, a father obsessed with the honour of his name. But the novel is in no sense a pastiche. It represents the best of d'Annunzio, free as it is of the excessive preciousness of *Il Piacere* and the vulgarity of *verismo*. It is essentially d'Annunzian because, despite pages that bear the imprint of the period, written in a mood of grey and morbid languor, the irrepressible vitality of the author bursts forth in dazzling passages, exciting even when his exuberance becomes entangled in fantasies and is expended in the pursuit of creatures belonging to another world.

The hero (closely akin to those of Maurice Barrès) is descended from a man who was admired by Leonardo; he retires to his estate in a remote province of the former kingdom of Naples and pays a visit to his neighbour, Prince Castramitrano, who has two timid and slightly backward sons and three beautiful and intense daughters, Anatolia, Maximilla and Violante, all of whom are profoundly disturbed by their visitor, even the daughter who is due to enter a convent. He hesitates and then chooses Anatolia, but she refuses happiness so that she can look after the household, lost in its dreams and which survives only by her will-power.

In this novel d'Annunzio treats a theme common among the Symbolists: the prestige of an aristocracy awaiting its extinction. It is a novel that needs to be illustrated by artists of exquisite delicacy and able to depict the princesses in flowing gowns gathering flowers, seated by the fountain gushing in the courtyard of the mansion, gliding like shadows through badly lit galleries, or leaning over a swamp as if inviting fevers. He wanted to write 'a work of style presenting the character of a great symphony through which the four themes of Hair, Hands, Waters and Rocks move like ever-recurring melodies'. D'Annunzio, who was obliged to work in very difficult material and emotional circumstances, sought refuge in this book as if in a dream. It is hardly surprising that in the novel he should greet Ludwig II of Bavaria as a brother: 'His efforts to make his life conform to his ideal are desperate in their violence. All human contact makes him shudder with disgust and anger; all pleasure seems nauseous to him unless it is what he himself has planned. Exempt from the venom of love, hostile to all intruders, for years he has seen no one, save the resplendent heroes which a creator of beauty has given him as companions in super-terrestrial regions.' (From the translation by Agatha Hughes.)

Le Vergini delle Rocce was to have a sequel and form the first part of a cycle (indicating the influence of Wagner) entitled *I*

Romanzi del Giglio ('The Romances of the Lily'), by contrast
with another cycle, *I Romanzi della Rosa* ('The Romances of the
Rose'), of which *Il Piacere* had been the first part. D'Annunzio
did not intend thereby to pay homage to the medieval *Roman
de la Rose*, but to group his erotic tales under the sign of the
'rose', which to him symbolized the feminine sex. Finally there
was to be the 'Pomegranate' cycle (*I Romanzi del Melograno*).

THE TRANSLATOR

When d'Annunzio expressed his regret at not being able to lead
a monastic existence, he was writing to a Frenchman on whom he
wished to make a good impression, Georges Hérelle, thanks to
whom his name was becoming as famous in France as in Italy.
Hérelle, a teacher of philosophy at the lycée of Le Havre, was a
man of immense curiosity and enthusiasm, qualities that might
seem unexpected in a fifty-year-old academic. After having chanced
to read *L'Innocente* in serial form in the *Corriere di Napoli*,
Hérelle wrote to the poet asking to be allowed to become his
translator. *L'Innocente* was thus published in France in 1893,
under the title of *l'Intrus* ('The Intruder'); *Il Piacere* (*L'Enfant
de volupté*—'The Child of Pleasure') and *Giovanni Episcopo*
(*Episcopo et Compagnie*) in 1895, *Il Trionfo della Morte* (*Le
Triomphe de la Mort*—'The Triumph of Death') in 1896 and
Le Vergini delle Rocce (*Les Vierges aux rochers*—'The Virgins of
the Rocks') in 1897. Within four years d'Annunzio had conquered the French public, offering it fashionable themes treated
with a vigour lacking in both the French Symbolists and the
Society writers. Soon his novels were selling much better than in
Italy, thanks to an excellent publisher, Calmann-Lévy, who was
always extremely generous to Gabriele. The leading reviews vied
with each other for priority in publishing his latest work, while
Doumic and Bourget wrote laudatory articles. In 1895 the critic
of *La Revue des deux Mondes* even delivered a lecture on d'Annunzio at the Sorbonne. When the foreigner became altogether
too successful, Bourget and another ladies' author, Marcel Prévost,

condemned his immorality. Hérelle's translations have been criticized for their rather academic style, for their reticence in the treatment of the more sensual passages, and for pruning many of the superlatives and images which might have seemed too extravagant for French taste. On more than one occasion, d'Annunzio himself reproached Hérelle for his 'mania for futile clarity'. Having an excellent knowledge of the French language, d'Annunzio was in a position to write: 'I expect and demand wonders'; but he defended Hérelle when the latter was attacked for his translation of Il Piacere: 'I do not want your prose to resemble the jargon of certain Decadents, above all because I am a traditionalist. I have formed my style on old Italian authors with the rigour of a purist.' (M. de Montherlant has compared the translation of Il Fuoco [Le Feu] with the finest pages of Chateaubriand.) To no other person would the poet have confided that his early works were 'those of a child allowing himself to be thrilled by the sonority of the rhyme without caring if it corresponded with the sentiment or the thought'. Hérelle, an erudite bachelor of delicate health, dedicated himself to the works of d'Annunzio; a solid friendship was born between the two men, at first by the exchange of letters. The poet expressed himself more freely to this foreigner than to his Italian friends, revealing to him his intimate thoughts, his aspirations and his aversions. The letters written to Hérelle—admirably edited by M. Guy Tosi—thus form the best guide to d'Annunzio's inspiration over a period of fifteen years.

The meeting between the author and his translator took place in Venice, during the summer of 1894, and it appears that Hérelle was immediately captivated by 'the slender, fair, seductive and charming young man'. After working together on the translation of Trionfo della Morte, they walked with their guide, the Venetian aesthete Angelo Conti, the 'fervent and sterile ascetic of Beauty' and a great expert on Giorgione. In the evening a select circle of friends gathered at the Caffè Florian around the poet's table; but this delicious existence had to be cut short for lack of money. Returning to Francavilla and Maria Gravina, d'Annunzio wrote to Hérelle: 'Alone with a creature suffering from a terrible nervous illness that makes her almost demoniacal; a being who wants to possess me absolutely like an object and whom I do not love . . .', for he had ceased to love Maria Gravina since his meeting in Venice with Eleonora Duse, the woman who was to become the most famous of his mistresses. For Hérelle, d'Annunzio wrote in French some 'Cisalpine sonnets' (1896) which indicate an astounding knowledge of the most unfamiliar French writers, from Charles d'Orléans to Jean Lorrain:

> *Assises dans le sang du soleil moribond,*
> *Près des noirs cygnes nés de l'ombre des carènes,*
> *Plus d'une fois j'ai vu les divines Sirènes*
> *Et j'ai miré mon rêve en leur regard profond.*

('More than once have I seen the divine sirens, seated in the blood of the dying sun, near the black swans born of the shadows of hulls, and I have beheld my dream in their deep gaze.')

(From *Les Donatrices.*)

and:

> *Les paupières couvraient, lourdes, ses yeux ardents*
> *Toutes rouges encore des voluptés fiévreuses*
> *Et je croyais sentir battre en ses tempes creuses*
> *La secrète fureur des rêves obsédants.*

('The heavy lids covered his burning eyes, still red with feverish pleasures, and I thought I felt the secret fury of haunting dreams beating in his hollow temples.')

(From *Aestus.*)

(The lines from *Les Donatrices* are sort of pastiche of the Symbolist poet Albert Samain, while those from *Aestus* are not far removed from another French Symbolist, Jean Lorrain, who had just dedicated to d'Annunzio his *Princesses d'ivoire et de rêve.*) In sending these poems to Hérelle, the poet had added: 'In a few years I should like to publish a book of French verse, since

I have broken my Italian lyre.' (Without enjoying the same success in England as in France, d'Annunzio also had the good fortune to be excellently translated by Arthur Symons, and by Georgina Harding and Agatha Hughes, excerpts from whose translations are quoted in this book.)

In 1895, the year following the meeting in Venice, d'Annunzio persuaded his friend Scarfoglio to organize a cruise to Greece on his yacht *Fantasia*. They were to take with them the explorer Guido Boggiani, a rather mysterious person of lively intelligence and melancholy temperament who was killed by the Indians of South America a few years later, and, in contrast, Pasquale Masciantonio, a boon companion; Hérelle was also invited, for he was an excellent Greek scholar and could serve as tutor to these *enfants terribles*; naturally, the countess was to remain on land, with her rages and her little ones. This voyage to Greece was indeed to break the evil spell that had held d'Annunzio in the *mondo cane*, and allow his genius to blossom.

A HAPPY ODYSSEY

As an observer on the great voyage, Hérelle was often grieved. Certainly, the yacht was elegant, the company intelligent and Greece divine, but d'Annunzio was constantly to shatter the academic Hérelle's idea of a great poet in Greece. As they prepared to depart, the Frenchmen watched amazed while as many trunks were piled on board as a *cocotte* would need for a month in Monte Carlo; the trunks contained shirts with frills, a suit for embassy occasions, smoking-jackets for evenings on board, jackets of alpaca and shantung, countless panamas and a variety of footwear with assorted gaiters. Fortunately, the poet also brought with him the notebooks in which he haphazardly recorded sublime impressions, laundry notes and women's addresses; these notebooks and, later, some of his most beautiful poems reveal that this voyage brought infinitely greater benefit to d'Annunzio than might have seemed possible. Scarfoglio, skilled journalist that he was, forewarned the public of the ambitious nature of the expedition, which thus began amid the hubbub of reporters and the curious that henceforward regularly surrounded the poet. At every port of call there was a rush to the post office to send masses of telegrams. They weighed anchor at Gallipoli on 29 July 1895, where Hérelle suffered his first shock when he saw d'Annunzio lying naked in the sun on the bridge and then cooling himself by having the sailors throw buckets of water over him. As he dried himself, the poet made this note: 'In my total lack of physical modesty I feel myself Hellenic to the marrow. I should have been born in Athens and exercised my youth in the gymnasium.' There was not a woman on board and, once his relief at having left the countess on land was forgotten, d'Annunzio could not help longing for 'the nocturnal caresses in our great bed'; he spoke of nothing but women, and in terms which appalled Hérelle. The Rabelaisian vigour of the poet seemed indistinguishable from the delirium of an erotomaniac. He noted his exhilaration at the bow of the yacht; 'the bowsprit is like an extension of my body, a monstrous phallic extension that gives me the sense of an irresistible virility.'

As they passed by stony Ithaca and the vines of Cephalonia, d'Annunzio filled his little book with detailed notes. How great was the disappointment of the group when they landed at Patras and found only heat, flies and poverty! A pimp promised to lead the tourists to some women. The first woman he showed them, a frightful old hag, seemed to d'Annunzio the image of Helen in her old age. They were hardly more successful farther on: 'At the house of a procuress and her niece, at the top of a shaking staircase, the two women appeared. Horrible! We fled. At the end of a dark street he promised us a woman from Pirga with very white arms. Her face covered with red spots, the sick woman appeared in her chemise, like one of the Fates with a mane of white hair; a tragic masque, deeply furrowed . . . Finally, the procurer promised us a fifteen-year-old maiden who would give everything except her virginity. We walked a long way before arriving at her

house, only to find that the mysterious child was receiving no
one. But it was too late . . .' From Patras they made their way
to Olympia on a wretchedly slow train. To refresh himself, d'Annunzio threw himself into the Alpheus: 'This bathe reminded me
clearly and forcibly of my early life. My body and my mind absorbed joy from everywhere. I relived an hour of ancient youth,
the youth that glowed on the immortal limbs of Hermes . . . I
feel that the secret of Joy is enclosed forever in that marble.' At
Piraeus, they invited on board some women from a German music
hall who were hardly in the bloom of youth. They also encountered disappointment in their hopes of social life, for the dip-
lomatic corps left Athens in August.

Luckily the museum remained open and d'Annunzio was
fascinated by the treasure of the Atrides which Schliemann had
recently discovered at Mycenae, by the Hermes of Praxiteles,
which was to inspire a fine poem, and by the *Korai* recently
found at the Parthenon. At the French Institute, with the
director, M. Homolle, d'Annunzio studied the Auriga found at
Delphi. He watched the meticulous cleaning of this bronze,
which became one of his favourite works of art; he was to have
casts of the original in all his homes, and would allow no one but
himself to apply the patina to the plaster, with a mixture of tea
and ammonia. From Athens the party went on to Delphi, where
they wandered among the ruins in the moonlight; it was here that
the poet invented the tenth Muse, Energeia. At Mycenae, in
torrid heat, he conceived his play *La Città morta* ('The Dead
City'). Among the stones they found a snake whose skin he
demanded as a decoration for his panama. It was hoped to continue the cruise to Constantinople, but a violent wind blew up
and d'Annunzio, suffering from sea-sickness, returned to Italy on
a large steamer. A note made by the poet after a conversation
with Hérelle sums up what he had learned from the voyage: 'The
Greek spirit was formed by the constant reaction of man against
the exact and powerful personality of things. The land which
they inhabited stimulated their will continually.' When he returned to Greece three years later, with Eleonora Duse, he

declared in a speech delivered in the presence of the royal family: 'I owe to Greece the maturity of my mind, the fullness of my life and the mastery of my joy.'

The three years that passed before he attained this 'mastery of joy' would, for another man, have been made excruciating by the relationship with Maria Gravina. D'Annunzio certainly suffered intensely when he was with her; but, endowed with the capacity to obliterate from his mind what he could not see, he was able to banish his cares simply by travelling. Indeed, he travelled much between September 1895 and September 1898, when he settled in Florence for ten years. He went to Rome to fulfil his functions as a deputy, and to Venice, where he had found a circle of intelligent acquaintances; he travelled throughout Italy and even in the Near East, following La Duse, and finally made the journey to Paris. During this period Maria Gravina remained alone, in her house by the sea, for increasingly long periods. Dramas of a truly d'Annunzian character awaited the poet each time that he came back: when the countess found herself pregnant once again, was she to procure an abortion or not? Drama erupted when Dante Gabriele was born, for the countess threatened to kill the baby unless her lover stayed with her. Having read *L'Innocente*, she soaked the baby in cold water and exposed it to the open window; the child resisted, as did d'Annunzio. It almost seems as if the Sicilian had cast a spell on him, for during these four years he always returned to her, despite 'an insatiable amorous frenzy which was jeopardizing my reason and my health'. It was in this almost criminal atmosphere that he wrote his best play, *La Città morta*. Finally, one fine day in February 1898, d'Annunzio casually announced that he was going to spend twenty-four hours in Rome to meet the editor of the *New York Herald*; he set off with a small suitcase in his hand, never to return. The countess remained in the villa beside the sea with her bastards and her Japanese draperies, without becoming much more demented than she was already.

7

La Duse

D'Annunzio's break with Maria Gravina was also a break with his native province. Like a snake growing a new skin, the poet left behind him in the Abruzzi the remains of his passion and, with it, a whole manner of writing; this process had been slow and painful. Unlike Rome, which he had had to conquer, Venice offered itself to the poet rather as an ageing courtesan offers herself to a young lover. Venice was the scene of theatrical love-affairs, provided the background for one of the finest novels and much later, like a mistress who has become a mother-figure, was to restore his strength between two battles.

At the end of the nineteenth century Venice was becoming fashionable once more, for the city found itself in that intermediate state between luxury and decrepitude which delighted the Decadents without repelling high society. It was the capital of refined souls who loved the crumbling but comfortable palaces, the churches which look more like ballrooms, the cafés as intimate as sacristies and the canals which, like the tarnished window of an antique-shop, reflect walls the colour of old damask. In the city one might pass John Addington Symonds, the author of the *History of the Renaissance in Italy*, guided by a handsome

106

gondolier, or Henry James visiting Isabella Stewart Gardner; from
his boat Baron Corvo offered small boys to old Englishmen; and
on the Piazzetta, Maurice Barrès paraded his profile and Jean
Lorrain his eyelashes. Rilke and Proust were to frequent this vast
'salon' and Wagner had died in Venice in 1883. Austrian princes
hailed the Carlist pretender to the Spanish throne, who surrounded himself with outmoded pomp, and impecunious families
sold their treasures to Americans who could not bring themselves
to leave the city, where men's thoughts turned easily to Byron and
Casanova, who had so much in common with our hero. If Greece
enabled d'Annunzio to enrich his repertoire of myths, to put aside
sordid Realism and imported Symbolism, Venice endowed his style
with all the wealth of its painters, even though he spent much less
time in it, the city closest to his own works, than in Rome, Florence or Francavilla.

D'Annunzio had found great difficulty in tearing himself away
from Venice when he had met Barbara Leoni there in 1887, and
again in September 1894 when he met Hérelle there, for this was
the occasion of his meeting with Eleonora Duse. He returned in
February 1895 and again at the end of September of that year, a
sacred date in the history of his love-affairs; he entered this date
(26 September), marked with an asterisk, in his notebook with
the following words, which were to inspire the title of Barrès'
finest book: 'Amori et dolori sacra . . . Hotel Royal Danieli.'
On 8 November, a week after the closing of the first 'Biennale',
he delivered a speech to the glory of Venice which is reproduced
in *Il Fuoco*; the speech was made not in the great hall of the
Doges' Palace, as in the novel, but in the more modest Liceo
Marcello. A year later, d'Annunzio came back to Venice to make
notes for his novel—notes on paintings ('At San Alvise, Tiepolos
eaten away by damp'), commentaries on the Tintorettos in the
Scuola di San Rocco, walks to the Franciscan friary of San
Francesco del Deserto and to the Capello palace, which was to
become the residence of his heroine, along the Gradenigo gardens.
He was particularly enchanted by the house of Prince Hohenlohe,
who became Prince Hoditz in the novel and who lived among

curios (described in the style of the Goncourts) with a *donnatta bergamina* ('a little lady from Bergamo'). D'Annunzio listened there to the *Aria* of Benedetto Marcello and lovingly noted the flowers growing through the iron railings of gardens and the fruits carried by heavy barges.

The great disadvantage of Venice was the impossibility of working there: the city contained too many delightful people. Most agreeable of all was Angelo Conti (Daniele Glauro in *Il Fuoco*), who showed the poet his city's hidden corners and took him to the Accademia, initiating him in Venetian painting. This aesthete, pledged to Beauty as others pledge themselves to religion, talked as readily of Wagner as of Pisanello. A small man, prematurely bald, with a fine face, bright eyes and a short beard, Angelo Conti was the most eminent of the admirers who, throughout d'Annunzio's long career, acted the part of acolytes to the high priest of Beauty, dispensing their erudition with the incense of flattery. D'Annunzio also went to the antique dealers with Prince Hohenlohe and visited the studio of an American woman who devoted her talent as a sculptor to the restoration of statues; this saint-like person earned the nickname of 'Clarissa d'Oltramare'. With one or other of his women friends he would linger in the studio which Mariano Fortuny, the son of the Spanish artist, had installed in the Mocenigo palace at San Gregorio. Inspired by a collection of ancient fabrics, Fortuny designed materials and even dresses in the manner of Carpaccio or Veronese which enjoyed such a great vogue that Proust was to give one to Albertine. Fortuny was a cousin of the French musician and composer Reynaldo Hahn, who used to bring ladies to the studio; for their benefit the poet, caressing brocades, would evoke the splendours of *La Serenissima*. During his earlier visits to the city, all that d'Annunzio had seen of the two queens of Venice, 'La Marcello', lady-in-waiting to Queen Margherita, and 'La Morosini', said to be the most beautiful woman in Italy, had been a brief glimpse as they had passed in their gondolas. And how could the poet possibly tear himself away from the spectacle which unfolded in front of the tables at the Florian, when the autumn brought to the capital of the Decadence the *Settembrini,* the disciples of Jean Lorrain, Stefan George and Oscar Wilde?

The Venetian novel *Il Fuoco* ('The Flame of Life'), begun in 1896 and published in 1900, was a splendid but morbid tribute to this capital where the Byzantine mingles with the Rococo. The theme of the novel is simple: an ageing woman, a great actress, 'La Foscarina', finds the courage to leave her young lover, the brilliant poet Stelio Èffrena. The story begins with a lecture given by Stelio in the Great Council Chamber of the Doges' Palace, in the presence of the queen. A fine evocation of Venice is followed by pages describing the women descending the famous staircase (a Veronese come to life) and the Epiphany of Fire which illuminates Venice (reminiscent of the shimmering effects of Guardi). A young musician, Donatella Arvale, arouses the jealousy of the actress who, despite her misgivings, yields to Stelio. This woman who has lived her life to the full discovers love but also anguish: 'I must die before you leave me . . .' she repeats to her lover. Fortunately, a plan to provide Italy with a theatre on the Wagnerian model brings the writer and the actress together. They go on splendid walks which are always spoilt by scenes, leading up to a sinister game of hide-and-seek in the maze at Stra. La Foscarina finally resolves to devote herself to Beauty, to carry its message to the 'Barbarians' and to return with enough money to give Stelio the theatre which his genius deserves. The novel ends with Stelio Èffrena carrying the coffin of Richard Wagner.

In *Il Fuoco,* d'Annunzio revenged himself for having loved a woman by betraying her secrets, a nasty trick which he often used. Was this a misogynist's need for vengeance, or a dislike of half-remembered pleasures which no longer brought excitement? Probably both. The following lines are written with a knavish lyricism: 'And a heavy sadness urged him into the last embrace of the lonely, wandering woman, who seemed to him to carry in herself, mute and gathered into the folds of her garments, the frenzy of the distant crowds in whose dense bestiality she had stirred the divine lightning-flash of art, with a cry of passion, a pang of pain, or the silence of death; an impure yearning forced him towards this experienced, desperate woman, in whom he believed he could trace the marks of all pleasures and all pain, towards this body no longer young, softened by every caress, but still, to him, unknown.' (From Angus Davidson's translation of Mario Praz's *The Romantic Agony*.) But what would the novel be without this attitude? It would be merely a dazzling tour of Venice. The poet sacrificed tact to Beauty. The difference between *Il Piacere* and *Il Fuoco* is like that between a richly stocked antique-shop and a famous museum; but, as in the first novel, *Il Fuoco* is a book dedicated to a city and one which for a long time was read as a supplement to Baedeker by visitors strolling through Venice. With the ease of a Veronese or a Tiepolo, d'Annunzio gave an allegorical quality to characters set against a background of architecture and gardens; perhaps these characters, like the figures in the frescoes, possess more movement and colour than personality. There is a greater vigour in the Roman novel, a greater languor in the Venetian one; if d'Annunzio had imagined himself as Andrea Sperelli, it could be said that, ten years later, he was almost Stelio Èffrena. Venice was indeed the perfect theatre for the loves of two great actors, but unfortunately too many episodes were to take place in the wings and in sleeping-cars. Undoubtedly, d'Annunzio and Eleonora Duse were sincere actors who, while weeping real tears, knew how to assume the most moving attitudes and how to deliver lines that would shatter the audience—actors who lived this love-affair as much for the public as for themselves.

LA DUSE

The actress Eleonora Duse, the one and only rival of Sarah Bernhardt, had much more in common with the symbol of the French theatre than her very different art and life might suggest. The simplicity of La Duse was no less theatrical than the extravagances of Sarah; she, too, had many love-affairs and in all walks of life, although her most illustrious liaison caused these to be forgotten.

1

D'Annunzio at 18

Barbara Leoni

2

Count Primoli

4

The Vow, by Michetti

5

The engraving for *Il Piacere* by Sartorio

Donna Maria and her eldest son, by Count Primoli

The Virgins of the Rocks. Three cousins of Count Primoli

Gabriele d'Annunzio in Rome, 9 March 1897, by Count Primoli

Maria Anguissola Gravina Cruyllas di Ramacca

10

Matilde Serao, Eleonora Duse and Count Primoli

La Duse in Venice, by Count Primoli

12

La Duse, by Baroness Alphonse Rothschild

13

Countess Giuseppina Mancini

On the other hand, her public was different from that of her older rival. Leaving the bric-à-brac of late Romanticism and a large international following to the interpreter of Sardou, La Duse succeeded in bringing the spirit of Symbolism into the theatre of Realism; in the words of Romain Rolland, she came 'from a land without boundaries, that of the soul'. She loved Ibsen, Maeterlinck, Beethoven, the paintings of Carrière, the Nihilists, scorned panache and glitter, and played for those who had suffered. As Max Beerbohm wrote with some irony: 'Signora Duse has inspired much awe through her contempt for the art of making up.'

She herself had suffered much since early childhood. Born in 1859, she had been brought up in the theatrical profession (her grandfather had been a friend of Goldoni) and at the age of five played the part of Cosette in a melodrama based on *Les Misérables*. Her mother died of consumption and Eleonora, exposed to the promiscuous life of a travelling company, felt herself condemned to unhappiness, so much so that her greatest successes and her greatest loves brought only the sad smile of one who no longer possesses the strength to be happy. The lover who caused her the greatest suffering before the meeting with d'Annunzio was a friend of Matilde Serao, Martino Cafiero, whom she had met in Naples in 1878 and who might have served as a model for Andrea Sperelli. The actress was an aesthetic experience for this dandy, who abandoned her with a child after having given her 'lessons in Beauty', to use the phrase in vogue at this time. She then married a third-rate actor, Tebaldo Checchi, out of pity. Later she had an affair with Arrigo Boito, the composer who strove to introduce a German gravity into Italian music; the creator of *Mefistofele*, and librettist of some of Verdi's greatest works, was a deeply serious man.

With some ups and downs La Duse had been famous since the age of sixteen when, playing the part of Juliet in the amphitheatre at Verona, she had had the idea of scattering roses on the body of Romeo. She enjoyed an equally great success shortly afterwards in the role of Thérèse Raquin, and she was a stunning 'Lady of the Camellias'. *'O grande amatrice'* ('O great lover'), d'Annunzio said to her after seeing her for the first time in this role. Her favourite part was Ellida in Ibsen's *The Lady from the Sea,* a character usually played as a madwoman and whom she alone had understood. Mme. Simone has left some useful notes on the woman whose rival she became for a brief time: 'A smooth, bronzed skin plentifully covered with white cream; a very slight limp; carelessly dressed, lined forehead; a few white hairs. Wonderful smile on a face dedicated to despair. She suggests dark propensities, unconscious fears, with the strange arabesques formed by her hands . . . her desperate giving of herself . . . a grave and sensual face.' To please her lover, Eleonora covered her weary shoulders with Fortuny's brocades and walked through palaces disguised as a dogaressa, but her most appropriate attire was the grey costume of Hedda Gabler or the flannel dressing-gown of the Lady of the Camellias in her sick-room.

The name of Eleonora Duse had appeared two or three times in d'Annunzio's newspaper articles around the year 1883, but without the superlatives accorded to princesses. In Rome the actress had an influential worshipper in the person of Count Primoli. Using this passion (which he would have been greatly distressed to find gratified) as a cover, 'Gégé' was able to indulge in pleasures which at this time no one admitted. The count, sensing that great things would issue from the conjunction of the actress and the poet, prepared Eleonora by persuading her to read everything written by d'Annunzio. After reading *Trionfo della Morte,* a few days before the fateful meeting, she wrote to her lover Boito: 'Another thing. This infernal d'Annunzio! I have read his book. We poor women think we have found the words we need. But this infernal d'Annunzio also knows them all. I would rather die in a corner than love such a soul. The great test of courage—the great strength to endure life—, the great and painful sacrifice which is life, all this the book destroys. No, no: despise me if you will, but neither Falstaff nor d'Annunzio . . . or perhaps not, I hate d'Annunzio, and yet I adore him . . .'

In Venice the actress occupied the upper floor of a palace belonging to a Russian, Count Volkov, who had been a great friend of Wagner. It was here that the poet was presented to her. That love should not be born of this meeting between these two illustrious Italians would have been as impossible as an opera in which the prima donna has not a single duet with the tenor. They owed a great romance to their country and to their own glory. That she should be older than he mattered little to Gabriele; on the contrary, he was more excited by women who had lived. For her, he was youth, art, a devastating sun myth—an Apollo. One of her first love-letters shows to what extent La Duse entered into the d'Annunzian myth and gave it substance: 'I see the sun and thank all the good forces of the earth for having met you.' They became lovers not in the days immediately following their first encounter, but only on 26 September 1895, which was to remain a sacred date. Eleonora then received her new name: 'Ghisola' or 'Ghisolabella'. Shortly afterwards, she wrote this letter: 'My soul is in you, all my soul. I feel it impatient to reach beyond my body. I have found harmony. Oh! blessed is he who has found that! I have struggled so long to restrain my soul. And now, if you look at me, I am what I feel. I have felt your soul and discovered mine. I do not know how to tell you this, but you understand, don't you? Squeeze my hand hard.'

The happiness of the lovers was soon spoilt by the jealousy of Eleonora whenever a younger woman appeared on the scene. All these dramas are recounted in *Il Fuoco*. On the same evening on which the actress had given herself to d'Annunzio, one of her friends captured her lover's attentions. The Donatella Arvale of the novel was in fact a Florentine harpsichord-player, Giulietta Gordigiani. A few years later, d'Annunzio, having failed to attain his ends, gave La Duse her revenge by writing: 'I saw Giulietta Gordigiani pass with a heavy step (where is that gait as light as the wing of a Victory?), dragging her fertile flanks towards the Arno.' Another cause of instability in their relations was the contradiction which made La Duse always dissatisfied with herself: to the world she wanted to appear a source of inspiration and a sister, but, since she loved intensely the pleasure which d'Annunzio

gave her, she found herself in the position of a bacchante compelled to deceive the muses. Romain Rolland, despite his adoration of the actress, recognized that it was her senses that bound
her to the poet; one should also allow for the uncertainty of an
ageing woman ashamed of her body and of her past. But there
was always Art! In this glorious *fin de siècle*, every kind of pain
and ridicule was suffered for the sake of Art. Alas, Eleonora Duse
did indeed appear ridiculous to reasonable people, as can be seen
from this reminiscence by d'Annunzio's secretary: 'She turned
towards the poet and, draped in a fourteenth-century dressing-
gown (which she even wore at home, no doubt in homage to
tragedy), with the attitude and gestures of a Niobe watching the
massacre of her offspring, she repeated several times in a dreadfully theatrical tone of woe: "Gabriele! Leave me my swallows . . .
My poor swallows! I want my swallows!" This was a line from
d'Annunzio's play *The Victory of Samothrace*'.

La Duse offered all her sufferings at the altar of Beauty, with
such nobility and such disinterestedness that one is a little
ashamed to observe that her physical love for the young poet
verged on madness, a madness which often showed the symptoms
of mental masochism. Her whole life, tinged by some obscure
illness, predestined her for this role of the humiliated woman, in
which she was incomparable. In the very first week of their relationship, Eleonora and Gabriele resolved that this union would
be much more than a liaison: 'One dawn, I was alone after
a sleepless night; suddenly I saw him in front of me emerging
from a gondola . . . We spoke of art . . . of the poverty of art
in the theatre of today . . . We said nothing which bound either
of us, but between us, tacitly, a *pact* was signed.' The actress
might well believe that she had dedicated herself to the poet and,
indeed, her influence was extraordinarily enriching, but it was she
who received the light, as a nun receives light from Him whom
she adores: 'I was pitied when he forsook me. Yet people do not
know that there was no bitterness in my heart . . . and that,
even in the agony of my soul, I still blessed this great giver of
life who had made me what I was. Before him, I did not exist.'

LA CITTÀ MORTA

The sublime 'pact' was to result in a number of plays which lifted the Italian theatre out of its mediocrity and which, even more than the novels and poems, established the reputation of their author in his own country. Eleonora Duse wanted her lover to provide her with the kind of drama that she found in her favourite authors, Euripides and Ibsen. D'Annunzio responded to the challenge with a certain degree of success. He did not set to work at once, although his visit to Mycenae had given him an excellent idea for a subject. His life was still too complicated; the attractions of society and politics were still too strong for him to devote his energies to the play which he had promised Eleonora, who in any case was leaving for a tour of the United States.

After Venice and the events which, condensed in time, formed the subject-matter of *Il Fuoco*, d'Annunzio returned to Francavilla to appease the countess, charm the electors and comfort his mother, Donna Luisetta. During the electoral campaign his mother received anonymous letters that drove her almost to distraction. D'Annunzio also had to meet the demands of his publisher, who had advanced a great deal of money and was waiting for copy. Emilio Treves, a Milanese Jew, was a good fellow at heart and always ended by sending a cheque after receiving letters such as these: 'I am an animal of luxury, the superfluous is as necessary to me as breathing; so I need these three thousand lire . . . Don't try to resist me . . .'; and, written a day or two earlier: 'I am a man of disorder and wish to remain such, for my style is never to go against my nature. In almost ten years of relations you have not yet been persuaded of this necessity.'

And then social life brought the temptations that never fail to confront those who claim to have renounced such things. D'Annunzio discovered fox-hunting, with all the pleasures which that sport offered—elegance, danger, speed and pretty women; twice a week in winter the poet, dressed in his red coat and riding an excellent horse, frisked across the countryside. He used a monocle to observe his female fellow-riders and, with a courage that was possibly boosted by short-sightedness, jumped over gates and

gullies with the casual ease of a true 'gentleman'. When in Rome
he often went to have tea with his wife who, it will be remembered, had recently extricated him from a difficult situation. He
even accompanied his elder son to the college of his childhood at
Prato, but thereafter hardly concerned himself further either with
this son or with his younger boy; the Cicognini college still possesses letters in which d'Annunzio asks that his sons be allowed
to attend the premières of his plays, 'whose beauty will be beneficial to them'. He returned to Venice to work with Angelo Conti
on those parts of *Il Fuoco* that concerned the history of art. In
October 1896 he went on an excursion into the Abruzzi with
Hérelle.

It is understandable that La Duse should have written him
some uneasy letters. Eleonora, true to their 'pact', performed in
Paris a one-act play in verse, *Il Sogno d'un mattino di primavera*
('Dream of a Spring Morning'), which harked back to the Pre-
Raphaelite mood of *Isaotta Guttadauro* and included a rather
Shakespearean madwoman. Her other performances had been
such a triumph that the *Sogno* passed for a masterpiece in the
eyes of the aesthetes. A French translation was published by the
Revue de Paris in a number which also contained Rodenbach's
Nocturnes, a chapter of *Les Déracinés* by Barrès, and an article
on La Duse by Primoli. 'Gégé' had made himself his idol's social
impresario and strove to reduce the friction between her and
Sarah Bernhardt, whom he adored equally. Paris was divided; one
day Robert de Montesquiou replied to Bernhardt's devotees: 'Yes,
you are right, there is only one Sarah . . . La Duse.' Eleonora,
rather surprisingly, had friends in high society, unlike Sarah;
among these friends were the Countess Greffulhe and the Baroness Alphonse Rothschild, who took a fine photograph of her.
Duse's performance, no less than the success of the novels, justified these words of Gide, published in an Italian review in
November 1897: 'M. d'Annunzio has drawn the attention of all
Europe to Italy.'

But meanwhile what had become of *La Città morta*, the
play that was to be the first fruit of the 'pact'? Today, d'An-

nunzio's first drama, which is still the most admired, seems weighed down by interminable monologues and by a rhetoric that does not bear translation (these rhetorical passages must be seen as an imitation of the Wagnerian recitative). The influence of Maeterlinck is as evident as in *Le Vergini delle Rocce*; the play owes to Maeterlinck its blind character (nearly every Symbolist drama had one), the monologues interspersed with repetitions and silences, and the stage-directions which could almost have been taken straight from *Pelléas et Mélisande:* 'The loose hair spreads over the shoulders of the virgin and falls onto the blind woman's dress, flowing like water, Anne's hands follow its streams . . .' The last act, with the brother and the lover beside the girl who has drowned in the pool, is pure Maeterlinck, but in the character of the blind woman there is also an echo of Sophocles; the idea of the right of the creator to cultivate his ego belongs to Nietzsche, and the style of the play is strongly influenced by Leconte de Lisle's archaic translation of Homer. Yet the vigour of d'Annunzio, the incredible richness of the images, the underlying harshness and the suggestion of incest, give the play its originality. In a theatrical world whose masterpiece was *Cavalleria rusticana*, it represented an extraordinary step forward; the whole text of the play seems to have been written with the purpose of grouping the protagonists sculpturally against an immortal backdrop, which should have been that of the Roman theatre at Orange; alas, the effect was more like a museum of plaster-casts.

Although the play was written for Eleonora Duse and at her suggestion, with the role of the blind woman one in which she could have given one of her most stunning performances, it was in fact created by Sarah Bernhardt, her one and only rival. This act of treachery on d'Annunzio's part was to be followed by many others. There was treachery in the very writing of the play, for d'Annunzio confided to a friend that in composing the last act, he had been 'guided' by the imagined gestures and posture of Sarah. Almost as soon as the translation was completed, it was sent to Sarah who immediately replied with this telegram: 'Have read your tragedy stop Admirable stop Admirable stop My heart-felt thanks'; she decided to have the play performed as soon as possible at the Théâtre de la Renaissance. D'Annunzio had dreamed of Sarah since adolescence; as a journalist, after a performance in Rome, he had presented her with a copy of the *Cronaca Bizantina*, 'a triumphal issue printed in honour of La Divinissima with brilliant inks'. Sarah, the magnificent idol of questionable reputation, was much more his type than the righteous Eleonora.

In January 1898, accompanied by Scarfoglio, d'Annunzio arrived for the first time in Paris, staying at the Hôtel Mirabeau in the Rue de la Paix. Announcing his arrival with an avalanche of roses, he rushed round to visit Sarah in the Boulevard Pereire. On the threshold of the studio he stopped, as if petrified by the apparition of the actress lying on bearskins: 'Divine . . . Yes, Madame, you are d'Annunzian . . .' Sarah, who was not so easily astonished, found her author amusing but not in the least seductive. Later, she made this curious comparison in speaking of the poet to André Germain: 'And those eyes, Monsieur, they are *petits cacas*' ('little blobs of shit'). One cannot help regretting that the woman whom Wilde called 'this serpent of old Nile' did not fall passionately in love with d'Annunzio. How many outrageous moments, how many great dramas there would then have been, with Sarah probably having the last word!

The première took place on 22 January before a brilliant audience, which reacted cautiously and even seemed rather amused by the archaeologists dressed in bicycling clothes and their female companions in smocks, in a museum of casts which looked rather like a jeweller's shop, for, carefully protected under glass, glittered a replica of the gold of the Atrides. According to d'Annunzio's dedication, Sarah 'had one evening in her eyes the blindness of the divine statues', but the Parisians were bored by her monologues. After the première Jules Renard noted: 'This is woman as seen by this poet who never penetrates the truth . . . This is poetry as gold is a precious metal.' In his review Jules Lemaître wrote of the 'poetry of an Asiatic'. Modish young people and artistic ladies were ecstatic, but Paris was not ready for poetic drama and *La Città morta* was given only a dozen performances.

Little is known about the three weeks which d'Annunzio spent in Paris. They were certainly very busy, if one is to judge by the addresses entered in his notebook: 'Love-nests [*chambres d'amour*] Rue Saint-Lazare . . . Countess de Vogüé from 5 to 7, Mrs. Henneman, saddle-horses, 55 Avenue Bugeaud . . .' He was invited to a musical evening at the house of Princess Bibesco, to dinners with Mme. Beer (who wrote, and quite well, under the name of Jean Dornis), to the house of the Countess de Béarn, the collector, and to the house of Mme. Aubernon where he was bored, though he thanked his hostess by sending her a book with a flattering dedication. He noted the addresses of the critics Brunetière, Gandera (editor of the *Revue de Paris*), Maurice Barrès, Anatole France and Marcel Prévost. But did he meet them all? He had a grand lunch with Countess Cahen d'Anvers. Primoli, an admirable public-relations officer, had alerted all his friends, but the fickle Italian disappointed a number of these, arriving late for a dinner with the Princess Mathilde and forgetting a tea at the house of Mme. de Heredia. Did he have tea with the famous *demi-mondaines* Liane de Pougy, whose novel *Idylle saphique* had just been published, or Émilienne d'Alençon? He was certainly on the best of terms with these two beauties. He also spent hours looking at Gustave Dreyfus's collection of Florentine bronzes. Perhaps he also kept the assignations proposed by unknown ladies who had been enraptured by *L'Enfant de volupté*. He certainly saw his great friend Ernesta Stern, an imposing and luxurious woman from Trieste who wrote under the name of Maria Star. He had already visited her at her Byzantine villa at Cap Ferrat.

In Rome, on the evening of the première, late hours were kept in three houses, as the telegrams announcing the number of curtain-calls were eagerly awaited. At the house of Count Primoli a group had gathered round La Duse, sublime in her self-abnegation; Donna Maria had invited a few fashionable friends, and in Michetti's studio there was a gathering of d'Annunzio's Bohemian circle, among them Barbara Leoni. After the decision to entrust the creation of *La Città morta* to Sarah Bernhardt, Eleonora Duse resolved to break with d'Annunzio and resume her liaison with Boito. There were dramas in which Axel Munthe was involved; Eleonora had gone to Capri to find a little peace. Letters were exchanged between the three protagonists on a common theme: 'Oh! how it hurts me to hurt you!' There was even a brief reconciliation between the poet and Donna Maria and explanations with Maria Gravina. In other words, during this year of 1897 Gabriele and Eleonora provided enough heart-rending situations to fill the works of ten playwrights. They were actors on a stage, involving irresistibly in their own lives all the subsidiary characters essential to any drama. There is no reason to be surprised by extravagance in the dramatic works of a writer whose daily life was so tumultuous. Primoli, unable to tolerate the separation of the incomparable couple, smoothed things over. Shortly after the Parisian production, Eleonora Duse played the *Sogno d'un mattino di primavera* in Rome, at the Teatro Valle and in the presence of Queen Margherita. The author sat in a ground-floor box with a princess. Fashionable Rome filled the auditorium, but fashionable Rome was not very cultured and the beauties of the text were lost; out of respect for the queen, the play was not booed; at the end, the only names to be called and applauded were that of La Duse and, derisively, that of Goldoni from whom d'Annunzio had borrowed a situation.

MARTYRDOM ON TOUR

The year 1898 was to be the happiest that the lovers enjoyed. At Settignano, outside Florence, the actress owned a little house where the poet would join her between tours. They went on excursions together and visited museums. In his hand d'Annunzio clasped 'the hand of the desperate nomad woman'. At the end of the year, he followed his mistress on a tour of the Levant. Far from temptations, he proved an incomparable lover, as his notebooks indicate, and they had a sort of honeymoon on the boat taking them to Egypt. '27 December 98. We are alone and far away. The whole world is in us, it lives in the embrace of our bodies . . . When I see her again, I embrace in that fragile, trembling body the whole strength of a people, the barbarous and disparate people [the Americans] which only yesterday was acclaiming her, which only yesterday was overwhelmed by the chaotic revelation of Beauty that she brought them. A minute of incalculable profundity, of infinite sweetness. When I am above her, in her arms, she caresses my lips with a bunch of violets . . . Then vague words, stories, smiles, the exaltation of arriving in the city of Alexandria, in the East.' But to what dream does the following note allude: 'The whole night the moist green mouths of the sirens suck my voluptuous blood. My gums have become as white as my teeth'?

In Cairo, the poet became passionately absorbed in archaeology, made a thorough study of the old city, went riding with the Bedouins between the pyramids of Sakkarah and Gizeh, revelling in the sun, and had a sudden revelation of eternity. In a prince's garden, planted with thick bushes like a labyrinth, he amused himself by losing Eleonora who, in anguish among the cacti, called out for him in desperation; in *Il Fuoco* this rather sadistic game of hide-and-seek takes place in the labyrinth at the villa of Stra. They returned via Greece, where the poet shared in the triumphs of his mistress, and stayed for a while in Corfu, in a villa situated near the Island of the Dead which had been made famous in the painting by Böcklin.

February 1900 was spent in the serenity of Settignano; then d'Annunzio followed Eleonora to Vienna, where the grandeur and richness of the city seemed barbaric. The poet's notebook contains the record of some sacred moments: 'Remember the 10th of April as a peak in your life. Isa.' The 12th of April is marked with an asterisk: 'God is protecting our love.' Soon, however, the ample buttocks of the Viennese women brought d'Annunzio back to more earthly considerations. He followed Eleonora's tour; at Basle, in front of the pictures of Böcklin, he wrote these lines reflecting his abhorrence of the Germanic world: 'Usurped reputation of a Nordic who has a yearning for the mythical world. Confused sense of sacred mystery, strident colours, frightful women, yet the Tritons show a certain sense of mystical bestiality.' At Frankfurt, he set about a veritable inventory of Goethe's house, then they went to Zurich where they met Romain Rolland and his wife, who was secretly in love with the poet. Mme. Rolland, beautiful, intelligent and highly 'artistic', was one of Eleonora's dearest friends. This intensely intellectual household was utterly devoted to d'Annunzio, though sometimes taken aback by his levity.

During this visit to Switzerland the friends met a young actress and her husband, the celebrated actor Le Bargy; the actress, Mme. Simone, has left a colourful account of the dramas of which she was the innocent cause. After lunch one day the poet asked Simone to recite a poem by Hugo, and then threw himself at her feet: 'In that first look I saw burning the spark which signifies the choice of Apollo.' The next day they all met again (by chance?) in a mountain hotel and had tea together. Suddenly, Eleonora dragged Simone into the corridor and pushed her into the bedroom where d'Annunzio was having a siesta: 'Look, look, since you love him, there he is!' Then she double-locked the door. 'Our friend is mad', d'Annunzio said simply, and they started talking quite blithely about one thing and another, waiting for the ladder which would enable them to climb out of the bedroom. That same evening Eleonora cancelled her performance and threatened to leave for Florence. But peace was restored and the friends spent an enchanting evening around the piano at the hotel, listening to Romain Rolland playing and talking about Götterdämmerung. After this eruption, d'Annunzio wrote to Angelo Conti: 'I have just experienced one of the most cruel hours in my life; everywhere she sees nothing but lies and deception. This gentle creature is becoming unjust to me and to herself.' Eleonora's judgement of her lover has more style than his whimperings: 'His life is an inn through which all and sundry pass.' Later, she wrote: 'I gave him everything . . . even suffering.'

To make his mistress appreciate the divine quality with which he endowed grief, d'Annunzio spent three summer nights on the terrace at Settignano reading to her *Il Fuoco*, which he had just completed. Eleonora heard herself described as a time-worn woman, and learnt that the memory of past pleasures excited the young lover more than her beauty or her love; she realized that, from the very first day, she had been observed by a pitiless eye. When the book appeared, arousing a storm of indignation that proved an excellent stimulus to sales, Eleonora feigned surprise; but she knew what to expect and had truly offered her grief to the novelist. Fortified by the thought that she was considered the most unfortunate woman in Europe, the actress continued for another four years to devote herself to her lover's theatrical work, despite constant disloyalty even on the professional level.

As soon as Eleonora had regained her composure, they had to leave. A letter to Mme. Romain Rolland, the nervous handwriting marked by the thick cross-strokes of the t's and by the lines under the words that she would almost shout, gives an idea of her manner of delivery:

'The *earth* awaits the spring. It knows how to wait . . . My little house is *very, very* small . . . Olive-trees and roses all around . . . *Not* a sound . . . In the evening, over there, you can see the light of Florence, the city—*Here* the stars . . . I must leave.'

Mme. Romain Rolland, the daughter of the philosopher Michel Bréal, was just the exalted spirit whom Eleonora Duse needed as a confidante. She suffered as much from the moral severity of her husband as did Eleonora from the waywardness of her lover. Music was a great bond between the two couples, for Clothilde Romain Rolland had been the favourite pupil of César Franck. Inevitably, she was to fall in love with d'Annunzio, confessing one day: 'What grief one would be ready to bear for the love, however brief, of such a poet.' The coolness with which Romain Rolland began to treat the poet around the year 1900, after his extraordinary fervour, can perhaps be explained as much by the attitude of his wife, whom he was in the process of divorcing, as by his admiration of Eleonora Duse. Passing through Florence when Eleonora had returned from a tour, the Frenchman noted that d'Annunzio had become 'a little fat man with bloated features, a rake with an unnerving expression'. Yet, after asking Romain Rolland to play the piano, d'Annunzio had this to say: 'Music makes me ashamed of myself, makes everything which I write seem empty.' Perhaps the entire career of d'Annunzio could be regarded as an heroic effort to rise above this vulgar appearance; in particular, his dramatic works may be seen as expressing the need to project in flesh and blood a sublime, criminal, irresistible d'Annunzio, as far removed as possible from the petty-bourgeois of Pescara.

After a trivial jealous scene, in May 1904, Eleonora Duse had the courage to leave her lover. In the 'guest-room' that was reserved for her in the poet's house, she had found a scarf that did not belong to her. After a frightful explosion in which d'Annunzio's manager, Palmerio, had to stop her setting fire to the villa, she broke off all physical relations with the poet. On the professional plane, she continued to place her hopes in him. It will be seen how she was to be rewarded. D'Annunzio slipped back into his old extravagant ways. The departure of La Duse was truly a catastrophe, for the actress had compelled him to lead a relatively sober life; under her influence he had written his finest poems and his most famous plays; he had even paid his debts. She had been his muse, but also his mother. Much later, a curious confusion was to arise in the poet's mind between the two tutelary divinities whom he worshipped, Donna Luisetta and 'Ghisola': did not the latter call him 'my son' and 'my little one'? Eleonora had known how to soothe him when, after working at his table for ten or twelve hours, he would come down into the garden, totally exhausted, the veins bulging out from his forehead; she had spoken his language and, equally accustomed to glory, had been able to look at the world from the same viewpoint.

8

How to Become
a God

HEAD OF BRONZE AND FEET OF CLAY

Mme. Simone, whose meeting with the poet in Switzerland was described in the previous chapter, was to remember d'Annunzio as an amusing rather than a dazzling figure. The perspicacity and the lack of indulgence which characterize her reminiscences seem closer to the truth than the vague, lyrical memories usually conjured up by his name: 'The author of these verbal pyrotechnics would emphasize what he was saying by waving his beautiful white hands in the air, the little finger of the right hand bearing two emeralds mounted on a thin gold thread. Dressed with an excessive luxury in a close-fitting suit, a silk shirt with jewelled buttons on the cuffs, and elaborate footwear in two colours, he disconcerted you as much by his feminine coquetry as by his shortness of stature, his shoulders narrower than his round hips, his tiny feet, his thick arms, thighs and legs which afflicted his body with a bisexual softness . . . The head, on the other hand, displayed the full and virile lines of some antique busts. There is no doubt that, under the fingers of a sculptor, the fine volume of the forehead, the powerful nose, the regular mouth and the wilful chin would have become so many objects of beauty. But in living form, deprived of the flawless matte quality of marble, their nobility lost all power of attraction because of their ghastly colour. The sparse hair, of a dingy satin texture, vanished in an ugly point. The bulging eyes, with neither lashes nor brows, neither grey nor blue, resembled soapy water. The pallid lips revealed funny little teeth, jagged and decaying, while the thick skin, sometimes pale, sometimes rosy, provided an uneven covering for a face that ended in a beard in the style of the Valois.' How can this portrait be reconciled with that of Stelio Èffrena, the hero of *Il Fuoco*, which had only just appeared that same year? It seems incredible that such a person could ever have been irresistible. A study of photographs confirms the description given by Mme. Simone, for the camera proved no more susceptible than she had been to the prestige of his genius or the mask of bluff. The story of d'Annunzio's successive conquests invites the same sceptical reaction as the traveller who returns with tales of miracles performed by fakirs: 'I saw a rope rise into the sky, covered with flowers . . .'; when the photos taken by the traveller are developed, they show only a man who appears to be asleep, encircled by curious onlookers. One very important element is lacking which would enable us to appreciate the charm of the seducer—his voice: 'His clear, penetrating voice, which gave a precise contour to the musical form of each word, set in even greater relief this singular quality of his speech.'

Cagliostro, another Italian who had had a good deal of success in France, had also managed to disguise his rather common appearance with a strange charm; but, whereas the magician relied on mere hocus-pocus, the poet must visibly have possessed what people like to call the flame of genius. D'Annunzio found difficulty in accustoming himself to the contrast between this flame and the body that fed it. Through love he attained a universe worthy of him; in 1908 he wrote thus to a mistress: 'I have spoken divine words to you, my entire soul entered into the slave of Michelangelo, into the only body appropriate to it.' His physique, revealing the mediocrity of his origins, was an abominable blunder on the part of destiny; that Gabriele d'Annunzio was, on the contrary, as handsome as a god and as noble as a Braganza, he convinced himself and many other people quite easily, for rarely did social scruples or a sense of humour allow him to remember the unwelcome truth. When the poet reached the age of thirty-five, the image of himself which he had fostered had been moulded in the imagination of his contemporaries and immediate posterity—and, according to d'Annunzio, for Eternity.

Yet his attitude was not a pose like that assumed by Barrès, an attitude expressed by a glorious profile on a patriotic medal. D'Annunzio was a Baroque statue carved in the round, every detail meticulously sculpted in a bronze of an incongruous alloy to which the years were to add a delicate patina here and patches of verdigris there. Before long, legend became the accomplice of vanity and spread abroad all the clichés of black Romanticism: the houses in which he lived were said to be the scene of strange feasts at which he drank champagne from the skull of a virgin; it was rumoured that his slippers were made of human skin and that he slept on a pillow stuffed with the locks of more than a hundred mistresses; he had been seen, at Viareggio, riding naked into the waves and emerging to be rubbed dry by Eleonora Duse in a robe of red silk. The legend was vulgarized in caricatures and his outline became familiar to the readers of popular newspapers: the prim figure, in pointed shoes and straw hat, with a carnation in his buttonhole and a monocle. As he was extremely short-sighted, he wore spectacles whenever he shut himself up to write.

Nietzsche had prepared the ground which this masterpiece would occupy in society; d'Annunzio assumed quite naturally the role of the superman above good and evil. He elaborated the rites of his cult, the law which only he and a few other heroes were capable of following: 'In my insight, I know that today, as tomorrow and to the very end, the work of flesh is in me a work of spirit, that the one and the other harmonize to attain a single beauty' (*Splendore della Sensualità*, 1907). One cannot help sharing the sense of wonder of a man enchanted by the ever more profound knowledge of his own genius, who made that genius the object of his finest meditations: 'Qualis artifex valeo. What a marvellous instrument have I become! The violin which emerges from the hands of a master violin-maker is merely a well-born child; but I, during years of sonorous life, have multiplied its qualities and have brought it to perfection. Music, by passing through the fibres of the wood, renders them more sensitive. It is the artist who gives the instrument its inimitable tone. Thus, the exercise of my art has refined my brute matter and has rendered it capable of ever greater resonance . . . My vision is a sort of common magic practised on the most ordinary objects. I keep still warm within me the ideal imprint of the forms which I have engendered. I delve into the depths of everything low and vile, as into the depths of an enigma that cannot resist my skill . . . Always the genius of art is succeeded by the demon of execution. Have I, in addition to the faculty of creating, the ability to take and refashion matter already gathered at will, without fatigue or a false note, because there is no resistance? Thus the potter's wheel turns wildly when the hand of the artist ceases to follow the clay' (Il Venturiero senza Ventura, 1899). When he felt himself growing old, d'Annunzio exclaimed: 'I shall keep fresh the inextinguishable vein of my laughter, even in the extremes of sadness. I shall never halt at the junction of our roads. I shall never wish to be a prisoner, not even of glory. And I say that, if I am not, tomorrow another shall be by virtue of me' (Contemplazione della Morte, 1912).

D'Annunzio considered himself the last of a line of wise men—artist-princes, the greatest of whom was Leonardo. Wagner had passed the torch to him; the pages of Il Fuoco where Stelio carries the composer's body on his shoulders underline this continuity. What Wagner had been for the Barbarians, d'Annunzio wished to be for the Latins, a role which he expounded in a speech celebrating the centenary of Victor Hugo: 'But All is in him. In his bosom—is contained the world. Every beam—every shadow descends from him—begins from him—His wild and divine spirit darkens and then shines again—as Night and Day—He is Pan, the substance of the Heavens—of the Earth and of the Sea—the Argioste, the Sonorous—the Vagabond—the God with the goat's foot and the lunar horn—the Choir-master—the leader of the eternal return—who supports the stars—inspires the races—opens the door—of eternal visions . . .' (From the French of d'Annunzio himself.)

This cult of d'Annunzio which spread so rapidly through Italy and France stopped when it reached the Channel. D'Annunzio was never considered seriously in England although he was very well translated by Arthur Symons, a friend of Wilde and Verlaine, and author of *The Symbolist Movement in Literature,* and then by Miss Georgina Harding. Symons, who preached 'the universal science of Beauty', knew Italy very well and he finally went mad there in 1906. Max Beerbohm compared Symons' translations to those of Maeterlinck by Sutro. Beerbohm also related d'Annunzio to Maeterlinck when reviewing an extremely bad play by Howard Marion Crawford on Paolo and Francesca da Rimini: 'D'Annunzio has given us their hearts' passions, Maeterlinck (changing but the names) has given us their souls' pathos' (an allusion to *Pelléas et Mélisande*).

The only English writer who really treated d'Annunzio seriously, in an extremely important and intelligent article in the *Fortnightly Review* of March 1897, was unfortunately not highly regarded in her own country. Ouida lived a long time in Florence, an old lady of absurd passions, but these passions had given her a good knowledge of the Italian character. Talking of an article by the French academician, Melchior de Vogüé, who hailed d'Annunzio as 'the Renaissance of the Latin genius', Ouida regretted that the French translations had been so heavily bowdlerized; of course she deplored the 'recurrent obscenity' in d'Annunzio but this enabled her to compare him to the realism of Zola. She recognized that 'd'Annunzio has a total lack of perception when the ridiculous mars the pathetic'. She was also irritated by his preciousness. But apart from these criticisms Ouida is full of fervour for the irresistible writer whose novels she analyses very carefully—and whom she had often met in Florence. She adores his descriptions of palaces and gardens, and she praises him for avoiding so completely the 'Superstitions of Science' and of fighting against the vulgarity of capitalism and democracy; in other words she sees in him the Apollo whose radiance destroys the monster of modernism. She would like to have seen him escape from all outside influences, and she finished her article with these lines: 'Genius, like the river at its source, takes the colour of the earth it springs from. It is only when it has reached its full volume, its deepest currents that it becomes clear and reflects the sky alone.'

Poor Ouida! How happy she would have been if she had lived to read an article by Vernon Lee in the *Westminster Gazette* of 1907. D'Annunzio is there compared with her: his heroes have 'the golden dust-cloud of past greatness which makes a halo round every one of Ouida's Italian personages'.

THE MAGICIAN

Some lines from *The Virgins of the Rocks*, which were wisely omitted in the French edition, place d'Annunzio among the caste of prophet-princes who know no service other than that of Beauty: 'Fortunately the State, erected on the foundations of popular suffrage and equality, and cemented by fear, is not only an ignoble structure, it is also precarious. The State must be an institution perfectly adapted to favour the gradual elevation of a privileged class towards an ideal form of existence.' This impudence on d'Annunzio's part caused him to be regarded as a public enemy by many of his fellow-countrymen. At the beginning of the century he could boast of being one of the most hated men in the kingdom (yet another point in common with Byron).

The idea of the poet-magician, the poet-prince, comes straight from Péladan. The name of Péladan, whose influence was immense and whose works were unreadable, raises the question of d'Annunzio's borrowings. Professor Mario Praz, in the preface to the anthology compiled in collaboration with Signor Gerra, offers a clear analysis of the problem. In his view, the works of d'Annunzio constitute a complete monument to the Decadent movement in Europe, by virtue of his prodigious capacity for assimilation—the assimilation, but not pastiche, of writers in vogue—Péladan, Swinburne and Jean Lorrain—rather than the more difficult authors, such as Rimbaud or Mallarmé. It is the 'Decadent' work of d'Annunzio that is today enjoying a revival of interest, rather than the plaster allegories or the realist stories. The d'Annunzio who is returning to favour is the writer with an affinity to Gustave Moreau, whose paintings are beginning to take their place among the greatest works of the nineteenth century. In his book *The Romantic Agony*, written thirty years ago, Professor Praz was rather more severe and compared d'Annunzio to a Barbarian looting Florence or Paris for gems with which to adorn himself. There was undoubtedly something of the Barbarian in this child of the Abruzzi, but this was not incompatible with the role of the magician; one must come from a pre-rational culture to believe in magic, and d'Annunzio was the first to believe in the power of his spell. The critic Bini has offered an admirable definition of d'Annunzio's work: 'an exploration of the world and of the ego leading to the discovery of a world *metampirico e metaspirituale* and culminating in the investigation of music as a mystical, supra-logical mode of knowledge'.

The whole of d'Annunzio's work is permeated with the assurance of one who possesses the Truth: 'To discover the secret of the low-born Universe in grains of sand, in grains of corn or in the stars of the constellation Spica Virginis, in the pip of a grape, in the shadow of lowered eyelashes; to discover the secret of agony in the heart of a rose devoured by a beetle no less beautiful than the fallen petals; to gather the infinite in the hollow of the hand that holds rain-water or a swallow fallen from the eaves . . . To bring everything, every event, every phenomenon into my art, into my works of art: that is my law' (*Libro segreto*).

Perhaps this aspiration conceals a regret at not having been able to gather disciples around him. In his youth, d'Annunzio had liked to imagine himself in the role of Socrates, to whom he devoted nearly twenty pages of *Le Vergini delle Rocce*; but, by choosing to pursue the path of pleasure, he had renounced the discreet way of life which alone can attract a coterie of admirers (d'Annunzio himself lamented the fact that he preferred the love offered by women to the deference of young men). In his periods of serenity, he would at once assume the Socratic role which Wilde played so well. In the cafés of Florence he assembled round him poets and musicians, among them a friend of Gide, the violinist Giuseppe Vanicolo, one of the strangest figures of the Italian Decadence. A little later, after a tempestuous affair, he sought relief among the students of the University of Pisa. One of these students, Baron Tancredi, still remembers the poet's simple and yet brilliant conversation; but as soon as a woman approached, the simplicity was forgotten (Berenson, it will be seen, had the same impression). D'Annunzio called this dark descendant of an old Sicilian family 'the Saracen with the Norman name'. To another student at Pisa, the poet dedicated *La Contemplazione della Morte* (1912). He had been struck by the quiet intelligence of this boy and in the dedication recounted how, in Paris, he had met a poor young man who could have become a disciple if d'Annunzio had not been so preoccupied with the social world: 'The last but one evening of April, I saw in the street a fellow of about twenty, with a beardless face modelled by the iron thumb of Destiny, like the face of Beethoven, a closed heart in which, perhaps, the four formidable notes of the Fifth Symphony resounded.' The poet sought other disciples in this social world: Maurice Rostand and Illan de Casa-Fuerte.

He must have had these young friends in mind when he wrote: 'The greatness of a work is measured not by the number of approving voices by which it is received, but by the impulse that it arouses in rare and closed spirits, by the sudden anxiety that it provokes in a man of action, a man of leisure or a man of commerce, by the torment of perplexity that it creates in a destiny which is already fixed' (*Libro segreto*).

These lines were a belated retort to the critics who had been insensitive to the magic of his spell, to the sceptics in whose eyes the inspired poet had appeared a mere charlatan. The most notable of these critics was Benedetto Croce who, in a series of articles written at intervals throughout d'Annunzio's career, accused him of corrupting Italian taste and blamed him for all the bizarre movements in vogue at the beginning of the century, such as sensualist Spiritualism, internationalist Idealism and an erotic mysticism of a vaguely Slav or Buddhist character. It would be futile to reiterate the strictures of lesser critics who, both in Italy and in France, pointed to borrowings from Maupassant, Dostoevsky and many other writers: such critics have not succeeded in persuading us that the phoenix was a magpie; d'Annunzio was a phoenix, but he was a fashionable phoenix.

The great magicians, who are the first to believe in their gift, always share some of the absurd foibles of those who follow them blindly. D'Annunzio was aware of this danger and wrote: 'But it is not always in vain that I have chewed laurel-leaves, like the soothsayers, though I fear the divinations of my heart.' Incapable of overcoming the innumerable taboos inculcated by his primitive homeland, d'Annunzio allowed himself to be guided by superstitions. He always carried with him a box of dice which he consulted before taking an important decision. He had his favourite numbers: 9, 11 and especially 7. Sometimes he would recite his list of the '27 sevens', in which the seven books of his *Laudi* were included together with the seven gifts of the Holy Spirit and the seven gates of Thebes. He always had an aversion for even numbers, but the number 13 filled him with such horror that he would never write it: in the year 1913 he dated his letters '1910 + 3'. Like many of his fellow-countrymen, d'Annunzio believed in the evil eye (*iettatura*) and attributed to *iettatori* the dark periods in his life when catastrophes resulting from his own carelessness accumulated one upon another. His faith in fortune-tellers was absolute. It will be remembered that in Naples he had organized a spiritualist circle with a Russian woman. On several occasions he consulted Eusabia Paladino, who undoubtedly was prodigiously gifted. In 1908, two fortune-tellers predicted to d'Annunzio, within a day of each other, that he would die that year, on 17 July. On the morning of the fateful day he was grazed by a tile falling from a roof; he then mounted the most refractory of his horses, tempting providence with incredible recklessness and emerging unscathed.

One of the most bizarre aspects of the d'Annunzian religion was the cult of St. Francis of Assisi, manifested by countless statues of the *Poverello* and devices surrounded by the Franciscan cord. Perhaps his communion with nature induced d'Annunzio to regard himself as a disciple, or even possibly a reincarnation of the saint. It is true that he despised money, even while seeking it avidly; he could endure periods of asceticism, and in his old age he was to prove no less courageous than St. Francis had been in his youth. Yet the manifestations of this fervour were usually sacrilegious: he allowed himself to call Colette 'my sister in St. Francis'; the equivocal Burgundian was indeed far from being a Tuscan saint.

For the figure of Christ, d'Annunzio showed the mistrust of the magus confronted with the new god: 'Although I am not afraid of a God without sinews, I never had occasion to look deep into his eyes' (*Contemplazione della Morte*). On the whole, Catholicism was merely a source of the marvellous, from which to draw an image, an idea, an attitude. It received not the slightest respect from one capable of inventing the figure of Elabami, a son of Christ and Mary Magdalene and a sort of Christian Adonis (how Wilde would have envied such a piece of folly!). D'Annunzio had nothing but contempt for popular rituals, writing to a mistress on Christmas evening: 'While everyone abandons himself to Christian debauchery, I drink a solitary cup of tea.' It is hardly surprising that the Roman Church should have adopted a severe attitude towards him. After Leo XIII, a humanist who resisted those prelates anxious to see such unseemly works on the Index, more ordinary popes took it upon themselves to condemn the poet: in 1911, Pius X condemned d'Annunzio for *pravae doctrinae . . . fidei et morum offensiva* ('depraved teaching . . . offensive to the faith and to morals'); in 1928, Pius XI, in an *ex cathedra* pronouncement, reminded the faithful that d'Annunzio had 'embraced so many *genres* and so many different domains, always leaving traces of impiety and blasphemy, profaning the most sacred things, and at the same time indulging in a revolting sensuality'. D'Annunzio's official rupture with the Church took place in 1905. He was to have opened an exhibition of Abruzzian art at Chieti, but the bishop declared that if the poet appeared, he would withdraw all the objects lent by the Church; d'Annunzio stayed away, in order not to empty the exhibition rooms.

SUPERMAN IN PYJAMAS

Around the year 1895 a man entered the poet's life, one of those characters to be found in all picaresque novels, and who assume in turn the roles of buffoon, procurer, confidant and secretary. Tom Antongini, a Milanese publisher, was something of a Leporello to our Don Juan, but a Leporello more handsome than the seducer, well-bred and cultured, and who left two large volumes of reminiscences on his master which are highly diverting for those who, when contemplating the statue, prefer to study the feet of clay rather than the head of bronze. With much less ill-humour and just as much verve as Brousson (the author of *Anatole France in Slippers*), Antongini compiled over a period of forty years a catalogue of the absurdities and the superstitions of a man whom he admired passionately.

Like all magicians, d'Annunzio loved perfumes and considered that nothing was as precious as that which was to enter into contact with his person. His consumption of toilet water was extraordinary and he changed his shirt twice a day; he took a bath daily with the utmost fastidiousness, at a time when people were usually content with a fairly cursory wash. By 1900 the number of his suits was quite unbelievable. Fortunately, the best tailor in Milan was a fervent d'Annunzian and many a bill was forgotten in return for a dedication. In his notebooks d'Annunzio would make an inventory of his wardrobe from time to time. One day he replied to his friend Conti, who had reproached him for his love of finery: 'You attach too much importance to the concern

I show for my body. Plato wore the most delicate bands round his perfumed hair. Richard Wagner covered his divine fever with velvet. After an aromatic bath, my thoughts become more agile and fresh. By what strange reasoning do you find a connection between my choice of cravats and the nobility of my meditations?'

Like Balzac, the poet wore a monkish gown to write. But, if he was expecting a woman, he would change the rough wool for silk, *crêpe de Chine* or velvet. He chose these fabrics for the 'combinations' which he had tailor-made, and which were rather like pyjamas, with a long jacket that could pass as a dressing-gown. D'Annunzio always adored fancy dress, not only for costume balls, but in all the activities in life that offered the opportunity for a change of clothes: the red foxhunter's jacket and the lancer's uniform conferred an imaginary prestige on a body with which he was not quite at ease. Undoubtedly, these perfumes and silks aroused women in a way which other men, with the hideous undergarments of the period, could hardly emulate. A luxurious and rarefied creature, like his women, the poet might well call them 'sisters'. Like Andrea Sperelli and the heroes of Willy and Rachilde (two authors abundantly represented in his library), d'Annunzio knew how to prepare the refinements of the hours from five to seven (the *'cinq à sept'*): the lamp-shade, tea and port on a low table, cushions inviting a tumble in the most unexpected places and masses of flowers everywhere. The décor used for bachelor apartments in plays by Bernstein and Bataille, and which can be found in the old *Illustrations théâtrales,* gives an exact idea of the kind of setting that awaited d'Annunzio's women friends. The décor was easily reconstructed when the poet was on his travels; as a true aesthete unable to tolerate the mediocrity of hotel furnishings, he always took with him the trappings of his personal opera. A room in which he was to stay only one night would be draped with brocade, fumigated with burning joss-sticks and adorned with all kinds of objects—half trinkets and half fetishes to remind him of the darling of the moment. Often, to escape from the mistress whom he had installed in his home (a mistake that he was always making), he would borrow his secretary's rooms to indulge a temporary liaison. One day Antongini found these lines scribbled on a piece of paper under a pillow: 'In the bitterness of your armpit, my mouth seemed to chew the bitter leaf of the laurel.'

All those who entered these places of perdition were immediately given a nickname: when the woman had told him her name, d'Annunzio would inform her that henceforth she would be known as Donatella, Isa, Nontivoglio, Cinerina, Meliadusa, Nidiola, Chiaroviso, Basiliola, Nectarina, Trivellina, Gigliola, Pivetta, Barbarella, Coré, Sirocchia, or by some other such name. This fetishism with names was matched by a fetishism with footwear, a preoccupation common among readers of Sacher-Masoch. When Antongini was in Paris, he would receive messages of this kind: 'I beg you to fetch me a pair of lady's court shoes in gold fabric or with gold brocade, from an elegant shoemaker. The prettiest there are, with high heels, either gilt or coloured.'

But perhaps this concern with detail should be seen simply as the mark of the sculptor chiselling a bronze cast. D'Annunzio 'chiselled' everything that might glorify his image. He had a passion for mottoes which he had carved above his doors, painted on the beams of his ceilings and embossed on his writing-paper: 'When I wanted to choose a device worthy of my obedience, I hesitated between *Per non dormire* and *Per non morire* within an open crown of laurels. Then I wished to have them both carved on the sides of the solitary tomb which my friends and relatives have promised me at the mouth of my native river.' Other mottoes were *Ardisco, ma non ordisco* ('I dare, but I do not plot') and *Io ho quel che ho donato* ('I have what I have given'). At Fiume, the Comandante was to have two mottoes, one noble, *Semper audeamus* ('Let us always dare'), the other somewhat more popular, *Me ne frega* ('I don't give a damn'). Only the finest parchment was worthy to receive the immortal word of the poet. D'Annunzio's handwriting has been described thus by Colette: 'The handwriting of Pierre Louÿs, Anna de Noailles and d'Annunzio, rolling, breaking like a wave, ringed like the tendrils of a viburnum.' A graphological analysis of his writing is interesting. It is the hand of a man of action rather than a man of imagination, one who lived in the present, a materialist. It indicates that his vitality, though extraordinary, came in waves. Only the o's, like large eyes, suggest an aptitude for meditation, and even a certain mediumistic faculty. The writing is that of a man with an irascible, sanguine temperament who suffered fits of vertigo. It is, in many respects, that of a megalomaniac.

Antongini mentions the care with which d'Annunzio, ostensibly such an unmethodical person, corrected his proofs and also his appreciation of beautiful typography. In fact, the first editions of most of his works are masterpieces in this respect, rather in the style of the books published by William Morris. An excellent draughtsman and wood-engraver, Adolfo de Carolis, spent his life illustrating the works of d'Annunzio. It was Carolis who was responsible for his book-plates, with the exception of one highly ambiguous drawing by Sartorio which showed a young man, naked and sprawled over laurels, his throat swollen into the shape of a phallus. Carolis was also a painter of rich colours who sometimes recalls Frank Brangwyn, an affinity which he shared with d'Annunzio.

D'Annunzio rarely replied to letters, leaving *billets-doux* and invoices to pile up chaotically in baskets, but when he did write it was with the elegance of a Chinese calligrapher; the envelope was usually written in two different inks. He had a primitive mistrust of the post; he registered all his letters and, better still, preferred to have them delivered by hand. But he sent an enormous number of interminable, lyrically phrased telegrams which must have stupefied the post offices. Consequently, his postal bills were fabulous and often remained unpaid. Only Proust showed such extravagance in his use of the telegraph service.

After reading Antongini, one has an impression of d'Annunzio quite different from that which he wished to convey through the heroes of his books, and yet, despite the absurdities and the contradictions, the charm of the man emerges triumphantly. Berenson, who was both fascinated and irritated by d'Annunzio, seized on an important characteristic: 'I much preferred seeing him alone or in the presence of other men. The presence of a woman, or worse still of several women and the atmosphere of adulation they created, brought out something boastful, cheap, and vulgar in him. And yet women found him irresistible.' Mme. Simone was to be an exception. That Anglo-Roman *grande dame* the Duchess di Sermonetta tells in her memoirs how she hesitated to meet d'Annunzio, because she was afraid of finding him a *poseur*: 'One day he came to see me at the Crillon. "How can I prove to you that I am not a *poseur!*" And for a whole hour he talked to me with the simplicity of a college-boy. He explained to me the beauty of the soul of St. Francis of Assisi, and when he left me we were friends for life.'

Gide, who had met the poet in Florence in 1895, also succumbed to the magnetism: 'He speaks with a charming grace, without seeming much concerned to make an impression. He is small; from a distance, his figure would appear ordinary or even familiar, so devoid is he of any external show of literature or genius. He has a little pointed beard of a pale blond colour and speaks in a deliberate voice, slightly frigid, but supple and almost caressing. His look is a little cold; he is possibly a little cruel, but perhaps it is the appearance of delicate sensuality that makes him seem so to me. On his head he wears simply a black bowler.'

9

Florence

It was in Florence, where, between frequent absences, he was based for the first ten years of this century, that the already prodigious literary personality of Gabriele d'Annunzio burst into full bloom. In Florence he wrote his finest verses—a vast quantity of poetry amounting to some twenty thousand lines, plus another twelve thousand lines of dramatic works—and also a large number of pieces in prose, mostly autobiographical. Cities counted for much more than women in the poet's works; d'Annunzio considered that a kind of mystical marriage existed between him and the city of Dante. Venice had been a glittering mistress, Rome his first passion, Naples a mistake, while Ferrara or Mantua had merited a week's adoration: but it is on a hill overlooking Florence, in the Piazzale Michelangelo, that d'Annunzio should have his bronze statue, surrounded by masses of flowers to hide the feet of clay. Quite apart from the poet's own glory and the prestige of the city, how many good reasons there were for this union! First of all, the memories of his youth, the love of the schoolmaster's daughter, the walks through museums, the discovery of pleasure with the girl 'with the hair of Medusa', the escapades of the college-boy of Prato which on more than one occasion had been crowned with success. For the child of Pescara, Florence was the city of perfection, the city that was to see him in his greatest splendour: 'To please one of the spirits which held dominion over me at this time [Cola di Rienzo], I rediscovered effortlessly the tastes and manners of a Renaissance lord, surrounded by dogs, horses and beautiful furniture.' Since d'Annunzio lived at the end of that phase in the history of decoration known as Historicism, everything in his life was to have a historical reference, just as the buildings erected in the capitals of Europe and America from the middle of the nineteenth century were called 'Gothic' or 'Renaissance' or 'Queen Anne'. Thus, all the prose works which he wrote in Florence, and which for the most part concerned his youth (*Il secondo amante di Lucrezia Buti*), are studded with famous sayings, with bookish and aesthetic allusions: even the most banal event in such a momentous life had to have an illustrious resonance.

At the beginning of this century, no city could compete with the prestige of Florence. A museum city, the capital of the Aesthetes, its principal industry consisted of selling Alinari photographs which reproduced the great masterpieces in sepia halftones. The city was frequented by a great many English ladies, some the disciples of Vernon Lee, who looked like a page with a *pince-nez* and wrote on the Renaissance, others readers of Ouida, the most romantic of novelists, an old maid who died of love for a Tuscan count. Rich Americans, Germans and Russians had bought villas, to which they had restored the splendour of the Medicis, with the help of resourceful antique dealers. The young Bernard Berenson had just bought a villa at Settignano, with the proceeds of his early finds. Florentine society, less imposing than that of Rome, but infinitely more cultivated, was composed of the families that had brought greatness to the city in the fifteenth century—Rucellai, Strozzi, della Gerhardesca; the women were ravishing, the men affable, but the hospitality limited. Whoever settled in Florence felt they were participating in the rarest of civilization's achievements. During these years in Tuscany, d'Annunzio, so sensitive to atmospheres, was to attain in his poems a perfection which hitherto had eluded him.

On a hillside to the north-east of the city, near the little house owned by Eleonora Duse, the poet had rented in 1898 a large but simple villa, bordered by terraces that looked out over the olive-trees onto the domes and towers of Florence (it might be wondered where he found the money, for he had left debts of seventy thousand lire in Francavilla). Settignano, less spectacular than Fiesole, has a more rustic charm; it lies against the mountains, where flocks of sheep graze; thick woods adorn the gorges, guarded by cypresses as in the pictures of Böcklin, who also lived there. D'Annunzio called the village 'Settignano di Desiderio', in memory of the sculptor born there; his house was called *La Capponcina*, somewhat inappropriately, for the name suggests 'the house of the capon'. La Duse's house was named *La Porziuncola*, after the church annexed to the basilica of Assisi.

A more regular life, much larger royalties, and the excellent Benigno Palmerio, the manager and veterinary doctor appointed by La Duse, enabled Gabriele to develop his tastes. He began by indulging freely in what Balzac called *bricabracomanie*: refectory tables, chairs, lecterns, angels of gilded wood and hangings of brocade rapidly transformed the interior of *La Capponcina* into a state of even greater clutter than could have been found in the dwellings of Victor Hugo himself. The décor was a less bizarre version of the furniture with which Des Esseintes surrounded himself. As a visitor remarked, there was not an object which was not adorned with some other object: there was a necklace round a statue, flowers on the necklace and grains of incense on the flowers. In a fifteenth-century stone niche, behind a Rococo grille, was a Byzantine triptych. The rooms were small and dark, with furniture that was too large; the bedroom was draped with velvet of 'deceived-hope green' (d'Annunzio's own phrase) and had a wrought-iron bedstead. There was also a 'Room of Fire' in which everything was red. A distinguished Florentine lady, the Marchesa Serristori, whom d'Annunzio showed round the villa, stood speechless when confronted with the horror of this décor: 'But', she admitted, when describing her visit, 'the poet's commentaries were so marvellous that one ended by thinking the Room of Fire sublime.' There was a 'guest-room', more feminine, with masses of cushions, where Eleonora Duse stayed when she was not on tour and when she had not, yet once more, resolved to break with the traitor.

For five years no other person occupied this room. But d'Annunzio had two bachelor apartments in the city for his amours, one in the Piazza Indipendenza, the other in the Via Capponi, with a small garden. The soothing influence of La Duse enabled d'Annunzio to establish roots in Tuscany and to give free rein to his inspiration, without too many distractions, amorous or political. For this he thanked her with the dedication written with the delicacy of a calligrapher, as if on marble, on the first page of the manuscript of *Alcione,* which he presented to the actress four years after the end of their liaison:

> Incipiunt Laudes
> creaturarum quas fecit
> Gabriel Nuncius ad laudem
> et honorem divinae Heleonorae
> cum esset beatus
> ad Septimianum,
> A.D. M.D.CCC.XC.
> IX

('Here begin the creation's praises sung by the Angel Gabriel in praise and honour of the divine Eleonora when he was blessed at Settignano in the year of the Lord 1899'). 'Gabriel Nuncius' is a pun on the poet's name referring to the Angel of the Annunciation.

LIVING IN STYLE

During the early years of his liaison with Eleonora Duse, d'Annunzio had mingled little in Florentine society. He had delivered a brilliant lecture on Dante in the church of Or San Michele, in December 1899, and then, several months later, he had stood as a parliamentary candidate; but he declared that the social world of Florence was 'a deep bath of stupidity'. However, a tempter soon appeared to plunge him into this bath, which was certainly less stupid than Roman society. Carlo Placci, who bore a certain resemblance to Savonarola, played in Florence the role that Count Primoli performed in Rome and, like the count, had French connections. He knew 'everyone' in Europe. His knowledge of history was as profound as his knowledge of society: in short, he was a delightful companion. Another Florentine friend, the Marchese Origo, was descended from Byron by 'La Guiccioli' (he gave his ancestor's ring to d'Annunzio); an accomplished sculptor and a generous host, Origo gathered round him all the most agreeable women of a highly exclusive but provincial society. Like d'Annunzio, he was a convinced spiritualist. One day, at a séance, the spirit that they had summoned, declaring itself to be a well-known person who had died recently in a motoring accident, began hurling insults at d'Annunzio; the table rose from the floor with such force that he was pushed against the wall of the room.

Between two important liaisons, d'Annunzio paid his respects to various foreign ladies. The Princess Abameleck-Lazarev was a superb Russian who had inherited the Demidov estates. Brought up in the Caucasus, she had retained the oriental habits of her province; in private she improvised dances which d'Annunzio was to remember in his next novel. Another semi-oriental lady had less success with the poet, possibly because her beauty was that of a woman of exceptional intelligence. After a dinner at the house of the Countess Rucellai, d'Annunzio wrote to a friend: 'I was to be introduced to a Greek beauty; it was Princess Soutzo [now Mme. Paul Morand, and who was a great friend of Proust]; a little ram, not stubborn enough, with two white breasts displayed like two things foreign to her person, two bloodless, motionless things surrounded with gold. We were left alone and I had to talk painfully for two whole hours, before glazed eyes like those of the bronzes of Aegina . . .'

At the Muravievs', the poet heard Felia Litvinne sing: 'She

sang for me. She was radiant with joy. The enormity of her face seemed to herald the appearance of a sun-god. I intoxicated her with fine words. I knew that I would have been rewarded . . . Suddenly, the artificial world vanished and I saw her rooted in the deep earth, like a primitive Moira, like an ancient soothsayer of the trees, perhaps like the great oak of Dodona which sang oracles. She had accomplished the miracle of eternal Poetry: she had transported me beyond the Veil. May she, too, be praised!'

Almost as exotic were two Sicilian sisters: the Duchess Massari, whom d'Annunzio nicknamed the 'Regina Carbonilla' because she was extremely dark, and the Countess d'Orsay, much more beautiful and on whom the poet conferred, like a diadem, the name of 'Basilissa Irene'. In her memoirs, the countess, of notoriously easy virtue, writes at great length of d'Annunzio and of the armfuls of roses or lilies that preceded his visits. There was no shortage of pretty women at the gatherings of the Countess d'Orsay and d'Annunzio called her apartment 'the jewel casket'. It was also a hotbed of gossip; every day Carlo Placci came to inform himself of the latest society news, and it was almost impossible to prevent him from discovering who was frequenting *La Capponcina* and whom the poet was keeping shut up ('cloistered') in his villa. In a drawing-room on the banks of the Arno, in a half-light that enhanced the beauty of the countess, the young Harold Nicolson, who had come to learn Italian, saw, or rather heard, the poet. The enthusiastic and pretentious Marquis de Chaumont had just declaimed some verses by d'Annunzio, in a loud enough voice to dominate the conversation:

'A voice—a woman's voice?—no, a man's voice, a voice like a silver bell, broke in upon us from the corner of the room. The sonnet was being repeated by someone else and with an intonation of the utmost beauty. I leant back in the large red sofa revelling in the languors of that lovely voice, in the amazing finish of that lovely sonnet. There was a hush when he had finished. Visconti whispered to me, "It's d'Annunzio himself." I was too excited to be sorry for de Chaumont.

'D'Annunzio then recited some further poems, and notably that splendid metrical achievement called "the rain among the pines". I was enthralled. I crouched back among the cushions, conscious of an emotional pressure such as I had not as yet experienced. He finished and refused to recite again. The sun, as it illumined the green slits of the shutters, had turned to red. Our hostess went to them and flung them open: the room was lightened. I could now see d'Annunzio sitting there playing with an agate paper-knife. I could not have believed that anything not an egg could have looked so like an egg as d'Annunzio's head. He was not very polite either to me or to de Chaumont. I wished rather that he had remained a voice in the dark' (*Some People*).

One afternoon in May 1904, the Marchesa Viviani della Robbia, who lived near *La Capponcina*, heard a noise coming from the road that led through the olive-trees to d'Annunzio's house. She leaned over the terrace and saw women strewing the path with rose-petals, as if for a procession, and servants in livery standing in a line. At last, through the trees, she saw d'Annunzio appear in a costume of white silk and, on his arm, a tall and beautiful woman walking towards the villa like a bride approaching the altar. The marchesa's curiosity soon turned to indignation, for the proud sinner was her own cousin, the Marchesa Alessandra di Rudinì Carlotti, the daughter of one of the most important men in the kingdom, the Marchese di Rudinì, a senator and only recently the prime minister of Italy. The curious Marchesa della Robbia should have lamented a disaster much worse than the scandal with which her family was being smeared: the almost total sterility that was soon to overcome the greatest Italian poet. The arrival of Alessandra di Rudinì at *La Capponcina* exposed d'Annunzio to all the temptations of social life, giving full rein to his frivolity and snobbery. For two years he was to produce only hastily written works, his poems were merely occasional pieces, and it seemed that his genius, if not his verve, had been extinguished. The fact was that d'Annunzio, now forty years old, could no longer lead a life of pleasure and a life of creative activity simultaneously. The life of pleasure won the day, to be succeeded in due course by the heroic life; unfortunately, neither was to prove favourable to a resurgence of the inspiration born under 'the enchantment of the sun' (*incantesimo solare*).

Married at an early age to the Marchese Carlotti, whom she did not love, Alessandra had given birth to two children by him. A widow at the age of twenty-six, she was rich and independent. The encounter with d'Annunzio had taken place a year earlier, on the occasion of the marriage of her brother, a great friend of the poet. According to Berenson, this perfect gentleman had managed to turn his mistress, Lina Cavalieri, into a fashionable woman and his friend, d'Annunzio, into a man of the world. Alessandra, who did not immediately take to d'Annunzio, and was a little afraid of him, had asked that the poet should not be introduced to her; but it was hardly avoidable that this sovereign beauty and the magician should not come together. A week later, d'Annunzio organized a party to hear a concert in Milan; Alessandra was among the group. The autumn found them in Rome, fox-hunting side by side. An intrepid horsewoman, the marchesa seemed to fly as she rode; even when she walked, she reminded d'Annunzio of the soaring quality of the Victory of Samothrace, hence her nickname 'Nike'. Soon, indiscreet journalists uncovered the liaison; Alessandra's family was furious and Eleonora Duse resolved to leave the poet once and for all. D'Annunzio followed the marchesa to her villa on Lake Garda and it was probably there that they became lovers. When, on 4 September 1917, d'Annunzio flew over the lake, he noted: 'Memories of the great Alessandra, that Diana the Huntress—the summer visit—the heat—the foaming horses—the long hours in bed—imperious love—the boat motionless on the lake at dawn—the frenzy of luxury. The melancholy of the innocent prisoner.'

Once again Gabriele was to feel himself the prisoner of the woman he loved, a woman who wrote him letters like this one: 'Do you know that since your lips took possession of mine, I have hardly been able to eat? I am hungry and thirsty for you . . . Until now I have lived like a virgin, cold to the desires of men. But you came and took me. There will be nothing low or

ordinary in our romance, no lies . . . I fear that terrible suffering
awaits me. So much the worse.' Indeed, there were some dreadful
scenes, first of all with Alessandra's family, infuriated by the
scandal and by her threats of suicide. From the very outset of
their romance, the marchesa was to resort to threats: 'If one day
you deceive me, I shall throw vitriol at you!'

Having sacrificed her position, Alessandra wanted no clandestine
happiness. Intoxicated by the poet's words, she too imagined herself a Renaissance figure. No sooner had she settled herself at
Settignano than the relatively simple life of the villa was transformed. There were footmen and grooms, the stables were filled
with thoroughbreds and the kennels with greyhounds. The prod-
igality terrified Palmerio, Gabriele's manager: the favourite dogs
slept on silk and had collars studded with emeralds. D'Annunzio
bought one of the first automobiles, in which he raised clouds
of dust on the roads of Tuscany; he emptied the antique-shops
and, so that he might dress his mistress to his own taste, cheerfully cut up old velvets and silks obtained from China. Followed
by the gilded youth of Florence, the lovers rode on their horses
through the woods of the Cascine. For the summer they rented a
large villa by the sea at Marina di Pisa, near the pine-tracts where
Shelley and Byron had walked; they spent the autumn at the
villa on Lake Garda. This life of splendour was frequently interrupted by rows. One day, as they were riding, a quarrel flared up
and the marchesa made her horse jump into the lake; without
hesitating, d'Annunzio followed her in and managed to save her;
he was riding his favourite mare, Undulna. With intermittent
crises of this kind, their frantic happiness lasted until June 1905.

Then the marchesa had to undergo operations for a tumour; the
operations were painful, her convalescence long and interrupted
by relapses. It is generally admitted that d'Annunzio's grief was
not merely loudly proclaimed, but sincere, and that he made no
attempt to seek relief in affairs with other women. But, with
the morbid relish typical of him, he made detailed notes of the
operations. He dwelt on the idea of that magnificent body being
butchered and took down the delirious words uttered under the

influence of chloroform. When, after six weeks of watching by her bedside (the doctors admired his stamina), the marchesa was saved, the poet exclaimed: 'I have won!' He now thought of marrying Alessandra. In fact, the senator di Rudinì, in an effort to minimize the scandal, offered to pay his daughter a large pension if she would regularize her position. But divorce did not exist in Italy, and so Italians who wished to obtain a divorce had to adopt another nationality. D'Annunzio, casting patriotism aside, took steps with a view to obtaining Swiss naturalization. Donna Maria, for her part, would have been quite happy to regain her independence; a liaison with a charming man, the painter La Gandara, had brought her consolation for the suffering endured twenty years earlier. Gabriele and his wife met in Zurich, where they conferred with the most famous lawyers. Matters seemed to be taking a promising course when d'Annunzio told a journalist that, were he to become Swiss, it would be solely for the purpose of securing a divorce. The Grand Council immediately made it clear that naturalization would never be granted and d'Annunzio returned to Florence. Antongini had accompanied him on this journey and the two cronies had such a wild time together in Zurich that the reports made by the police had probably influenced the Council's decision.

Although only recently he had envisaged marriage with serenity, d'Annunzio suddenly found the affair a burden; relations between the lovers deteriorated. The marchesa had unfortunately become addicted to morphine during her illness; the drug was disfiguring her beauty, she was losing her allure, the 'Nike' quality that had so captivated the poet. D'Annunzio began to fear that Alessandra would become hysterical, as Maria Gravina had been, though he did nothing to restore calm to this troubled mind which, between passionate reconciliations, was tortured by a jealousy that was justified only too often. For instance the poet showed an interest in a provincial poetess, Giulia di Sesto, whom his patronage failed to raise from obscurity, and also a Dutch lady, an artist who had settled in Florence and whose *art-nouveau* embroideries had enjoyed a brief fame; he wooed Rosita Finaly, whose father, a banker, owned a large villa on the road to Bologna. Rosita spent her holidays at Cabourg and was one of Proust's '*Jeunes Filles en fleurs*'. He turned his attentions briefly to a noble Florentine, the Countess Amatino-Spina, who resembled a Renaissance youth painted by Perugino; he sent her a postcard of the portrait: 'This is your secret portrait, your spiritual portrait.' There was also an Englishwoman, but a typically d'Annunzian incident, accompanied by dark forebodings on the poet's part, put an end to this friendship. In the *Libro segreto* d'Annunzio relates how he had wanted to give the lady a present. His most cherished possessions were his greyhounds, and he told her to choose one. Without hesitation, she chose Timbra, his favourite. Alarmed, d'Annunzio warned her that Timbra was dangerous, that she could take any one of his magnificent animals, but not that one. But she insisted so forcefully that he eventually gave way. Having offered her plentiful advice, d'Annunzio watched in anguish as she set off with Timbra up the high hill on which she lived. A little later, d'Annunzio suddenly caught a brief glimpse of something white dashing over the lawn—it was Timbra. He called the dog's name, but it had vanished. A few hours afterwards, a man arrived from the villa where the young woman lived. A terrible thing had happened: the woman had tried to play with the dog, which was not used to her. It had leapt at her face and had bitten her horribly. The servants, who had come running when they heard her cries, had caught and killed Timbra, at precisely the moment when d'Annunzio had seen the dog running across his lawn.

Alessandra withdrew to her villa on Lake Garda, pestering the poet with letters and telegrams whose only effect was to hasten the end of their affair. When *La Nave*, which she had inspired, was performed with great success, the marchesa did not attend the première. The journalists then announced the rupture officially and claimed, though without formal proof, that Alessandra had ruined her children financially for the poet's sake. In her grief the marchesa turned to religion; she went to Lourdes and a year later, in 1911, entered the Carmelite order after burning all d'An-

nunzio's letters; hardly a trace of her appears in his literary output, of which she had been too successful a rival.

THE CONTESSA

In the parody of *Don Giovanni* which d'Annunzio's life became
from 1904 onwards, the role of the countess would have been
better played by the Marchesa Alessandra than by the countess
who in fact replaced her. The poet, caught in a web of amorous
successes, between two affairs that brought him dazzling happiness, was on more than one occasion overcome with disgust: 'I
am a pig with wings', he noted one day on a scrap of paper. But
there was no stopping him. After all, did not these brilliant
women who threw themselves at him enhance his prestige? He
had made easy conquests, but he wanted the difficult ones. He
therefore set his sights on the charming Countess Mancini, the
wife of a rich wine-grower. A sentimental woman, quite cultured
but subject to melancholia as a result of her childlessness, she
had a soothing effect after the imperious 'Nike'. With a pretty
body, a rather insignificant face and a fondness for bright dresses,
she would have been no different from many other young women
if she had not had a keen interest in automobiles and poetry. A
well-bred Madame Bovary, she resisted for quite a long time and
her hesitation caused Gabriele's desire to grow into an obsession.
Every day he would write her two letters: one which she could
show to everybody, the other of a more intimate nature. These
private letters were later published under the title *Solus ad solam*.
Finally, on 11 February 1907, the countess surrendered and spent
the night at *La Capponcina*. The Marchesa Carlotti had left the
villa in January; frequent letters and promises to meet her, in
Rome or in Bologna, kept her out of the way. D'Annunzio never
failed to remember the anniversary of this date; a few years before
his death he noted: '11 February 1934. O sweet and cruel memories . . . This was my last happiness.' It was certainly not his
last amorous success, but it was, perhaps, the last time that he

experienced the happiness of a young man, untarnished by the anticipation of fatigue or of difficulty in waking up the following morning. Gabriele nicknamed her 'Amaranta with the Face of Light'; at other times he called her Giusini. After her 'fall', the young woman rapidly became, in the words of Antongini, 'a veritable demon of lust', which is rather surprising when one hears the poet compare her to a 'white rose'. Here is d'Annunzio's description of her: 'Her hair is of that tawny brown which the painters of statues in Hellas used for women's hair; the colour of her skin reminds me of the marble of the temples at Delos which the servants used to impregnate with an essence of roses slightly gilded with some mysterious compound.'

D'Annunzio charmed the husband, who invited him to stay with them in the country. He also stayed with the couple when they were on holiday and, in the meantime, wrote one of his worst plays, *Più che l'amore* ('More than Love'), a propaganda piece on the dignity of sin which was very badly received. The absurdity of the situations brings to mind the famous line from *Antony* by the elder Dumas: *'Elle me résistait, je l'ai assassinée'* ('She resisted me, I murdered her'). The public, sated with the 'sublime', jeered both at the poet's attempt to give adultery the dimensions of a Promethean myth, and at the defence of his play which he published after its resounding failure.

In the spring of 1907, d'Annunzio began to detach himself from *La Capponcina*. There was no space in the house for any more furniture, nor in the garden for any more flowers. Moreover, his creditors had found their way there and were becoming a great nuisance. He made frequent visits to Rome, where he met the Countess Mancini, rented various villas on the Tyrrhenian coast, and went to stay first with one household, then with another. During a stay with the Marchese Origo, the collector Albert Henraux, a French cousin of Carlo Placci, met the poet and made this entry in a notebook: '11 April 1907. . . . Gabriele d'Annunzio is here. Very simple, a little dull, he talks of La Duse and of the performance yesterday, in which he admired her costumes. He does not like the play (*L'Autre Péril* by Donnay):

"The only interesting act is the fourth, even then the situation is not new." Origo is leaving after lunch for Venice, to choose a site for his works at the exhibition, and d'Annunzio has been chaffing him for his mistake in favouring this exhibition; he approves only of exhibitions in international cities; he does not approve of them in Venice, where Venetian painting should reign alone. When I take no fruit, he is indignant: "*Non le piace la più bella cosa della Natura!*" ("You don't like the best thing in Nature"). He has a taste for unbridled luxury; twenty-five thousand francs in a season is the least that a fashionable woman should spend on dresses. As soon as he climbs into a motor car, his only thought is to exceed a hundred and ten kilometres an hour. He finds rare and wonderful words to describe a pretty woman. Magnificent words and phrases slip even into his small talk. After lunch he goes back to his room, where he has been working for two days.'

D'Annunzio's ways irritated the Tuscans immensely. To these purist provincials, he was an adventurer. They reproached him for his slight southern accent. The Accademia della Crusca, founded in the seventeenth century to preserve Italian in all its purity, seized on all the little faults in his writings, but he retorted: 'I am myself *cruscallissimo*.' It is sometimes tempting to think that this union with Tuscany had been a marriage of convenience from which he sought escape as often as possible. His neighbour at Settignano, Bernard Berenson, also a Tuscan by adoption, shrewdly observed the trait which, in d'Annunzio, annoyed high society and charmed artists: 'Like so many Latins, he was more of a monologist than a conversationalist. With his voice, his gestures, the sequence of the words he used, he created a sort of magic spell. Politics did not preoccupy him yet. Philological, grammatical, stylistic problems provided him with admirable subjects of conversation. I almost never talked to him about my work, as he lacked all sense of quality for the visual arts. He had exquisite taste for handling words but none for art or for how to furnish a house. To the beauty of nature and of landscape he had a more direct and genuine reaction' (*Sunset and Twilight*).

Casting all discretion aside, 'Giusini' followed the poet to the villas where he was trying to work and to the cities where he used to watch motor races. At Brescia, the lovers enjoyed 'an unforgettable night': 'The breath of Tristan passed over us.' All that remains from this period is a series of very fragmentary autobiographical stories, published in newspapers in serial form under the title *Le Faville del Maglio* ('The Sparks from the Hammer') and dedicated to Count Mancini; the stories reflect the admiration with which the poet contemplated even the most trivial episodes of his existence. There were also numerous projects that d'Annunzio mentioned to his publisher in order to obtain advances— a project for a play, *La Madre folle*, two dramas which, after *Francesca da Rimini*, would continue the 'Malatestian' cycle, and plans for two novels which, with *Il Fuoco*, would form a cycle entitled *I Romanzi del Melograno* ('The Romances of the Pomegranate'). Eventually, the count's eyes were opened to the lovers' indiscretions and he made their meetings difficult. In his notebook for the month of July 1907, d'Annunzio described a rendezvous with his mistress in a country inn. The madness that was creeping upon the countess can already be discerned:

'Arrived at Borgo San Dannino, stormy sky. I find Amaranta at the station, trembling all over and afraid. I was not expecting her. She was wearing her black silk costume and the hat with a feather. Agitated conversation on the square. In terror, flashes of love. We climb into the carriage. I speak in that low, rather rough voice which upsets her. So as not to hear it, she covers her ears with a crazy gesture. We stop at a little inn called "The Roman Eagle". We are given a room with an enormous bed. Feverish caresses interrupted by her childish agitation. Slight taste of iodine on her white skin. The body is still marvellous and my desire still frantic. A meal is brought which we do not touch. She wants to return to Salsa. After long kisses we go down the wooden staircase. On the square, a concert of guitars and mandolins. A cold wind has made a stormy sky. The carriage is drawn by a white horse. The wind blows her veil, through which I seek her mouth. Under the street-lamps I see her terrified face.

It is raining. Sadness. Sadness. Why did I let her leave? She goes back into her hotel and takes the two boxes of orchids. I find my bed impregnated with her odour; impossible to sleep . . . How exquisite and yet trivial life is. I keep the inn bill. So much intoxication and so much anguish has cost only twenty-one lire.'

The father came to the assistance of the husband and, at the beginning of August 1908, the two men compelled Amaranta to write to d'Annunzio saying that she was returning to 'the path of duty'. However, the countess managed to escape surveillance to make two pilgrimages with her lover, one to the shrine of Cosentino, where d'Annunzio asked the organist to pray for his interior peace, the other to Assisi, from 15 to 17 August. Was she hoping to lead Gabriele back to faith at the shrine of his dear St. Francis? Her fanciful hopes were rewarded with a copy of the *Little Flowers,* inscribed with a long dedication recording in detail those 'three mystical days' and signed 'Friar Gabri, sinner'. The end of this affair was to be related with the utmost exactness in the work which d'Annunzio was now contemplating, *Forse che sì forse che no.* Real life provided him with the appallingly sordid dénouement of what is the finest of his novels.

D'Annunzio, losing patience with his mistress, had gone to Bologna to meet a new conquest, giving an excuse which the countess had believed. No sooner had he arrived than he received this telegram: 'I am dying of grief and of love stop Come stop Come for pity's sake.' If one is to judge by the novel, Gabriele intended to join his mistress immediately in Florence; but, alas, the carriage broke down most inconveniently. In the novel he used this mechanical delay and the anguish that accompanied it to great literary effect. In fact, he could easily have caught the train and arrived before the final paroxysm of despair drove the Countess Mancini, haggard and without hat or gloves, into the streets; she was eventually found in a church and taken to a nursing-home that was more like a prison. As if this drama was not quite complete, d'Annunzio degraded his mistress even further in the novel, delivering her for an entire evening to two sinister individuals and suggesting all kinds of horrors.

As soon as he was separated from 'Giusini', the poet suffered atrociously from the parting, even though she had begun to be a burden. The lines that he wrote on his grief are admirable and provide the most beautiful pages of the novel. But the poor woman, the victim of a persecution mania, began to hate her lover. She refused to see him and after several months in a clinic returned home, where she was hardly less a prisoner, no longer demented but always a little abstracted, as if she had been loved by a god. D'Annunzio must have had more than one occasion to regret that his victims were not transformed into constellations like Selene. Three years later, when he was no longer living in Italy, he resumed a melancholy correspondence with Countess Mancini. In one letter he assured her: 'I believe I suffered much more than you, who were lost in a shadowy dream, while I was wounded constantly by brutal reality.' Often, d'Annunzio would savour his remorse with a kind of masochism. In his old age, he frequently thought of three of the women who dominated his life in Florence, and wrote: 'The martyrdom of Ghisola, the dishonour of Donatella, the perdition of Amaranta beat in torrents against my masked face, against my heart.' It will be seen later who was this 'Donatella', another martyr who was to suffer both 'perdition' and 'dishonour'. But let us first of all trace the influence of Eleonora Duse on the poet's dramatic works and on his development as a politician.

10

The Heroic Aesthete

A NATIONAL THEATRE

As soon as d'Annunzio was conscious, in the words of Gide, of having 'drawn the attention of all Europe to Italy', patriotism became one of the forms in which he expressed his genius. His country, to which he was bringing a long-awaited glory, would be raised—if necessary against its will and, above all, in spite of the politicians—out of the mediocrity dotted with scandals that it had known since unification. In the last year but one of the century, d'Annunzio began to exalt in his works Italian countryside, Italian history and Italian passions. The artist whose only fatherland had hitherto been the Beautiful became *italianissimo*. In the face of Italy's intellectual decrepitude, he wanted to create an art that would glorify the forces of Latin culture. It is interesting to observe his readiness to use a Latin word, more imperial in range than the corresponding Italian word. In his works for the theatre he presented characters of lofty sentiments, too exalted perhaps for non-Italian taste, posed in historical settings. The theatre also seemed to him the best means by which 'to bring everything, every event, every phenomenon into my art, into my arts: that is my law' (*Libro segreto*).

Encouraged by Eleonora Duse, d'Annunzio dreamed of founding near Rome a national theatre, a 'Latin Bayreuth', where not only his own plays but also those of the Greeks and Racine would be performed. All his ideas on the theatre are developed in *Il Fuoco*; the novel reflects his desire for a return to ancient modes, to a Dionysiac inspiration, and often brings to mind the Nietzsche of *The Birth of Tragedy*. Above all, as in ancient Greece, this theatre must be built in a sublime setting: 'Both saw in their dream the marble theatre on the Janiculum, the multitude overcome by this idea of truth and beauty, the great starry night stretching over Rome; they saw the frenzied crowd descending the hill, carrying in their rude hearts the confused revelation of poetry; they heard the clamour spreading through the shadows of the immortal city.'

In conceiving this theatre, which he dreamed of building at Albano, d'Annunzio was influenced by what he knew of the fine performances given at the ancient theatre of Orange. In a long article entitled 'The Rebirth of Tragedy' and published in *La Tribuna*, but which aroused little public response, he maintained that it was necessary to commune with Nature in the open air, that conventional subjects and eroticism had robbed the theatre of all grandeur, and that the religious spirit must be rediscovered. His theatre would be 'a sanctuary beside the lake, among the olive-trees whose twisted branches imitate the convulsions of the maenads'. A committee was formed; the inauguration was to take place in March 1899 with a *Persephone* written by d'Annunzio himself; but the great scheme dragged on until thirty years later, when d'Annunzio had a Greek theatre built in the gardens at his Vittoriale. How could he have expected that the government would provide the funds for a National Theatre, when Italy's only actors belonged to travelling companies (the most famous were the rival groups of Eleonora Duse and Irma Gramatica)? Nevertheless, with this ideal theatre always in mind, d'Annunzio wrote profusely, nearly one play a year over a period of six years. And to obtain her forgiveness for his treachery in connection with *La Città morta*, he dedicated his next play to 'Eleonora Duse of the beautiful hands'.

PROPAGANDA FROM THE CHARNEL HOUSE

La Gioconda, a drama set in modern times, is a propaganda piece on the rights of genius. The action takes place in Florence. The first act is set in the house of the sculptor Lucio Settàla; his wife Silvia tells us that he has returned to her after trying to kill himself for a *femme fatale*, Gioconda Dianti. Lucio appears, 'his eyes extraordinarily dilated by suffering, with a weak smile that softens his sensual mouth'. There follows a long conversation with an explorer who has come back from Egypt (the explorer was the hero of an Italy as yet without victories of which to boast), and then a tender love duet between husband and wife. In the second act, Gioconda finds Lucio and tells him that she goes to his studio every day. Alas, she is his inspiration! Silvia decides to go to the studio and drive her out. The studio is decorated with a cast of the *Victory of Samothrace*; behind a drape is Lucio's latest work in clay. Her beauty gives Silvia the courage to confront the mistress, who enters with a veil over her face. After a great scene Silvia orders her to leave, but Gioconda, not content with hurling curses, tries to destroy the statue which she has inspired. In the course of a struggle, Silvia, in saving the statue, has both her hands crushed beneath its weight. The last act takes place in a villa by the sea. La Duse was wonderful in these final scenes: 'There is in her bearing something incomplete which suggests a vague image of clipped wings, a vague feeling of a strength that has been humiliated and mutilated, a nobility debased, a harmony destroyed. She wears a garment of an ashen colour down which runs a thin black strip, like a band of mourning. The long sleeves conceal the stumps which she lets hang at her sides, or which she sometimes holds against her, as if to hide them in the folds of her dress, in a pitiful gesture of modesty.' There is a conversation with a beggar-woman which brings little consolation (the scene is reminiscent of the Symbolist theatre); we learn that the sculptor has returned to his *femme fatale* and has started work again, but has refused to give the statue hands.

The character of Gioconda was inspired by Maria Gravina; one can almost hear the redoubtable countess speaking, and the stage directions are surely based closely on the author's memories of her: 'Her fury makes her choke and quiver. In her the wild beast is awakened, vindictive and destructive. Her whole body, lithe and powerful, is filled with the same strength that contracts the murderous muscles of felines about to pounce. The veil, which she has all the time held over her face like a sombre mask, gives an even more formidable aspect to her person, ready to inflict injury by any means, with any weapon.' La Duse, on the other hand, was certainly the inspiration for the wife willing to make any sacrifice, however futile. The gesture with which she held out her stumps to her daughter seemed unbearably beautiful.

La Gioconda triumphed at Palermo in April 1899, but a few days later, in Naples, *La Gloria* was a resounding failure. This play, in which d'Annunzio projected his desire for power into all the characters, without regard for balance, is a prophetic summary of the career of Mussolini. The action takes place in the 'Third Rome', a Rome which is once again the first city of the world. His stage directions, precise as ever, almost suggest that d'Annunzio had a prevision of the famous office in the Palazzo Venezia: 'A large, bare room, its powerful stone vertebrae visible to the eye. A heavy table stands in the middle, cluttered with maps like the table of a strategist, still animated by recent deliberations, by the meditations and then the unanimous agreement of the men who had been gathered round it only a short time ago: a motionless support from which is radiated and propagated a central thought, a regulating energy. On each architrave of the four doors, two to the right and two to the left, is carved the emblem of a flame that is revived by the breath of a contrary wind, with the motto: VIM EX VI. At the back of the room, a balcony opens onto the vast city.' It was just such a décor that d'Annunzio chose when, at Fiume, he was himself to live *La Gloria*.

In March 1901, Eleonora Duse, at last playing *La Città morta* in Milan, enjoyed a triumph which she repeated every evening on a tour across Italy. Although he did not follow the tour to all its stops, d'Annunzio joined it in the major towns, where he delivered morning lectures. There was great excitement, with ovations and banquets that gave the Italians the impression of entering on a second Renaissance. When the company appeared in the Austrian towns of the Adriatic, Trieste or Goritz (Gorizia), the performances degenerated into demonstrations at which d'Annunzio improvised speeches on the glory of *la più grande Italia*. And yet, despite these political successes, nearly all his plays were badly received at first, some so badly that they never recovered, like *Francesca da Rimini*, first performed at Rome in December 1901. This latter play was a financial catastrophe for La Duse, who had spent four hundred thousand lire, a figure never before reached in any theatre in Italy—not even when La Scala had introduced a locomotive and a buffalo hunt into their production of *La Fanciulla del West*. The machinery, too complicated, broke down, while the costumes, too meticulously copied by Fortuny from the drawings of Pisanello, hampered the actors' movements. (Zeffirelli's *Romeo and Juliet* might, perhaps, today give an idea of what d'Annunzio had wanted, a blend of violence and splendour.) *Francesca da Rimini* was to have been the first part of a trilogy devoted to the Malatesta family, but d'Annunzio wrote only the second play, *La Parisina*.

In 1902 and 1903, Eleonora Duse made three tours in the United States, imposing on theatre managers who wanted *The Lady of the Camellias*, or perhaps Ibsen, the d'Annunzian repertoire which she played to auditoriums three-quarters empty. She sent her lover large royalties, and journalists smiled when the author boasted of being famous in the United States. But her stratagem was soon uncovered and d'Annunzio was left with a reputation for living on women.

At last, in March 1904, in Milan, d'Annunzio enjoyed a dazzling success with his play *La Figlia di Iorio*. The fact that this triumph was achieved at the cost of an insult to Eleonora Duse mattered little. This was indeed the national work for which the Italians had been waiting, a *Cavalleria rusticana* on a Shakespearean scale. In an isolated village in the Abruzzi, during a journey with Michetti, d'Annunzio had seen a girl in a red dress running onto the square, pursued by a band of peasants who wanted to rape her. Michetti had already achieved a great success with a painting inspired by this scene. When d'Annunzio decided to use it for a regional drama written in an archaic style, in the manner of a mystery-play, Michetti designed the rustic décor and costumes with scrupulous precision. And yet, how far removed from reality were the stilted, operatic movements of the actors, the crowd of extras reminiscent of the choruses of antiquity, the silences which brought the action to a halt so that the audience might be thoroughly imbued with the atmosphere of this 'inimitable life'.

'The high quality of the drama *La Figlia di Iorio* lies in its melodic design, in the fact of its being sung as a pure popular song and containing the musical representation of an ancient people. My effort (though I should not say "effort", for I composed the whole of this pastoral tragedy in eighteen days, between sky and sea, as if obeying the demon of the species who was repeating his songs within me), my obedience, rather, lay in following the music, even though I felt that I was inventing it' (*Libro segreto*).

D'Annunzio had found the model for this genre in a Celtic drama by Henri Bataille, *La Lépreuse*; Bataille on the other hand had already been strongly influenced by *La Gioconda*. The new play also echoed the Provençal epic *Mireille*, as well as *Peer Gynt*; like Ibsen's play, *La Figlia di Iorio* became a national drama. In places it even calls to mind Claudel's *L'Annonce faite à Marie*, which d'Annunzio did not know. This last comparison shows that, in the case of d'Annunzio, one must not speak of pastiche, but of influences, of experiments that were common at the time, experiments which, in the case of this particular work, would have been *avant-garde* ten years earlier.

D'Annunzio had written *La Figlia di Iorio* for Eleonora Duse, who was by his side during its composition, but friends told him that the Milan audiences much preferred her rival, Irma Gramatica. The latter's unsophisticated verve and plebeian physique possibly suited the part better. On the pretext that La Duse was convalescing and would not have the stamina for an exhausting role, d'Annunzio entrusted the play to Gramatica and her company. On the evening of the dress-rehearsal Matilde Serao visited her friend, whom she found alone and prostrate in a hotel bedroom. Eleonora raised herself on her bed and cried out: 'It was mine, it was mine, and they have taken it from me!' Taking the manuscript from under her pillow, the actress began to read it, to act her part and soon all the other parts, for she knew every line. Then, exhausted, she sank into a stupor. Shortly afterwards, in a fit of jealousy, exasperated by her lover's faithlessness, she broke with him once more.

As soon as Eleonora Duse went out of his life, success in the theatre deserted d'Annunzio. However, if a verse drama entitled *La Fiaccola sotto il Moggio* ('The Light beneath the Bushel'), a story of a vendetta in the Abruzzi, was coolly received, *La Nave* ('The Ship') triumphed in Rome on 11 January 1908; but the triumph was political rather than literary.

One of the reasons why d'Annunzio's plays did not enjoy the same success in the rest of Europe as his novels is their author's lyrical but intensely physical realism, his taste for gaudy horror. The reader of a novel can be amused or moved by a sordid description, or he can skip the pages that he finds repellent. But this is not possible in the theatre, and the plays of d'Annunzio are full of the kind of horrific scenes which in France were reserved for *Grand-Guignol*. In *La Nave*, Orso Faledro and his four sons have their eyes and tongues torn out; in *Francesca da Rimini*, Malatesta has an eye gouged out; in *La Fiaccola sotto il Moggio*, Guigliola plunges her hand into a tank full of snakes. The martyrdom of St. Sebastian and the suffocation of 'La Pisanelle' with flowers take place on the stage. In the wings, the courtesan of *Sogno d'un mattino di primavera* dies in the flames; the heroine of *La Città morta* is drowned; in *La Gloria*, Comnena stabs her lover; in *La Figlia di Iorio*, the girl is burnt to death. In *La Nave*, Basiliola prefers to throw herself on to the pyre of a pagan altar rather than be nailed to the prow of a ship. And how often one is reminded of the speeches of Théramène in *Phèdre*, when d'Annunzio's massacres are too complicated to produce on stage! In

Francesca da Rimini, a naked woman is hunted with mastiffs; in the prologue of *Sogno d'un mattino di primavera*, we learn that Isabella woke up to find herself bathed in the blood of a lover who had just been murdered; Fedra plunges a pin into the young slave-girl loved by Ippolito. Certainly, the Greek tragedians and Shakespeare had set a precedent and the Parisian Mounet-Sully's gouged eyes streaming with blood in his performance of *Oedipus* offered a tempting example, but d'Annunzio's historical butcheries were closer to the Byzantine tragedies of Paul Adam and Péladan, in which people were blinded, crucified and stoned to death with gay abandon.

These grandiloquent dramas with artificial and usually revolting subjects were always mounted with the greatest care and at considerable expense. D'Annunzio looked on them as the sacred ritual of the cult of the Beautiful, a cult of which he was the high priest. It would really be necessary to have seen these performances to have a true idea of the d'Annunzian aesthetic creed; the photographs available clearly do not do justice to their dramatic effect.

THE ENCHANTMENT OF THE SUN

During the same years in which he was producing this theatre of horror, and was still under the influence of Eleonora Duse, d'Annunzio wrote the largest and the most beautiful part of his poetic work, verses that placed him in the front rank of contemporary writers and which remain the perfect model of the Italian language. The nobility of these poems inspired by Mediterranean myths was, perhaps, only made possible by the cruelty of his dramatic works; the plays were a kind of blood-letting which purged d'Annunzio of his impurities, leaving him free to evoke the extraordinarily sensitive impressions which he received from a landscape or a work of art. Liberated from physical matter by his plays and his realistic stories, the poet saw himself in a heroic perspective and identified himself with the heroes of mythology, and in particular Ulysses.

The sudden blinding illumination which transformed a prodigiously gifted writer into a great poet happened in Tuscany, shortly after he came to know Greece. He was at Pisa with Eleonora Duse, in January 1896, when he experienced what he described as the 'enchantment of the sun' (*incantesimo solare*). On 16 January he wrote to his publisher: 'I am still in Florence, held by the enchantment of the sun . . . Here in Florence, and in Pisa, I have lived a month of marvellous dreams.' A little later, he wrote to Hérelle, his translator: 'It is a glorious day. I am going to San Rossore, into the woods . . . and then to Gombo on the shore of the Tyrrhenian sea scattered with seaweed, where the youthful spirit of Percy Shelley roams. For weeks now, rivers of poetry have been pouring into my soul.'

As soon as he had settled himself in Florence, in a villa over-looking the city, d'Annunzio started to write the poems known by the general title of *Laudi*. In 1897 d'Annunzio wrote *Maia* and *Laus vitae*; *Elettra* and *Alcione* followed during the years 1900–4. Later came the patriotic poems *Merope* and the *Canti della guerra latina*. On his return from Greece, as he embarked on this enter-prise, d'Annunzio wrote: 'From my furnaces has emerged the only poem of total life, the only true and proper representation of Soul and Body, to have appeared in Italy since the *Commedia*. This poem is called *Laus vitae* . . . He who is able to read these great stanzas . . . stands on the threshold of the future and glimpses the first lineaments of the being who is soon to take shape, the son of our wondrous anguish and of the most divine myth . . . May this being retain, among all that he has been taught, these two poles of the new spiritual axis, two heroic arts: the art of inventing each day his own virtue and the art of preserving his purity.'

The principal figure in the poem is a Ulysses who bears a distinct resemblance to the poet, a Ulysses whom he places above Christ:

> O Galilean,
> You are worth less than, in Dante's fire,
> The pilot-king of Ithaca, Odysseus.

His Pallas was like a Valkyrie; the style, according to M. Guy Tosi, is 'Dante contaminated by Zarathustra'; his itinerary is that taken by Scarfoglio's yacht. Even more than the contemporary French poets, who were equally disgusted by Realism and bored by Symbolism, d'Annunzio owed much of his inspiration to Greece: the olive-branch had succeeded the orchids. Only Anna de Noailles succeeded in certain of her poems in conveying a sense of blinding illumination similar to that experienced by d'Annunzio; occasionally Charles Maurras achieved this quality, but in a highly academic manner. Another French writer little known at this period, Saint-Pol Roux, was alone in formulating the theory of 'magnificism' which urged that 'the effects of word and light be blended' (1893). A little later, in a long article in *Le Mercure*, Saint-Pol Roux explained what this 'magnificent art' was to be; it was the very art practised by d'Annunzio, who may have read the article, for he always kept himself informed of new literary trends. But the most certain literary influence was, once again, that of Nietzsche's *The Birth of Tragedy*.

After the pilgrimage to Greece, the poet ventures into the modern city, Rome, to stigmatize the modern world, and finds solace only with the sibyls and the *ignudi* of Michelangelo (M. de Montera has here observed the influence of *Les Villes tentaculaires* by Émile Verhaeren). He then seeks refuge in the desert and in his memories of the journey to Egypt, questioning the Sphinx (one is reminded of Flaubert and *La Tentation de saint Antoine*) and learning what are the four metaphysical metals of which the bronze of his own statue is composed: Will, Pleasure, Pride and Instinct. On completing *Laus vitae* in April 1903, d'Annunzio was able to write to his translator: 'This is the first modern poem that combines the incandescent matter of the new life and the memories of the majestic past.' The reader encounters two obstacles in these poems: first, it is difficult to distinguish between dream and narrative; and secondly, the excessive erudition makes certain passages rather ponderous. But some of the impressions of the Florentine countryside are even more beautiful than the poems evoking walks in Rome.

The collection entitled *Alcione* is warmer and is inspired by the sun-scorched beaches of the Tyrrhenian sea; it achieves a true fusion with Nature. Clearly, the Great Pan is not dead:

> *E la mia forza supina*
> *si stampa nell'arena,*
> *diffondesi nel mare;*
> *e il fiume è la mia vena,*
> *il monte è la mia fronte,*
> *la selva è la mia pube,*
> *la nube è il mio sudore.*
> *E io sono nel fiore*
> *della stiancia, nella scaglia*
> *della pina, nella bacca*
> *del ginepro; io son nel fuco,*
> *nella paglia marina,*
> *in ogni cosa esigua,*
> *in ogni cosa immane . . .*
> *E la mia vita è divina.*

('And my recumbent strength is pressed into the sand,
  spreads into the sea; and the river is my vein
  and the mountain my forehead, the forest my pubis,
  the clouds my sweat . . . I am in the flower of the reed, in the
    scale
  of the pine, in the berry of the juniper;
  I am in wrack, in seaweed, in everything tiny,
  in everything vast . . . And my life is divine.')

One can believe the poet when he writes to a friend: 'I am in the clutches of the Furies who seize and agitate me for six or seven hours and then leave me almost dead.' In some poems he rediscovers the accents of Virgil; in others, such as *La Pioggia*, he achieves a *tour de force* of onomatopoeic harmony. (A poem that can be compared with the *Laudi* is Hugo's *Booz endormi*.)

The poems of Carducci seem, in comparison, to be no more

than noble rhetoric. Carducci died in February 1907 and d'Annunzio went to Bologna to extol a glory less brilliant than his own. Did he know that the modest Carducci used to sigh whenever anyone spoke of d'Annunzio as 'the poet of the new Italy'? Pascoli, who despite his reserve was the only other Italian poet with whom d'Annunzio maintained friendly relations, was rather like the French poet Francis Jammes, a Virgilian of largely rustic inspiration.

As far as the glory of his country was concerned, d'Annunzio had confidence only in himself. If he looked down on other writers, he deliberately ignored contemporary artists. In the iconographic study by Mazzarotto, *Arti figurative nell' arte di d'Annunzio*, among the hundreds of reproductions of works of Antiquity or the Renaissance that inspired a few lines or even entire poems, there are barely a dozen contemporary works. In *Elettra*, he devoted a few lines to Segantini. The only artist of great talent who conveyed in his works the aspect of the d'Annunzian protagonist was the sculptor Trubetskoi; in his studio near Lake Garda, Trubetskoi carved a statue of the poet and another of a great passion of his later years, the Marchesa Casati. But the poet makes no mention of the sculptor Wildt or the painter Zeccino, whose bizarre style ought to have attracted his interest. D'Annunzio, appalled by the contrast between what Italy had produced in the past and what it was now producing, turned his back on his own age; in this respect, he was quite unlike Oscar Wilde, but close to Barrès. His taste, which in his youth had been Pre-Raphaelite, was fundamentally academic. This remoteness from his own period is brought out in Angelo Conti's book *Beata Riva*, a collection of aesthetic conversations with the poet.

It is therefore hardly surprising that d'Annunzio should have remained silent when Futurism, founded in 1907, began to disseminate its violent tracts, seeking to sweep away the old art and to anticipate the mechanism of the city of the future. Conversely a marked d'Annunzian influence is to be found in Marinetti's first manifesto, published in *Le Figaro*, in French, on 22 February 1909: 'The world has enriched itself with a new beauty . . .

speed—the racing car more beautiful than the Victory of Samothrace. There will be no beauty without struggle. A work that is not aggressive cannot be a masterpiece. We want to glorify war, the only hygiene in this world, militarism, patriotism, the destructive gesture of the libertarians, the beautiful ideas for which one dies.' It is interesting to note that d'Annunzio's *Forse che sì forse che no* was written in this same year. But the Futurists proposed to do things that were inconceivable for d'Annunzio: 'Destruction of syntax . . . Unbridled imagination . . . Geometric sensibility. Futurism the exacerbation of irrationalism . . . Ethics and aesthetics fused in action.' In 1908 Marinetti had published a pamphlet attacking the poet and entitled *Les Dieux s'en vont, d'Annunzio reste* ('The Gods are leaving, d'Annunzio remains'). After having started as a fervent d'Annunzian, Marinetti ended by tolerating only the most frenetic of the plays, *Più che l'amore.* What was intended to be a reaction against d'Annunzio proved a monstrous exaggeration of his style. His verbal sensuality was the Futurist ideal. The Futurists could, however, claim the credit for uprooting the prevalent academicism.

There is a growing recognition of the importance of artists such as Boccioni, who died in 1916 and who gave the initial impetus to Cubism, and the architect Sant'Elia, the author of the *Sonografia futurista,* whose ideas are based on the use of light. The Futurists were also the forerunners of *musique concrète.* Admittedly, there existed a 'd'Annunzian' style in the painting that preceded Futurism—macabre subjects, erotic antiquity, hysterical portraits. In the décor of his plays, also, d'Annunzio had a considerable influence on Italian architecture at the beginning of the century. A modest prosperity finally allowed the Italians to erect some public buildings, to flatter their need for glory: suffering from a kind of 'giantism' and crammed with allusions to an heroic antiquity, the buildings have all the faults of d'Annunzio's plays. One of the most characteristic constructions of this period is the bizarre group of buildings known as the Arch of Coppedé in Rome, cluttered with trophies, Medusa masks and prows. Milan railway station gives the same impression of bombast. The purely decorative structures erected in this same style are more successful —for instance, the huge fountain on the Piazza dell'Esedra in Rome, in which the sculptor breathed a Baroque spirit into d'Annunzian myths; the beautiful women struggling with octopuses and riding dolphins, the heroes writhing as if to raise the world aloft, straight out of the *Laudi*. In painting, Sartorio re-created the same larger-than-life world in canvases which, though academic, have a morbid and ambiguous quality, with their naked warriors trampled under the feet of implacable goddesses. D'Annunzian art, with its tinge of Roman severity, blossomed under Fascism. It is not at all unlikely that, in a few years, this art will be found to possess qualities that seem to be lacking in the d'Annunzian theatre.

POLITICS

The enthusiasm which he felt for his current writings gave d'Annunzio an almost divine self-confidence, by comparison with which his previous performance seemed mere impudence; in the same way, his political ambition now was not so much to make people talk of him, as to restore the Italy he loved to her rightful place in the world. A quotation from Anatole France carefully copied into his notebook defines the poet's feelings at this time: 'I should like to see the Latin peoples unite to erect on some illustrious and deserted beach a monument to the dead Mediterranean, which once bore on its charming waters the most beautiful thing in the world, the Greek genius, and the greatest, the Pax Romana.'

D'Annunzio's patriotism, impatient of all government, despised systems of alliances and bargains no less than economic and democratic theories. The downfall of the Italian prime minister Crispi after the disaster of Aduwa in Abyssinia in 1896 no doubt justified his attitude, but his hatred of the Italian politicians who tried to extricate themselves from the Triple Alliance (with Germany and Austria-Hungary), while clinging to its advantages, was more often than not unjust. During his short political career d'Annunzio had, it is true, provided ample evidence of his capacity for contempt. As we have seen, in 1894 he had decided to offer himself as a parliamentary candidate, perhaps less from ambition than from a desire to escape from the ill-starred period in Naples, and, despite a few upsets, Pescara bore its child triumphantly to victory. Most of his friends had been stupefied that a man so contemptuous of politicians should wish to be a member of a discredited Parliament. This is what he had to say in reply to his publisher Treves: 'I have just returned from an election tour, and my nostrils are still filled with a sour stench of humanity. This enterprise may seem foolish, and it is foreign to my art, contrary to my style of life; but, before judging my attitude, you must wait for the result to which my purpose is directed. Victory is assured. The world, my dear fellow, must realize that I am capable of everything.' In fact, he captivated the Abruzzians; he knew their language and was familiar with the vocabulary of the vine-growers, the blacksmiths and the masons whose votes he sought; unlike his adversary, a socialist lawyer, he was of the soil. Having gained their confidence, he spoke of Dante, Michelangelo, Beauty and *la Patria*. Even the ageing Crispi was moved when he read d'Annunzio's speeches: 'Amid the cowardice and the degradation of modern youth, I heard beating in my heart the greatness of Italy.'

The 'Representative for Beauty' sat on the Extreme Right, but soon the atmosphere of Montecitorio (the Parliament) depressed him. He found in the hall of the Chamber of Deputies a combination of the two things which he could not tolerate: ugliness and stupidity. When an usher asked him for his voting number, he retorted: 'Tell the President that I am not a number.' In March 1900, exasperated by the mediocrity of the representatives of law and order, he moved from the Extreme Right to the Extreme Left: 'After today's spectacle I know that on one side there are a lot of men who howl, and on the other side a few men who are alive and eloquent. As a man of intellect, I am moving to the side of life.' He attacked the 'great parliamentary lie' and, when subjected to a campaign of vilification, replied with an article in

Il Giorno: 'Of all manly enterprises, I admire that of the person who breaks the law imposed by others and who establishes his own law . . . Between the socialists and myself there exists an insurmountable barrier; I am and shall remain a whole-hearted individualist, a ferocious individualist. For a time I wanted to be in the lions' den, but I was pushed into it by my disgust at the other parties.' The article continued with an anarchist profession of faith.

D'Annunzio ought to have known that an aesthete does not meddle in public life, that a hero does not vote. However, in May 1900, this time with the backing of the Left, he stood as a candidate for the San Giovanni district in Florence. The Florentine setting endowed the campaign with a special charm and d'Annunzio wrote to Hérelle: 'On some evenings I have had a perfect illusion of living in the fifteenth century and inciting the Ciompi to set fire to the towers of the nobles.' But he was defeated and henceforward his patriotism was to find strength in his hatred of politicians. His experience of a parliamentary life that was worse than mediocre explains the readiness with which d'Annunzio was to welcome Fascism.

A NATIONAL POET

D'Annunzio's patriotism reacted against the international spirit of democracy, which he cursed when, during violent riots in May 1898 (the 'bloody spring'), 'drunken slaves' had thrown stones at Michelangelo's statue of David. He had indignant articles published in the American press; had he not written, in *Le Vergini delle Rocce*, that the mob was 'the monster that rebels against the hero' and predicted, in *Il Piacere*, the 'grey deluge of democracy'? He was thus resolutely nationalist for the same reasons as Barrès, but without the Frenchman's justification he turned the Adriatic into the Alsace of Italy. The success that d'Annunzio enjoyed in the Dalmatian towns under Austrian domination strengthened his determination to save his country from mediocrity.

In *La Vita di Cola di Rienzo,* a quite short and, as always, solidly documented book, d'Annunzio projected his ambitions into Cola di Rienzo, the first hero of Italian unity, who had inspired a canto of Byron's *Childe Harold* and the first opera of Wagner. Cola, a handsome young man of great eloquence, made himself master of Rome in 1347, during one of the darkest periods in Italian history, and had himself crowned in the Capitol. For five years he succeeded in restoring the capital to its former importance; in his speeches he urged the Pope to return to Rome. He had chosen a red flag embroidered with the words *Roma caput mundi.* His dream of reviving ancient Rome succeeded in uniting nearly all the Italians whom he had been able to dazzle with his magnificence, but a rival faction compelled him to leave the capital and to wander across Europe. He regained power in 1354, but his cruelty and cupidity soon made him hated. When the mob invaded the palace, Cola thought that he could escape the massacre by disguising himself as a man of the people and joining in the shouts of 'Death!' But, recognized by his rings, he was murdered and his body burnt on the ruins of the mausoleum of Augustus. As Barzini has written, men like Cola di Rienzo have a prophetic intuition of what their fellow-countrymen expect: 'You must ignore their explanations, which are often ridiculous. You must watch them. Listen to them talk to the crowds. They speak as if they are giving words to the crowd's own dumb sentiments. They awaken an echo in men's hearts. They drive them to great deeds' (From *The Italians*). Although his ideas were confused, Cola had put his finger on the problems that were to dominate Italian history up to the present day. Already, in *La Gloria* (1899), the portrait of the young dictator in the illustrious setting of the Capitol had been modelled on Cola di Rienzo.

In 1908 d'Annunzio again glorified nationalism in *La Nave* ('The Ship'), a historical drama which, extolling Venetian expansion, was a lyrical piece of colonialist propaganda. Before the performance he wrote: 'I have finished an extraordinary work forged with the gold of Byzantium and the sand of the lagoon; in it blows my greatest Italian passion, which is pained at not being able to raise a vast fleet and nail to the prow of the ship a victory, not of bronze, but of flashing metal. I want the actors to hear the first reading of this sometimes lyrical, sometimes cruel story in Trieste, in the Fiume that used to seem so mysterious to me in my childhood when one of our brigantines would set sail towards it.'

The first performance of La Nave, at the Argentina theatre and in the presence of the king and queen, was an outstanding triumph. The ovation was even carried into the streets. For Italians this play meant that the time for great enterprises had arrived. D'Annunzio the aesthete was forgotten, the man of scandal forgiven. As Italy's national poet, he replied to a toast by the minister of education, drinking to 'the most bitter Adriatic'. With these words, d'Annunzio was laying claim to all the Venetian possessions of the Dalmatian coast.

The presence of King Victor Emmanuel and Queen Helena at the first performance of La Nave showed the political importance that they attached to the play, rather than their esteem for its author. In fact, d'Annunzio was not popular at the Quirinale, where the royal couple led a quiet family life. The queen mother, in spite of some highly flattering pages in Il Fuoco, only became favourably disposed towards the poet during the war, for reasons of patriotism; her son could never hear the name of d'Annunzio uttered without muttering 'Ah! that dog!' The Aosta branch, on the other hand, was full of admiration. The dowager duchess, one of the most extravagant of the Bonapartes, found her own weaknesses reflected in d'Annunzio's novels, and the young Duchess Hélène of France, daughter of the Count of Paris, was a princess after d'Annunzio's heart. Very tall and very beautiful, with a long face, blue eyes and a mass of wavy blonde hair, the Duchess Hélène hardly concealed her contempt for the rest of the royal family, calling the queen 'my shepherdess cousin', for the queen came from poverty-stricken Montenegro. The duchess was an ardent colonialist, thrilled by the expeditions in Africa of Savorgnan de Brazza (as has already been seen, the explorer was a favourite myth of the regenerated Italy—the hero of d'Annunzio's worst

Clotilde Bréal
a few years after
her marriage
to Romain Rolland

14

Donna Maria d'Annunzio,
by La Gandara

15

16

D'Annunzio hunting

EX LIBRIS GABRIELIS NVNCII

17

Book-plate by Sartorio

La Figlia di Iorio, by Michetti

D'Annunzio with Blériot

The Marchesa Casati, by Vitellini, around 1900

La Casati
around 1913

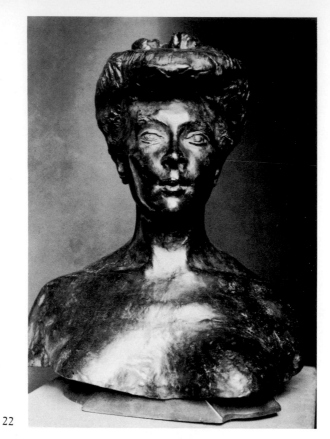

22

Mme. de Goloubeff, by Rodin

23

D'Annunzio, by Sem, 1913

Ida Rubinstein   24   25   Self-portrait

26   27

D'Annunzio, the poet in exile   The Comandante Gabriele d'Annunzio

28

Miss Nathalie Barney and d'Annunzio

D'Annunzio and Mme. de Goloubeff at the races, 1913

29

play, *Più che l'amore*, was an explorer, and the hero of *Forse che sì forse che no* had been an explorer before becoming an aviator). The duchess herself explored Africa; she even brought back two black children whom her sister, the Queen of Portugal, secretly baptized. The woman who had nearly become the fiancée of the Duke of Clarence (eldest son of the Prince of Wales), and as such would have become Queen of England, yearned for a colonial empire; it will be seen in a later chapter how in 1919 her ambition, enhanced by the prestige of the poet's support, was to prompt her to seek the crown of Italy, the stability of which had been undermined by the war.

Three years after the triumph of *La Nave*, Italy declared war on Turkey and occupied Libya, Rhodes and several islands of the Dodecanese. The whole Italian press became d'Annunzian and, according to Benedetto Croce, 'plunged into a Dionysiac delirium, investing the slightest incidents of the war and the most trivial manoeuvres with dazzling images and monstrous hyperboles'. From France, where he was leading a far from heroic existence, d'Annunzio addressed poems to the combatants. Croce passed a harsh judgement on these poems: 'The *Canzoni della Gesta d'Oltremare* are rather cold metrical exercises, despite the luxurious sounds and images. He [d'Annunzio] wanted to glorify the enterprise and the heroes of the enterprise, the valiant Italian officers and soldiers who, without theatrical poses and words, were performing their harsh duty, who were astounded by this magnificent warrior's cloak, this verbal *paludamentum*, which was thrown over their shoulders, and who showed themselves naïvely grateful for a homage which seemed to be sublime.' The prime minister, Giolitti, was alarmed when, under the pretext of warlike fervour, the poet insulted the Emperor of Austria. The government demanded the withdrawal of the offensive lines and the edition of *Merope* appeared with blanks and the words 'Mutilated by the police of the leader of the Italian government'. Victories gained over the crumbling Ottoman Empire gave the Italians an exaggerated idea of their strength, encouraging them to expect a rapid success when, in 1915, they again threw themselves into war.

D'Annunzio's humanist nationalism bore a close affinity to the ideas of *L'Action française* and of Barrès. No such intellectual movement existed in Great Britain, too confident to boast of its strength except in the poems of Kipling and some others and then in a very different style; indeed, d'Annunzio was altogether taken much less seriously there than in France or Germany. In reading these poems, one cannot help thinking of the massive monument to Victor Emmanuel in Rome, which overwhelms the Capitol with its colonnades of white marble and its allegories of gilded bronze. It has a bombast that is displeasing to all non-Italians; fundamentally, however, this patriotic Baroque is no less sincere than the religious Baroque which, two centuries earlier, had erected those theatrical churches at one time despised but so admired today. It is conceivable that in a few decades, a performance of *La Nave* or *La Gloria* on the esplanade of the Victor Emmanuel monument may seem unutterably beautiful.

11

Living Dangerously

ICARUS

D'Annunzio, preoccupied with his love-affairs, his travels and his worldly pleasures, wrote little between 1904 and 1908. His poetic verve appeared to have been exhausted. But in 1908 he started work on a story which he intended at first to call *Il Delirio* and which, after two years of writing, was to become the best of his novels, the most 'd'Annunzian': *Forse che sì forse che no* ('Perhaps so, perhaps not'), a title taken from a motto painted on the ceiling of the ducal palace in Mantua. Beside this work the other novels are rather like museums, antique-shops of the aesthetes or the ready-made products of realism. In *Forse che sì forse che no* d'Annunzio recorded the memories of his great love-affairs, but without retracing them in the same precise detail that had characterized *Il Fuoco* and *Il Trionfo della Morte*. He succeeded in embellishing the descriptions with the poetic *élan* of the *Laudi*; at the same time, the great scenes in the novel have a dramatic power unequalled in the tragedies. The hero of the novel was, of course, d'Annunzio himself, in a new incarnation both mythical and very modern: Icarus the aviator.

From its opening pages this novel is dedicated to speed. Paolo Tarsis makes Isabella Inghirami, a rich widow, ride with him in his powerful motor car, to frighten her into giving herself to him.

They arrive at Mantua and visit the palace, but their kiss is interrupted by Aldo and Vana, the brother and sister of Isabella. Then, at Brescia, Tarsis arranges an aviators' meeting with his friend, Giulio Cambiaso. They fly higher than the others, but Giulio crashes and Vana, who thinks that she is in love with him, goes to look after him. After a stay by the sea the lovers, Paolo and Isabella, withdraw to the Inghirami palace at Volterra. The novel describes the haunted atmosphere of Volterra, the music, the walks along the sulphurous ravines and through ruined chapels. Everyone is in love with Paolo, even Aldo, who challenges him to races on horseback. Rivalry comes between Isabella and her sister, Vana, who tells Paolo that Isabella has become her brother Aldo's mistress. Paolo has a dreadful scene with Isabella; she goes mad and is shut away by her evil-minded family. Vana stabs herself, and the aviator, in a last flight towards the sun, crashes on a deserted beach with these words engraved in his thoughts: 'There is no God if you are not one.'

Icarus also dominates the collection *Alcione* (1904) and to an even greater degree than Ulysses dominates *Laus vitae*. The poet imagines Icarus in love with Pasiphaë and as the horrified witness of her intercourse with the bull. Icarus wishes to rival the gods, a desire inspired by contempt for humanity and by the need to become God himself: 'He was my body, he was my anger of a man without wings, my anguish to fly', noted d'Annunzio during the composition of the poem, longing for a destiny similar to that of his hero:

> *Icaro, Icaro, anch'io nel profondo*
> *Mare precipiti, anch'io v'inabissi*
> *la mia virtù, ma in eterno in eterno*
> *il nome mio resti al Mare profondo!*

> ('Icarus, Icarus, may I too be swallowed
> In the depths of the sea, plunge there
> My courage, if only, for eternity, for eternity,
> My name might remain on the deep sea.')

D'Annunzio was the first writer of his time to understand that speed would become the great need and pleasure of the modern world. The aesthete, abandoning his trinkets, became a mechanic and valued the beauty of an engine almost as much as that of a work of art. At first, he was fascinated by the automobile less as a means of transport than as a machine in which to play with death. The beginning of the novel is a glorification of danger such as was to be seen fifty years later in the film *Rebel without a Cause*, in which James Dean foreshadowed his own death. The now familiar images of a life cut short by speed are to be found for the first time in *Forse che sì forse che no* (begun in 1908 and published in 1910), the only one of d'Annunzio's novels that nowhere invites comparison with any foreign work. As always with d'Annunzio, dramatic thrills ranked equally with aesthetic pleasures. With his friend Carlo Placci, another pioneer of the automobile, he set off to explore places which previously could be reached only after hours of travelling in a crawling train or by stagecoach. These excursions along dusty roads, in the company of ladies as heavily veiled as Arab women, enchanted d'Annunzio. Cars play a most important part in the novel, transporting the lovers to half-dead towns, or breaking down and thus preventing them from meeting.

The other myth which has such a hold on our minds today is the sun myth. D'Annunzio adored the sun, as was evident at the time of the journey to Greece, and even in his childhood. At a period when people wore a great deal of clothing, he demanded warmth and beauty from the sun; the sun was the furnace from which the bronze of the poet's imaginary statue was to emerge. On the beaches of the Tyrrhenian coast which he visited frequently from Florence—Marina di Pisa or Versilia—he led a 'divine existence', exposing himself to the sun with his horses, his dogs and a superb mistress, and in constant contact with the sea.

Other reasons prompted d'Annunzio to take an interest in the motor car and flying, to follow the first races, to try the most precarious prototypes and to risk his gaiters in dirty oil. Patriotism was one reason; the new Italy, which had found so little success in its colonial ventures, was to win respect by sporting victories and economic achievements. In 1910 d'Annunzio made a lecture tour, with 'the empire of the sky' as his theme. At the beginning of *Forse che sì forse che no*, he quotes himself: 'Suddenly, the Latins remembered the first wing of man to fall on the Mediterranean, the wing of Icarus made with the shoots of the hazel-tree, the dried membranes of the ox and the feathers of the great birds of prey. *Un'ala sul Mare è solitaria* ['A wing on the sea is alone'], the poet of the race had cried.'

And then he remembered that Leonardo had made drawings of flying machines. Full of these ideas, he went to Brescia to meet Blériot, who had just crossed the Channel; he climbed into the Frenchman's aircraft and discussed the prototypes at great length. One of the roles of the modern hero was to make the conquest of the air, and d'Annunzio was also the first to realize this. He even attempted to invest the hero with a humanist prestige, by forging a vocabulary for the new machines and their components; he tried to establish the use of the word '*vélivole*', which he had found in Chateaubriand: '*Le pêcheur napolitain qui va dans sa barque vélivole . . .*' ('The Neapolitan fisherman in his boat with flying sails'). He consulted mechanics about the best names to give to the various parts of the machine, but it seems that nobody listened to him.

D'Annunzio had another reason, more profound and only half-conscious, for pursuing this new activity—the need to remain young. The machine removes the obstacles of age: a horseman gets out of breath, but not a motorist; speed restores to man the vitality of the twenty-year-old. As any young man of today is aware, a car is essential to his sexual prestige. With this extension or, rather, this rediscovery of youth, there re-emerged in d'Annunzio the sentiment that had occupied such an important place in his adolescence—friendship. Around an engine, or in the hangar where the aircraft were repaired, the famous writer and the ladies' man became the comrade of the youths who shared his passion. Women were excluded from this world, and how peaceful it was! Léon Blum, an excellent critic, shrewdly observed that *Forse che sì forse che no* was primarily a novel of friendship. The memory of the friend who had crashed to his death dominates the book; by comparison, the rival sisters seem dangerous nymphomaniacs.

Perhaps the women on whom the sisters were modelled had been reduced to nymphomania by contact with the poet. Yet, while each of the earlier novels had contained an almost exact portrayal of a woman who had been loved, then abandoned and viewed with a pity not always devoid of contempt, Isabella Inghirami owes only certain traits to the author's Florentine mistresses. She is a widow, with the high social position of Alessandra di Rudinì and with her taste for luxury, but she also has a perversity lacking in both the future Carmelite nun and the Countess Mancini. The only contribution that the countess made to the novel was the dénouement of the liaison, the decline into madness and its sordid consequences. On the other hand, at the time of the novel's publication two other women were playing a prominent part in the life of the author: Mme. de Goloubeff and the Marchesa Casati. Mme. de Goloubeff's role was undoubtedly the more important. The poet's acknowledged mistress for at least two years, she managed to stay with him much longer than any other woman. But the singular character of the Marchesa Casati was to continue to intrigue d'Annunzio even in his old age.

'THE ONLY WOMAN WHO ASTONISHED ME'

It was in these terms that d'Annunzio was to present the Marchesa Casati to his friend Robert de Montesquiou, and indeed the marchesa astounded all Europe right up to the day when she disappeared after a magnificent ball in 1936. She was the most d'Annunzian of the poet's heroines. He nicknamed her 'Corè', because of her 'archaic' smile, and compared her to a unicorn, for he found her pure. *Née* Luisa Annam, the heiress of a Milanese industrialist, she had married into the nobility at an early age and seemed determined from the very beginning of this union to follow in the steps of the Princess Belgiojoso, whose macabre beauty, scandalous affairs and patriotic deeds had captivated romantic Europe. Casati had a slender figure, with slim hips, long legs, the face of one of Gustave Moreau's sphinxes, huge grey-green eyes, a very white skin and flame-coloured hair that was often hidden by gilded wigs, powdered with white or mauve and intertwined with necklaces, like the serpents on the head of Medusa. The marchesa was, indeed, the Medusa of the great hotels and more than one of her admirers is said to have perished. She was Boldini's best model, for he preferred her style, reminiscent of Beardsley and the costumes of Bakst, to the excessively formal elegance of his more conventional sitters. She was painted by more artists than any other woman—Zuloaga, Driant, the Futurists, Augustus John and even van Dongen. In his portrait Boldini shows her as Scheherazade, covered with peacock feathers and arched over cushions like a panther about to pounce. The elegance of the heroine of *Forse che sì forse che no* owes everything to her:

'She, too, loved to enhance the freshness of her twenty-five years with black and red; she always darkened her eyelids around the bright irises, and sometimes she would steep her mouth in vermilion. But her alchemy was much more complex, producing many other marvels. By what fire did she transmute the substance of her life into beauties of such moving power? Certain expressions on her face condensed the poetry of a garden, a tragedy, a fable. The ordinary acts of daily existence—slowly removing her glove, allowing the doeskin to slip over the light down of her arm; sitting on the bed and taking off the long silk stocking, delicate as a flower that fades in an instant; taking the pins from her hat by raising her arms in an arc and letting the sleeve slip down to the curly gold of the armpit.' For La Casati, Fortuny invented his finest fabrics: 'She was wrapped in one of those long scarves of oriental gauze which the alchemist-dyer, Mariano Fortuny, soaks in the mysterious pigments of his vats, stirred with a wooden pestle, sometimes by a sylph, sometimes by a gnome, which he draws out tinted with strange dreams, and with his thousand instruments marks with new generations of stars, planets and animals.'

In evoking the character of Isabella, d'Annunzio borrows his images from the world of magic. La Casati, a devotee of the bizarre, was regarded as a sorceress, as one familiar with all the necromantic extravagances that had flourished at the close of the century. Even in her appearance she called to mind the enchantress Circe; she could be seen followed by a handsome Tunisian prince as dark as night itself and whom she drove to desperation, by Afghan hounds and ocelots which she pretended were panthers. The queen of decadent Venice, the marchesa lived in the Palazzo Non Finito (now the Guggenheim Institute), where she gave entertainments of theatrical splendour. When there were too many guests, she borrowed St. Mark's Square, illuminated with torches held by Negroes dressed in the manner of Tiepolo. She lured the poet with sibylline telegrams: 'I have a fierce turtle-dove . . . The glazier has given me two large green eyes as beautiful as the stars, do you want them?'—'Corè is dead because she wanted to draw too close to the gods; her heart is asleep for ever.' But this telegram, sent from St. Moritz in 1913, was not the last, as one might suppose. From time to time, until the end of his life, d'Annunzio would receive unexpected information of this kind: 'I have a live monkey' or simply 'Pure turquoise sky'. Sometimes words were scribbled, in the handwriting of a schizophrenic, on black visiting-cards decorated with a pink skeleton. La Casati was certainly d'Annunzio's mistress on more than one occasion, but there was no regular liaison between them, for neither was willing to suffer, to make the slightest sacrifice of pride, for the only person whom either could treat as an equal. She was the only woman to lead the 'inimitable life' without weakening, the only one capable, in her love of luxury and of the fantastic, of anticipating the poet's every whim. Her dresses and her postures provided d'Annunzio's writings with many a troubled image; but her influence on fashions did not make itself truly felt until fifteen years later; Luisa Casati was the original model for the 'vamp' of the silent films, as played by Napierovska and Theda Bara.

Through the Marchesa Casati, whom he met in Milan in or

around 1906, d'Annunzio entered an international social world
that made Italian society appear a little provincial, a world which
then had Venice as its capital and which is nowadays known as
café society.

DONATELLA

In March 1908, in Rome, d'Annunzio had met a woman who also
belonged to international society, a twenty-five-year-old Russian,
Nathalie de Goloubeff, with an immensely rich husband who was
an eminent orientalist and a collector of Persian miniatures. M.
de Goloubeff was also a Tolstoyan spirit, for the generosity and
self-effacement with which he viewed his wife's passion made him
the perfect d'Annunzian husband. The Goloubeffs lived mostly
in Paris, in a huge apartment on the Avenue du Bois, but they
also felt quite at home in the midst of a brilliant Russian colony
in Rome. Nathalie's great beauty had inspired Rodin, whose
bust, modelled in 1906, shows the bosom swelling as when she
drew her breath before singing, for from this superhuman body
there emerged a marvellous voice which was compared with that
of Litvinne, a voice to sing Isolde. When this goddess was in his
arms, the poet could imagine himself a new Michelangelo whose
caresses gave the attitudes of the 'Caucasian Diana' an immortal
quality: 'When she lay on the divan, her body submerged beneath the waves of muslin or tulle, she perhaps resembled the
Libyan Sibyl only in the arch of the protruding foot. But if she
suddenly sat up and leaned from the shadow towards the halo
of the lamp, to have her say in an excited argument, the quality of
her relief was such as to suggest a creation, a vision, of genius.'

Music brought d'Annunzio and Mme. de Goloubeff together.
The ageing Primoli had prepared the ground with these lines
written after hearing the society lady sing: 'Only the poet of *Il
Fuoco* could describe the harmonious silence accompanying those
final chords during which one can follow, on the calmed lines
of the beautiful face, in the veiled look and the vague smile, the
voice that seems to continue the song which the human voice

has ceased to render.' The meeting took place on 16 March 1908. The next day the Russian received this letter, with a mass of flowers:

'The great white clouds have gone to tear themselves asunder on the tops of other cypresses. We shall not be going to the Villa d'Este today! The golden miracle of your voice will not fill the solitude of the statues and the waters . . .

'Yet my day will be still warm with the melodious memory. You gave me, yesterday evening, an emotion so sudden and so profound that it seems as if a whole life has been transformed.

'Please accept, Madame, the humble expression of my gratitude.

'I should like to live in Armida's gardens for ever.'

Other letters followed in the style of the *Elegie romane*. In the meantime, the poet pursued his liaison with the Countess Mancini and even his brief affair with Frau Weingreif-Grafstein, the Dutch lady who made artistic embroideries in Florence. Mme. de Gouloubeff decided to go to Florence and give herself to d'Annunzio on 18 September, at the very time when the countess's madness, which had assumed the most alarming proportions, was revealing to d'Annunzio a hitherto neglected vein of compassion in his genius. In *Solus ad solam* he was to say that he had thought only of the unfortunate countess when he was in the arms of the beautiful Russian. But the lovers met again a month later at Marina di Pisa, when the Countess Mancini had been shut away, and were deliriously happy. Since Mme. de Gouloubeff's home was in Paris and the poet was busy with lectures, they were frequently separated and wrote an enormous number of letters to each other. Their correspondence has been faithfully published by M. Pierre Pascal; a few extracts will set the tone of this superhuman relationship. Even when they were only separated by the partition-wall of a hotel bedroom, the letter-writing continued: 'My soul tells me: "Thank life, O brother, and death, for the gifts you have received." This evening I am like the son of Grief born of Joy.'—'. . . I always slept curled up at your feet, like the greyhound. From time to time you would put your toe in my mouth.'—'. . . I wish that, by the splendour of my images, I could make you forget the poverty of my kisses.'—'Ah! that strange, harsh whinnying, that sweet, wild sound that rose from your throat, while pleasure, as visible as a juicy liquor, as some rare sap, flowed between your shoulders from vertebra to vertebra.'

30 November 1908.—'Do you remember, on that magic night of Blood, do you remember those repeated embraces when we fell, unable to separate? You and I were a single red cluster which you pressed with your burning hands. Do you remember? Spicanardi! Spicanardi! Spicanardi!' (A d'Annunzian phrase, perhaps not entirely meaningless in the circumstances.)

2 December 1908.—'My soul is harsh and disdainful this evening. For hours and hours I have been giving birth to beauty. It is still warm and palpitating in front of me, and my entrails are burning. I love my pain and my genius. You are distant and your two hands are the only laurel-leaves that I should want on my temples. They are held out to other lives.'

The sublime is intermingled with the erotic:

5 December 1908.—'I am dying from the desire to bite the nape of your neck and lick your armpits, and to intoxicate myself with your odour, Spicanardi, Spicanardi!'

8 December 1908.—'. . . I am sending you three jonquil flowers: the first for the furrow of your shoulders, the second for the shadow of your rose, the third so that you can soak it in the moisture of your tongue and send it back to me.'

In d'Annunzian language the 'rose' signifies the female sexual organ.

+ 28. 1909.—'Balm of my wound, sheath of my sword, I am drunk this evening. All night, as I worked, I felt on my chest the hard nipples of your little breasts. All day, as I slept, I felt your warm mouth run all over me.'

26 March 1909.—'Your divine mouth rendered my body divine. The fusion was so perfect that I no longer felt the living form of your lips, but only the essence of your music. Ah! why did I awaken with this heavy rancour deep in my happiness? Why, so unexpectedly, should a horrible image have been imposed over the same mouth which had sung that silent song through all my

veins? The inevitable sadness of passion! The obscure vengeance of vanquished pleasure!'

These last two extracts refer once again to the oral pleasures particularly dear to the poet, who had already sung their praises in his youth. And what can one say of the note slipped under a door after a night in a hotel: 'Ah! the savour of armpits!'?

These letters were signed in various ways: sometimes 'Gabri', as the loved ones like to call their master; or 'Stelio', like the hero of *Il Fuoco*; or 'Elabami', like the son of Christ and Mary Magdalene, the Christian Adonis invented by d'Annunzio. In the lovers' telegraphic code, 'Alis' signified 'Do you not feel my hand on yours?' 'Adel' meant 'The great fire of my soul and your soul is impenetrable.' But there must also have been terrible scenes between them, as this letter suggests:

21 May 1909.—'. . . I am filled with an unutterable agitation. All tenderness is swept away. The only memory that remains is the memory of the atrocious times when savage instinct awakened to offend you.

'Be indulgent, my dear. A time comes, in love, when one must almost die or kill. I realize this full well. There is the middle course, which is to depart.'

That there were scenes is evident too from the latter pages of *Forse che sì forse che no,* where the hero assails his incestuous mistress with the vilest insults and even strikes her. Moreover, one can believe that a scene from d'Annunzio must have been something quite dreadful. A god cannot be expected to behave like a gentleman. But what is strange is that the novelist should involve a heroic figure such as Paolo Tarsis in a despicable scene of this kind.

From all this sublimity and drama, from these pleasures and chimeras, two works emerged. Nathalie de Goloubeff was certainly the inspiration of the first, the play *Fedra* ('Phaedra'), which was dedicated to her. This is a verse drama of great erotic violence, for Phaedra proves herself a worthy daughter of Pasiphaë. It was written during a period of separation; on 15 December 1908 the poet informed his mistress that he was setting to work:

'. . . And I must renounce you, Donatella!

'I have had some bad times. I have a hard task in front of me. I have difficult engagements to fulfil, promised works to complete. I cannot interrupt my work. I am chained to this rough walnut table on which you laid your immortal huntress's hands. I am once again a slave with stubborn brow, after two years of the most avid debauchery.'

D'Annunzio sometimes identified his Muse with the memory of Nathalie de Goloubeff.

'The tragic Muse is too cruel to the laurelled Messenger. I should like, from time to time, to have her tongue sticky with honey against my dry tongue. And on my mouth she puts only her buskin spattered with black blood!

'Ah! Melitta' (another nickname for Mme. de Goloubeff), 'great naked bee with beautiful tresses, I am dying of the moist cell that I cannot suck, from which the thickest honey drips.

'. . . I comfort myself a little by thinking that everyone is at this moment indulging himself in the Christian orgy [Christmas] and that you, too, are sitting at an interminable dinner, while I drink a perfumed tea which has the colour, not of your hair, but of the talisman. I am fasting. It is good. God bless you!'

These lines give one an idea of the mood of *Fedra*, written in verse with music by Ildebrando Pizzetti. Mme. de Goloubeff had been promised the role of Phaedra and had had made some Mycenaean robes of rare splendour, but her Italian was not pure enough to convey the music of the verse and the part was given to a Milanese actress. Veniero, d'Annunzio's second son, played Ippolito; he was a handsome young man, but without character. The play was a flop in spite of a sumptuous production; the audience was bored because nearly everything happened in the wings, with long narrations replacing action (like Théramène's narration in Racine's *Phèdre*). The play was given a respectful burial, though it was not quite the resounding failure that *Più che l'amore* had been.

Long separations helped to keep the poet's love for 'Donatella' burning. Meanwhile, his holidays were occupied by a Russian singer, Salome Kruscensky, who was creating Strauss's *Elektra* at Milan, and by trips to Venice with the Marchesa Casati. The summer and early autumn of 1909 found the lovers reunited at Marina di Pisa and d'Annunzio set to work in earnest. Part of the novel was written in the Villa Paratonare (renamed Villa delle Tempeste), and part at Volterra where they spent two weeks; the pages describing the town are as dramatic as El Greco's *View of Toledo*. D'Annunzio worked intensively on the novel. Finished in January 1910, *Forse che sì forse che no* is pervaded with the essence of the woman by whose side it was composed and who immediately undertook its translation. As has already been seen, Nathalie de Goloubeff's contribution to the character of Isabella was physical rather than psychological. To the heroine's sister, Vana, the Russian gave the power of her voice:

'Then Isabella would feel intoxicated and bewildered, for everything was dominated by Vana's singing, and all passion went to her, as the untamed unicorn of the fable goes up to the virgin and places its head on her unviolated knees. The wave of the voice seemed sometimes to throb in the singer like the midday heat on burning rocks. Her whole body resounded as an instrument resounds through all the fibres of the wood. The vein of the bare neck disappeared into the dress and seemed to extend as far as the heel. As her sides, her thighs, her legs trembled at the loud notes, it really seemed that the vibration of the long melodious vein had passed through her whole body.'

The other main character, Aldo, the incestuous adolescent, was based on a young friend of d'Annunzio, a Parisian who owned a mansion near Rome, Illan Alvarez de Toledo, marquis of Casa-Fuerte; the marquis, handsome as 'a young fallen god', had fascinated the poet almost as much as he had fascinated Robert de Montesquiou and, for a time, Marcel Proust.

To an even greater degree than *Il Fuoco*, d'Annunzio's last novel is a splendid example of the 'inimitable life'. In this book the poet's different inspirations are expressed with a greater perfection. The aestheticism of *Il Piacere* is evident in the description of the palace of Mantua and of the heroine's dresses; the dramatic intensity of *L'Innocente* in situations which are shattering but not at all implausible; and, finally, the realism of *Giovanni Episcopo* in the sordid dénouement. The book is scattered with lyrical passages that recall the finest poems of the *Laudi*, especially in the final pages describing the flight on which the aviator was to share the fate of Icarus.

Even more than his other works, this novel reveals the sadism inseparable from d'Annunzio's character; the episode of the bats burnt by the flames of a torch is particularly unpleasant. The mad scene taken from the life of the wretched Mancini is made even more distasteful by the complaisance with which the author delivers his heroine into the hands of two ruffians. Here, and in the ignoble scene that precedes it, there is a relish in degrading a charming creature, a relish partially disguised as pity. Surely, a man who had been responsible for such a horror would have tried to bury it in the depths of his memory? But perhaps, in the eyes of the Master, the dramas of which he was the cause showed that mortals were consumed merely by contact with him: to a god like d'Annunzio, the odour of incense and the smell of burning flesh were equally acceptable, and from the second he often drew finer effects. When the book was published, the Italian critics, completely failing to appreciate its qualities, remained largely silent. By contrast, the French edition was immensely successful, the translation appearing under Mme. de Goloubeff's pseudonym, 'Donatella Cross'; it had been revised by Charles Muller, who shortly afterwards, in collaboration with Paul Reboux, was to write those witty pastiches *à la manière de* . . .

DÉBÂCLE

The death which Paolo Tarsis had encountered, on a sandy beach and in broad daylight, was just the kind of death that d'Annunzio would have welcomed to escape from the cares and the humiliations which his extravagances had brought upon him. He conceived the most fantastic schemes to extricate himself from his difficulties. In 1908 he thought he could make himself a million-aire by putting on the market a perfume which he had blended himself; the perfume, called 'Acqua Nunzia', was supposedly derived from an old recipe used by nuns. He installed a sort of laboratory at *La Capponcina* and ordered hundreds of bottles of a medieval shape which he delivered to traders with seals of red wax. Alas, 'Acqua Nunzia' was a total failure. In 1910 d'Annunzio fell once again into the clutches of money-lenders, as he had done in his youth, but for sums a hundred times larger. He turned to a second-rate impresario, Pilade Frattini, who arranged for him to give lectures on flying, in northern Italy. He certainly had his triumphs: in Turin the students pulled his carriage from the theatre to the hotel, and everywhere he was greeted with banquets and bouquets. But eventually he found this transient glory ab-horrent. He was bored with travelling and was writing nothing. Sometimes, he had to speak to a half-empty hall; after a fiasco of this kind, in a dilapidated music-hall in the suburbs of Genoa, he broke with the impresario.

Hoping to move his publishers to pity, d'Annunzio reminded them of his responsibilities: the education of his sons and of the illegitimate daughter who, thanks to the patronage of the Rudinì family, had been placed in the aristocratic boarding-school of Poggio Imperiale in Florence, and the mother and sisters whom he had been obliged to keep since the ruin of the Casa d'Annunzio in Pescara. As Italy grew more prosperous during the early years of the century, his Renaissance manners were regarded with the utmost disapproval. There was no longer room for an Aretino or for the Machiavelli who wrote: 'Few people know how to conduct dishonest affairs honourably.' The bourgeoisie now took its revenge and the bailiffs came to *La Capponcina* to seize the horses; d'Annunzio did not dare go out into the streets of Flor-ence for fear of meeting exasperated creditors. One creditor sold the bachelor apartment 'where for two years I celebrated rites that were more than Dionysiac'. Since Florence was intolerable, he settled in Rome, at the Grand Hotel, where he at once started

giving brilliant dinners. There was certainly something of Cagliostro about the poet, a genius for improvisation and for throwing
dust in people's eyes.

In 1910, d'Annunzio became involved in an unfortunate business which was to blacken his reputation even further. A certain
Del Guzzo, a native of the Abruzzi who had made a fortune in
Brazil, offered the poet large sums to make a lecture tour in Latin
America; he even gave an initial advance of fifteen thousand lire,
and then several further payments of nine thousand lire. D'Annunzio gaily presented Del Guzzo with a copy of his most recent
work, with this dedication: 'To the Messiah who was invoked and
appeared, to Giovanni Del Guzzo, with a hosanna.' Perhaps
d'Annunzio thought that such a compliment was sufficient repay-
ment for all the advances he had received and even released him
from the obligation to compose the ode which he had promised
for the centenary of the Argentinian Republic. Del Guzzo organized the tour and made reservations on the best steamer, for
the poet, his servants and his favourite dogs. Gabriele was quite
determined to make the tour, for he went to Pescara to say goodbye to his mother, whom he had not seen for three or four years
and was not to see again for another five. How piously and
tenderly d'Annunzio described this meeting to his mistress! Perhaps he respected Donna Luisetta primarily as the mother of a
god. From Pescara he went to Naples, on 23 March, to sign a
'pact of alliance' with Del Guzzo and to supervise the loading
of his motor car on board. Suddenly, however, he discovered an
urgent need to have his teeth treated—they had always been
frightful; he would have to go to Paris and travel to Argentina by
a French boat. On 28 March, ignoring Del Guzzo's protests,
d'Annunzio jumped into a train for Paris, where he stayed for five
years. Del Guzzo lost no time in seeking revenge, publishing a
pamphlet in which he exposed the poet's swindles. But he met
with little sympathy, for decent people said, 'How could he have
trusted d'Annunzio?' and the others were amused by such a
splendid trick, worthy of Casanova himself.

In fact, there was no question of calculated fraud; d'Annunzio had simply panicked at the idea of leaving Europe. Since Italy had become intolerable, there remained France, where he was almost as famous, fêted by his fellow-writers, played in the most important theatres, and where he would soon, he had no doubt, be adored by the most beautiful women. In France, d'Annunzio was to lead an intense and, on the whole, delightful existence. At the same time, these years became the 'Exile' of his legend. Dante and Garibaldi had been exiled, as had Machiavelli and Leonardo; it was therefore necessary that the greatest of poets should undergo this test. Events were to justify his decision. He arrived with several trunks of clothes, the crimson hangings with which he always adorned hotel bedrooms, his manuscripts and nothing more. A year later, in May 1911, the furniture of *La Capponcina* was sold by auction. Among the objects sold were the doorbell (a bronze chestnut inscribed with the words *Noli me tangere* to deter unwanted visitors), the drawing-room chandelier, in the form of a crown, the chairs and the wooden chests; and so all the bric-à-brac returned to the antique dealers of Florence, who were again able to do excellent business. When a large crucifix with a very thin figure of Christ was offered for sale, somebody shouted: 'There's Ida Rubinstein!' A walnut refectory table fetched nine hundred and twenty-five lire; the horse Malatesta seven hundred lire. The library was saved by the intervention of a banker friend.

12

Paris

Mme. de Goloubeff awaited the poet in Paris with a beating heart, for two reasons. First, she believed that the adored lover was leaving Italy and renouncing the treasures of Argentina for her alone. Why should she not have thought so? He had told her so in the letters and telegrams in which he had sought her advice on the best train and the best hotel. He wanted to be entirely hers: 'I wish to remain incognito and to see only indispensable people.' He was at the end of his tether, exasperated by the turn his affairs had taken and depressed by the visit to Pescara. Yes, Donatella might well believe that Gabriele was coming to her as to a refuge of peace and pleasure. With this happiness that filled her whole being, there was mingled a joy of a more worldly kind. In spite of her beauty, her voice and the important position of her husband, she did not occupy the place in Parisian society to which she felt entitled. She was thought affected and was seen in the company of slightly flashy people, for discrimination was not her strong point; she was said to be stupid and, since she had not yet had an affair, her beauty had brought her few social advantages. Now she would have the most brilliant man in Europe at her beck and call; he would be seen only in her salon, or only with her permission; she would be for d'Annunzio what Mme. de Caillavet had been for Anatole France during the past twenty years; she would continue the tradition of the great Slav Egerias, Mme. Hanska and the princess of Sayn-Wittgenstein. The success of the Russian Ballet placed her in a particularly favourable position, for stage-designers and dress-designers constantly sought permission to copy the Persian miniatures of the Goloubeff collection. She spent hours with the fashion-designer Callot and was one of the first to risk herself with another famous one, Poiret. All this made her feel very Parisian and ready to do the honours of the city to her 'Gabri'.

In an apartment much more modest than that on the Avenue du Bois, a disillusioned heart still throbbed a little at the thought of the poet's arrival. Donna Maria felt that her husband should, after all, pay her some attention and enhance by his presence the prestige which she enjoyed in her own select circle. The sacrificed spouse had become what was known at this time as a *madone des tantes* ('madonna of the fairies'), for she fulfilled all the conditions necessary to charm faded homosexuals: a great name, a great love-affair and an elegance achieved by manners rather than by dress. She belonged to that class of women, quite numerous at this period, who wore grief well, like the colour mauve; women who were the victims of love, eternally reclining on chaises longues where they would receive a comforter from time to time. Although she had had affairs, Donna Maria wore the halo of the martyr like a veil. Her liaison with the painter La Gandara had attracted to her all those who sighed, in vain, for that charming and handsome man. Among these brilliant friends were the writer Jean Lorrain, the composer Reynaldo Hahn and, more rarely, the prince of aesthetes, Robert de Montesquiou. The rich dilettante André Germain served her as page, a role which he continued to play until her death. Donna Maria was to be less disappointed than Mme. de Goloubeff, who in moments of despair about Gabriele had no hesitation in seeking her advice.

Who were the 'indispensable people' who alone, according to d'Annunzio, would be allowed to steal a few moments from the life which the poet was to devote to his mistress? Undoubtedly, they included Jacques Rouché, a middle-class Maecenas, slightly pompous but endowed with excellent taste, the editor of *La Grande Revue* and future director of the Opéra. It was in his review that *Forse che sì forse che no* was being published, and d'Annunzio was counting on obtaining from him sums even larger than those already received in advance. There was also Calmann-Lévy, the ever-generous publisher, as well as a number of distinguished critics. But 'Donatella' had surely not imagined that these 'indispensable people' would also include actresses, the hostesses of salons, and all that the Paris of the *Belle Époque* could offer in the way of amorous adventures, from a princess kept by a baroness to the dancing-girl at a night-club in Montmartre or a black girl in Montparnasse (a fleeting affair that may have been an act of homage to Baudelaire).

On arriving in Paris, d'Annunzio forgot his debts and other cares; like the character in Offenbach, he could have sung: '*Je veux m'en fourrer, fourrer jusque-là! . . .*' ('I want to stuff myself with it up to here!'). He settled himself at the Hôtel Meurice, where he made the Pompadour-style lift famous, for its cushioned walls tempted him to behave as if he were in a bedroom. The most beautiful of the hotel's guests, Princess Bibesco, a young married woman, developed an unconquerable revulsion for the poet as a result of attacks of this kind. During his first week, devoted to Donatella, d'Annunzio behaved himself quite well, but soon the hotel was resounding with the loud complaints of the Russian lady, who found the bedroom where her lover had arranged to meet her empty; before long, he was caught up in a whirl of social events and love-affairs. For six months d'Annunzio led a life of utter futility, like a child let loose in a cake-shop who goes from cream buns and jam tarts to éclairs and rum-babas.

Since these Parisian escapades deserve a separate chapter, it is worthwhile concentrating at this stage on his more elevated social life, his meetings with the writers whom he admired, and about whom he was anxious to discover if their genius approached his own. He was also concerned, of course, that his genius should receive the seal of approval of Europe's intellectual capital. Owing to an immense appetite for reading, d'Annunzio had an excellent knowledge of French literature, from the driest academicians to the writers who had formed the *avant-garde* of his youth. In 1895 he had spoken to Gide of Mauclair, Régnier, Paul Adam (who was not genuinely *avant-garde*) and also Coppée, Daudet and Bourget. To this list he had added, fifteen years later, Henri Bataille, Marcel Boulenger and, above all, André Suarès, with whom he had much in common, in particular haughty aestheticism and a broad culture; but, unlike d'Annunzio, the author of the *Voyage du Condottiere* had no grasp of life. Romain Rolland, who had been an intimate friend, now disassociated himself from d'Annunzio the nationalist poet; on the other hand, Marcel Boulenger, an agreeable and at the time a highly esteemed writer, was to occupy an important place in d'Annunzio's swaggering social life.

THE MOST NOBLE DISCIPLE

The pleasure which d'Annunzio was to derive from meeting such writers was at first subordinated to the pleasures offered by Paris. The Paris of Willy was certainly more exciting than the Paris of Romain Rolland's hero, Jean Christophe. Mme. de Goloubeff had no salon in which he could have met his peers during his first week in the city, and so it was Donna Maria who presented him to that most distinguished arranger of introductions, Count Robert de Montesquiou. Admittedly, the count was no longer at the peak of his glory; his spitefulness was creating something of a social vacuum around him, and his writings received the compliments only of those who feared his wit; but he had recently bought a sort of Grand Trianon at Le Vésinet, where he intended to entertain on the grand scale. Over fifty years old, he still possessed a slender, lithe figure and a refined elegance. His erudition was prodigious; like d'Annunzio, he knew as much about Michelangelo as he did about lace, and was equally familiar with Wagner and the harpsichord composers. He had a taste for minor poets, bizarre painters and unusual trinkets, but his aesthetic taste was much more expert than that of d'Annunzio, for he had acquired his artistic education in the most sophisticated Parisian circles, and not in Pescara.

His elegance, his taste and his great name were bound to appeal to d'Annunzio, but the poet was truly enraptured when, at their very first meeting, Montesquiou showed an admiration that was both keen and intelligent. To this fervour d'Annunzio responded with the most charming blandishments and Montesquiou was able to write: 'I tasted the heady intoxication of believing myself tenderly loved by a man of genius. I did what I had never, I believe, agreed to do until then for any human being of either sex: I contracted, *motu proprio*, a sentimental, almost religious bond for a period of one year, in honour of the man who accepted this liege homage, who affectionately consented to my respectful fancy, and who, just as if he were dubbing me his knight, bestowed on me the accolade.'

However, since no physical emotion disturbed this devotion, Montesquiou entertained no illusions about his hero and his judgement of d'Annunzio shows a remarkable shrewdness: 'Do not conclude from this that he was a man to whom one could become attached; attachment must be reciprocal, and he did not seem to desire it. He ran through the whole gamut of urbanity and grandeur with the obvious desire to please, though, I think, rather for the pleasure which he took in excelling in this skill, as he excelled in his art, but without emotion infusing his grace with the shimmer that renders it divine . . .' After reading the pages on friendship in *Forse che sì forse che no*, Montesquiou noted: 'I read them zealously and was convinced that not one nuance of this sentimental manifestation had escaped him, which by no means signified that he was capable of feeling it himself.' This pen-portrait should also be quoted: 'One thing that will surprise many people, his conversation is not brilliant, but quite simple, substantial and directly related to everyday events; but sometimes it is pierced by a flash of lightning, or the luminous streak of a meteorite. He carries within him his own beacon, the lenses of which turn and play in his dazzled brain and for him alone. His face, which the blind do not consider beautiful, sometimes assumes expressions of beauty all the more striking for being imperfect and composed of contrasts. [. . .] The most moving of these expressive moments are those when his mask drops its affected aggressiveness and feigned gaiety; the sadness of the look hesitating on the threshold of the eyelids then brings, from the depths of the soul, something withered which refuses to come back to life; the nostrils become deformed like those of a face on a shield that has been dented in combat, and the corners of the mouth are lowered in such desperation that they express the unutterable horror of watching an agony which it is impossible to pity.'

All this is written in a highly serious tone, but nothing could have been more light-hearted than the meetings of the two friends. D'Annunzio loved to laugh and Montesquiou had a gift for saying the most amusingly spiteful things and indulging in the most salacious scandal; he was the best-informed guide to the ladies of Paris—society women, authoresses and actresses. With the enthusiasm of a rival, he brought the poet's attention to the weak points of all these potential muses, as he unearthed their past lives. D'Annunzio laughed loudly at these virulent portraits, but was wary of following advice that would have restricted the circle of his new relationships. He was often seen at the home of Montesquiou's favourite butt, the Duchess de Rohan, an excellent woman who perpetrated some execrable verses. At Josselin, her house in Brittany, together with more touching relics, is preserved the pen which the poet presented to the duchess. Her daughter, who had recently married Prince Murat, was a woman full of imagination with whom d'Annunzio became acquainted through Primoli. Marie Murat, who considered herself a painter, had undertaken a portrait of the count, an old friend, dressed in a doge's costume, but Primoli used to fall asleep during sittings, only to be woken by d'Annunzio's laughter.

Montesquiou on his side would laugh also, though condescendingly, when d'Annunzio told him of his escapades, such as the

night when his car broke down in the middle of the Bois de
Boulogne, as he was driving with two Rumanian ladies, the very
ugly Mlle. Vacaresco ('Helen of Asia') and the very beautiful
Mlle. Valcogano ('the fair chatelaine'). D'Annunzio had no
money on him and had to go to Anatole France, at the Villa
Saïd, to borrow enough to pay the mechanic.

'The only Rumanian worthy of you', Montesquiou told him, 'is
Marthe Bibesco; I am going to repair the results of your ill-timed
ardour.' He invited the princess and her husband to Le Vésinet.
A quartet played among the hedgerows during tea; on the princess's shoulders he placed a cape that had belonged to the beautiful Countess Castiglione, and in the poet's hand the Count
d'Orsay's walking-stick; then he lured the husband into the picture
gallery, but nothing could change the princess's dislike. The
influence of Montesquiou can be discerned in the list, which
d'Annunzio sent to the publisher of *Le Martyre de saint Sébastien*,
of people who were to get presentation copies: 'Japan (paper):
Sarah and Duse—Holland (paper): the ladies Rothschild, Mme.
Édouard André, Muhlfeld, Rohan, Guiche, Haussonville.' These
ladies had all been interested in various degrees by d'Annunzio's
project for a Festival Theatre, a huge iron rotunda that was to be
built on the Champ-de-Mars, a sort of Bayreuth of the Latin
world where the lighting, 'corresponding to the sentiments expressed', would be much more important than the décor. Montesquiou had connections with three Italians who also acted as d'Annunzio's public-relations officers: the journalist Luigi Gualdo; the
art publisher Manzi, who organized lectures; and a fascinating and
highly gifted person, the violinist Vanicolo, also a friend of Gide.

During the first few months in Paris, d'Annunzio spent so much
time with Montesquiou that he acquired a dubious reputation.
The love of Beauty and a taste for gossip were not the only links
between the two men; both were also interested in spiritualism:
Montesquiou was a keen devotee of the world beyond, while
d'Annunzio, as a true native of the Abruzzi, believed in witches.
Together they consulted clairvoyants; one of these women, who
lived in a hovel behind Notre-Dame, particularly astonished them.

Montesquiou's cousin, the Countess Greffulhe, shared their curiosity. But the countess's son-in-law, the Duke de Guiche, a future member of the Académie des Sciences, viewed such things with scorn, and so to overcome his scepticism, Mme. Greffulhe summoned the most famous clairvoyant, Eusabia Paladino, whom d'Annunzio, according to Mme. Greffulhe's grandchildren, had invited from Italy. The three devotees and the sceptic assembled round this woman in a huge library. An hour passed without anything happening to shake the duke's materialist convictions. But, just as he was taking his leave of the others with a shrug of the shoulders, an enormous paper-knife carved from an elephant's tusk rose from the table on which it had been lying and slowly circled the room; the scholar had to agree that there were certain phenomena which escaped rational explanation.

OLYMPIAN ENCOUNTERS

Montesquiou found that the great men of France were in no hurry to welcome d'Annunzio. He decided that if he could win over Maurice Barrès, the man who in so many respects was closest to d'Annunzio and who had also moved from aestheticism to nationalism, the rest would follow. But Barrès, concerned as always to present his chiselled profile to the world, had no reason to want to associate with this Baroque bronze that had arrived in Paris. He was familiar only with the early novels, which he considered as improper as the newcomer's private life. Perhaps the 'spectacle of such an unbridled life' was a little bitter to such a respectable man: 'At a first view, I do not like this Italian', he replied to Montesquiou's first advances, but he agreed to meet d'Annunzio at a dinner at the Pré-Catelan given by Cécile Sorel, arranged by Montesquiou and paid for by Whitney Warren. The irresistible lover flirted indiscreetly with Cécile Sorel. At the other end of the table, Mme. de Goloubeff burst into tears: 'She is beautiful only when she cries', the poet replied to his alarmed hostess. During the dessert the tragedienne Mme. de Bartet read passages from *Il Fuoco*. D'Annunzio, who found her dreadfully bourgeois, continued to make up to his hostess, explaining to her how to set about making love with a lion. He spoke also to Barrès, believing that his gracious manner and compliments, and the fact that they both worked in front of reproductions of the Sistine Chapel, made them friends. But his charm was to take much longer than the duration of one meal to have its effect.

These first encounters between d'Annunzio and the great names of France were rather like two squadrons of ships that meet at sea, hoist all their flags, and continue on their way without further incident, leaving the diplomats to shudder at the thought of the sparks that could fly from such confrontations.

The meeting with Anna de Noailles proved an even more delicate occasion. Surely the conjunction of two such stars would set the literary heavens ablaze? Wisely, but to the dismay of the gallery, the two poets preferred friendly chatter to sublimity. The first visit took place in the presence of the witty Mgr. Duchesne, the director of the French Institute in Rome. When he saw the flowers with which d'Annunzio announced his arrival, the prelate murmured: 'They smell of the devil's brimstone.' D'Annunzio entered and the countess rose from her chaise longue, with outstretched arms: 'You are a god!'—'One is too many, madame.'—'Ah! monseigneur,' said the countess, 'absolve him from the deadly sin of pride. How sure of himself he seems! How he appears to carry his destiny in his hands! Does he know, this Don Juan, what love is? Only pride causes his heart to tremble . . .' After this fine beginning there were silences. Anna thanked Gabriele for wanting to write in French. D'Annunzio on his side was disconcerted by 'this puny, delicate organism, which suddenly is fired by genius'.

A few days later, Mme. de Pierrebourg assembled *le tout Paris* for another 'first meeting'. As always, Mme. de Noailles arrived very late, but to her amazement d'Annunzio was even later. As soon as he appeared, she led him off into the dining-room where the poet, exhausted by a tumultuous '*cinq à sept*', devoured the fancy cakes. Their conversation was held in a low voice and the guests, disappointed but respectful, gathered not one immortal word. Mme. Greffulhe also organized several luncheons for the two poets, but, as well-bred people, they unleashed no fireworks. One morning, on the Avenue du Bois, d'Annunzio was seen in his car with Mme. de Noailles at his side. 'And what did you talk about?' asked the countess's close friends. ' "Are you not glad to be seen with me?", d'Annunzio said to me. I looked into his eyes and replied: "Glad, dear friend? No . . . but truly happy, as one should be in the company of an equal." ' This sentiment guided the pen of Mme. de Noailles in the following dedication: 'To the dazzling and total genius in whose goodness I also believe, and to whom I should like to address the praises which he himself has given to Earth, Fire, Water and Air.' Her few letters generally begin with 'Illustrious and magnificent friend . . .' It was rumoured, for a time, that the countess used d'Annunzio to rouse the jealousy of Barrès. Teas were organized by Mme. Siekievich and by André Germain, anxious to arrange other historic confrontations, but for d'Annunzio the only women who mattered were those with whom he could go to bed, and so the meetings between the two friends became less frequent. Yet d'Annunzio continued to have a high regard for the poetess and always spoke of her with fervour to the French visitors who were later to come to his retreat.

If there was a true fellow-feeling between d'Annunzio and one of the great Frenchmen of the period, that man was Anatole France. D'Annunzio had long admired this representative of Latinity. He had read and re-read *Sur la pierre blanche*, and was captivated by the archaic language of *Le puits de sainte Claire*. Like himself, the old pagan was sensitive to the charm of St. Francis. In his copy of *Les sept femmes de Barbe-Bleue*, d'Annunzio had underlined this passage: 'Life without vice is merely tedium, heaviness of heart and sadness . . . Vice is man's only originality, his only creative power . . . I call vice a natural disposition towards what the majority considers abnormal and bad, that is to say, beauty, power and genius.' On a copy of *Le Martyre de saint Sébastien*, d'Annunzio wrote this poetically cynical dedication: 'For Anatole France, for whom all the faces of truth and of error smile together divinely'. They had first met either at the house of Dr. Couchoud, Montesquiou's confidant, or as guests of Édouard Champion, the medievalist. At this first dinner the two writers, more interested in female flesh than in talking literature, discussed the necklines of the women guests. Marie Siekievich, a Russian blue-stocking who was more discriminating in her invitations than Mme. de Goloubeff, provoked this exchange of epigrams: when d'Annunzio remarked 'Her complexion is so white that it seems to have been made with the curdled milk of Cossack mares', France replied 'To play with such a moon, one would have to be a sylph.' D'Annunzio teased the Frenchman: 'Your great writers use only five thousand words and there are forty thousand in your language, so what do you do with the other thirty-five thousand?' The creator of innumerable neologisms could not understand such reticence. A photograph of the two friends taken after a lecture calls to mind a French proverb, '*Deux augures ne peuvent se rencontrer sans rire*' ('Two soothsayers cannot meet without laughing'). A sly malice illuminates the faces of the two men and one can almost hear the twittering of mutual compliments. Politics were later to divide the pacifist France and the bellicose d'Annunzio.

At the beginning of his Parisian period, d'Annunzio seems to have had even more arrangers of introductions than persons to whom to be introduced. There was Hélène Vacaresco, Jane Catulle-Mendès, Marcelle Tinnayre and others whose names would mean nothing today. If one is to believe René Boylesve, only Marie Siekievich (a friend of Proust) kept her head: 'In a box, surrounded by swooning women, he acts the god with Mme. Siekievich, takes her two arms as they leave the box and asks: "What will you be for me?"—"The one who will say no to everything you suggest."—"But one should never say no to a man who gives so much pleasure."—"Nonsense! For three francs fifty I can buy the best you have to offer; I do not ask for the rest."' And Boylesve adds: 'He takes a pride in having all the vices and making people suffer.'

To launch d'Annunzio in the world of non-academic literature, Jacques Rouché gave luncheons in his honour. Gide, who attended one of these, noted that evening in his *Journal:* 'D'Annunzio, more prim, repressed and irritable than ever, and also more jaunty. The eyes are without goodness, without tenderness; the voice cajoling rather than caressing; the mouth cruel rather than greedy; the forehead handsome enough. Nothing in him suggests genius rather than talent. Less will than calculation; little passion, or only of a cold kind. He generally disappoints those who have taken to (that is, who have *mis*taken) his work. "He sums up all Italy", says Mme. Rouché, who is one of the latter. "Dante apart", adds Suarès [a literary figure—a poor man's d'Annunzio], who told me eloquently how little he likes the "braggart". The amusing thing is that d'Annunzio smiles only for two people, Suarès and myself (for me less than for Suarès, whose grandiloquence not surprisingly impresses him).' But Suarès was delighted when d'Annunzio invited him for a ride in his car. Gide poisoned his pleasure by whispering in his car: 'You have had your day, it will be another's turn tomorrow.' At this luncheon there was another of d'Annunzio's disciples, Henri de Régnier, whose inspiration bore an affinity to the minor modes of the Italian (deserted gardens, antiquated music, bizarre passions), and whose ravishing wife was to be one of d'Annunzio's first Parisian conquests.

SWEET FRANCE

Of all French writers d'Annunzio preferred Marcel Boulenger, who had shown his admiration in letters and enthusiastic articles. This slender and attractive person, an excellent horseman, had nothing of the intellectual in his appearance; above all, he was a highly cultivated dandy. A dandy also in his literary style, with a scrupulous regard for syntax, he wrote short stories rather like those of Henri de Régnier but much less interesting. The meeting took place on 10 July 1910, at a reception given by Countess Greffulhe at the Crillon, in honour of the Russian Ballet. D'Annunzio, seated on an enormous couch, was surrounded by women in gowns of lace, bedecked with plumes and with boas that emphasized the curves of their bodies. That year the fashion was for white. Even Nijinsky and Rodin could not emulate d'Annunzio's success on this occasion. Montesquiou strutted around, keeping away the small fry, while Maurice Rostand and Jean Cocteau played the part of pages. Marcel Boulenger immediately made a favourable impression. He was with his wife, Suzanne, a superb blonde five years older than himself. D'Annunzio at once became an intimate friend of the couple and was invited to their house at Chantilly overlooking the race-course: 'The maternal house stood there, tranquil, protected by its old trees; a beautiful and comfortable French house, light and clean, illuminated by order even more than by its windows, slightly Italianate like a sonnet by the Pléiade' (Ronsard's circle of poets).

At Chantilly the poet found himself near Vallières, where he had been invited to hunt by the Duc de Gramont; the duchess insisted that he take a house in the area. He was enchanted by the scenery and by the well-bred elegance that reigned around Chantilly. The Duc de Chartres, the grandson of Louis-Philippe, still had his hounds, and the races were too far from Paris to attract the vulgar throng. Most important of all, d'Annunzio found himself involved in a romantic situation. He had taken a fancy to Mme. Boulenger, whose beautiful face earned her the nickname 'Chiaroviso'. Mme. Boulenger was not going to be cruel to him, for her husband was wildly in love with a gorgeous young neighbour, Mme. Hubin, who had a passion for horses and dogs. To avoid hurting his friend Boulenger, d'Annunzio publicly informed Mme. Hubin that he did not desire her and called her 'Nontivoglio' ('I do not want you'). The Boulengers initiated him into greyhound-racing and on 26 October he accompanied them to one of the first races held at La Chapelle-en-Serval, which was won by Mme. Hubin's greyhound; on these occasions d'Annunzio was quite simply charming, so much so that the things he said in the places he visited are still remembered today, sixty years later. Of Mme. Hubin's house he said: 'It was so cool, as if the garden served it as a fan.' One of their friends, the writer Fernand Vanderem, lived in a scrupulously well-kept house; at a joke-shop d'Annunzio bought what looked like overturned ink-pots, which he placed on the carpets or the arm-chairs for the pleasure of watching Vanderem turn pale. The conversation was of books and horses, pictures and dogs. The women were gay and elegant, the men cultivated and fond of sport. D'Annunzio thought seriously of settling near his friends, who still knew the 'sweetness of life'. His new translator, Doderet, younger and more Parisian than Hérelle (who had retired), also became a friend of the Boulengers.

D'Annunzio took his distinguished friends and a few rather overdressed ladies to listen to Louis Vierne at the cathedral of Notre-Dame. He had asked the organist's 'humble permission' to hear the 'mystical din' of his organ, so that he could compare it with the great organ of the master glassmaker which he had in-vented for his novel *Il Fuoco*. Vierne improvised a solemn march. In the nave, surrounded by swooning women, d'Annunzio im-provised a poem which followed the inspiration of the organist. These sublime moments were repeated on other occasions, in the presence of an ever-increasing number of ladies. All this was con-sidered rather shocking and d'Annunzio was soon to hear about it from the archbishop's palace, especially after Mme. de Goloubeff had thrown a fit of jealousy in the Place du Parvis in front of the cathedral.

Poor Donatella! Her jealousy was the talk of Paris society: spiteful people imitated her mournful cooing, with the Russian accent and the sobbing: 'Gabri . . . Ah, Gabri . . .' One night she went to waken Mme. Simone. Armed with a revolver, she cried: 'He's at Dieppe with a woman! Come with me, I want to kill him.' To which the quick-witted Mme. Simone replied: 'The sea air does me no good.' One evening, after finding her lying across his doorway, d'Annunzio called her a 'tyrant'. She felt that the poet was slipping from her grasp. Had the separation from her husband (and an enormous pension) been in vain? The pension, the amount of which everybody pretended they knew, led to a rumour that it was not just her beauty that had kept d'Annunzio by her side. If he went to Villacoublay to try a new type of '*vélivole*', the anguished Mme. de Goloubeff would proclaim the rights which she thought were hers; the dinners in a restaurant near the airfield, where d'Annunzio used to meet the pilots after the trials, would be ruined by scenes. It is strange that, about this same time, Proust should have brought to this same airfield his heroine Albertine and, in real life, his chauffeur Albert, for whom he bought an aeroplane.

An intriguing meeting with a woman of great talent, entirely independent and possessed of a masculine intelligence, opened the poet's eyes to the futility of his life in Paris and revived the desire to work. He stopped looking for a house between Chantilly and Senlis, where Mme. de Goloubeff or some other admirer would have found it too easy to disturb him, although he kept a nostalgic affection for this district and for the Boulengers and their circle of friends, who had enabled him to discover a France other than the France of the boulevards. In fact he needed to go far away, if he was to escape the vigilance of Mme. de Goloubeff and of his Italian creditors, whose importunity knew no frontiers. Montesquiou, who was in favour of the new friendship, arranged the departure as carefully as the flight to Varennes, and with more success. This romantic escapade thrilled him; d'Annunzio's luggage was taken piece by piece from the Meurice to the Hôtel d'Isly, near the Gare Saint-Lazare; then cabs with blinds drawn took the poet from one hotel to the other and, at the very last minute, to the Gare d'Orsay and the Sud-Express. D'Annunzio assumed the name of Guy d'Arbes and Montesquiou that of Robert Lecomte. On 6 July 1910, the poet arrived at Arcachon, where Miss Romaine Brooks awaited him.

13

Arcachon

ROMAINE BROOKS

When one sees Arcachon today, one is amazed that d'Annunzio should have chosen such a place for his retreat. The prosperous mediocrity of the villas, piled one above the other between a silted-up harbour and the stifling forest, was at that time much less apparent. The villages at the edge of the bay still retained the simplicity of the period when the *Landes* were poor, but here and there citizens of Bordeaux, more adventurous than those who clustered round the 'Moorish' casino, were erecting pretentious chalets. In the *Ville d'Hiver* ('winter city') tuberculosis patients waited for death among the mimosas. The great dune of Le Pyla rose high above a deserted coast and an endless forest. The vast golden beach and the pines were reminiscent of Marina di Pisa, where the poet had known his finest inspiration, but the sea-pines on the *Landes* did not possess the beauty of the Italian umbrella-pines. The tepid, humid climate was enervating rather than bracing. In the surrounding countryside there was no important architectural monument to provide the kind of aesthetic inspiration which, in Italy, had stimulated d'Annunzio wherever he went; there was no aristocratic or intellectual companionship, for the people of Bordeaux who were settling in the Arcachon basin were neither aristocrats nor intellectuals. Perhaps this absence of distractions made the village of Le Moulleau, five kilometres from Arcachon, an ideal retreat for someone determined to work; it was also quite an effective snare in which a woman could keep the man she loved far from temptations, for Arcachon was not even on a direct railway line.

Romaine Brooks, who had selected this retreat and rented the villa with Montesquiou's approval, was also much in need of solitude. Too intelligent to have any illusions about holding d'Annunzio for long, she believed that she could influence his art and, by her example, encourage him to work. A greatly talented portraitist, she had found herself in fashion as soon as she arrived in Paris in 1905, at the age of thirty-five. She was one of those Anglo-Saxon beauties, long in body, with clean features and an unadorned elegance, who look more like boys than women, and whose emotional life confirms this ambiguity. Soon after she arrived in Paris, where she was fêted by immensely wealthy women such as the Princess de Polignac and the Baroness van Zuylen, the young artist made friends with another American, Miss Nathalie Barney, who was also beautiful and endowed with an intelligence which charmed even the most unresponsive persons; their friendship was to last for more than sixty years. As if to compensate for a lonely youth, she cultivated passionate affairs and an active social life with equal intensity. Totally neglected by a mother obsessed with spiritualism, Romaine Brooks was determined to be a painter, but she had had a very difficult life up to the age of twenty-five, when the death of her mother brought her a large fortune. At Capri she was briefly married to an Englishman who had been good to her when she was poor; she then lived for a time in Chelsea. In Paris she selected a fine studio at Passy, which she furnished in the white, black and grey hues that characterize her paintings. Like Whistler, whom she admired above all, Romaine Brooks had a great influence on the taste of the society people whose portraits she painted. The bare, unadorned style fashionable after the 1914 war owed much to this artist, whose austerity made a refreshing contrast to the Russian Ballet, then in its heyday.

D'Annunzio relished this simplicity founded on great wealth; he was intrigued and excited by a world of which he knew little; he was fascinated, and sometimes also irritated, by an intelligence that was quite unfeminine. He nicknamed Romaine Brooks 'Cinerina' ('the pale one'). They met in the studio of the artist Capiello. On his first visit, d'Annunzio said such wonderful things about her melancholy portraits that the young woman's whole life seemed to change: 'He changed the world about me and lifted me from a state of deep despondency. His enthusiasm, his hero-worship, his erudition and love for the English poets; his complete detachment from all petty prejudices, scandals and gossip. I never heard him speak maliciously of anyone.' But, Miss Brooks adds: 'He was vain and showed a certain "mauvais goût" in his braggadocio, belonging as it did to a more rococo period. When I took him to task for what seemed to me a lack of discrimination, he would reply "*Ma! Io appartengo al mondo intero!*" ("Why! I belong to the whole world!").' (Of Mme. de Goloubeff, Romaine Brooks was to write: 'She was a composite of vanity and humility; a beautiful statue whose emotional ego had been quickened by a careless Pygmalion.')

The Villa Saint-Dominique, where d'Annunzio finally established himself, a huge chalet-style building with bare beams, offered a fine view onto the Bassin d'Arcachon and Cap Ferret. The first days here were happy. At peace under the open sky, Gabriele was able to begin his drama *Saint Sébastien*. Romaine, in her blue artist's smock, made sketches for the large portrait which she completed the following year, at Saint-Jean-de-Luz, with the waves breaking against the dyke. The portrait inspired a poem in French:

> . . . *C'est la pourpre de Tyr qui double ton mantel*
> *De bure; c'est le vent du courage immortel*
> *Qui seul de tes cheveux rudement te couronne* . . .

('It is the purple of Tyre that lines your cloak of sackcloth; it is the wind of immortal courage which alone gives you your rough crown of hair.') The 'crown' was indeed a meagre one, for the poet now had only a greying halo encircling a shining dome. Luckily, a hairdresser in Arcachon had a lotion which for a time created the illusion of hair growing.

After several dramas, Romaine Brooks became an oasis for d'Annunzio; her letters suggest tenderness rather than exaltation. How peaceful it was! 'We shall again ride together in the car, hand in hand, me watching the trees and you . . . asleep. I can still see your dear face, enclosed in a leather helmet lost in a great fur collar. Do you remember your great sadness as you listened to the bells in the evening and your reawakened tenderness at the hotel? . . .' Unlike other women, she never believed that she could keep her hold on d'Annunzio: 'I am not theatrical . . . I cannot show my feelings by howls or by exaggeration, and since subtle, half-concealed feelings escape you, I have not been able to communicate to you the full depth of what I feel . . .' Romaine Brooks had her eyes quite open from the very outset of this liaison; not for a moment did she harbour illusions about the man she loved and admired. Once when she left him, she wrote to the 'Maître de l'Amour' a letter which is more like a dialogue with herself:

'. . . Romaine, you are a great artist, all your strength and all your thought are in your art, then why do you attempt another role which, if successful, means slavery and imbecility? . . . By taking refuge in your art you can scorn nature and its snares. Now you come down from your throne to join in the intrigues of the herd. You are a chosen one and yet you are becoming an ordinary female, you are meddling in things which the common people of the streets will always know more about than you . . . So I speak, dear friend, with much vanity no doubt, but also with a little sadness, for I should have liked sometimes to sit on a stool beside a throne higher than my own. Alas! the King is hardly ever there . . . it seems he descends from his throne each evening to give dreams to a woman on the dunes, and when he returns he sleeps nearly all the time with his feet on the stool . . . it is sad.'

DRAMAS

Two weeks after his arrival at Le Moulleau, d'Annunzio received several trunks of clothes from Italy. Happy as a child, he donned his red hunting-jacket and asked his friend to make a sketch of him in this colour, so foreign to her usual palette. Suddenly Miss Brooks's chauffeur rushed into the studio: 'There's a tall, fair lady, very upset, asking to see Madame . . .' As Mme. de Goloubeff was known never to go out without a revolver, Romaine told the chauffeur to deal with her gently but not to let her in. Howls could be heard behind the iron gates; the poet sighed and stretched himself out on the divan; then the cries ceased and it was discovered that the wretched woman, who had been trying to clamber over the gates, had been forced to let go of them. D'Annunzio seemed more sombre than ever; in fact, he had arranged by devious means that 'Donatella' should learn of his hiding-place, for he no longer found comradeship sufficient. Romaine Brooks in fact felt really in the way when she discovered the next day that Mme. de Goloubeff had rented a house in the forest, where she had fallen ill after her attempted invasion had been thwarted. The American tactfully returned to Paris, where she wrote the letter just quoted.

An echo of these dramas is to be found in the unpublished journal of Henri de Régnier, in a passage which only confirms d'Annunzio's sorry reputation: '26 October 1910.—I have seen Miss Brooks again. She was at Arcachon this summer with d'Annunzio, whose portrait she was painting and whom Mme. de Goloubeff came all the way to reclaim. A big scene, whereupon d'Annunzio explains to Miss Brooks that he needs thirty thousand francs a year, that Mme. de Goloubeff gives him this, but that if she, Miss Brooks, will provide this sum, she will have preference. As a practical American, Miss Brooks declined the offer.'

Mme. de Goloubeff sent for her two sons, her servants and her dogs; Antongini was instructed to go and fetch the poet's favourite horses, which had been left at Marina di Pisa, but for the sake of decorum (and also to preserve a little independence) the lovers lived in different villas. To escape Donatella's frequent scenes, the poet arranged meetings with Romaine Brooks at Saint-Jean-de-Luz; nevertheless he continued to live at Le Moulleau. From the Louvre he ordered casts of the *Victory of Samothrace* and of Michelangelo's *Slaves*, which he needed so as to create an atmosphere of beauty around him, and from Alinari he ordered large photos of the Sistine Chapel. In the garden he had an improved type of kennels built and hired a man to look after the hounds, more numerous than ever and which eventually were to be his only link with the 'Caucasian Diana'. As always, to obtain an exact picture of the life of the poet at this period, one must refer to his writings, and in particular a short tale which is more a curiosity than a thing of beauty, *La Leda senza Cigno* ('Leda without the Swan'). In this story poor Donatella could read a description of herself: 'one of those sweet but tiresome creatures who stubbornly and endlessly cling to their defunct love.' It also contained a description of her attempt to get through the gates. Between one villa and the other there were ridiculous games of hide-and-seek, absurd and painful scenes. The Russian, knowing that a rival had rented another chalet, went to the wrong house and slapped the face of some perfectly respectable mother in the presence of her family. Eventually she became really ill and M. de Goloubeff came to take her home.

LA CONTEMPLAZIONE DELLA MORTE

The hero of *La Leda senza Cigno* is called Desiderio Moriar. The name (literally, the desire to die) is a clear indication of a wilful melancholy: the heroic period of Paolo Tarsis is past. On the fringe of the mournful *Landes*, d'Annunzio contemplated himself with the admiration that one might feel for an instrument which no one is worthy to play: 'An adventurous sensuality suffering no constraint, but which, though impulsive, is capable of choosing, seems, merely as he turns, to be counterpoised by the resignation of one who never fails to discover the same empty horror beneath the easiest and the most difficult of life's caprices. His beautiful hands, one moment vigorous like those of the great violinist between the bow and the finger-board, the next moment slack and gentle like those of the famous dress-designer as he tries the garment on his client—from time to time these beautiful hands, with a sudden gesture, make the fingers crack as if to assume the timbre of the hidden skeleton . . . Ah! this wonderful living instrument, which with a gesture, an accent, a pause, a sign, a look, reveals the qualities of things visible and invisible!'

The mysterious heroine, who is in the clutches of a sinister procurer, eventually kills herself. As always, d'Annunzio followed real life closely. The woman on whom his heroine was based belonged in fact to a family which had been ruined by gambling; she had caused the death of her fiancé, the heir to a porcelain firm in Limoges, by means of a drug. It would be futile to recall the real names of these persons, whom their own families have succeeded in forgetting. D'Annunzio had become acquainted with this circle through the composer Gabriel Dupont, who was shortly to die of tuberculosis. The young woman had not found the poet to her taste, but she did not commit suicide; in real life, she ended her days as a lady of the manor in Béarn, surrounded by greyhounds; if d'Annunzio was to become interested in a story, however, it was essential that death should be constantly present.

Death also dominates the other work written at Arcachon, in 1912. M. Bermond, his landlord and a local worthy with whom d'Annunzio had struck up a friendship, died at about the same time as the Italian poet Pascoli—the timid Pascoli whom d'Annunzio had also charmed. Their deaths led Gabriele to compose *La Contemplazione della Morte* ('The Contemplation of Death'). La Duse had her niche in this chapel: 'A noble creature chosen by me, who ruined herself for me, through vicissitudes and across the distances sends me this message: "change wings".' Between two meditative passages the poet becomes obsessed with the characters of his new play, Ugo d'Este and Parisina Malatesta: 'They were to me two explorers of the shadows. I modelled two bodies full of black blood and I lived entirely in them so that I might understand sin.' Alas, these lofty notions led merely to Shakespearean tirades:

> To live or to die? Tell me,
> To live or to die . . .

Side by side with lyrical pages are to be found, as always, pages of the most gruesome realism—a description of a drowned man and the death of a litter of puppies which their mother was unable to feed.

D'Annunzio took the opportunity of a visit to Pau to see Robert de Montesquiou in his castle of d'Artagnan. Here the grand style and the tawdry existed happily side by side; there were a real cloister, numerous plaster casts, authentic family portraits and not a few daubs. When, some ten years later, d'Annunzio began to erect the shrine to his glory, he was to remember his friend's dwelling, and probably also Arnaga, the great Basque villa with its Versailles-style gardens which Rostand had recently built near Cambo, an excellent example of the way successful poets spend vast royalties. Did he like Rostand? He must have preferred him to other celebrities, for Rostand spoke little. At Arnaga this letter from d'Annunzio has been preserved:

'My dear brother, I am sending you the box for the rehearsal of *La Pisanelle*. *O Virtù della chiara presenza!* as an old Italian poet said. O virtue of your bright presence! I love you with all my heart. After your harmonious strophe, I should like to add two wings to the laurels of *Per non dormire* and enclose it like the winged wreath that adorns the tomb in Florence, for I must soon die.'

While he awaited this death, he was kept amused by a number of visitors and neighbours: André Germain, who had come on a d'Annunzian pilgrimage, was shocked to see the poet in the company of 'a veritable maenad of the *Landes*, who was nearly always on a horse and only dismounted to fall into the arms of d'Annunzio'. 'He praised her carnal merits to me in front of her and quite brutally. "She is extraordinarily impure", he said to me. Then, without apologizing for neglecting the appointment, he dashed off with her into the depths of the woods. Indeed, as he pushed his maenad before him, he had the appetite and made the whinnying sound of a faun who, sure of the complicity of the forests, rushes off to seduce a nymph.' Then there was Henri de Régnier and his ravishing wife. Mme. de Régnier has left a delightful description of the Villa Saint-Dominique: 'He loves to impregnate his entire house [with perfumes]. In a half-light reminiscent of a yacht's cabin, simple but comfortable pieces of furniture drowse, the friends of siestas and dreams, of a greygreen sea colour like the countless cushions in the drawing-room, where the great bay-window veiled with green curtains looks out on to the sea. An open piano . . . bouquets everywhere, flowers arranged with charming taste, with the care of an artist, very pale casts of ancient sculpture in shadowy corners, and bottles, trinkets, photographs of living women and dead beauties, fragrant petals in dark bowls. In the dining-room, all yellow and gold, the table is laid and is succulent even to the eye . . . fruits piled up in the most beautiful disorder tumble from full dishes or bulge from precious bowls. On the staircase, all the photographs of all the St. Sebastians that have been painted or carved over the centuries. The mysterious study contains a large writing-table along the entire length of which, among the photographs, papers and letters, there lies in dense rows, like a thousand thin blue keys, a veritable keyboard of telegrams . . . A large cast of the Apollo of Delphi stands opposite this table. The outstretched hand holds a sort of blue stone which, it appears, is a violent poison. Then, on a revolving bookcase, lies a large manuscript, that of the work in progress, like a huge black and white butterfly . . . Then more books, a large bouquet of white carnations and, as an inscription on the wall, *Ecce Deus.*'

The *Landes* were a primitive region with traditions which, though of a much less colourful kind, recalled those of the

Abruzzi. On more than one occasion d'Annunzio consulted a sorceress at Gazinet, Mère Mathie, who predicted that he would become 'a kind of king'. Mère Mathie was a highly gifted healer, but dabbled in occultism with a herbalist from Bordeaux, Mme. Ortarix d'Alonzo, and surrounded herself with renegade priests, one of whom consecrated himself archbishop of Gazinet (a village near Arcachon). It is a great pity that the poet never devoted a novel to this provincial Là-bas. At one time he thought he had fallen under the influence of an old shepherd who had the evil eye. Fortunately, this was also a land of hunting and shooting— pigeon-shooting in October and, most important of all, fox-hunting throughout the winter, either with a hunt from Bordeaux or with the Duke of Westminster, who had a hunting-box in the heart of the forest near Aureilhan. This great lord would have lived à la d'Annunzio if he had possessed a little more imagination and fewer principles, for he married nearly all the women he loved. D'Annunzio had probably made the acquaintance of the duke through the Duchess de Gramont, of whom the duke was a great admirer.

FEVERISH TORPOR

The climate of south-western France, pleasant but much too humid in winter, rapidly depressed a temperament as highly-strung as d'Annunzio's; in the summer the heaviness of the air, interrupted by violent storms, the stifling heat under the pines, the frequently low-lying cloud and the south wind combine to make work extremely difficult. Le Moulleau, so solitary during the first few months, became in the spring of 1914 a fashionable and romantic place. D'Annunzio ploughed across the bay on a pinnace decked out like the Bucentaur of the Venetian doges, with damask trailing in the water, a silk tent erected on the stern and two sailors dressed as gondoliers; indeed, the marshes of Arès and La Teste are quite evocative of the Venetian lagoon. For a short while d'Annunzio was seen in the company of a young man of stunning beauty, Illan Alvarez de Toledo, marquis of Casa-Fuerte,

the model for Aldo in *Forse che sì forse che no,* who was everything that the illusionist d'Annunzio had merely succeeded
in appearing in the eyes of his mistresses. He also translated into
French *Le Chèvrefeuille* ('The Honeysuckle'), a play which
d'Annunzio had promised Paris for the winter of 1913. Adored
by women, Illan also welcomed the attentions of men, though
from a distance; among these male admirers were Robert de
Montesquiou, his mother's best friend, and in particular the
painter Chaplin (this artist had painted a fine portrait of the
young man whom a jealous victim had mutilated). Illan's great
name, that of a Spanish viceroy of Naples, and his castle at Bal-
sorano, not far from Rome, unfortunately demanded much greater
means than he possessed. Even more than their taste for women,
and at one time for the same woman, music created a close bond
between the poet and the young marquis, and d'Annunzio bestowed on Illan the name 'Fratello' (brother). In Paris they met
mostly at the home of a Jewish banker's wife, Ernesta Stern,
where they found a rich and cultivated circle where little fuss
was made about morals (Mme. Stern had a strong fancy for young
Italians).

In spite of his excursions, social visits, frequent journeys to Paris,
and the climate, d'Annunzio produced almost as much at Arcachon as he had done in Florence in the time of La Duse; but, alas,
the quality of his output proved distinctly lower, though *La Leda
senza Cigno* and *La Contemplazione della Morte* are considered
models of Italian prose. At Arcachon he wrote two long dramatic
works, *Le Martyre de saint Sébastien* and *La Pisanelle,* the play
entitled *Le Chèvrefeuille,* and *La Parisina,* a libretto commissioned by Mascagni, the composer of *Cavalleria rusticana.* He
would have much preferred to see the successful conclusion of a
projected collaboration with Richard Strauss, a realistic opera
about a day in the life of a Montmartre prostitute, but in Imperial Germany the name of d'Annunzio represented the depths
of decadence and the indignation of the press put an end to
the negotiations. Perhaps there is less cause for regret in the failure of another project, an opera about the Children's Crusade

entitled *La Crociata degli Innocenti* ('The Crusade of the Innocents') with music by Puccini. The composer of *Madame Butterfly* came to Arcachon to confer with d'Annunzio, at the time when the poet was writing *La Contemplazione della Morte*, but d'Annunzio could not bear Puccini's music and was not offered enough money to overcome his dislike. Another collaboration was suggested by Sarah Bernhardt, who was convalescing at Arcachon after the amputation of her leg. Together d'Annunzio and Edmond Rostand were to write a *Joan of Arc* for Sarah. The idea was often talked about, but never seriously considered.

D'Annunzio also wrote at this time numerous articles for the *Corriere della Sera*, poetic meditations on the events of his adolescence which were subsequently gathered together under the title *Le Faville del Maglio* ('The Sparks from the Hammer'). These articles were very well paid by Albertini, the paper's editor, who managed to persuade the poet's creditors to be patient by letting them have his fees from time to time. With the help of the Banca di Roma, this devoted friend succeeded in preventing the library at *La Capponcina* from being sold (the library contained over ten thousand volumes). As we have already seen, d'Annunzio also composed patriotic songs on the occasion of the Italo-Turkish war of 1911, in which he sometimes echoes Paul Déroulède, the French writer, politician and patriot. It is interesting to compare d'Annunzio's songs with those of another imperialist poet, Kipling. While d'Annunzio's are mostly abstract and adorned with mythological images, Kipling's songs seem to be written for soldiers in their own language. When the songs were published in book form, purged of a few lines considered insulting to Austria, d'Annunzio received a curious visit from the editor of his youth, Sommaruga, who had been reduced to living off his wits by a series of unfortunate court cases. The cunning old man had just bought five hundred volumes of the songs and offered d'Annunzio three hundred francs for every copy into which he would insert the suppressed lines; the poet demanded six hundred francs and the deal came to nothing. Yet d'Annunzio was short of money.

The month of August 1912, oppressively hot, was particularly depressing for d'Annunzio, who realized what his work was worth. He sent a telegram to Antongini: '*Va subito dall'usuriere*' ('Go quickly to the money-lender'). A little later, he sent his factotum to London to deposit with Sutton's, the pawnbrokers, three emeralds (a ring and two cufflinks), presents from La Duse. These financial worries did not prevent him from engaging a comely chambermaid, Amélie Mazoyer, who was intelligent and also willing, and who was never to leave him (d'Annunzio called her 'Aelis'). D'Annunzio was always adored by his servants, despite the irregular hours, the unexpected guests and his eternal capriciousness. He was so generous with his tips that arrears of wages were forgotten; his manner was always natural and gay. For twenty-five years he kept the same valet from the Abruzzi, a man who knew how to discourage indiscreet persons and to put jealous women on a false trail. Although he did not live in the princely style that he had maintained in Florence, he found his debts with the leading tradesmen of Arcachon mounting rapidly: in south-western France he had become a gourmand and had learned to know his wines, while remaining the height of sobriety; Mouton-Rothschild, his favourite château, did not, however, prove conducive to inspiration.

Twenty years later d'Annunzio, always the first to believe in his own legend, wrote in the *Notturno* ('Nocturne'): 'Five years of exile in the Far West, on the thorn-covered slope of the ocean dune, a long succession of days and work, a long patience, a long waiting.'

14

St. Sebastian

IDA RUBINSTEIN

Of all the women visitors that d'Annunzio received at the Villa Saint-Dominique, none was more fascinating or more impatiently awaited than the dancer Ida Rubinstein. She came frequently, accompanied by impresarios, a large staff of servants and innumerable trunks, to work with the poet on a composition which her determination and beauty succeeded in passing off as a masterpiece. What sort of life had the dancer led before she met the man who became her god (but hardly at all her lover), and for whom she was to become the most generous of patrons? Born in St. Petersburg, of a very rich Jewish family, she was from childhood accustomed to having her every whim gratified. Ida wanted to dance, so she was entered at the Opéra school; Ida wanted to see Greece, so she was sent to Athens with a famous Hellenist. At the age of twenty, too tall, too thin and with much too large a nose, there could be no question of Ida becoming the rival of Pavlova or Karsavina, but she astounded Diaghilev by her prodigious stage sense and became a star in roles which demanded no pirouettes— Cleopatra, Scheherazade, a queen or idol carried by slaves, swathed in Bakst's most opulent creations without being overwhelmed by them. She also wanted to try the theatre; her Russian accent proved as much of an impediment as her figure was for dancing, but once again Ida overcame her disadvantage, for her extraordinary appearance and the use which she made of it captivated the most discerning among her audiences. Others were not always so impressed. At first it was rumoured that her parents were giving Diaghilev millions to allow Ida a prominent part in his ballets; then these largesses were attributed to a Greek lover, Mavrocordato, and finally, from the time with which we are concerned and for a period of many years, to one of the richest men in England, the brewer Walter Guinness, later Lord Moyne.

Ida Rubinstein's first disciple in Paris during the famous season of 1909 was Robert de Montesquiou, who saw that she was bringing something new into dancing. The following year she broke with the Diaghilev company and commissioned Bakst to create some glittering décors for Strauss's *Salome*, which she performed only a dozen or so times. Rubinstein was concerned not so much to win applause as to create a spectacle that corresponded exactly to her idea of Beauty and in which, with the aid of a musical score, text and décor that should be as modern as possible, she would become the incarnation of that Beauty. For this priestess, who spent money with an oriental lavishness, her art was a ministry in the service of Divine Beauty and it mattered little whether the public offered its support.

D'Annunzio, naturally sympathetic to such an attitude, spoke of her: 'Before dancing, she sat down in silence like a sibyl listening to the god within her . . . She is motionless in the discovery of herself.' Romaine Brooks, who was very fond of Ida Rubinstein, wrote: 'She seemed to me more beautiful when off the stage; like some heraldic bird delicately knit together by the finest of bone-structures giving flexibility to curveless lines. The clothes she wore were beyond fashions, for without effort everything contributed to making her seem like an apparition. The banality of her surroundings, to which she paid no attention, made the effect even more striking. I remember one cold snowy morning walking with her around the Longchamps race-course.

Everything was white and Ida wore a long ermine coat. It was open, and exposed the frail bare chest and slender neck which emerged from a white feathery garment. Her face sharply cut with long golden eyes and a delicate bird-like nose; her partly veiled head with dark hair moving gracefully from the temples as though the wind were smoothing it back. When she first came to Paris she possessed what is now so rarely spoken of—mystery. Hers was a mask whose outer glow emanated from a disturbed inner depth . . . She was cultivated in so far as it suited her. She knew by heart pages of Goethe and Nietzsche and would declare Dostoevsky to be greater than Shakespeare, making her point open to discussion.'

Rubinstein seemed in her element as soon as she saw the artist's covered terrace, with its black and white décor and the masses of white flowers: it was, she thought, an ideal place in which to kill oneself. Romaine Brooks found her very difficult to paint, for Ida would pass suddenly from exaltation to despair. When Montesquiou saw the dancer against such a setting, his fervour redoubled: 'Your soul beats its wings continually, like a great gull over the sea.' Having placed his artistic taste and social position at the service of d'Annunzio with an almost feudal oath, Montesquiou sent his liege-lord to the Opéra where Rubinstein was dancing Cléopatre. D'Annunzio's enthusiasm was total. As soon as she appeared, he said to his secretary: 'She has the legs of St. Sebastian, which I have been looking for in vain for years.' To Montesquiou he wrote: 'I cannot conquer my agitation, what shall I do?'—'Create for her the exceptional work which such an artist deserves', Montesquiou immediately replied.

D'Annunzio, in a state of trance, declared to all and sundry: 'Among the frivolous actresses of Paris, Ida creates the effect of a Russian icon among the trinkets of the Rue de la Paix.' The mystery with which the dancer shrouded herself excited the poet. He believed the Russian to be a difficult person to meet and chose a ceremonious approach. Montesquiou pulled the strings of this little comedy, the dénouement of which was bound to be a masterpiece—that no one doubted. And indeed at their first encounter the poet and the dancer found themselves fascinated by each other, and soon Gabriele left for Arcachon to set to work.

The idea of St. Sebastian had long haunted d'Annunzio. The poem *Adonis,* written in 1883, foreshadows the theme of the drama: 'Thus died the Adolescent, in a great mystery of Pain and Beauty as imagined by my Dream and Art.' Later, contemplating a picture by Mantegna, he called St. Sebastian 'the Athlete of Christ'. In the early days of his liaison with Nathalie de Gouloubeff, he compared her with the ravishing martyr, for she had those long boyish legs which excited him so greatly. He took Mme. de Gouloubeff to see Gozzoli's great painting of St. Sebastian at San Gimignano. On 7 December 1908 he wrote to her: 'My suffering is like a carnal magic, O St. Sebastian . . .' Shortly afterwards she replied: 'Today is the triumph of St. Sebastian—he is abandoned on his bloody couch, but never has a more feeble life concealed a more conquering mind and a more knowing body—for him it is the greatest pleasure to relive his martyrdom—superhuman is his inspired body—by an unparalleled magic he has brought back to his pallor all the stigmata of his torture—the bites in the legs, the blows on the back, the scratches on the shoulders and the wounds of the arrows flowering with blood—he loves his executioners—he calls to the archer who loved him with an abundant heart, with an absorbing passion.—The basilisk with serpent's eyes, the guardian of swirling death—come to St. Sebastian stretched on his burning couch.'

This letter, which, not without naïveté, expresses highly physical emotions in mystical terms, suggests that d'Annunzio was acquainted with an apocryphal version of the legend according to which the handsome archer, having fallen into the hands of the Infidels, was pierced not with arrows of iron, but with the arrows of lust.

The drama which d'Annunzio composed at Arcachon during the summer and autumn of 1910 crystallized around the long legs of Ida Rubinstein. He asked Montesquiou, a great collector of reproductions, to send him all his St. Sebastians, both engravings and photographs. He went to the Bibliothèque Nationale to ask the medievalist, Gustave Cohen, to guide him through the mysteries of the story; he bought everything he could find on *The Golden Legend*. Then, from Arcachon, he sent Antongini to consult the most abstruse works in the library at Bordeaux. Utterly absorbed in his subject, he found inspiration even in the pines of the *Landes* gashed by the resin-collectors: 'Each tree had its own martyrdom, as if in each lived a spirit eager to suffer and to bleed like the divine hero chosen by me.'

BAKST

As soon as she was sure that the poet was at work, Ida Rubinstein came to Arcachon. The 'heraldic bird' was accompanied by a large cat with *pince-nez*, Léon Bakst, who, to the fury of his previous patron, Diaghilev, had agreed to work separately with Rubinstein. He alone would be able to deck out the stage with splendours worthy of the genius of d'Annunzio, the beauty of Rubinstein, and the Guinness fortune. Bakst wanted to transform the theatre into a cathedral, as Max Reinhardt had just done at the Olympic Hall in London, in his production of *The Miracle*. But he had to lower his sights.

As soon as Rubinstein descended from the train, the poet and the dancer launched straight into the sublime:

—'Madame, you have come to me to bring the ultimate glory.'

—'Master, I am merely the humble servant of your sovereign word.'

The next day the people of Arcachon saw a slender young woman practising shooting arrows at the pines. The poet's notebooks contain these jottings, written in French and dating from the time of the first working sessions with the two Russians:

'The character. The sick young man—suggestion by colour—yellowish brown—a sad yellow. A woman green like a larva—with bloodshot eyes.

'Asiatic voluptuousness—the spots in concentric circles as on the lamprey—the blue and black mantles—star-spangled.

'The dryads, the leaves of the tree changed into a veil. The young Boeotians. The bounding strength, the vitality of the muscles of the spotted garments which makes them resemble young winged panthers, powerful butterflies.

'St. Sebastian against the tree—a Daphne. The unity of beings —the boundaries between species abolished—the leaf and the beak.

'A kind of corporeal topography—a human body with valleys, hills and plains.

'The direction of the wind—the fluttering of the garments and the hair.

'The prodigious invention of the costumes and accoutrements. The art of showing patches of living skin, in the openings—the evocation of the beast by gesture.'

DEBUSSY

The greatest problem was to find a composer for the music. Roger Ducasse was considered, then Henri Février. When Montesquiou was consulted, his immediate reply was: 'Debussy!' D'Annunzio had admired the composer since the time when the young musicians with whom he liked to surround himself in Florence had acquainted him with Debussy's chamber music, and he immediately wrote a beautiful letter. The offer came just at the right moment. Debussy had recently confided to a friend: 'I am like someone waiting for a train in a sunless waiting-room.' In December, d'Annunzio went to Paris and the two men at once found themselves in sympathy. In the poet's own words, Debussy, whom he baptized 'Claude France', 'showed surprise, but only to love me, to give himself entirely, he who seemed still wounded by the obtuse presumption of another poet'—an allusion to Maeterlinck, who had not liked the music of *Pelléas* and had tried to insist on Georgette Leblanc, his mistress, for the part of Mélisande; d'Annunzio could not stand the famous Symbolist, as is often the case when one artist is indebted to another. ('I find him artificial and monotonous', he had said fifteen years earlier to Romain Rolland.) The composer's family on their side were overwhelmed by the simplicity of d'Annunzio, who boasted of being a great friend of little 'Chouchou', Debussy's daughter, sending her dolls and letters signed 'The sorcerer with the yellow beard'.

Debussy submitted readily to this claim made by d'Annunzio: 'The *Martyre* contains music between one syllable and another, between one line and another.' But the work required was enormous, for there were only four months available; the text arrived piecemeal, the first act in January, the third a month later, quickly followed by the second act. Debussy wrote to Arcachon: 'What do you want to become of me, faced with the torrent of beauty of your double consignment?'—'I am working like a slave day and night', he wrote to his publisher friend Jacques Durand; and then: 'This, if you do not mind, will be St. Sebastian's last cry.' D'Annunzio's letters are commentaries on his texts, written, so it seems, while listening to the Passions of Bach on the pianola. He yielded to Debussy's request that liturgical Latin be omitted. Sometimes d'Annunzio would recommend an actress: 'I beg you to engage Mlle. Paz Ferrer; she has eyes of dark flame and a warm voice in a plaintive mouth . . .'

D'Annunzio spent the month of March 1911 at Versailles, in the Trianon Palace Hotel where Rubinstein had an apartment. In spite of the passionate messages which page-boys carried from one bedroom to the other, it is almost certain that d'Annunzio was not Rubinstein's lover. What little desire she had for men she offered to her protector; it was her soul that burned for the poet.

The reading of the text (after it had been pruned of Italianisms by Montesquiou) took place in the apartment of the impresario Astruc, 'that Hebrew Volpone' (in d'Annunzio's phrase), in the Pavillon de Hanovre on the Boulevard des Italiens. The impresario was enchanted, as were the actors. Montesquiou went everywhere declaring that the *Martyre* was the most beautiful thing one could hear, not only in a season, but in a whole lifetime. The press, counting on Rubinstein's generosity, published some wild gossip. In short, at a time and in a society where people lived in the superlative, *St. Sebastian* was awaited as something tremendous. A week before the first performance, Cardinal Amette, archbishop of Paris, issued a very firm pastoral letter reminding the faithful that the whole of d'Annunzio's work was on the Index and that they must not attend. D'Annunzio and Debussy defended their work in a respectful letter, but *L'Action française*, in whose eyes author and composer represented the worst decadence, supported the archbishop and jeered at 'this Italian who comes to have his macaroni cooked French-style in Paris'.

The social world was divided and Montesquiou broke many a lance defending his hero's honour. Tough methods were used to silence 'respectable' people: for instance, when Paul Bourget, academician of ponderous respectability, inveighed against the unbeliever and debauchee, he was discreetly informed that letters written by him in his youth had been discovered, letters addressed to young men whom he had loved around the year 1875. Montesquiou had kept those which he had himself received, and Hérelle, the poet's translator, had got hold of some even more alarming letters.

Indeed, when one hears the clergy of today recommending the film *Theorem*, one cannot help thinking that the Church was closer to her mission in 1911, when she banned the *Martyre*. These two Italian works, separated by some sixty years, both contain some very beautiful images combined with a false profundity, the glorification of sexual ambiguity under cover of the miraculous. The film, whose setting is secular, is, however, both more absurd and more shocking than the *Martyre*, in which pagan fable is made to blend harmoniously with Christian legend.

Everything was helping to prepare public opinion; a rehearsal in the Italian manner (that is, as an oratorio, without acting), conducted by Capelet and with Inghelbrecht as chorus-master, enabled the musicians to spread the news that Debussy had composed his masterpiece. 'This is the French *Parsifal!*' declared d'Annunzio. It was said that Bakst had rediscovered the splendour of Byzantium in the act set at the imperial court and the mystique of the great cathedrals in the act with the angels. In short, too much was said in advance. The public's curiosity is like a soufflé that must be served just at the right moment, otherwise it sinks:

the twelve performances, from 29 May to 19 June 1911, were not a triumph but merely a success; moreover, at the Châtelet this success went to the designer, then at the height of his career, and not to the author or the composer. The sets for the *Martyre* were judged the finest achievement of Léon Bakst, who had faithfully followed d'Annunzio's sumptuous stage directions:

'The red of the embers floods the entire portico with crimson; but already the evening is falling over the gardens, which turn more blue. The arcades are filled with azure. In the dark azure, the tall sheafs of lilies begin to shine with a supernatural whiteness, as if they were clustered round a celestial spirit.'—'An elliptical vault can be seen, of such a polished substance that it reflects every image, like a concave mirror. A double rectangular door, as huge as the portal of a temple, stands closed in the far wall. Leading up to it are seven steps painted in the colours of the planets, like the seven levels of Nineveh, the seven enclosure-walls of Ecbatana. Two sun idols, two colossi completely covered with serpentine whorls down to the winged and clawed feet, holding in their two hands two symmetrical keys, support the monolithic lintel on which is engraved a Chaldean inscription. The face of the Sun and the face of the Moon shine on the bronze door-leaves with their enormous hinges.'

The stage directions for the third act, a description of all the gods of Asia, begins: 'In the centre of the ceiling with its blue lacunae, a circular opening which is closed by means of a round shield like those of the Curetes, manoeuvred by chains, allows the fumes from the spices to escape. On the other walls are movable sheets of ivory, which cover the niches where the sublime theogonies and the unutterable conjunctions are hidden.'

The décor for the last act was the finest: 'The ancient laurels of the wood of Apollo can be seen, on a hill round like a breast. They are close and thick-set, dark and motionless like their bronze votive images offered in sanctuaries. Their trunks, bristling with leaves sharp as the tips of spears, rise against the sky, which is streaked with the long sulphurous trails of the fleeting day.'

After Bakst, the limelight went to Rubinstein, an ascetic hermaphrodite who moved with a breathtaking beauty. (She had even
gone to Monte Carlo for five days to rehearse with Fokine, who
had created a dance for her.) In the first act, in her breastplate,
she looked a little too much like Joan of Arc; but in the final act,
almost naked under the ropes binding her to the cypress, she
stunned even the severest members of the audience. Cocteau
skilfully explained the hieratic postures in language that regular
frequenters of the Opéra would understand: 'She suggests some
piece of stained glass miraculously brought to life, in which the
image, a little ill at ease and filled with motionless memory, silent,
translucent and sacred, has not yet acquired the free use of its
recently created voice and its new movements.' Cocteau was at
the age of enthusiasms. Proust, on the other hand, who had
yielded to Montesquiou's insistence that he go to the Châtelet,
was more readily drawn by the magnetic power of the 'professor
of Beauty' than by the genius of d'Annunzio: 'I was so happy to
be able to listen to you in the intervals, and to listen by your side
during the last act when, joined to your enthusiasm by your wrist,
as if by a metal electrode, I stirred in my seat with ecstasy, as if it
had been electric.' To Reynaldo Hahn he admitted the tedium of
that evening: 'Everything that is foreign in d'Annunzio took
refuge in the accent of Mme. Rubinstein. But, as for the style,
how can one believe that it is the work of a foreigner? How many
Frenchmen write with such precision? . . . But I found the piece
very boring, despite certain moments, and the music pleasant but
thin, insubstantial, crushed by the style . . . It is a flop for both
poet and composer. Nobody even came to call their names.'

Music-lovers, for their part, were exasperated by the restlessness
of the production, the incessant entrances and exits which distracted attention from the singing. When, two years later, in the
production of *La Pisanelle*, d'Annunzio was completely overshadowed by Bakst, Debussy wrote to him in these words, which
describe precisely the impression left on him by the twelve performances of the *Martyre*: 'Why occupy the eyes so much when

the ears have everything to absorb? For some years we have been submitting to influences in which the North has been combining with Byzantium to stifle our Latin genius . . .'

Fashionable society was severe; it had been bored, which is a hundred times more serious a matter than to be shocked in one's most sacred convictions; the performance had not finished until half-past one in the morning. Very few shared the fervour of Montesquiou, for people were beginning to realize that 'his thunderbolts were of cardboard', as Proust was to say of the Baron de Charlus. The press was reticent; only Léon Blum showed any real enthusiasm.

Many influences are to be discerned in the *Martyre*, which is so close to Wilde's *Salomé*, also written in French, and which echoes all the different aspects of the Decadence. Above all, there is Flaubert. D'Annunzio pillaged *La Tentation de saint Antoine*, as can be seen even in the stage directions. All the sorceresses of *La Chambre magique* (the Magic Chamber scene) prophesy like the apparitions in the novel:

> I am Phoenisse, the guardian
> Of Dilbat who is named Venus,
> The mother-goddess of Rome,
> The flower of the flowering wave,
> The pleasure of men and gods.

La Fille malade des fièvres ('The Girl Sick of the Fevers') is in places reminiscent of Maeterlinck, but mostly of Edmond Rostand's *La Samaritaine*. As for the idea of the emperor falling in love with the archer, this is the counterpart to Wilde's invention of a Salome in love with Jokanaan. D'Annunzio certainly manipulates the French language with much greater virtuosity than Wilde. His marvellous ear seized all the nuances of the new instrument; Wilde's play, on the other hand, is better performed with an English accent. D'Annunzio's vocabulary is prodigious; on the other hand, despite borrowings that border on pastiche, Wilde's *Salomé* is a truly dramatic work. First of all, it is short;

the *Martyre,* in contrast, which has recently been revived at the Paris Opéra without either Rubinstein or Bakst, is an extremely tedious affair. Perhaps one is bothered by the insincerity of d'Annunzio, who endows the finest images—of which there are many—with a rhetorical tone. The mere idea of a comparison between the *Martyre* and an inspired genuine work such as Claudel's *Le Soulier de satin* is quite ridiculous.

The *Martyre* has another fault: it was dated, written fifteen years too late. It should have been produced at the time when the Decadence was in full bloom, like a picture by Gustave Moreau. Montesquiou was delirious because he had rediscovered in this work everything that he had adored in his youth, but the public was no longer excited by ambiguous martyrs and emperors. All that had become the domain of De Max, a male Sarah Bernhardt; people had been sated with lilies and tiaras; only Bakst, still a fashionable genius, could make such things acceptable. What is truly d'Annunzian in the *Martyre,* apart from the dazzling images, is not very pleasant: the sadistic realism, the *mondo cane* of *The Golden Legend,* the smell of burning flesh and freshly spilt blood, the fondness for degrading lovesick women by making them idiots like 'The Girl Sick of the Fevers'.

BARRÈS

D'Annunzio wanted to dedicate the *Martyre* to the greatest living French writer, in an act of homage that would serve to contradict all his detractors in social and intellectual circles. By this homage he hoped to overcome the reticence of the only man whom he found close enough to himself: Maurice Barrès. Montesquiou was involved in the preliminary approaches, which filled him with a resentment for which he soon found solace in the embarrassment of Barrès. The text of the *Martyre,* which defied religion and morality, seemed a poisonous bouquet to the president of the League of Patriots. Could not Montesquiou take the bouquet somewhere else? But the pose assumed by Barrès at the historic meeting at the Pré-Catalan had annoyed the sensitive aesthete; what would he have said if he had been able to read what Barrès had written in one of his notebooks shortly after that dinner? '23 June 1910. He is a portrait by Clouet, a little Italian with a hard face, from the world of our Valois and painted by our artist. He says that the art, the style, of the Venetian eighteenth century is interesting in regard to the French eighteenth century because it is impure. In him I find the faded tradition of the Jean Lorrains and the Wildes . . . But he is something else. What? A businessman looking for providers of funds. In my opinion, as I see him, he is like a bird which, with its hard beak, scratches about for seeds, for the words which he gathers from books and conversation, the images which he seizes from life, using women and money for his own ends . . . This hard little soldier, this grasping conqueror, pecking and hurting the palm of my hand, a Jean Lorrain—but he finds a serenity, a solidity, a peace. One can chat with him because he is of the soil, has common sense.'

It was d'Annunzio's dedication rather than the work itself that conquered Barrès. Clearly, of all the arts which the Italian practised, the art of pleasing was the one in which he excelled. These pages are better than a pastiche, they are Barrès himself: 'And it seemed that I was returning to my primitive homeland, with a soul more vast than all my thoughts; and the thin notes of the mournful flute seemed to accompany the immortal chant of the dead which you have heard so many times across the plain of Metz, or in the gentle breath of the river of Lorraine, or on the height of Sainte-Odile, between the Druidical wall and the Latin castle.'

The dedication contains references to everything that might touch the great Frenchman—the cult of the dead; the crusaders; Valentina of Milan, mother of Charles d'Orléans; Joan of Arc; the Italian sculptors of the court of Nancy; Chartres and Sparta. Barrès was overwhelmed. Nevertheless, the dedication of a book on the Index was highly embarrassing. Without attending the performances, Barrès thanked d'Annunzio in a letter almost as beautiful as the dedication itself. Then, in his notebooks, in a long meditation addressed to the poet, he developed the contradictory but no longer reticent sentiments which d'Annunzio inspired in him: 'You have expressed pleasure well and the giving of the heart badly . . . I have travelled in my imagination through your country, the kingdom of Frederick II, the moral confluence of so many diverse currents, its impieties, its creduli- ties . . . You were born on a pagan shore. Christian, pagan or Mohammedan, how violent a beauty is the soul on that shore! . . . It [i.e. the *Martyre*] is a hymn to pleasure; you do not like to mingle with pure beings . . . I do not wish to go where there are fevers. You offer me an excommunicated book, a fruit of your sad shores. I would have been like you had I not belonged to a country that has duties. You do not have a duty.' D'Annunzio must have had an inkling of this attitude when, much later, he described Barrès as 'a castrated eagle'.

Shortly afterwards d'Annunzio published his *Canzoni della Gesta d'Oltremare*, inspired by the Libyan campaign, whereupon Barrès found him a true place in his heart. The Italian aesthete, like the French aesthete, was to be saved by nationalism; at last he had a 'duty' to accomplish. Each time that he went to Paris, d'Annunzio would pay a visit to Barrès on Boulevard Maillot and would then leave him for a rendezvous. The great Frenchman sighed at such vitality: 'He's a soldier of the Abruzzi.' Barrès was a little envious of an existence devoted to pleasure and heroism. Suarès and Romain Rolland also felt this bitterness. Beside these French men of letters, so bourgeois, even petty-bourgeois in the case of Suarès, prudent in their daily life, thrifty by nature or by necessity, and with mediocrity the hallmark of their emotional life, d'Annunzio was a *grand seigneur*, a veritable Don Juan.

If Barrès's friendship for d'Annunzio grew with the years, the fervour of Montesquiou ran dry. The vow with which the count had dedicated himself to the poet's glory for one year was not renewed. Montesquiou had suffered too much from never being able to be alone with his hero; some woman would always arrive and he would find himself obliged to talk dresses instead of ex- changing immortal words. D'Annunzio was not aware of this estrangement and continued in his relationship with Montesquiou to make the delicate gestures that succeeded in making sensitive persons believe that he possessed a heart. Thus, on the anniversary of the death of 'the other Gabriele' (Yturri, the poet's charming and patient friend), Montesquiou, who was taking flowers to the grave in the cemetery at Versailles, found d'Annunzio waiting for him beside the 'Angel of Silence'. After a lecture on d'Annunzio, with a recitation of poems (mostly by Montesquiou himself) delivered by the most famous actresses to an audience of duchesses, the Italian presented the Frenchman with a 1522 Petrarch in an Aldine binding which had been salvaged from his library, and which bore a book-plate inscribed: *'Gabrielis Nuncii Porphyrogeniti'*. The 'Porphyrogenitus' makes one smile when one thinks of the house in Pescara. On another occasion, overcoming his horror of prefaces, d'Annunzio wrote one for a deplorable book by Montesquiou on Castiglione; in the preface, as Montesquiou could not refrain from remarking, he said 'such beautiful things that one would have thought that he was speaking of himself'.

The advice and enthusiasm of Montesquiou were lacking two years later, when Ida Rubinstein produced at the Châtelet *La Pisanelle ou la Mort parfumée* (an imitation of a pastoral poem by Honoré d'Urfé called *Silvanière ou la Morte vive*). D'Annunzio kept Ida fully informed of his anguish: 'Dear brother, I am working in pain, but joy will come. Dear brother, one day I shall tell you of the harsh intellectual tragedy of *La Pisanelle*. I needed to write a work absolutely different from *St. Sebastian*, but of the same intensity.' The poet was mistaken, for *La Pisanelle* is not very different from *St. Sebastian*. It is a story of redemption through love in the Christian East, but it is also a farce: the nuns who are expecting the arrival of a saint are confronted with a courtesan. It shows, moreover, a distinct decline in intensity. Once again the applause went to Bakst for his costumes inspired by the paintings of Carpaccio; Rubinstein, seen as a nun and then as a beggar-woman crushed beneath a shower of roses, and De Max, a corrupt prince of Tyre swathed in silk, also had their share of applause. But the public was unimpressed by the magnificent spectacle, which came after a season of the Russian Ballet that had included *Boris Godounov* and *The Rite of Spring*. The Monteverdian music of Ildebrando de Parma was, like the text, a high-quality pastiche. 'Comoedia', in Rubinstein's pay, wrote: 'An orgy of beauties, a tempest of lyricism, a lake of subtlety, the new work is to French letters a rare, marvellous, immortal offering'; but his colleagues offered only lukewarm praise: Schlumberger, in the *Nouvelle Revue française*, deplored 'the Beauty which is as deadly to the theatre as obscenity or commercialism'. The drama was described as 'an aesthetic bazaar' and the Futurists gloated. People remembered the simplicity of the *Carnaval des Enfants* by Saint-Georges de Bouhélier or turned to the plays of Claudel, which were beginning to be appreciated after the excessively rich dishes offered by the Italian. Léon Daudet called the poet 'a mixture of Wilde and Scaramouche'.

Quite clearly, d'Annunzio the French poet had not caught on. He felt no resentment, regarding the public with a contempt that was in no way affected and finding his female admirers ready enough to lavish praise on to justify any new work.

15

❧❧❧❧

Mill'e tre

After the performances of the *Martyre*, d'Annunzio's visits to Paris became so frequent and so long that Arcachon, still his official residence, was relegated to the position of an 'out-of-town' resort. The poet, now 'a truly Parisian personality' like his compatriot Boldini, was caricatured as a dancing-woman by Sem (see illustration 23). René Boylesve's portrait combines Sem's verve with a little more indulgence: 'At first sight he has the familiar, rather common look of a little man who could quite easily become grotesque. An unprepossessing figure, bald head, uncertain beard, large hooded eyes, a large thick nose bulbous at the tip, especially in profile. A soft almost honeyed voice. He enters like a character from Italian comedy: one could easily imagine him with a hump. But there is a simplicity in all this; he does not pose, he is at ease, one senses that he is well-bred, he does not monopolize the conversation. He speaks slowly, without an accent, sometimes looking for his words, but finding just the ones he wants . . . He did not make a pleasing impression at first, but I have seen him grow animated in describing something beautiful. He is a man whom the spectacle of beauty transforms . . . He has gracious-

Mme. Marcel Boulenger

D'Annunzio, Mme. Boulenger and Mme. Hubin in Venice, 1917

The wounded poet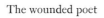

D'Annunzio at the greyhound races

34

Mussolini and d'Annunzio. Propaganda card

35

D'Annunzio and Chicherin
('You think you have fooled me,
but you are mistaken'),
10 June 1922

Benito Mussolini and Gabriele d'Annunzio at Gardone di Riviera, 1925

a Don Antonio de Candarillas
il Lanciere bianco e l'Aviatore azzurro

Gabriele d'Annunzio
di Montenevoso.
23. X. 1928

38

D'Annunzio Museum: entrance

39   The auditorium: the aeroplane in which d'Annunzio flew over Vienna

40

The cruiser *Puglia*

St. Francis of Assisi, by Giacinto Bardetti

41

43   The 'Officina'

30 | 31
32 | 33

ness. He is a child; he gives himself away with a thousand lies and tricks.'

On the fashionable Gabriel-Louis Pringué, whom he met at dinner with Mme. Guillaume Beer, he made a worse impression: 'With his little beard, he looks like an inverted Riquet à la Houppe. He shows a sadistic relish in listing the women he has made suffer.' To another memoir-writer, the Duchess de Clermont-Tonnerre, more intelligent and more intimately acquainted with him than was Pringué, d'Annunzio seemed 'eternally drunk and always sober'. His audacity made her smile when, on coming out of the Opéra, she heard him declaring to a woman: 'Come, we shall have a profound night.' Obviously, he was not taken seriously.

D'Annunzio stayed at first at the Hôtel d'Iéna, a small establishment, well-situated rather than elegant; then he found it more convenient to have a *pied-à-terre* and for a year rented furnished apartments, first at 4 Rue de Bassano, then at 44 Avenue Kléber. These bachelor flats were immediately cluttered with trinkets of all kinds, and in particular a host of Buddhas of every size and colour which he bought on credit, for money was becoming difficult to find in spite of Antongini's ingenuity. His secretary nevertheless secured some handsome contracts, including a series of articles for Hearst's newspapers and a contract for the film *Cabiria* (the title means 'born of fire' in Greek), for which d'Annunzio was paid the enormous sum of fifty thousand francs. The film had already been shot in Italy: utterly d'Annunzian in spirit, it was a mixture of *Salammbô* and *Quo Vadis?* The poet was simply asked to give some coherence to the story and to write the sub-titles. This extravaganza, a forerunner of *Metropolis*, filled the cinemas in Italy, where no one doubted that it was entirely d'Annunzio's own work. The poet always felt ashamed of it.

In his various abodes, or in Antongini's *pied-à-terre* when he had to avoid unexpected encounters of the kind found in Feydeau farces, d'Annunzio yielded to every woman whom his reputation ensnared. A prisoner of his own legend, incapable of becoming attached to any one of them, he nevertheless found some delicious creatures among these blue-stockings, adventuresses and third-rate actresses. The Paris from which he had fled with Romaine Brooks was regaining its hold and draining him of all creative energy; but he had probably never really stopped thinking of the city. The young Duchess de Gramont, born a Princess Ruspoli from Rome, entertained the poet as soon as he arrived in Paris in 1910, both in her house on the Champs-Élysées and in the château of Vallières. It was at Vallières that d'Annunzio had discovered the Senlis region, which for him came to represent the very essence of France. Scandalmongers poisoned this friendship; in Paris there were people who, jealous of the duke's continuing success with women, were only too ready to excite his jealousy. In order not to compromise the duchess, whom he called 'Piccola', d'Annunzio made his visits less frequent. Nevertheless, the friendship continued.

Two extracts from some unpublished society memoirs, which were quite widely circulated before the 1914 war, echo the rumours to which d'Annunzio's love-affairs gave rise in good society: 'M. de Gabriac tells us that if d'Annunzio did not rent a villa at Saint-Nicolas, near Senlis, it was because of a financial disappointment of a highly inelegant nature. At Biarritz he is said to have had two mistresses—women of quality—one of whom was a great Russian lady. The other offered him a pension. D'Annunzio did not consider it high enough and asked the Russian for a larger sum. This lady loved him very much, but after reflection said that she did not wish to give any fixed amount . . .' —'Yesterday evening Masson (Frédéric Masson, the historian of Napoleon) was quite scathing about d'Annunzio, saying that he was the son of a Neapolitan fisherman brought up by public charity; he insisted that he is being kept, and that he has placed one of his mistresses in a brothel . . . He is indignant that he should have dared to reply to Mgr. Amette's letter forbidding people to go to see *St. Sebastian*.' Maurice Rostand, though utterly devoted to his great friend, was later to write that d'Annunzio's rich mistresses paid his hotel bills. D'Annunzio might have answered, 'Why not?' The idea that men should not live off women is a prejudice that is not shared by the Mediterranean world. He brought them everything—glory, pleasure and pain. Curious situations certainly arose; Berenson tells the story of an American woman, apparently perfectly respectable and extremely wealthy, a woman of advancing years with silver hair, who let d'Annunzio know that a single night spent with her would be generously rewarded: 'Is she white all over?' said the poet to the go-between.

In this dubious world with its inordinate pretensions, in which people believed only so that they could continue to cherish illusions about their own connections, d'Annunzio, credulous like all adventurers, allowed himself to be easily dazzled by a woman such as the Princess de Colloredo-Mansfeld or by other ladies who, bristling with plumes, covered with emeralds, and with necklines too low for their age, made spectacular entrances at the Pré-Catalan or at Poiret's gatherings. In elegance or intelligence not one of them could hold a candle to Rubinstein or Casati.

A superior brilliance showed its final flourish in the person of the Baroness Deslandes, who had been loved by Wilde and Barrès, and whom d'Annunzio had known for some time, for she used to stay in Florence. From time to time, in an apartment inundated with lilies, Elsie Deslandes would give esoteric receptions for a Hindu dancer or a Scandinavian muse. With her diaphanous quality and child-like voice, she seemed a princess out of Maeterlinck, but one endowed with wit, for it was she who said: 'My eyes are a luxury, for they do not see but are beautiful.' Through the baroness's lorgnette and the poet's monocle passed knowing and provocative looks: 'I swear to you, I shall violate you.'—'And when, poet?'—'In your coffin, baroness.' Circumstances did not permit the vow to be fulfilled; in any case, Baroness Deslandes, who ended her life a lesbian, would hardly have appreciated this belated homage.

At the gatherings of Elsie Deslandes, d'Annunzio met a strange creature of vaguely German origin, who was a mime and a singer, but primarily a graphic artist, in the manner of Beardsley but even more bizarre. 'Alastair' (as he was known), poor and quite young, had the morbid beauty of the plumed hermaphrodites which he drew. With very little persuasion, he would dress up in costumes which made him look like something between an archbishop and an Indian dancing-girl and would then perform occult dances. The young man fascinated d'Annunzio and many an evening was organized so that the poet could watch him dance amid the smoke of perfume-pans and the scent of tuberoses. Later, d'Annunzio was to record this scene in his notebooks for *Notturno:* 'At Ilse's, around a Burmese golden unicorn, Alastair, dressed in an azure tunic brocaded with gold, performs Gothic dances. The bronze deer seem to browse among the cushion-covers. A wax figure. A poet dressed as a bishop. The wind blows the flames from the hearth into the room. An Indian singer, Isnayat Khan . . .'

With the cellist Barjansky and a young Russian, Catherine, who modelled wax figures as morbid as his own drawings, Alastair formed a strange trio. During the spring of 1914 d'Annunzio saw much of these young people and wooed Catherine, but without success; shortly afterwards, she married Barjansky. In her memoirs, the Russian describes an evening at d'Annunzio's apartment, with Mme. de Goloubeff in tears and covered with emeralds, and Cécile Sorel laughing and talking too loudly, a long chain of pearls hanging from her forehead to her shoulders and fastened above the knee on a brocaded dress; the room was hung with Indian tapestries, there was a circular mirror on the black velvet ceiling, a shadowy awning and bunches of peacock feathers: 'That brings bad luck', said one woman.—'Not if there are three hundred and eighty-seven or three thousand and eighty-seven', the poet replied coolly. When the cellist played Bach and Gluck, d'Annunzio selected from his 'library of perfumes' the scents which seemed appropriate to each composer. 'He listened to music with as much intensity as if he were creating it himself.' Then he presented the young woman to La Casati, who commissioned from her wax statuettes of herself, with eyes of emerald, flame-coloured wigs, a waxen complexion with black and white make-up, dresses studded with cabochons and open in the most unexpected places.

La Casati came to Paris from time to time, and then the poet would leave his duchesses and baronesses for 'the Divine Marquise'. This homage to de Sade influenced their relationship: 'The evening at Saint-Germain-en-Laye, the stinging kiss on the neck, the mad return to the hotel, the red mark which she shows . . .' D'Annunzio needed a confidante with whom to share his successes; this role was filled by Mme. Simone, the most intelligent and least shockable of actresses, but a woman who knew how to use irony to rebuff importunate entreaties. Of a lesbian mistress, he said to her: 'I have taught her everything, even the parting of the legs'; about a very young woman, he commented: 'She is discovering everything, like a spring beneath the moss.' In this native of the Abruzzi, vulgarity often bordered on poetry.

THE NYMPH AND THE ACTRESSES

A woman as different as possible from Casati or Rubinstein, and no longer in the first bloom of youth, had for some years enjoyed a good deal of popularity both with the general public and the aesthetes. Isadora Duncan had only two points in common with Ida Rubinstein: a love of Beauty (though not at all the same beauty) and a very wealthy patron. Paris Singer, the sewing-machine heir and the nephew of the Princess de Polignac, enabled Isadora's simplicity to spread itself on a royal scale. This, after all, was the *Belle Époque* when beer and sewing-machines gave artists the freedom to indulge their extravagances. After the Byzantine Greece of the Russian Ballet, the Classical Greece of Isadora Duncan seemed a refreshing change. Naturally, the dancer had an affair with d'Annunzio; the passage from her autobiography (*My Life*) which describes it is worth quoting, for it explains the fascination exercised by the poet: 'When d'Annunzio loves a woman, he lifts her spirit from this earth to the divine region where Beatrice moves and shines. In turn he transforms each woman to a part of the divine essence, he carries her aloft until she believes herself really with Beatrice, of whom Dante has sung in immortal strophes. There was an epoch in Paris when the cult of d'Annunzio rose to such a height that he was loved by all the most famous beauties. At that time he flung over each favourite in turn a shining veil. She rose above the heads of ordinary mortals and walked surrounded by a strange radiance. But when the caprice of the poet ended, this veil vanished, the radiance was eclipsed, and the woman turned again to common clay . . . D'Annunzio can make any woman feel that she is the centre of the universe. I remember a wonderful walk I had with him in the Forêt. We stopped in our walk and there was silence. Then d'Annunzio exclaimed, "Oh, Isadora, it is only possible to be alone with you in Nature. All other women destroy the landscape; you alone become part of it." (Could any woman resist such homage?) "You are part of the trees, the sky; you are the dominating goddess of Nature." '

The affair was brief. In the studio which the American dancer occupied at Neuilly, d'Annunzio had displayed an incredible zest in playing charades in the company of Cécile Sorel, the woman whom Barrès called 'our national tart' (a rather tasteless remark considering he had been her lover). Sorel, a member of the Comédie-Française, lived amid the Versailles-style décor of her apartment on the Quai Voltaire, like a royal favourite, surrounded by the furniture presented to her by the American architect Whitney Warren. What this coquette wrote about her relationship with Don Juan does not quite tally with what was said in Parisian society columns. According to the actress's memoirs, d'Annunzio declared to her: 'You are the only woman who can hold her own in the presence of a greyhound, of that perfect breed with a small head, a swan's neck, a stomach like a lyre, and long, wiry legs . . .' 'His look burned with such a fire of passion that it seemed impossible not to be burnt. Ah! dear Gabriele, how many times . . . But no, at the last minute I would flee . . . my pride feared your dream.' In fact, Cécile was reluctant to be parted for a second from the great man when she had him around her. One day, d'Annunzio and Romaine Brooks were the last to leave a grand luncheon given in her flat. From the top of the staircase the mistress of the house, in a ringing voice, called Gabriele: 'Poet, two more words, I beg you . . .' Cécile would have found it difficult to utter those words, for the particular homage that she offered the poet, who had gone back up to her, made all conversation impossible. A comment by Miss Nathalie Barney sums up the situation at the beginning of 1914: 'He was all the rage. The woman who had not slept with him became a laughing-stock. But he was running after Illan de Casa-Fuerte.'

With the staging of his play *Le Chèvrefeuille* ('The Honey-suckle'), at the Porte-Saint-Martin, d'Annunzio's connections with the theatrical world became a matter of business rather than of pleasure. The play had been written in Italian and the author had supervised the translation which Illan de Casa-Fuerte had come to Arcachon to undertake. In writing it, he had frequently sought the advice of Mme. Simone, advice which, unfortunately for him, he was careful to ignore. The amused confidante became the screen behind which d'Annunzio hid from jealous women, saying: 'I am working with Simone.' She always managed to refuse the parts that he offered her, for she scented disaster. Her opinion of him did not change over the years: 'He is the only man I have seen with teeth of three colours, white, yellow and black; his behind was even fatter. In short, he was a *rasta* [an exotic vulgarian] . . . but nevertheless delicious.' D'Annunzio attributed the failure of his play to the actors. He wrote to his friend Albertini: 'The actors are massacring the text . . . What a dreadful world! You would have to see these dogs from close to and smell their odour to feel the nausea which I feel. I should like to start writing a novel so that I might breathe.'

In order to breathe the poet went to watch his dogs run at the La Fouilleuse racing-track at Saint-Cloud. There he renewed his acquaintance with the Countess Greffulhe—who was introducing greyhound racing into France—the Boulengers and Mme. Hubin, one of whose dogs won the 'd'Annunzio Cup' in 1913. This beautiful huntress with light blue eyes and foaming blond hair, surrounded by dogs but always dressed in the very latest fashion, possibly attracted d'Annunzio more than Mme. Boulenger, but she continued to earn her nickname of 'Nontivoglio'. Nathalie Barney and Romaine Brooks sometimes joined Robert de Montesquiou to watch the dogs being trained. Mme. de Goloubeff, reduced to managing the kennels, clung to these opportunities of seeing her lover. At Villacoublay, near Meudon, she had rented a farm which she called the *Grange de la Dame Rose* and where she lived with twenty or so dogs.

Mme. de Goloubeff joined the expedition to England which d'Annunzio made with the Boulengers and Mme. Hubin in February 1914, to attend the great greyhound-race, the Waterloo Cup. There she made herself quite unbearable with scenes as out of place as her sumptuous attire. The visitors were received by another breeder, the Duke of Leeds, and the splendour of the English aristocracy made a great impression on the Italian. He met a certain Lalie Pearson, whom he called 'Nectarine' and who rejoined him in Paris for several days. The photos taken by Mme. Hubin at the race-track show Donatella smothered in an interminable ermine stole with a bunch of feathers that made her seem even taller—a clear indication of her lack of tact, for beside her d'Annunzio, in a cape with sealskin collar, simply looked squat. In London the poet spent a great deal of time in front of the Italian paintings in the National Gallery; he was fascinated in particular by the portrait of a man who bore quite a close affinity to himself, Titian's *Aretino*; he noted: 'The brown eye of an Arab horse, a red, sensual mouth.' His notebook also contains this sketch made from his room at the Savoy: 'A red sun in an opal sky. The bridges are veils of lace—a symphony in grey.' On the boat, on 13 February 1914, he noted: 'Englishmen returning from winter sports, red-faced, as if varnished.'

There was a sharp contrast between the world of Chantilly and the other rather more dangerous encounters in which d'Annunzio also liked to involve himself. Antongini has left a record of these escapades, in which he was an accomplice. There was the negress who kept the poet for a whole week in a seedy hotel in Montparnasse, and the dancing-girl at a tavern in Montmartre who managed to lure him into a private room, where he lost some precious cufflinks. After several rendezvous with 'a person above all suspicion', d'Annunzio discovered that he had caught syphilis. Immediately he proclaimed the news. Was it not extraordinary, at the age of fifty and for the first time, after leading such a life? But he recorded his true feelings thus: 'I can say that I have suffered the true and ignominious mark of Paris, the truly ignoble and unmerited punishment.' With this accident and the failure of Le Chèvrefeuille the year 1914 was beginning very badly: 'The life of Paris is a ferment of putrefaction.' He felt homesick for Italy; after seeing, at the home of the Hellenist Victor Bérard, some fine photographs of the temples of Sicily, he wrote to Albertini: 'I do not know what stopped me taking the eight o'clock train, so powerfully was the yearning for my distant homeland gnawing at my heart.'

The Caillaux affair came, like an abscess, to drain away all his feelings of disgust, giving him an opportunity to express himself with a fine bitterness; in evoking the horror of the court which acquitted the murderess (the wife of the minister Joseph Caillaux had shot the editor of Le Figaro), d'Annunzio recaptured the realism of Giovanni Episcopo, but with a contempt which ennobled the realism. 'Eternal France' seemed to him at her nadir: had she not voted for the Left, for a reduction in the length of military service and for a rapprochement with Great Britain? Of the French Parliament he wrote: 'The geese of the Capitol are coming down to paddle in the sewer.' In the course of a conversation with Maurice Paléologue, the French ambassador to Russia, he did not conceal his disillusionment with his country of adoption: 'The crisis through which France has just passed has shaken me in every fibre of my patriotism. We are living in an infamous epoch, under the tyranny of the plebs . . . Never has the Latin genius fallen so low . . . A great national war is its last remaining chance of salvation. Only war saves the peoples, bastardized by their decline.'

16

War

With the coming of war our syphilitic, debt-ridden Don Juan, whose now mediocre works brought compliments only from broken-down women and bored snobs, was transformed into a d'Annunzian hero, discovering a second youth much more exciting than the first had been. This rather fishy individual, now the comrade-in-arms of soldiers much younger than himself, outshone them in bravery and gave magnificent expression both to the intoxication of this new life and to its inevitable horror. D'Annunzio's energy was from now on directed too much towards action to give him time to write a single long work; later, haphazardly gathered together under various titles—*Envoi à la France, Notturno, Per la più grande Italia, Il Libro ascetico*—he published the proclamations and the dreams, the memories and the polemics, the meditations and the projects of this period; through these pages, as beautiful as the broken sculptures and overturned columns of an overgrown ruin, we can follow five of the most exhilarating years in the poet's life. These fragmentary texts, like the pieces of a broken bas-relief which enable us to appreciate its quality, possess a truth not to be found in the sumptuous façades of the d'Annunzian basilicas. Once again, however, one must refrain from moral judgements; for d'Annunzio the heroic life became a work of art, and what matter if it struck reasonable people as absurd, if to the erudite it sometimes seemed difficult to reconcile with the dull reality of the facts?

In this new life, in his battles as orator and soldier, d'Annunzio discovered an intoxication that he had never derived from success, women or speed. This enthusiasm, which went under the name of patriotism but was often devoted to the furthering of personal politics, crowned the struggle for the greatness of Italy begun twenty years earlier. Sixty years ago, war seemed a sublime ordeal, both to the Continental intellectuals who followed Nietzsche and Charles Maurras and to the French middle classes intent on revenge; it was not yet seen as the cosmic calamity that we dread today. The British intellectuals were unusual in their outspoken pacifism.

It was at the races at Chantilly, on 27 July 1914, in the company of the Boulengers, that d'Annunzio sensed the approach of a new life. 'Can you still remember, O Chiaroviso, that summer day, raw and murky like midday in a premature spring? It was the last spectacle of the idle life, the rapid concourse of grace and ardour transmitted by the blood . . . A touching hour of beauty and divination, unforgettable like the surviving fragment of a frieze in a ruined temple . . . The smell of future blood seemed to rise from the sweet bosom of the Île-de-France; but from the soft horizons of Valois the visage of War seemed to loom, blowing its suffocating heat of decay and conflagration.'

When he returned to a feverish and silent Paris, he found this telegram from La Duse: 'Change wings.' Immediately he realized that he could not remain a bystander: 'I followed the great tanks that crossed the white street, heading northwards, full of sacrificial flesh and drunken singing, all the men sitting in their red uniforms as if in their own carnage, like that battalion that had been mowed down, shot through the groin, lying on the ground in a congealed puddle and still crying out. Every night I went to the gloomy stations to greet the wounded, to adore the splendour of blood, to breathe the strength and power of the people, to feel the heroic quiver deify the undernourished mass.

All the centuries of the race became intermingled in the waves of my constant emotion. The nearer danger was, the more beautiful and strong the city appeared to me' (*Envoi à la France*).

In the meantime, d'Annunzio found time to go to Augé's, the grocer on Boulevard Haussmann, to lay in a stock of food, and to move from the eighth *arrondissement* to the Marais district. The Châlons-Luxembourg hotel, rented to the artist Huart, in a street at the top of Saint-Gervais, had the decrepit mystery of the Venetian palaces. From there the poet, who previously had known only the '*beaux quartiers*' and had seen the city only by car, carried his anguish with him on long walks, discovering Paris as he had discovered Mantua and Volterra. In his notebooks, written in French, historic memories are mingled with scenes suddenly encountered in the shadow of a doorway, inscriptions found in churches and his own meditations. The idea that Dante should have prayed at Saint-Séverin inspired some great pages. He refused to be 'an Italian of this uncertain Italy, corrupted and polluted by the hands of old men'. Observe how this great lover often expressed his patriotic emotions in erotic terms. When he came across Barrès on the Place Vendôme, he said: 'Ugh! writing when the others are fighting!' On the announcement of the German advance, most of his friends fled to Bordeaux. Marcel Boulenger was already at the front; d'Annunzio returned to Chantilly to console his fair friends. His notebooks were filled with bitter comments: '2 September. It is being said that Paris will not be defended, that the Imperial Prince will be allowed to make his entry into the impure city. *Incredibile*. Everywhere flabbiness, chaos, resignation. The race is lost. Miserable procession of Belgian refugees.' Another note reads: 'The dogs are a great worry; can enough meat be found to feed them?' One day, calling at the *Dame Rose*, he found Donatella 'smartly decked out in a summer dress to go to lunch at Versailles and visit the wounded; in that costume!' Later, however, he paid her this compliment: 'The young woman, disdaining all counsels of prudence, was ready to perish with her admirable dogs, defending the walls of her retreat. Her teeth shone even more than the whites of her eyes, illuminating the face of a handsome, stubborn child. She already saw herself unleashing with her guttural cry the fearsome pack against the first invaders to appear, commanding the strange battle amid the red glow of flames.'

D'Annunzio claimed to have coined the phrase 'the miracle of the Marne'. When the invaders were halted, he was enraptured. He wanted to visit all the fields of battle.

On 16 September a friend introduced him to General Gallieni, who was of Lombard origin: 'He is a tall, thin man with a direct look and simple manners, grieved that Italy is still hesitating.' And so d'Annunzio set off for the front. On the way he noted this little scene at Senlis, a town dear to the Boulengers, and which shortly afterwards was to be captured: '20 September. The little streets around the cathedral; the walls covered with virgin vine. Everything is clear, everything is grey and silver. Rue du puits Saint-Saintin, the grass grows between the paving-stones. Tiles covered with ivy and vine; the paving-stones are pinkish, the milestones greenish; the last house on Place Mauconseil has two gargoyles and a pepper-box turret. The sixteen chestnut-trees of the Place du Parvis, dry leaves and brown nuts; Saint-Frambourg in ruins beside the cathedral; the red honeysuckle.'

From Senlis d'Annunzio visited the former abbey of Longpont, which belonged to a cousin of Robert de Montesquiou, and went to Soissons, where he claims to have seen the cathedral and Saint-Jean-des-Vignes burning. In this fire, and later in the fire of Rheims, he is supposed to have had a vision: 'The cathedral was aflame with resurrection and the soul of France stood there like the one risen from the dead.' When the poet met Cardinal Luçon—and, of course, the unbeliever charmed the prelate—he begged him not to have the church restored nor the statues re-erected: 'The great Gothic ruin, black and disembowelled, must keep this desolate splendour.' In fact, d'Annunzio had no more witnessed the burning of Soissons than he had that of Rheims, but had made good use of Rodin's book on the cathedrals. At the same time he wanted to keep himself informed of what young Frenchmen were thinking, and received delegations of students and even *lycéens*, to whom he would say beautiful things. M. André Malraux remembers having been invited to one of these gatherings, in a hotel on the Champs-Élysées. The poet, in uniform (but which?), seemed above all anxious to please: 'He displayed the same concern with verbal invention, the same fastidiousness as Jean Cocteau'.

NEGOTIATIONS

To obtain a more prosaic, but not necessarily more exact, idea of d'Annunzio's activities during the early months of the war, one must refer to his secretary. In the opinion of Antongini, these were the reasons which kept d'Annunzio in threatened Paris: first, he wanted to see from close quarters what war was, after years of *grassa pace*; at the same time, he was anxious to save his dogs; but above all, he could not go back to Arcachon, where innumerable creditors awaited him. To meet their demands, d'Annunzio considered trying to secure a privileged position, in which he would not be subject to orders from anyone, by becoming a war correspondent for the Hearst press, to which he had been sending well-paid articles. But the sublime has its price, a price which the newspaper proprietor decided not to pay in spite of this telegram: 'M. d'Annunzio cannot be an ordinary war correspondent. Consider the sum of ideality that he represents. Conditions five thousand francs per article all expenses paid plus secretary and servant.'

Between journeys to the front, d'Annunzio visited the Franco-Italian hospital founded by the Duchess de Camastra (a descendant of Marshal Ney and married to a Neapolitan). For *Le Figaro* he composed an *Ode à la résurrection latine* ('Ode to the Latin Resurrection') reminiscent of Péguy and Paul Déroulède:

> . . . *Je suis une offrande d'amour,*
> *Je suis un cri vers l'aurore,*
> *Je suis un clairon de rescousse*
> *Aux lèvres de la race élue* . . .

('I am an offering of love,
I am a cry to the dawn,
I am a clarion of rescue
On the lips of the chosen race . . .'
                    —the Italians, naturally.)

D'Annunzio wrote another four sonnets, *Sur une image de la France croisée* ('On an Image of France as a Crusader'); the painting to which the title refers, by Romaine Brooks, was of a nurse with veil flying in the wind, Gothic in its severity. When not at the front d'Annunzio was seen in the restaurants frequented by supposed *éminences grises*, among others Gheusi, an ex-impresario who had become General Gallieni's secretary. This friendship gave colour to the rumours that the poet was being paid by France to accelerate his country's entry into the war. Certainly, the creditors in Arcachon had been mollified; moreover, d'Annunzio believed for a long time that the French government would offer him the house at Arcachon, the Villa Saint-Dominique, which had been put up for sale. When he plunged into the interventionist campaign, it is possible that the poet, always short of money, allowed his spontaneous fervour to be subsidized; however, it would be too much to say that he was a man to change his convictions for the sake of advantages. Furthermore, if d'Annunzio did receive something, it must have been less than he expected; when, later, his relations with France became strained, parsimony was one of the chief accusations which he levelled at that country.

The two trump cards that d'Annunzio brought into the French game were not so much a reputation that had been compromised by a long absence, as his friendships with Albertini, editor of the *Corriere della Sera*, and with Giuseppe Garibaldi. The latter, as his father had done in 1870, had just raised a battalion of Italian volunteers to fight beside the French. On 14 February, Garibaldi, whose men had recently covered themselves with glory in Argonne, dined with the Boulengers. He and d'Annunzio swore that within six months Italy would be at the side of France, or the legionaries would descend on Rome!

In his notebooks d'Annunzio kept an exact record of the decisive moments in these negotiations: '7 March 1915. Jean Finot comes to talk about the Garibaldian venture. A small, bent man who stands only by virtue of the vanity with which he puffs himself. Jewish accent. Balances on his chair. With his aid and Clementel's consent, all is obtained. Arms, money, red shirts, the legal status of legionaries. Two thousand red shirts are offered by Mme. Paquin. The intermediary is full of the affair and at times this messenger smothers the whole project with his verbosity. He talks of his political power, his victorious campaigns, his review, his courage, his disinterestedness. So this philosophizing little Jew is the *homunculus ex machina* of French politics today. Story of the traitor Caillaux and the loan to Turkey (five hundred million) proposed by him. When the little bore leaves, all crooked, I remain alone, perplexed and uneasy. All the material difficulties are overcome, but what is still lacking? The inspiration, the afflatus, something inevitable and necessary, the rhythm of destiny, the certitude of an irresistible success . . . I am still tormented with fever, and by this bitter cup: to be no longer young. Visions in the darkness, sepulchral silence, midnight chimes at Notre-Dame. I wait for sleep as for a gift of death.'

The notes made on the following day are even more significant, for they reveal that a sense of almost divine predestination overshadowed all the sordid bargaining. On awaking, the poet remembered that the municipality of Genoa had just written to him about a monument in honour of Garibaldi and his first thousand companions who had landed at Quarto to liberate Italy. D'Annunzio searched feverishly for the letter among the pile of mail awaiting Antongini on the tables; eventually he found it: 'Sunday 3 March. The municipality of Genoa has asked me to inaugurate the Garibaldi monument. Suddenly, everything becomes clear. Here, truly, is an Apollonian Providence . . . I shall go . . . I shall carry the Garibaldian legion with me. No opposition, no machination shall stop me; where the Thousand departed, the new thousand will march off . . . from the rock of Quarto the army of Italy will go straight to the frontiers. I shall go to Quarto not as a distinguished orator, but as the guide of youth, the mediator between two generations. I shall cross the sea in a ship full of blood impatient to be spilt. In sacrifice I offer my heart and all the strength which I believe to be in me.'

That afternoon 'Pepino' Garibaldi came to see him; what he wanted to do coincided precisely with the wishes of the French government: to leave for Italy with his legion in twenty days . . . *Alla ventura dunque!* There followed a great patriotic scene. 'Tomorrow there will be a secret committee at Jean Finot's. Clementel and Dr. Guelpa will be there. I shall speak, I shall demonstrate, I shall persuade . . . I remain alone, lost in a torrent of interior music.'

D'Annunzio made a short visit to Arcachon to prepare his speech, to put the house in order and, above all, to collect his thoughts before leaving for Italy; he then spent a week in Paris, a week about which nothing is known, in the house which seemed to have become one of the great d'Annunzian residences, already cluttered with Buddhas, pieces of armour and books. At last, he departed, like a conspirator, informing only three people: Nathalie de Goloubeff, Romaine Brooks and the housemaid, whom he trusted implicitly.

CITIZENS, TO ARMS!

At Modane an excited crowd was waiting for d'Annunzio and gave him a hero's welcome. If Italy was desperately lacking in great men, it possessed a host of reasonable men whom the nationalist ferment antagonized; of these none was more reasonable than d'Annunzio's harsh critic, Benedetto Croce. The final chapter of Croce's *History of Contemporary Italy* analyses all the shades of difference separating the few adherents of the Triple Alliance, the large number of neutralists (led by politicians of long standing, capable rather than respected, such as Sonnino and Giolitti), and the warmongers. This last category included the army, all the nationalists intoxicated by the d'Annunzian ideal of a Mediterranean empire, the Futurists (prompted by a desire

for action rather than by patriotism), the royal family, especially
the Aosta branch, and the Socialists of the Extreme Left, led by
Mussolini. The mass of the people was only waiting for some bold
flourish to rally to the interventionists. The Vatican, on the other
hand, inclined towards the General Powers.

In the words of Croce, 'an entire youth impregnated with a
literary sensualism', but devoid of intellectual capacity, noisily
echoed the poet's speeches. Germany, though it had a very great
ambassador in the person of the ex-chancellor Prince von Bülow,
married to an Italian, alienated the sympathies of a great many by
following excessive promises with crude threats if the country were
to declare its neutrality. When d'Annunzio arrived on the scene,
pride rapidly prevailed over reason; Italy thought that a great nation should not stand aloof from the conflict, and threw itself
into it just when the allies it had chosen were suffering their
worst setbacks: the Russian front had collapsed, the French front
was immobilized, and America still neutral. The government,
cautiously entering into negotiations with the Allies, regarded the
poet as an unwelcome sparrow; but he rapidly became an eagle.

On that morning of 4 May 1915, when he set foot on Italian
soil at the railway-station of Modane, d'Annunzio became, like his
hero, Cola di Rienzo, a prodigious orator, an irresistible per-
suader, and, like St. Catherine of Siena, an impassioned polemicist.
The music of his sentences and a constant concern for the greatness of Italy took the place of honour, truth and reason. He
enraptured the crowd with fanciful promises interspersed with
cries of hatred. He swayed them with outrageous flights of fancy
to which a middle-class academician like Barrès could never have
aspired. Sentimental and unscrupulous, he talked of the Third
Rome; but, even at their most violent, his speeches remained
those of a humanist and an aesthete. He evoked Leonardo and
Dante constantly, speaking of the Beauty of which Italy was the
mother.

The tenor-poet tried out his voice at Genoa, on the balcony of
the Eden Palace Hotel. On the following day, 5 May, in front
of the Garibaldi monument at Quarto, d'Annunzio delivered the

speech which was to produce tremendous reverberations throughout the country. This contact with the crowd inebriated him,
became indispensable to him. A year later, wounded in the eye,
he wrote thus of the superhuman relationship between orator and
people: 'Faces, faces, faces; every passion from every face runs
through my wounded eye, innumerable as grains of warm sand
through the fist. Is it not the Roman crowd of May, the evening
of the Capitol? Enormous, swaying, howling. I feel my pallor
burning like a white flame. There is nothing of myself left in
me. I am like the demon of tumult, I am like the genius of the
free people . . . I see at last my Credo in blood and spirit. I am
no longer intoxicated with myself alone, but with all my race . . .
They sway and are swayed. I ascend to crown them and I ascend
to crown myself . . . The mob howls and writhes to beget its
destiny . . . The mob is like an incandescent metal. All the
mouths of the mould are open. A gigantic statue is being cast.'

D'Annunzio arrived in Rome on 12 May. Forty thousand
people were waiting for him at the station to lead him to the
Hotel Regina, demanding a speech that very day, and on every
succeeding day, each more violent than the last: 'The treachery
is being committed in the city of the soul, the city of life! In
your Rome they are trying to strangle the country with a Prussian
rope pulled by that blubber-lipped old hangman whose fugitive
heels know the way to Berlin.'

On the other side of the avenue, today the Corso Vittorio
Veneto, the queen mother listened to the poet behind the blinds
of her palace, her heart beating. But the king found that things
were moving too fast for his liking; he preferred negotiation to
violence and tried to achieve a balance between the prime minister, Salandra, and Giolitti, whose name d'Annunzio was dragging
through the mire. On 13 May the sovereign convoked the
Chamber of Deputies; if intervention were to be precipitated, it
needed to be legal. On that same day, from the balcony of the
Capitol like Cola di Rienzo, d'Annunzio, whose parliamentary
experience had left him nauseated, vilified the deputies with
scurrilous verve: 'These clowns rigged out in tricolour shirts, who

with their turds defile the sacred soil of Italy.' The populace, which understood such language, also adored the heroic tirades. The peroration, when the sword of one of Garibaldi's companions, Bixio, was brought to the poet, earned him a delirious ovation. From the Capitol the fever spread through the entire city and on that same evening d'Annunzio sent a telegram to Marcel Boulenger: 'I have won the battle. I have spoken from the top of the Capitol to a vast crowd. The great bell has sounded. The whole sky was on fire. I am drunk with the joy of war.' Barrès received this victory bulletin: 'They are singing the *Marseillaise* this evening around Trajan's Column. Until now we had two fatherlands, but this evening we have only one, extending from French Flanders to the sea of Sicily.' Some friends dragged the poet off to a banquet which ended in the early hours of the morning; d'Annunzio was the last to speak:

'My companions, it is dawn. Our vigil is over. Our intoxication is beginning. The frontier is crossed. The cannon thunders. The earth smokes. The Adriatic is grey at this moment, like the torpedo-boat which furrows it. Companions, is it true? . . . We are waging our war (*si guerreggia la nostra guerra*), the blood is gushing from the veins of Italy! We are the last to enter the struggle and already the first to reap glory . . . Here is the dawn, comrades. This is the reveille . . . Let us embrace each other and take our leave . . . May our God grant that we meet again, alive or dead, in a place of light.' After the violence of the orator, the poet had rediscovered the dignity of his finest verse. No translation can convey the powerful harmony of *si guerreggia la nostra guerra*. Such sonorous inventions stunned audiences more susceptible to music than to ideas.

YOUTH RECAPTURED

Having brought his country into the war, d'Annunzio wanted to go to the front at once, but this was not easy for someone who handled crowds better than he handled officials. Throughout his military career d'Annunzio was to pester his friends in power to send him into the front line, so that he might fight as a soldier, so that he might throw himself into enterprises which would bring greater prestige to his country than the strategy of its generals. This letter to the prime minister is a fine example of his bumptious demands: 'I am not one of those writers of the old sort, in skull-cap and slippers. It is easier to hold back the wind than me. "Who shall hold him?" was written on the great fireplace of the confiscated *Capponcina* . . . Who can prevent me, and by what means, from going to meet danger and, if I so choose, a certain death tomorrow, in the line of fire? . . . You want to save my precious life, you regard me as a museum piece to be hidden in oakum and sackcloth . . . I ask you, is it not to commit a crime against the spirit to call a man with my past and with my future, and to say to him: "By higher order, you are forbidden access to that heroic life which was the aspiration of all your years of anguish"?' Side by side with the conceited entreaties of a man who is aware of being a nuisance, one detects a kind of blackmail: 'Spare me the horrible sadness of feeling rancour grip my heart once more. Remove from me the temptation to resort, in vengeance, to unreasoning reprisals.'

D'Annunzio's detractors, unaware of the approaches he was making, gloated when, on the day that Italy entered the war, he appeared to resume the role of man of pleasure, fêted in the palaces into which he had wormed his way thirty years earlier. In the city which had acclaimed him, he found some of his former mistresses, and each day brought him new beauties. He hardly had time to reply to a 'foolish letter' from Donatella: 'The white uniform of the lancers makes me younger, but I cannot take advantage of this, for my heart is already at the front.' The war, he added, was going to last at least one winter and the dogs would have to be sacrificed. In fact, since the Goloubeffs were receiving no more money from Russia, Donatella found herself deserted at the *Grange de la Dame Rose*, surrounded by her starving dogs.

During this brief stay in Rome, d'Annunzio also rediscovered the stones that had inspired the most beautiful pages of his youth. A moonlit walk around the Maltese Priory, built by Piranesi on the Aventine Hill, inspired a passage comparable to an engraving by that master. How he had missed Rome when he had lived in France, in what he came to remember as a kind of 'Far West'. Finally, his efforts to gain admission to the army succeeded, thanks to generals whom he was already addressing as 'illustrious'. Before confronting death, d'Annunzio wanted to see his mother again and went to Pescara. There was no one waiting for him in the dilapidated house; he passed through dusty rooms, recognizing here and there a few wretched mementoes. His sister, who had just died, was no longer there to greet him in the hall on his mother's arm. At last he reached the little bedroom, where the paralysed Donna Luisetta did not recognize him, a haggard old woman in an unmade bed, looked after by a devoted, groaning servant. Fortunately, Michetti, the friend of his adolescence, was with Gabriele and advised him to cut short this visit, which recalled the most sordid pages of the *Novelle della Pescara*.

From Pescara, d'Annunzio made another pilgrimage, which was to give him strength, for he went to salute the stones that he was about to defend, the stones of Ferrara, one of the towns he loved most and to which he devoted a play, *Parisina*, and many pages of his notebooks. He presented the municipality with a manuscript bearing this inscription: 'Gabriele d'Annunzio departing for the holy war leaves these pages here and carries away in his intrepid heart the beauties of Ferrara.' Let us not smile, for he was only speaking the truth; he was quite determined not to imitate his French colleagues and act the sorry role of official letter-writer to the armies. However, his enthusiasm did not blind him to the literary challenge that awaited him, and he wrote to Albertini: 'I have begun the first Song of War, and I must admit that my situation in the *Landes*, at the time of the Libyan war, was more favourable to the lyrical vision, which requires remoteness and mystery . . . Here, I am constantly suffocated with anxiety, oppressed by the closeness of reality, troubled even by the cries of newspaper-vendors.'

As soon as he was among the troops, d'Annunzio established an extraordinary hold over them. He was able to speak to them just as he had spoken to the crowds, so much so that the high command decided not to post him to a particular corps, but to send him from cavalry to navy and from infantry to air force, often a nuisance but always an inspiration. A young French airman whose squadron had joined the corps of General Maistre (which came to the help of the Italians at the beginning of 1918, after Caporetto) found d'Annunzio's war an almost comic contrast with Verdun. Everything acquired a Homeric colouring; the speeches which d'Annunzio delivered to the mess after each expedition made a hero of everyone. D'Annunzio's cooks and batmen were trained to perfection, and while admiring d'Annunzio's courage and lyricism, the Frenchman was astonished to see the hero climbing into an aircraft in patent-leather boots with high heels.

The poet's example proved of more value than his literary contributions. The poem *Renato*, in which the 'Son of Man' is killed in a trench, is not good; the *Ode to the Serbian Nation* was so violent that the author was asked to suspend its publication. What was admirable were the blazing orders of the day, reminiscent of Caesar and Bonaparte, and the bulletins describing victories worthy to be carved onto the reconquered mountains.

COMRADES

In his notebooks the poet recorded the memorable moments of this anachronistic and magnificent war. These hasty scribblings between two alert, poetic illuminations inspired by a face, provided some of the finest pages of his books on the war. D'Annunzio went out to meet death with an impatience that won him the admiration of those to whom his writings and his way of life were anathema. This man around whom women had flocked, discovered comradeship; he had shown a feeling for it in *Forse che sì forse che no*, in those beautiful passages evoking the friendship that unites the aviators, a friendship whose purity was in contrast with the degradation of passion. In these years of war, it was not women but comrades that counted. Even in old age d'Annunzio could recall their features with the precision of one of Pisanello's medallions: 'I see again the feline eye of Maurizio Pagliano, greenish, phosphorescent, the iris cut by the half-closed lid. I see the insolent mouth of Luigi Gori, his blond hair like watered silk above his jaunty forehead, the boldness of a young Florentine partisan of the time of Buondelmonte, his habit of planting himself firmly on his wiry legs and placing his long hands, like jug-handles, against his slender flanks' (*Libro segreto*).

In another portrait, this time of a comrade remembered for his heroism rather than an alluring physique, the poet writes: 'A young grenadier of the Sardinia brigade, who had come back with a short, tawny rabbi's beard that had grown in the trenches, round a firm, clean face—as if redrawn in red chalk by the engraver of the *Triumph of Caesar*—, speaking to me of one of his companions who had not managed to die well, said: "Like so many others, he went to war without first making peace with himself."'

Of yet another comrade, d'Annunzio writes: 'He has close-cropped hair, like the Greek athletes, like the wrestlers in the gymnasium. I should like to give him the name of one of the Three Magi, the youngest, the one with swarthy skin, thick lips and protruding eyes, the one who brought myrrh. A Piedmontese of modern times, calm, headstrong, stubborn, not without a certain pliancy and with a love of gambling, precise, bold, determined to conquer and to enjoy. He is twenty-seven: he is at that peak of youth when, having satisfied the first cravings of hunger, one begins to linger over the savour.'

Beside this etching, how gloomy is the snapshot of himself on which the poet ponders: 'I see it clearly. There is something senile, which it is futile to regard as alien, which it is futile to feel is not in me when I walk, when I gallop, when I fly, when the air buffets me, when the wind whistles through my ears. The feeling I have of my face is unreal. I imagine I have the firm, smooth face which I should wish to have, and this is the wrinkled face of a little old man who has re-enlisted.'

On the deck of the *Intrepid*, during one of his sea ventures, he observed a Sicilian midshipman who looked like 'an Arab youth brought up at the court of Frederick of Swabia', and who was rubbing between his hands a leaf gathered from a garden in Venice.

D'Annunzio discovered that 'the most secret quiver of unspoken love is nothing in comparison with certain looks, exchanged by two companions in times of danger, which confirm their fidelity to the idea, the silent sacrifice of the morrow'. He was becoming a legend; a wounded airman whom he visited talked of no one but d'Annunzio: 'I am a winged shadow listening to its own myth.' The men in his squadron spoke in d'Annunzian language; a pilot, scribbling his flight instructions in a notebook, added: '. . . una ora incantevole ['an enchanted hour'] . . . Does not flying seem to bring us near to divinity?' All those who associated with d'Annunzio entered into the heroic game. Like a knight who leaves for battle surrounded by his pages, d'Annunzio climbed into his aircraft with young warriors in attendance, one handing him his gloves, another his helmet, and a third helping him into his fur-lined jacket. Before taking off he would touch his lucky charms and the capsule containing a fatal dose of strychnine, to be used if he should crash behind the enemy lines. Instead of the Virgin Mary, this knight would invoke the memory of his mother in the days when she used to fret about his rashness, Parsifal, Zarathustra, or, better still, that ideal d'Annunzio whom circumstances had hitherto prevented him from emulating. That one or other of the pages should share the hero's tent one night hardly shocked the officers, for d'Annunzio had a knack of making his entourage accept his way of life. His regiment became a Theban legion.

His favourite pilot was Giuseppe Miraglia; with him he dropped pamphlets on Trieste and bombs on Duino, where a few years earlier Rilke had been entertained by the Princess Thurn und Taxis. Miraglia crashed in the sea on a flight on which d'Annunzio had been prevented from accompanying him. It was to his memory that the poet devoted the finest passages of his next book, Notturno: the walks in Venice, the evenings in taverns among comrades, then the vigil for the dead man, written in a tone both romantic and grave, untainted by the sordid detail in which he so often indulged in his prose works. From this intimacy with death, d'Annunzio distilled a mystique expressed in many a page of the *Envoi à la France*. These are the closing lines of the book which he dedicated to his French lady-friends: 'And my loudest song, Chiaroviso, is the song which I shall not sing on that evening, but which I am certain of hearing again within me, when night falls and I find myself once more with my pilot, face to face.'

THE RAIDS

The Italian word *impresa* means a 'raid', but it can also be a *putsch* or a *razzia*, as we shall see; the *impresa* must be carefully prepared, but it must also be carried out with a flourish, for its purpose is spectacular rather than strategic—to boost the morale of troops disheartened by inactivity and to intimidate the enemy. D'Annunzio, quite lost amid the vast, sluggish movements of trench warfare, excelled in the more glamorous methods of the 'commandos' of more recent times which required only a handful of men, all under his spell and impatient for glory. To inspire his men he invented the battle-cry 'Eia, Eia, Eia, Alalà!', a Homeric cry that replaced the English 'Hip, hip, hurrah!' which he had used at first. All these raids were to be carried out from the harbour at Venice or from the airfields of the Veneto. Two phases must be distinguished in d'Annunzio's war: the first leading up to the wound that immobilized him for several months from June 1916, the second, the richer in heroic escapades, occupying the last two years of the war. In this second phase his influence was enormous in boosting morale, at the front and behind the lines, especially after the disaster of Caporetto. It is this phase of the fighting on which we shall concentrate, for the experience of being wounded and the death of his pilot gave a deeper meaning to the undisciplined enthusiasm that had marked his entry into the war and the early engagements.

D'Annunzio was compelled to spend a few weeks in a camp; no sooner had he recovered than he insisted once again on being sent to the front. During these weeks in camp, the life of servitude and squalor which is an army's daily lot gave him ideas of suicide. He found the men dirty and the officers stupid. A general informed him that he too was a poet and made him listen to two madrigals: 'I should like to see my face when I have to feign the most fulsome admiration.' Being the kind of man whose health deteriorates when bored, d'Annunzio began to feel anxious again about his wounded eye. By tricking the nurse he managed to have a very strong dose of strychnine administered: 'I knew that in most cases the fatal dose is ten milligrammes. I had succeeded in taking sixteen. I was alone, lying on my back, motionless and waiting. After a time I became rigid, and my body arched from the neck to the heels. With a mental lucidity that seemed to be changing my skull into a shell of rock-crystal, I observed my own poisoning. My eye-balls also became like crystal in their sockets.'

Then the raids resumed, mainly on the Carso where some fierce fighting took place between Venice and Trieste; a raid on Veliki-Hribach, in October 1917, earned d'Annunzio the rank of captain and was to inspire some very beautiful writing. In August there were three raids on Pola, and two months later a raid on Cattaro. With the bombs was dropped a vast amount of literature claiming Italian rights to the Adriatic ports and promising their restoration to the mother-country. Caporetto (October 1917) brought a halt to these knightly ventures, until the Buccari expedition (February 1918) was judged necessary to revive morale.

In semi-retreat at Padua, d'Annunzio put the finishing touches to his account of this expedition, which he called *La Beffa di Buccari* ('The Farce of Buccari'). Three torpedo-boats, each with ten men on board, and under the command of Costanzo Ciano, managed to slip between the islands and to the head of a sound near Fiume, sank an Austrian ship at anchor and returned miraculously unscathed, an enterprise which, to d'Annunzio, seemed to give him certain rights over Fiume. This account contains some

fine portraits of sailors; like the other writings on war, it suggests
a monument for the dead carved by a sculptor of genius; it is
also important because, under the motto 'Memento audere semper'
('Remember always to dare'), it affirmed Italy's rights over Istria.
In these pages d'Annunzio is already taking moral possession of
Fiume. Should one then believe him when he writes that he has
sought death rather than glory? On deck, in the grey dawn, he
noted after this victory: 'I taste salt and melancholy. After heroism, as after pleasure, the soul is sad.' The Canzone del Quarnaro
ends the narrative with this refrain:

> Siamo trenta d'una sorte,
>   e trentuno con la morte.
> Eia, l'ultima! Alalà.

('We are thirty, with one fate, and thirty-one with death'.) The
popular ballad style is strangely reminiscent of Kipling.

Then came the famous flight over Vienna; d'Annunzio obtained permission for the flight, though not without difficulty, on
9 August 1918. Taking off from Treviso at six o'clock in the
morning, the seven aircraft arrived over Vienna at half past nine
and dropped pamphlets written by d'Annunzio himself. One
pamphlet poured scorn on the Austrians, commanded by Prussians
and on the brink of famine; the second contained these words:
'We are flying over Vienna, we could drop bombs in tons. We are
only sending you a greeting in three colours: the three colours of
liberty.' The pilot who flew d'Annunzio's aircraft, Natale Palli,
helped to replace the memory of Miraglia; later, the poet was to
have Palli's handsome countenance represented on a bronze medal-
lion that was never to leave his working table. D'Annunzio always
remembered those 'ash-blue' eyes, and in his old age gave an
account of this flight in the Libro segreto. When one visits the
Vittoriale and sees the fragile machine that carried d'Annunzio
over enemy territory, one cannot possibly have the slightest doubt
about his courage. The raid on Vienna had the reverberations of
a mighty victory; some suggested that d'Annunzio should be

crowned at the Capitol (as Cola di Rienzo and Corinne, Mme. de Staël's heroine, had been crowned). On 22 September, again with Natale Palli, d'Annunzio took off for France to carry a message to the Italian soldiers fighting on the French front. He flew over Paris and stopped briefly at Épernay. He had refused in horror to preside over a Franco-Italian gathering at the Trocadéro. Now that the last German offensive had been repulsed, there was talk of peace and of the Wilson doctrine: 'It is to be feared that the last to come into the war are deciding this peace. I have the ghastly feeling that everyone except Italy has won the war', he wrote; on the eve of the armistice he confided in a friend: 'This stinks of peace.' As if to prolong the youth which he had recaptured, the Comandante hoped that the war would be continued in Austria so that Berlin could be bombarded from Bohemia. In December 1918 he was so exhausted that he thought he had caught Spanish flu and put himself to bed. Rarely had his mood been quite so grim, and he wrote to Antongini: 'With the war finished I find myself in the blackest misery and I have no desire to become a man of letters once again. Perhaps I shall become a Bolshevik, or perhaps I shall die of Spanish flu.'

But we must now go back two years, leave the front and its escapades, to observe our hero during the days of illness and intrigue that were to culminate in one of the most extraordinary incidents of the Great War: Fiume.

17

Venetian Nocturne

THE WARRIOR RELAXES

With the composition of *Il Fuoco*, Venice had become the d'Annunzian city *par excellence*, the capital of an empire both decadent and elegant whose temporary subjects were ready to sacrifice all to Beauty. Equivocal, fever-ridden Venice, where Thomas Mann's hero courted death, where a Polish countess was tried for murder (the countess was so beautiful that her guards were changed every day), Venice, the favourite city of Diaghilev before it became his grave, had been celebrated time and again by d'Annunzio since the famous discourse of November 1895, which he had delivered on the subject of Tintoretto's *Allegory of Autumn:* 'Venice or creation in joy . . . the most wondrous union of art and life . . .' He adored the city like a lover: 'The entire city heaves with desire and throbs with impatience beneath these thousand green girdles, like a woman awaiting her hour of joy. She holds out her marble arms to the wild Autumn, whose wing is fragrant with the exquisite death of the distant countryside . . . Indescribable impression of freshness and ardour.' But the bruises of this tainted beauty were as familiar to him as a woman's secret wounds; its odour—'the green odour of a damp tomb'—he breathed in apprehension rather than disgust.

However, it was because Venice was the city nearest to the front that d'Annunzio the soldier returned there. After a brief stay at the Hotel Danieli, where the indiscreet admiration of the Venetians upset him, the poet settled himself in the house (the *Casetta Rossa*) of his friend Prince Hohenlohe, an Austrian subject, who was only too glad to know that his collections were in good hands. In the *Casetta Rossa* (small red house) d'Annunzio lived among brocade hangings, innumerable glasses and porcelains, and the sound of clocks whose weird, cracked chimes delighted him. As in all his residences, the temperature was like an oven. A small garden lay between the red house and the Grand Canal; a gondola and a naval motor-boat stood by, night and day, awaiting the whim that would lead Don Juan to his pleasures, or to some deserted island.

From his capital, d'Annunzio planned his military escapades, while along its canals he pursued adventures of a less glorious kind, but which also brought the illusion of youth. These liaisons gave the poet nothing of the illumination which he had known with Barbara Leoni, La Duse or even Mme. Goloubeff; instead it was the comradeship of war that now provided the necessary inner renewal. Luckily, the proximity of the front, the mystery of the curfew suddenly torn asunder by a searchlight, the shells of the Austrians, all helped to shroud the most trivial rendezvous with a dramatic atmosphere, the feeling of living one last incomparable moment. And so the women followed one another, in a long procession of scenes and swoonings among the bouquets of roses; the old flames returned, some for longer than others, to relieve the new mistresses. Nearly always, the women he had loved in bygone days retained a nostalgic appeal for the poet; novelty, on the other hand, very often failed to hold him for long, once his curiosity had been satisfied.

During these war years, one woman played a truly important part in d'Annunzio's life—'Aelis', or, more prosaically, Amélie Mazoyer, the housekeeper who had entered his service four years earlier, at Arcachon. Possessed of a keen wit and a pretty face, '*ma petite Française*' did not try to keep the poet for herself, but she welcomed him with a smile in his moments of weariness; whenever he was ill, her 'weightless pity' was the only sympathy that he could endure. Both more and less than a servant-cum-mistress, 'Aelis' was to remain with d'Annunzio until his death, always standing aside to make way for newcomers, and even arranging things for them when necessary: the women-friends of long standing did not even notice her existence, although the new mistresses were invariably alarmed by her. These old friends flocked to see their hero as soon as they knew that he had made Venice his headquarters: Luisa Casati, Romaine Brooks, Mme. Boulenger and Mme. Hubin. La Duse, for her part, restricted herself to telegrams in which she implored the poet to save the city of their love.

The Casati palace was not far from the *Casetta Rossa*; the garden overran the truncated columns 'like a huge garland supported by the heads of the lions leaning over the water', and white peacocks strutted over the damp steps. In a strange tale written in French ten years later, d'Annunzio told the story of the little wax figure which La Casati always had with her, and which she dressed in the brocades and plumes that she herself wore; the figure was an effigy of Marie Vetsera, Crown Prince Rudolf's mistress, that had been made for some Viennese fetishist. A few lines from this story, which was left unfinished like the marchesa's palace, show how great a hold 'Corè' exerted over d'Annunzio: 'Everything above her head is superfluous, useless, disturbing—except a diadem, a crown, or two wings, or the thought of me . . . I am in the gondola . . . I can see the gold lace gleaming on the windows. The speckled carpet goes down into the water . . . She is there, with her brilliant teeth between her hard lips. She is in her costume of silver and pearls: the wide silvered trousers, the corsage of pearls, the splendid helmet, the vertical white feather . . . My heart stops. I have nailed her in the silver coffin. The world vanishes . . .'

It seems clear enough that d'Annunzio had, in fact, made love to Luisa Casati in a gondola. She inspired macabre images, and under her photo the poet wrote: 'Flesh is merely spirit betrothed to death.' If her visits were brief, she reminded d'Annunzio of her existence with strange telegrams, all of which he had carefully preserved since the first meeting ten years earlier; Casati still astounded him, just as she astounded the Futurists, who proclaimed her their 'Gioconda'. Marinetti saw in her 'the satisfied air of a panther that has devoured the bars of its cage'. The marchesa, who had become the best customer and the inspiration of Catherine Barjansky, the young wax-modeller who had intrigued d'Annunzio during his last Parisian season, never travelled anywhere without the macabre dolls, dressed in wigs and costumes as fantastic as her own, which she kept as companions for the Vetsera figure. What fantasies did these effigies represent, and for what magic rituals were they used? How perfectly they suited the atmosphere of dark enchantment which the poet loved to create around himself! The Casati–d'Annunzio conjugation was the final and the most perfect achievement of the Decadence. Casati truly obsessed d'Annunzio; once, in Milan, he was so strongly tempted to go back to her that only by thinking of La Duse, invoking her like the Madonna, could he keep himself at his work.

Romaine Brooks, utterly different, had a beneficial influence; she became that unique thing, the 'good friend'. 'Her strange face, full of genius, recalls the young Beethoven.' Romaine came for a long stay at the Danieli and rented a studio on the Zattere, where she painted a highly romantic portrait of the hero in his airman's jacket and blue-grey cape, against the wing of a seaplane and with the leaden hues of the Adriatic in the background (see illustration 27). He also wrote her some beautiful letters during the war years: 'I think I am invulnerable. I have been able to pass unscathed through machine-gun fire. My comrades were falling all around me, watching me. I saved two soldiers who were drowning in the Timave under fire.'—'It [the war] is becoming too monotonous; even heroism has exhausted its gestures, and the blood no longer has the brilliance that once thrilled us.'—'I am thirsty for bitter water. My very dear friend, I have so much sadness in me. I have not been able to overcome this dark anguish since my land was trampled underfoot. I am poisoned by hatred and humiliated by helplessness. And no one can say what this destiny of iron is preparing for us. All forces should be stretched to their uttermost; and yet there is still so much cowardice!'

NOTTURNO

On 16 January 1916, having taken off in a seaplane, d'Annunzio was forced by the wind to land on a sandbank. Thrown against the machine-gun in front of him, he lost his sight completely for several hours. He was taken to a hospital for the blind where, half-opening one eye, he found himself surrounded by soldiers with bleeding eyes and bandaged heads. He heard one of the soldiers say: 'Is that the man?' The sight of the right eye was definitely lost; to save the left eye, the doctors condemned the sick man to the two things most painful to him: absolute darkness and total immobility. He was then taken to the *Casetta Rossa*. Renata, his daughter by Maria Gravina and to whom he had devoted much more attention than to his other children, legitimate or illegitimate, came to nurse him. Renata, whom he called 'Sirenetta', was a big girl of twenty whom the role of Antigone would have suited perfectly: 'Under her thick brows, intent eyes shaped like the unconquered eyes of the Roman eagles.' The wounded man had to remain 'as rigid as an Egyptian sphinx hewn out of basalt'. Feeling as if he were 'at the bottom of a tomb', d'Annunzio let himself be carried away by the visions produced by the damaged retina, similar to those caused by a hallucinatory drug: 'An angel or a demon of the night breathes on the closed fire of my lost eye . . . In my wounded eye the whole substance of my life is forged anew . . . This night the demon takes my burning eye in the palm of his hand and blows on it with all the strength of his swollen cheeks' (*Notturno*).

This experience was to haunt him even in his last writings: 'For more than a year I enclosed my misery in my extinguished eye, which the demon of the retina rekindled with a primordial life, peopled with unknown worlds, and filled with beings and races without history, without destiny, without horizon. I took part in an unremitting toil, accompanied by an insane anxiety.' The doctor had said to him: 'Your eye is blind beyond hope, but with a blindness that sees beyond the retina, a blindness that lives on your most profound cerebral life, which it expresses constantly by the most diverse signs' (*Libro segreto*). He saw Egypt again, the rides over the burning sands to the pyramids of Sakkarah, and the sands of the Bocca d'Arno where he used to let his greyhounds run. Since he felt a terrible urge to write but hated dictating, his daughter had the idea of cutting out strips of paper just long enough for a sentence, 'like those oak-leaves on which the sibyls wrote their oracles and which were scattered by the wind'. With his fingers clutching a pencil, the poet managed to scratch these words: 'O my sister, why have you twice deceived me?'

D'Annunzio was saved! The ten thousand leaves that fell from the blasted oak became some of the finest pages of the collection entitled *Notturno*. This 'commentary of the shadows' is a series of meditations on death, on memories of flowers and music, written with the detachment of one who is no longer of this world. There is no apparent order: after the evocations of violets gathered with La Duse during a shower in Pisa, and of the paths of Sorrento strewn with orange-blossom, the images of death loom up like the skulls in paintings of the *vanitas* genre. As already pointed out, the most beautiful pages are devoted to the poet's comrade, Giuseppe Miraglia: the death of the pilot, in the sea, the return of his body to the chapel of the military hospital between candles and bayonets, the four days of vigil amid the stifling odour of the flowers, during which time the handsome face changed so horribly that d'Annunzio eventually fainted; and, finally, the procession across the lagoon to the Island of the Dead. This book is permeated with the awesome simplicity of those Baroque canvases in which ecstasy verges on the charnel-house, in which roses lie scattered over livid flesh.

The notebooks which provided the material for these fine pages in the *Notturno* are an indispensable guide to d'Annunzio's state of mind when convalescence enabled him to resume a 'normal' existence, for they reveal the mixture of buffoonery, licentiousness and heroism that constituted the very fabric of his life; they also reveal much self-pity, embroidered on a yearning for death. D'Annunzio was both Christ and the holy women who washed his body. Sentimental as ever, he was haunted by the memory of his mother; his thoughts also turned often to his little dog Fly, which had died before he left France, and more and more to La Duse.

A year after the poet received the wound in the eye, on 17 January 1917, when he had resumed the life of a combatant, Signora d'Annunzio died at Pescara; her image thus remained linked with the finest of his writings on the war. This cult of the *Mamma latina* seems somewhat lacking in decency to those not born on the shores of the Mediterranean, and one cannot help thinking of Don José's famous aria in *Carmen: 'Ma mère . . . je la vois . . .'* Until her son arrived to attend the funeral, Donna Luisetta lay in state in the parish church, and the whole of Pescara filed past the corpse, which had recaptured a kind of beauty: this was no longer an old paralytic, but a woman without age, one of the blest. When he saw her, d'Annunzio did not share the astonishment of the crowd, which was beginning to talk of a miracle; had the mother of the hero suffered the fate of ordinary corpses, he might have been surprised. He noted: 'Thus death was no longer a dark passage between two radiances, but the simple conjunction of two lights, and at that moment this is what death was for me.'

With his mother dead, La Duse took her place. Had she not often called him 'my son . . . my little one'? He made no attempt to see her, but sent her messages and noted the thoughts which she inspired in him. This transference of affection is of great significance in the d'Annunzian mythology. In Milan, in September 1917, he chanced to meet Virginia, the old chambermaid who served La Duse; the woman told him that La Duse still spoke of him: 'No woman loved me like Ghisola, either before or since. That is the truth, stabbed by remorse and allayed by regret . . . Ghisola helps me and saves me from a sentimental blunder [the temptation to see La Casati once more]. I take a sheet of paper and write to Ghisola as if I were speaking to her. I see her eyes, which must still be beautiful and passionate beneath the forehead encircled with the white crown. I always wear her two emeralds on my index-finger . . .' But the ambiguous tutelary image of Mother-Duse did not banish the obsession with death: '18 January 1918. I have never known such anguish, not even when waiting for the night of Pola or when sighing for the night of Cattaro. Why? Because I am ripe for death.'

Among the first visitors received by the convalescent were his old friends from Chantilly, Mme. Boulenger and Mme. Hubin. Leaning on the two women, his eyes hidden behind thick dark glasses, d'Annunzio was led round his favourite gardens. Sometimes he would let himself sink into despair, but Mme. Hubin, with her huntress's vigour, would restore his spirits: 'Life is beautiful!' he would repeat after her, cheering up a little. Mme. Hubin still has some yellowed photos of d'Annunzio in officer's uniform, in the rococo drawing-room of the *Casetta Rossa*, or leaning on the balustrade overlooking the Grand Canal; beside the two friends, Renata d'Annunzio has the glum look of one who has pledged herself to duty. To commemorate this visit, d'Annunzio dedicated to Mme. Marcel Boulenger the *Envoi à la France* which he wrote in June 1916, and which is full of his memories of Chantilly.

D'Annunzio's convalescence was occupied, first of all, with preparations for new raids, which have already been described, and then with love-affairs. Two women dominated the period from 1917 to the departure for Fiume in 1919. Olga Lévy, a native of Trieste and married to a lawyer, lived in an enormous gloomy palace on the Grand Canal; she was very beautiful, with milk-white skin, huge oriental eyes and black hair. She was, alas, of a sentimental nature and, often choosing the most inopportune moments, would visit the convalescent to make sure that he was really becoming his old self once again. Don Juan would send her away—in tears, of course: 'She is foreign to my spirit and to my tempest'. When he was annoyed with her, he would call her 'the White Goose'; when happy, 'La Venturina'. According to circumstances, she was also nicknamed 'Antilope', 'Balkis', 'Ni-

diala' and 'Vidalita' (she lived in the parish of San Vidal). With
her own hands she made a large tricolour banner which the Comandante took on his expeditions, and which was eventually to be
laid over his coffin. At first, 'Aelis' could not endure Olga Lévy,
who assumed a haughty air with her, but the woman's misfortunes
softened her heart and d'Annunzio must have smiled to see the
rival become a confidante.

La Lévy, a keen music-lover, lured the hero by organizing concerts in her palace. There, at a concert in honour of Debussy,
d'Annunzio met a woman whose stubbornness finally overcame
all his treacheries and intrigues, and who was to be separated
from him only by death. Luisa Bàccara, a young Venetian pianist,
was no more beautiful than she was rich or well-born, but was
quite simply tenacious. In Venice she behaved more discreetly
than could have been foreseen after the scandal of that first
evening, when she had gone straight from the piano to the poet's
gondola. To advertise the genuine talent of his young mistress
(the mere fact of a love-affair would never have induced him to
take such trouble) d'Annunzio in his turn organized concerts.
One evening he installed a piano and an orchestra on a *peatta*
(a barge used on the lagoon), and with a few guests followed the
concert along the canals in gondolas.

THE HORRORS OF PEACE

The negotiations between the Allies were being conducted by
three men, all of whom were blinded—Wilson by his principles,
Lloyd George by his ignorance and Clemenceau by hatred; this
trio, incapable of understanding each other, left little hope for
the Italians, who were represented only by politicians of distinction but without prestige. Wilson, 'smiling with his thirty-
two false teeth', became d'Annunzio's *bête noire*. The American
President, an advocate of a strong Yugoslavia, promised the new
kingdom the Dalmatian ports, some of which had been founded
by the Venetians and all of which, despite the Turkish and Austrian occupations, had retained a large population of Italian culture

and a Venetian architecture superimposed on majestic Roman ruins. D'Annunzio had always claimed Trieste as Italian, calling it 'the Gulf of Venice', and had just returned from combat in the Gulf of Fiume.

Feeling that he was not being supported by France, he wrote to the French (believing himself to be one of their famous authors) a manifesto entitled *L'Italia alla colonna e la Vittoria col bavaglio* ('Italy at the pillar and muzzled victory'): 'We have forgotten Nice and Corsica, we have forgotten Mentana, we have forgotten the bitterness of those who fought and conquered at Dijon [the Garibaldians of 1870], the astonishment of those who ingenuously allowed themselves to be caught in the snare of Tunis.' (This bitter litany was to be repeated in 1935, when sanctions were imposed against Italy's adventure in Abyssinia.) But his efforts were in vain, for the French no longer listened to their famous friend; they wanted the Rhine and a part of the Near East, and were ready to let Italy shift for herself. Minds as different as Maurice Barrès and Romain Rolland, writing within a short time of one another, noted their reactions to d'Annunzio's escapades. Barrès wrote: 'D'Annunzio opera poetry, scene-painting of virtuosity and brilliance. Neither severity nor excellence of taste. But he has, above all, virility.' Rolland, for his part, ends on a reserved note: 'A profound hatred of Wilsonian hypocrisy makes him brand the humbugs of liberty with an ineradicable stigma; they are plundering, holding to ransom and enslaving the universe; but, whatever he does, one feels too much that it is a part which he is playing in the opera of existence.' During the latter days of February 1919, d'Annunzio wrote a violent diatribe against the French, in their language, *Les Aveux de l'Ingrat* ('The Confessions of the Ungrateful One'), more a letter breaking off a friendship than a political pamphlet: 'Ah! what have I not done to get to know you better, to love you better. Yesterday, as today, my daring served my love.' He denounced the Treaty of Rapallo and its dispositions for Dalmatia as 'a document combining Viennese arrogance, Slav effrontery and Balkan voracity.' Demanding the whole of the Dalmatian coast, he found this argument with which to flatter French chauvinism: 'What in the Rhineland is not French is barbarous. What in Dalmatia is not Italian is barbarous.'

These pages, full of rancour and written in highflown language which ill-concealed the author's bad arguments, achieved nothing. The editor of Le Figaro, to whom d'Annunzio had sent them, telephoned Clemenceau to ask if their publication was opportune: 'Let d'Annunzio keep quiet', replied Clemenceau. Shortly afterwards, Georges Mandel called at the offices of Le Figaro with this message: 'Let him publish his "confessions" in a book; a book is never very important, but newspapers are a different matter!' The young publisher Bernard Grasset published the little book, but it brought no response. D'Annunzio had also hoped that the French government would make him a gift of his villa at Arcachon; the fact that it failed to do so rankled deeply with him. D'Annunzio left the contents of the house to M. Philippard, the new owner, and they were finally sent back to Italy. When the library was put up for sale to placate his creditors, it was bought by Romaine Brooks, who sent the books to d'Annunzio as soon as he had a house of his own, a generous gesture for which, contrary to d'Annunzio's normal practice, she was fully reimbursed within a few years.

The death in an aeroplane accident of Natale Palli, his companion in the flight over Vienna, merely intensified the gloom into which d'Annunzio was plunged, desperate because he too was not dead. But the gold medal with which he was presented by the Duke of Aosta in Trieste, and the choice of that city for the ceremony, appeared an encouragement to his Dalmatian policy. Disorder was spreading to Italy; would she, like Hungary and Germany, yield to Communist propaganda? His repugnance for parliamentary government enabled d'Annunzio to maintain a romantic view of the events in Russia; he did not take the October Revolution very seriously, merely wondering if the 'Russian tragicomedy' was affecting Donatella. The only ones who mattered were those who would support him against Wilson.

On 25 April 1919, d'Annunzio returned to his role of demagogue, delivering a speech on St. Mark's Square in Venice. The following week the Italian negotiators Orlando and Sonnino left the Versailles Conference to ask Parliament to support their policy. The mayor of Rome invited d'Annunzio to counter this move with a series of public speeches, which echoed those of May 1915. The first took place at the Augusteo, the orator in his lancer's uniform, a black monocle hiding the blind eye: 'Our epic May is beginning again, I am ready and you are ready.' He poured scorn on the ministers, accused both deputies and the Peace Conference of the basest compromises. The Italians must zealously oppose those who were busy tidying up. 'Over there, on the roads of Istria and Dalmatia built by the Romans, can you not hear the rhythmic step of an army marching? The dead are moving more quickly than the living . . .' On the evening of 6 May, d'Annunzio spoke from the Capitol: 'The heroism that blazed for four years of war is everywhere extinguished, save in Italy. Everything that emitted the brightest beams is now merely a dead coal, useful only for writing share-prices on the white wall.' He unfurled a huge flag, which was to fly over Trieste, then he covered the flag with twenty yards of crêpe, the symbol of the mourning that was to be observed until the Dalmatian cities had been recovered. As he reached his peroration, the great bell of the Capitol sounded the tocsin. Long after d'Annunzio had gone, the crowd stood there, motionless and thoughtful. The other demonstrations were banned by the government. 'Today the geese are placing the Capitol under interdict, so that they might seem, once again, to save it.' Among the messages of encouragement was this telegram from Mussolini: 'The entire family of the *Popolo d'Italia* gather close around you with an impetuous faith.'

The meeting with the young Socialist leader took place a month later, when d'Annunzio returned to Rome after a series of journeys in northern Italy; his movements there gave rise to rumours of a conspiracy to unite Venetia and Dalmatia in a republic, under the presidency of the Duke of Aosta and with d'Annunzio as head of the government. Some believe that the conspiracy was an invention of the Ministry of the Interior to discredit all the extreme patriots; a move of this kind would have been clearly ridiculous. But plans were afoot, meetings were being held, and the purely decorative role assigned to d'Annunzio might explain why the conspiracy remained a daydream. There can be no doubt that more and more people were beginning to think that d'Annunzio should put himself at the head of the government, both to prevent the injustices proposed by the Peace Conference and to restore order to Italy. Donna Maria d'Annunzio received society and ambassadors; her salon in the Piazza di Spagna briefly became a political centre; even her family, the Gallese, were at her feet, and d'Annunzio was elected to the *Circolo della Caccia* (the 'hunting club', a preserve of aristocratic Rome). A Central Committee for Action asked him to address them on 30 June, but the government banned the meeting. D'Annunzio retaliated with a call for disobedience: 'I have not given up one command with the intention of never assuming another. If I were to follow my instinct, this very evening, with the same petrol that took me on the Buccari raid, I would go and set fire to the Braschi palace [the Ministry of the Interior].' These were the words of a young man, uttered by one who was clinging to the youth which he had rediscovered in the war, and who wanted to prolong that youth in adventure. Once again, patriotism served as a mask for a passion which had nothing to do with the interests of the country. But how many moments of disgust d'Annunzio had to overcome before his triumph was fulfilled in action! He wrote to Aelis: 'I spend my day in conversation with men of action and ideas who are totally devoid of both. I am alone in my country and the struggle is desperate; everything is rotten with decay'. He comforted himself by imagining that Wilson had gone mad and that 'his thirty-two teeth have come loose from his jaw and entered his brain'.

In Dalmatia the situation was deteriorating. In Fiume, occupied by the French, some soldiers had taken Italian cockades from children, and agitators were threatening a repetition of the Sicilian Vespers. In October 1918, Grossich, heading a National Council, had declared Fiume Italian. This town of fifty thousand inhabitants certainly included a strong Italian majority, but it had been a free town for centuries, the enemy of Venice; above all, it was the port of Hungary, as Trieste was the port of Austria. Meanwhile, the ministry announced that d'Annunzio was preparing an air expedition from Rome to Tokyo and that he would be leaving almost immediately; the Paris Conference decided that, in order to avoid friction, the Italian and French troops stationed in Fiume should be replaced by British troops. D'Annunzio returned to Venice to be closer to the centre of events. If he had remained in Rome, would he really have fomented a conspiracy? By taking advantage of his immense popularity, he could undoubtedly have seized power and perhaps re-enacted the exploits of Cola di Rienzo. But he was destined for a scene less illustrious than Rome, for he preferred action to intrigue, the army to the crowd. Perhaps, also, he had not found in the Duke of Aosta the ally he had hoped to find, though it seems likely that the Duchess of Aosta, like her ancestor Philippe Égalité, Duc d'Orléans, would have had few scruples in removing the senior branch from the throne and reigning with d'Annunzio as dictator. (The duchess's grandfather, the Duc de Montpensier, had also tried to take advantage of general disorder and replace his sister-in-law, the Queen of Spain.)

The heroes of these troubled times owed it to themselves to consult the future: d'Annunzio would not have been a true Renaissance figure if he had failed to observe such rites. And who better than the Marchesa Casati could provide a link with the powers of darkness? In the *campagna*, among the tombs in the middle of the night, the lovers summoned the spirits as Benvenuto Cellini had done at the Coliseum. It was never known what answers these amateur necromancers received, but one can imagine the diabolical attire that the marchesa must have invented for such a ceremony. In the *Notturno*, d'Annunzio had just written: 'All is mere dream and occult destiny and predestination of the will.'

18

Fiume

In the early days of September 1919, d'Annunzio appeared frequently in society, apparently absorbed in his new love Luisa Bàccara and in music. On the 9th he gave a dinner in honour of Ida Rubinstein: 'She will dance for us to the music of Florent Schmitt . . . I have asked her to come to the *Casetta Rossa* for eight o'clock, in the silver jacket and the white and black shawl . . . I am full of sadness, but also of hope. And I constantly hear the beautiful and valiant voice singing "Italia! Italia!" ' Then he pretended to make preparations for the Rome-Tokyo flight. On the 10th he invited Luisa to an evening with some 'conspirators' from the Sardinian Brigade. As a farewell, she sang *Fuori i barbari*. The next morning he wrote to Luisa: 'Yesterday I had a fever of 39! This morning it is down. But I am leaving. I must.' He also wrote to Mussolini, who during the past two months had assumed a great importance in his life: 'The die is cast. I am leaving now. Tomorrow morning I shall take Fiume by arms. May the God of Italy help us. I got up from my bed with a fever. But it is not possible to delay. Once again the spirit will overcome the miserable flesh . . . Uphold the cause vigorously throughout the conflict.'

This was the letter of a leader to a second-in-command. In his diary the poet scribbled a few lines which show clearly that Fiume was a pretext, that he expected to secure power from the reconquered city rather than from the capital. He was deceiving himself: Fiume was a great adventure, but one in which he was to founder. This expedition was not really arranged by d'Annunzio, but was presented to him, like a fine horse that would take him a little too far. It is a great pity that d'Annunzio did not himself write the story of the intrigues which had grown out of disappointments, of the disappointments which he transformed into an ideal, and of the ideal which degenerated into violence. He would have achieved the tone of lofty contempt that is to be found in the memoirs of Cardinal de Retz. But oratory seemed to him a monument more worthy of such an enterprise; when one reads the innumerable speeches, the absurdity of the whole escapade is all the more apparent.

D'Annunzio and three companions were taken by car to Ronchi, not far from Trieste. There he found the conspirators—the officers and non-commissioned officers who had just left Fiume, and the comrades of the raids which he had led by land and sea. Most of them were deserters from an army they no longer wished to serve, an army which they considered to have been dishonoured by the peace treaties. Had they been captured before the raid began, they would probably have been shot. D'Annunzio knew well what power a leader wields over those who, having abandoned all, prefer death to failure; these patriots, some of them desperate men, who quickly came to be known as the 'Arditi', proved admirable companions but were intolerable as soldiers unless each day brought them some new opportunity for heroism.

Forty trucks were due to arrive from Trieste; as they were late, d'Annunzio addressed his handful of faithfuls, the Sardinian grenadiers: 'Yesterday, as I was about to leave, I wrote, to a companion in faith and in violence: "The die is cast. I am leaving now. Tomorrow morning I shall take Fiume by arms." The writing was in the best ink. Now I must—do you hear me?—I must take the town!' The forty lorries had to be requisitioned from a neighbouring camp; they were soon packed with soldiers. Other troops supplied by General Badoglio rapidly joined the vehicles, seven battalions in all, including a battalion of *bersaglieri* and a large number of officers. A little later, four hundred sailors arrived from Trieste. The ill-assorted column set off to follow the first vehicles, which were travelling at full speed.

At dawn the convoy had moved off along roads broken up by war, the commander, wrapped in a fur greatcoat, riding in front with four lieutenants, in a large open general's car with brasses gleaming and horn shrieking. Five armoured cars led the way. The adventure began cheerfully: 'The first resistances were swept aside by our assurance and the first threats stifled by our laughter.' At Castua the column found the road blocked by the troops of General Pittaluga. A Plutarchian dialogue ensued between Pittaluga and d'Annunzio, who was allowed to pass. As soon as the French and British officers saw the column of dust rising from the winding road that led down into Fiume, they decided not to risk the lives of their men and gave the order to lower the flag and prepare to move off. The British officer who went out to meet the Comandante's car later admitted to one of the latter's men that, although they were few in number, their sheer energy seemed to multiply them a hundredfold, and the fact that they had burnt their boats gave them strength. This rather un-English sentiment might almost be taken from *La Gloria* or *La Vita di Cola di Rienzo*. The poet was about to fulfil a destiny which he had already worked out in his imagination. No other writer, not even Byron, had succeeded in giving History the form of his own fantasies; but, alas, the alloy of d'Annunzio's mould was ill-blended, the founder was losing his touch.

IMAGINATION IN POWER

On the square in front of the town hall the entire Italian population of Fiume, roughly thirty thousand people, acclaimed d'Annunzio and his liberators. Flags were put up, songs were sung, and the poet uttered immortal words: 'Italians of Fiume . . .

here I am . . . Today I wish to say nothing more . . . Here is the man who has abandoned everything to be wholly at the service of your cause . . . Here I am. I have come to give myself entirely . . .' The speech, which makes long reading but must surely have been marvellous to hear, ended with these words: 'I the volunteer, I who have fought in all arms, I the wounded and the mutilated, I reply to the deep anxiety of my country by declaring the city of Fiume today restored for ever to mother Italy.'

D'Annunzio installed himself in a huge white palace, vaguely Magyar in style, which had been built by the municipality. Soon, casts of Michelangelo, banners and a grand piano had given it a d'Annunzian atmosphere. The rapidity of his success and the ovations went to his head. A letter written to the wisest of his political friends, the senator Albertini, who was also editor of the *Corriere della Sera*, reeks of megalomania. D'Annunzio urged Albertini to stir up opinion in his favour, which Albertini was careful not to do, for it was becoming clear to Italians that Fiume was only a springboard from which d'Annunzio hoped to gain control of the central power. Those who had acclaimed him in Rome a few months earlier now wondered if, after such an escapade, they were not about to entrust themselves to an irresponsible man. Mussolini, while not sparing in his praise, was to offer little support. The government, guessing the hero's intentions, deliberately avoided mentioning the affair and took precautions to prevent it from going any further. A blockade was organized which d'Annunzio's admirers made only partially effective, then it was decided to send an army and a fleet; but, ultimately, Fiume remained a local question and d'Annunzio the prisoner of his own victory.

While awaiting the opportunity to achieve mightier ambitions, the Comandante and his comrades regarded the administration of the little town as an end in itself, and decided to make it a model city in a Europe suffocated by capitalism. Fiume was a political experiment conducted in a vacuum, with that admixture of Viennese operetta characteristic of the Balkans—a Utopia which became more and more unreal as contacts with the outside world diminished. Unfortunately, the heroism of the soldiers soon gave way to brigandage and the eloquence of their leader became a delirium of words. Nearly every day, for sixteen months, d'Annunzio would appear on the balcony of his residence to reply amicably to the questions of the crowd, to make proclamations and threats against the hostile powers, and to lay the foundations of a new society with sublime phrases. The mornings were devoted to the army. Wakened by the reveille (as was the whole town), the Comandante would go to the drill-ground, returning quite late to lunch with his staff. The afternoons were filled with audiences and diplomacy, the evenings with music; always in a simple uniform which gave him a youthful look, d'Annunzio would play with a dagger (all the 'Arditi' carried daggers), his fine hands clenched round the hilt, as in a Florentine portrait. La Bàccara had arrived in the waggon-train, and so the Comandante could allow his decisions to mature to the strains of Beethoven's sonatas.

Before retracing the brief existence of the principality of Fiume, which was soon to be called the 'Regency of Carnaro' rather than the 'Republic of Carnaro', the title favoured by many, let us read the portrait of the Comandante left by two young English aesthetes, Osbert and Sacheverell Sitwell, who had been drawn to this Byronic figure. For the visitors the adventure began at Trieste station, where Slav peasants in folk costumes stared at the soldiers, dressed in the best Romantic tradition—eagle's plumes, daggers and black silk cravats. Young men eager to be enlisted in the 'Arditi' were slipping into the trains, asking for the officers' protection so that they could cross a frontier which was being guarded both by the Allies, who were anxious not to see the little army increase, and by the Regency, which already had too many mouths to feed. After passing along the vast docks (Fiume was the port for Hungary), where the flotilla that had joined d'Annunzio lay moored, the two Englishmen found themselves confronted with a town of modest size: 'Then the sun sparkled and it was possible to appreciate the disposition of the place, with its clustered houses and its bay, a spur of hills sinking into the opalescence of the far seas, and the quivering misty outlines of the islands.' On the square the governor had placed two flag-staffs, an idea imitated from his beloved Venice. All through the day a motley crowd loitered there: 'The general animation and noisy vitality seemed to herald a new land, a new system . . . Every man here seemed to wear a uniform designed by himself: some had beards, and had shaved their heads completely, so as to resemble the Commander himself, who was now bald; others had cultivated huge tufts of hair, half a foot long, waving out from their foreheads, and wore, balanced on the very back of the skull, a black fez.' There were also some Garibaldian veterans, with red shirts and white hair, and women in much more sober uniforms. Sir Osbert Sitwell continues:

'The hill was steep and we walked up it slowly to the Palace, built in the well-known Renaissance-elephantoid style that is the dream of every Municipal Council the world over . . . Every-thing was large and square—but in fact not quite large enough. You entered a large square hall, with pillars supporting a square gallery. D'Annunzio's love of the exotic had caused this apart-ment to be filled with hundreds of pale plaster flower-pots of every size, but all incised with Byzantine patterns or Celtic trellis, and containing palms and succulents. Soldiers lounged among the greenery, and typists rushed furiously through swing-doors. In the square gallery, and leading out of the side situated nearest the sea, were the rooms of the poet, always closely guarded: because he would often remain for eighteen hours at a time shut up in his apartment, and during these periods of thought he would take no food and must on no account be disturbed. Today, as it happened, one of these stretches of work had begun, and in consequence, since no-one knew when he would return to life, we were forced to pass two days of an in-credible monotony, broken solely by a lecture on the political situation of the Regency of Carnaro, which was delivered to us by the Foreign Minister. This gentleman held the unique distinction of being the only bore in Fiume . . . At five o'clock the following evening we were, accordingly, conducted to D'Annunzio's study. Our sole interview with him lasted only three-quarters of an hour, but it would be impossible soon to forget it . . . As we entered, I recall, a Portuguese journalist was just being shown out, reiterating fulsomely in Italian as he stepped backward out of the presence: "The Portuguese nation regards you as the Christ of the Latin World—the Christ of the Latin World—the . . ." When he had gone, in the ensuing silence, the repetition of the words could still be heard from the next room, and then gradually died away . . . The study was fairly large, and contained little furniture. Its walls were almost entirely covered with banners. On the inner side, supported by brackets, stood stiffly two gilded saints from Florence, their calm, wide-open eyes gazing out over the deepening shades of the Fiumian sea . . . At the central desk sat the Commander himself, with his pomegranate in front of him, behind inkstand and pens . . . The first thing that struck one was that he bore a distinct resemblance to Igor Stravinsky . . . The poet wore many ribbons and on his left shoulder carried the Italian Gold Medal for valour, the equivalent of our Victoria Cross. Though he was completely and grotesquely bald, though only his left eye remained—for he had lost the other in the war—, though he was nervous and exhausted, yet at the end of a few seconds the extraordinary charm he possessed, which had enabled him on many occasions to change mobs of enemies into furious partisans, had exercised itself on us' (*Noble Essences*).

D'Annunzio asked his visitors: 'Well, what new poets are there in England?' He talked to them of Shelley, whose death he wished to emulate at the age of fifteen, in the bay of Castellammare, and of greyhound-racing which, with poetry, he probably considered England's greatest title to glory. He described his confrontations with the people from his balcony, claiming that never since Greek times had such dialogues taken place. But he admitted his loneliness; the man who had always been surrounded with music and books found himself having to live among peasants and soldiers; perhaps the Italian government was hoping to make him leave out of boredom. Osbert Sitwell also tells of d'Annunzio's admission that he arranged mock battles to occupy his legionaries, who were likewise easily bored. One of these battles was organized in honour of a visiting orchestra; there was a long list of casualties, including a few musicians.

The soldiers found an outlet for their energies by plundering the inland villages, either in bands or in organized raids. Confident that the Comandante would always forgive them, they resorted to extortion and violence on such a scale that they were soon hated by the people of Fiume. The licence of the army knew no bounds, no more than the private life of its Comandante. Not content with seducing girls, the legionaries fought among themselves with knives to gain the favours of the young volunteers and carried off shepherd-boys. D'Annunzio closed his eyes to the morals of his Theban legion and on more than one occasion shared its pleasures. Three of his most brilliant comrades in Fiume were known for their homosexual relationships: Giovanni Commisso, Enrico Furst and Léon Kochnitzky. The first two were to write novels about sailors: Commisso wrote *In the Wind of the Adriatic* and Furst, who rather curiously was both an Anglophile and an admirer of Charles Maurras, *Simoun.* Kochnitzky, a Belgian Jew, wrote an excellent account of Fiume and also books on art. They all lived at a pitch of emotional exaltation which found its most familiar image in the beauty of the soldiers. The Comandante wrote: 'A well-trained greyhound or race-horse, the legs of Ida Rubinstein, the body of a true Ardito returning from the fords of the Piave, are among the most expressive beauties in the world.'

Fiume could not offer d'Annunzio magnificent women like those he had known in Florence and Paris. The jealous Luisa Bàccara quickly ejected the adventuresses who wormed their way into the palace; nothing escaped her. This twenty-five-year-old pianist was a strange creature, full of duplicity and devotion. Why, since she was so jealous, had she invited her sister to live with her? She knew that sisters invariably excited the lover. Yet she succeeded in asserting her personality, in persuading people of her genius by attitudes of profundity. When she played Bach: 'The first notes are laid like the foundations of a cathedral . . . At the organ she is a sibyl.' These words and the portrait that follows are taken from the *Ritratto di Aloisia Bàccaris* which the master of Fiume found time to write: 'The lines and planes of the face are simple and clean, arranged with a severity that is softened by melancholy only towards the base . . . Between the powerful arches of the brows the nose descends straight and slender . . . The mouth has an ambiguous life between the upper lip, shaped like a Cretan bow, and the contradiction of the lower lip with its soft pouting and its braced firmness. But her whole vigour rests in the neck . . . one is reminded of the nape of a caryatid supporting a vast, sonorous edifice . . . Her bushy, arid hair, like that of the frenzied Maenads, is composed of black strands, tawny strands and white strands arranged in masses whose intermingling is a secret of the night.' Imperious and possessive, the pianist soon made herself hated. D'Annunzio's comrades accused her of keeping him away from them and sapping his vitality; she became a public enemy who would have to be struck down. D'Annunzio, warned in time, sent the conspirators on a mission. And yet, at the piano, Luisa Bàccara became the incarnation of resistance. 'This little untamed Italian is a vital force of the city of life.' In rooms packed with soldiers, she would play Bach and Beethoven, then she would finish by standing at the keyboard and singing the song of Ronchi: '*Fratelli, fratelli, lodiamo il Dio vivente*'; whereupon 'the Arditi, long-haired like the Achaeans, would brandish their daggers at each refrain, making her a crown of vengeance'.

DAILY SUBLIMITY

The story of Fiume, which was only of minor importance in the mighty currents of the aftermath of war, was as rich in heroic episodes as the little wars of primitive Greece. The most colourful took place at sea. The prestige of the hero of Buccari was still immense among sailors, and several ships allowed themselves to be diverted from their route by the Comandante's flotilla, or even came of their own choice to swell his forces and replenish his stocks. Only a few days after occupying Fiume, d'Annunzio, for once listening to reasonable advice, abandoned the idea of taking Trieste, but as a result he found himself almost a prisoner on the land side. A projected union with the Croats, who had no desire to become part of the new kingdom of Yugoslavia, came to nothing, as did a chimerical alliance with the King of Montenegro, driven from his state by the same new kingdom. The accounts of the sixteen months of Fiume's occupation are mostly contradictory, distorted by hatred or by the desire to please the new master of Italy. At first, in a Europe that had been convulsed from Ireland to the Caucasus, Fiume was seen by dreamers as the great hope. Combatants came from all parts, but there were also the drop-outs, those who liked to fish in troubled waters and who found this part of the world more suitable for their ventures than the countries overrun by Communist revolutions. These parasites were as heavy a burden as the Arditi on the citizens of Fiume, who soon began to long for the return of the Austrians; it was the adventurers who earned the Regency of Carnaro its bad reputation.

It was possible to enter and leave the encircled city, but difficult enough to give every move a conspiratorial air. The most notable visitor was the Duchess of Aosta, in charge of the Red Cross which was bringing supplies. A fervent patriot and an admirer of the poet, the duchess attended the burial of a young hero, as if she were queen, and probably tried to gather together the threads of a conspiracy that would have placed her husband on the throne. Perhaps it was with such a *coup* in mind that d'Annunzio refused to declare Fiume a republic, preferring the title of Regency, which suggested a link with the monarchy. A few months later, he rejected another plan put forward by Mussolini, who wanted to overthrow the monarchy, intern the members of the House of Savoy on an island, and impose on Italy a republican triumvirate. The Duchess of Aosta's stay with d'Annunzio greatly annoyed the king, however. The other visitor of distinction was Marconi, the developer of radio and the most famous Italian in the world at that time after d'Annunzio and Caruso. From the yacht *Elettra*, the Comandante broadcast a message to the world. There were also a number of not very famous musicians, a Japanese poet, Harikuci Scimoi, and some young Italian writers; but, with the exception of Marcel Boulenger, who spent a week in Fiume, d'Annunzio's French friends did not make an appearance. However, four young volunteers came from Paris, led by Philippe d'Estailleurs Chantereine, a charming man highly esteemed by the French pretender, the Duc de Guise; these young romantics were disciples of Charles Maurras.

The most important Italian politicians kept their distance from d'Annunzio. De Nitti, the prime minister, was given the nickname 'Cagoia' ('the shit'—the language of the barrack-room was spoken in Fiume: on his personal banners the Comandante had had embroidered the motto *Me ne frega*—'I don't give a damn'). De Nitti, cleverer than most of the other politicians and no more dishonest, was replaced by Giolitti, who was hated even more by d'Annunzio, for he had mutilated the poet's patriotic ode in 1912. These two statesmen, swallowing the insults, spun around Fiume a spider's web which, though fragile at first and frequently penetrated, finally isolated d'Annunzio's Regency. Negotiations were never broken off, for both parties, as good Italians, abhorred final ruptures. General (later Marshal) Badoglio acted as intermediary between Rome and Fiume. In Milan, Mussolini was giving d'Annunzio his support, primarily through his newspaper; he also organized a collection, only a small part of which reached Fiume (a little money and provisions came from the Italians of the Argentine and the United States). In their effusive correspondence the poet and the demagogue both maintained a certain reserve, which enabled each to claim later that he had intended to hoodwink the other. But on the whole Mussolini could be counted as a brother.

Among the visitors to Fiume was Alceste De Ambris, a veteran of the trade-union struggles who had exercised a great influence on Mussolini. D'Annunzio charmed this austere champion of the workers, who remained loyal to him; the poet, for his part, accepted all sorts of demagogic measures proposed by De Ambris when the question of providing a constitution for the Regency arose. In complete contrast with this old professor, the aviator Guido Keller, a romantic and alluring young giant with a red beard, whom d'Annunzio listened to a good deal, urged all kinds of follies. He flew over Rome to drop a chamber-pot on the Parliament on the day of Giolitti's speech and to release a dove over the Vatican, with a message urging the Holy See to return to the austerity of St. Francis; he also dropped a bunch of red roses on the palace where the queen mother lived. Marinetti came to Fiume, for he loved the excitement of danger, and several of the Futurists accompanied him, but there was never any bond established between d'Annunzio and a movement wholly contrary to his own aesthetic creed. As for the faithful Antongini, he had been given the thankless role of ambassador at the Paris Conference. Rebuffs, wild hopes, long-winded documents, fine-spun but irrelevant negotiations, futility—these formed the daily routine of his mission, which achieved nothing except to invest the secretary with a prestige that he had hitherto lacked.

The history of the Regency of Carnaro can be divided into three phases, during which the various persons just mentioned, together with innumerable military personnel, spies and op-portunists, played their respective parts, some at the scene of events, others from a distance. The first phase, lasting a little over a month, was that of the régime's installation, the time of wild hopes and proclamations to the world. It could be called the 'springboard' phase. Immediately, difficulties arose between the three powers which were never precisely demarcated: the Com-andante, the National Council and the military. Each had its own police. Exciting but ineffectual sea 'raids' encouraged the Comandante and his men to believe that war was the most marvellous of games and that nothing could resist them. On 10 November 1919, d'Annunzio, on a gunboat at the head of his little fleet, landed at Zara amid scenes of tremendous enthusiasm.

Admiral Milo, the Yugoslav governor of Dalmatia, swore he would not abandon an inch of the territory awarded by the Treaty of London. This escapade caused Rome to tighten the blockade and aroused the indignation of the British government; Lloyd George called Fiume 'the shame of Italy'. Mussolini received this reprimand: 'I am surprised by yourself and by the Italian people. I have risked all, I have given all, I have possessed all. I am master of Fiume—the territory itself, a part of the armistice line and the ships; and of the soldiers, who intend to obey no one but me. There is nothing that can be done against me. Nobody can tear me from here. I have Fiume; as long as I live I shall keep Fiume, unconditionally. And you tremble with fear! You let yourself be grabbed by the collar by the most miserable pig among all the rogues who have ever adorned the history of the universal rabble . . . If only half of Italy were like the people of Fiume, we would rule the world. But what is Fiume, save a solitary peak of heroism where it will be sweet to die swallowing one last gulp of limpid air? There is nothing then to hope for? What about your promises? At least lance the belly that weighs you down and give it some air. Otherwise, it is I who will come when I have consolidated my power. But I shall not look you in the face. Come! Shake yourselves, you loafers enjoying your siesta! For six nights I have not slept, and I am gripped with fever. But I am still standing. If you want to know *how*, go and ask anyone who has seen me.'

The second phase, much the longest and marked by incidents both violent and picturesque, revealed d'Annunzio's incapacity as a statesman and even as a conspirator, for he had not been able to leap to Rome from his Dalmatian springboard. This was the period of political dissensions, when generals were arrested and admirals departed, and during which the quality of the new recruits dropped rapidly. The best troops, weary of skirmishes with the Arditi, wanted to return to the regular army. A feebly gerrymandered plebiscite failed to reassure the population; every morning in the newspaper and every evening from his balcony, d'Annunzio would give a boost to the town's morale. But how great an effort it cost him! This man who had always lived intensely would not recognize that routine is the worst enemy of the sublime, that a state of emergency cannot be prolonged indefinitely without inviting either catastrophe or ridicule, and without wearying even the most favourably disposed spectators. From time to time, his flotillas would bring back a freighter and its rich cargo, and for a few weeks there was no danger of starving to death. These seizures placed Italy in a difficult position and alienated middle-class opinion. One of the most spectacular captures was the cargo-ship *Persia*, en route for the Far East, loaded with provisions for Admiral Kolchak, munitions, champagne and uniforms. The pirates brought their booty ashore by night, in a gleam of torches. On another evening, they seized a strong-box from a steamer en route for Albania. When they broke the box open, gold coins and packets of bank-notes poured out, some three million lire in all. Kochnitzky, in his account of these doughty deeds, says that the torchlit scene looked like a painting by Delacroix. The National Federation of Sailors, well-disposed towards d'Annunzio in whom it saw the champion of Socialism, jeered at the fury of the shipowners.

The third phase covers a little over four months, from the anniversary of the march from Ronchi until Christmas 1920. Celebrating a year in power, d'Annunzio proclaimed the necessity for an independent State of Fiume, denouncing traitors and the faint-hearted. To talk of treachery was a sign that things were beginning to go badly. On 30 August 1920 the National Council resigned. The 'Carnaro Charter' published shortly afterwards is an interesting document for historians of Utopia. Its Socialist leanings show the influence of De Ambris, but d'Annunzio attached most importance to the last chapter of the 'New Order of the City of Fiume', which was devoted to music. At the end of August, Mussolini made a number of recommendations that sound more like instructions: 'March on Trieste. Declare the downfall of the monarchy. Appoint a governing directory with yourself as president. Organize elections for the Constituent Assembly. Proclaim the annexation of Fiume. Send loyal troops to land in Romagna [Ravenna], in the Marches [Ancona] and in the Abruzzi, to help the republican uprising.' D'Annunzio no longer possessed the energy for such an enterprise, even though he had been offered the presidency. He had allowed himself to become entangled in the day-to-day politics of Fiume; boredom was a constant hazard, and secretly he longed for an end to the whole business. There was a succession of 'raids', more or less successful, to keep the Arditi occupied, interviews with admirals in the government, and defections of senior officers no longer prepared to tolerate mismanagement. This was a period of frequent harangues. In his speech of 24 October, d'Annunzio preached 'the new crusade of all poor and free men against the usurping nations who are monopolizing all wealth, against the caste of men who live well in wartime and continue to live well in time of peace'. He wrote to Henri Barbusse to congratulate him on the victory of the proletariat against Kolchak's army. He wanted to establish a link with Moscow; he was indignant for Ireland, for Egypt and for India, oppressed by the signatories of Versailles.

The Treaty of Rapallo, concluded between Yugoslavia and Italy on 12 November 1920, endorsed Wilson's idea by declaring Fiume a free city. Naturally, d'Annunzio refused to recognize the treaty, though it did not contradict what he had himself proposed, and he attacked General Caviglia, who had come to ensure that the treaty was observed. On 29 November he wrote to Marcel Boulenger: 'I am in the greatest danger. *Morituri te salutant.*' The elections which had just been held in Italy, and in which not a single Fascist had been successful, had persuaded Mussolini of the necessity of coming to terms with the forces of order and abandoning the romantic socialism of De Ambris, whose spokesman d'Annunzio had made himself. There was collusion between Mussolini and Giolitti; the latter could attack Fiume knowing that the protests of the Fascists would be purely verbal. This sense of isolation stirred the Comandante. His notebooks during these last months of his reign are covered with feverish jottings: 'The feeling that we are acting at the very heart of the world. The remoteness, the anxiety, the hostile nations . . . Sense of historic inevitability . . . The atrocious song—the excitement—walking in the old town—the women weeping—the officers singing in the lower room, the kissing of hands and the sighs. The *aura del Soviet*—the intoxication of liberty—the passion for women . . .' There was another reason for this feverishness. D'Annunzio was beginning to take cocaine. His will-power undermined, he could now manage only theatrical effects and was incapable of following a considered plan of action. Responsibility frightened him.

WITH THE HONOURS OF WAR

At the beginning of December, the sailors of the little fleet of Fiume weighed anchor and rejoined the Italian royal navy. All the best men, disheartened or even disgusted, were abandoning Fiume. The poet's speeches now thrilled only the populace and the mercenaries. Giolitti, sensing that the time was ripe, tightened the blockade. On 21 December, both on land and at sea, the regular troops clashed with the legionaries: four men were killed. On the 25th a counter-attack was repulsed. General Caviglia then ordered the cruiser *Andrea Doria* to open fire on the government palace, which looked out over the town and presented an easy target. A shell struck the window from which, a few seconds previously, the 'Regent' had been observing the enemy through his telescope. D'Annunzio was slightly wounded: 'Oh! cowards of Italy, I am still alive and implacable. Though yesterday I had prepared myself for sacrifice and fortified my soul, today I am preparing to defend my life with every weapon. During my war I offered my life hundreds of times and with a smile. But today it is not worth throwing it away in the service of a people that does not care to be distracted even for a moment from its greedy Christmas revelries, while its government with cold determination murders a people of sublime courage, who for sixteen months have suffered and struggled at our side and are never weary of suffering and struggling . . .'

These fine words sounded the death-knell for Fiume. The mayor and the apostolic delegate had a long discussion with the

Comandante and then went to find the general who had arrived from Rome. The general told them that operations would continue until Fiume subscribed to the Treaty of Rapallo. To avoid the massacre of the population (surely an imaginary danger), d'Annunzio and the Regency Council resigned and a truce was called. All this happened without causing a ripple in the public opinion of Europe. The old fox Giolitti had chosen the right moment to fell his enemy, for the Christmas holiday prevented newspapers from appearing for three days. Everything had been settled by the time that the world learned of the city's surrender. On 2 January the Comandante appeared for the last time as head of the city, at a ceremony at the cemetery, before thirty-three coffins—ten Italian soldiers and twenty-three legionaries who had been killed on the last day of the resistance. To reach the cemetery, situated on a steep hillside, the mourners had to climb hundreds of steps. Women in black veils laid laurel-wreaths on the coffins. After a prayer by the bishop, d'Annunzio said a few words, much more touching than all his speeches: 'If He who wept beside the grave of Lazarus appeared among the lighted candles and the extinguished lives, if He appeared and raised these dead enemies to life, I believe they would rise only to sob, to forgive and embrace each other.' He knelt among the soldiers and the weeping women, then went down to shut himself in his palace.

On that day Italians were ashamed of allowing themselves to be governed by reasonable people. They despised ministers and Parliament, and dreamed of a new order.

De Nitti finally replied to all the insults with these unjust words: 'D'Annunzio entered Fiume as a combatant and hero, calling himself the "Corsair of the Adriatic". He left without glory, as a man, as a calculating individual who was altogether too shrewd.' Yet, despite the mutual contempt and resentment, the great Italian rule of life, *fare bella figura*, was respected on both sides. D'Annunzio left Fiume with head held high and the government congratulated itself that the city had fallen with so little damage. The autonomist party led by Zanella assumed power; two years later, the Fascists obtained its resignation and in 1924 the Yugoslavs recognized the *fait accompli:* Fiume was Italian. The reverse of this glorious medal was to be the insurmountable hostility of Yugoslavia towards Italy.

D'Annunzio did not leave the city until 18 January, surprised, perhaps, that his downfall had passed almost unnoticed by the world. Like his dramas, the Fiume affair had lasted too long and the public, gorged with heroism, had yawned. Might he have been consoled if he had known that, at this very moment, a French writer whom he had possibly seen briefly at the house of Anna de Noailles was thinking of inserting a homage to the poet-conqueror in his novel? Proust eventually omitted these pages, which were to have appeared in the Venetian episode of *À la recherche du temps perdu,* after giving them to the newspaper *Le Matin,* which published them in December 1919. M. de Norpois is explaining Fiume to Mme. de Villeparisis: 'Well, in spite of what I thought, De Nitti is not a Fiumist, though I believed d'Annunzio to be a true *ad latus* of his. At the minister's there was a completely unknown French writer, Marcel—I cannot recall his surname—who is ardently for d'Annunzio: he compares this man's voluntary exile in France with that of Dante; he has composed in advance, or rather in retrospect, three lines of Virgil in which Aeneas, passing by Fiume, evokes d'Annunzio; he quoted a line of Hugo, perhaps from *Le Petit Roi de Galice,* where the method of capturing cities is very similar to d'Annunzio's, and it seems that even in d'Annunzio's plays the soil oozes a historic past. But the Italian government takes the matter more seriously, if not more tragically. It naturally wants to save face. But there is no question of treating d'Annunzio as a hero, or even giving him a free hand. They want, somehow or other, to reduce him to unconditional surrender . . .'

19

Politics

In the eyes of Europe, d'Annunzio was leaving Fiume rather as a star quits the stage after occupying it for too long; the applause he received was prompted to a large degree by a feeling of relief, and even a touch of pity, for his style was no longer fashionable. But the Comandante was surrounded by too much brouhaha to be aware of this detachment on Europe's part; there were too many admirers, too many people who, having thrown in their lot with his, had everything to lose by his withdrawal. In an Italy sadly lacking in great men, d'Annunzio remained the outstanding figure of the war and now, naturally enough, became the outstanding political figure, the man who would lead his country towards a glory of which it had been defrauded by the Treaty of Versailles, towards an order which the country's immense social problems were daily making more difficult to achieve. To the enthusiasts he was a banner, to more reasonable people a vainglorious makeshift. Against him d'Annunzio had the royal court and the government (no great obstacle, it is true), but also the Vatican. It would be futile to retrace in detail the intrigues which, from January 1921 to August 1923, first brought d'Annunzio close to power, then removed it from his grasp, until a curious accident forced him to quit public life once and for all. In all the manoeuvrings, in all the speeches that stirred an enfeebled, frustrated and ruined Italy, though enthusiasm and *combinazione* played an equal part, there could be no questioning the patriotism of the protagonists, however different their aims.

The events with which this narrative is now concerned can be seen in a very different light, according to whether the witnesses of these events wrote of them during the period of the Fascist triumph or after its collapse. Should d'Annunzio be regarded as the St. John the Baptist of Fascism, or as its prisoner? No answer to this question has yet been agreed, and d'Annunzio himself played each role in turn. The truth is that he was, above all, the prisoner of his own image, of his love of luxury and his role of enchanter, a prisoner weakened by pleasure and by the increasingly frequent use of cocaine. Even so, the ambiguity remains, for in his mind he remained quite free, often caring little about his reputation provided that he retained the use of his prodigious intellectual faculties. Beside this life of the spirit which the poet sought constantly, glory, women and money were merely so many proofs of the vanity of an existence to which he clung in spite of himself. Never were these contradictions more evident than in these latter years of his life, years of extravagance and shame, but still illuminated by flashes of genius, as if old age and drugs were accelerating the pendulum movement that had always carried the poet to and fro between the sublime and the sordid. One may well be amazed by the man, but all judgements would be unjust, all moralizing absurd.

D'Annunzio left Fiume, amid flowers and tears, on 18 January 1921. Why had he dallied in the city after renouncing power? What had he been hoping for during those nineteen days? It is impossible to know. A car took him to Mestre where, waiting for him in a motor-boat, were Antongini and a naval officer, but no one else. Was this the beginning of an exile? The Comandante, dressed in his wolfskin greatcoat, his head almost hidden by a cap of the same material, embraced his companions without a word; vague glimmers of light could be seen through the mist that lay across the lagoon. It was dark by the time they moored in front of the black pilasters of the Barbarigo palace. Aelis was waiting for her master; she had decorated a superb apartment as best she could with the things bought during the stay at the *Casetta Rossa* (which had been returned to Prince Hohenlohe), with furniture from Arcachon that Romaine Brooks had salvaged and books saved from *La Capponcina*. In the empty rooms cases were piled up waiting to be opened, and the next day waggons arrived from Fiume with all the Regency documents, and also tapestries, weapons and La Bàccara's piano.

This removal operation started rumours of war booty. In his memoirs, the minister De Nitti openly accused d'Annunzio of having taken his share of the plunder seized by his pirate fleet. In fact, it was the same as with his rich mistresses: d'Annunzio was not a calculating person where money was concerned. He may have lived off the enemy, but he did not deliberately set out to pillage him. In any case, he had not returned from Fiume as rich as his detractors claimed, for he was soon piling up debts again. Despite the large royalties he received, he would with irresistible good grace demand enormous sums for articles (Hearst was still the best customer) and films (after *Cabiria*, still a great success, a film of *La Nave* was made with Ida Rubinstein). *Notturno*, published by the faithful Treves, was a triumph which enabled the author to secure an even more advantageous contract from Mondadori.

The money was coming in again, but not in sufficient quantity to allow d'Annunzio to live according to his requirements. Patriots and self-seekers offered him some fine residences, but he refused to be bound by ties of gratitude and opted for a villa, later to be called the Vittoriale, that Antongini had discovered on a hill overlooking Lake Garda, among the vines and olive-trees, near the village of Cargnacco. This simple and comfortable house, surrounded by cypresses, was a smaller version of *La Capponcina*, with terraces bordered by rose-trees and paths running down between the azaleas to the lake. Through the trees could be seen the great hotels of Gardone, the villas situated in ever-flowering gardens which give this shore the appearance of a luxurious suburb. The often misted lake and the distant mountains offered nothing dramatic; few architectural monuments, a luxuriant and carefully tended vegetation that suggests a botanical garden, and comic-opera villages. Switzerland was not far away. In such a setting it became rather unrealistic to try to evoke comparisons with St. Helena even when he wanted to do so. The position between Venice and Milan—between pleasure and business—was perfect: sufficiently isolated, but near the great international routes. After a brief stay in the Barbarigo palace, where he was an object of curiosity rather than of fervour, harassed by faithful followers who were expecting another grand escapade, and ill-informed about the state of Italy, the poet announced that the Comandante was making way for Gabriele d'Annunzio. The decision to establish himself at Gardone, while bringing him the rest that he needed, also allayed the fears of his political enemies. The hero was becoming a writer once again. So much the better!

The villa had attracted d'Annunzio because, quite apart from its comfort, it was imbued with the prestige of two heroes of his youth, Liszt and Wagner. The previous owner, Professor Thode, had married the daughter of Wagner and Cosima Liszt. In the rooms of the villa were still to be found Liszt's piano, portraits of Wagner, dark and mysterious German paintings, the library of Professor Thode, a great art historian, and all the imponderables that surround genius. Both Thode and Wagner's daughter were dead. The house, which was German property, had been confiscated by the Italian government and then rented to d'Annunzio at an absurdly low price. Matters became complicated when it was remembered that Thode had left a widow of Danish nationality, who had no intention of being robbed of her entire inheritance and was claiming the furniture. When she received no reply, Frau Thode, with the help of a friend, Mme. de Michaelis, quite a well-known writer, published a book in which d'Annunzio was described as a pirate; the Del Guzzo affair and some rather unpleasant gossip were dragged up. The idea of giving anything back to a German woman was inconceivable to d'Annunzio. In any case, was he not the natural heir of the geniuses who had lived in the villa before him? He kept the furniture; many years later, when d'Annunzio was dead and Hitler controlled Italy, Mussolini ordered that some articles be returned to the despoiled widow. When one visits this house, which must once have been a delightful place but is now rather sinister, one wonders if Frau Thode did not cast a spell on her villa, for it was to bring disaster to all who lived there.

SCARLET OR BLACK

Henceforth, the most important person in d'Annunzio's life, and until his death, was Mussolini. The progress of their relationship from the first meeting in Rome, in May 1919, is clearly marked by the manner in which d'Annunzio addressed Mussolini in his letters. At first, he used the friendly 'Caro Mussolini', then 'Mio caro compagno' or even 'Mio caro Benito'. After Mussolini's seizure of power at the time of the Ethiopian war, it was 'Mio Capo e Maestro' ('my chief and master'). An Italian historian has defined the relationship between the Comandante and the Duce by the adage: 'If you cannot beat your enemy, join him.' The aphorism applies appropriately enough to the theatrical aspects of their relationship, but ignores the great admiration which each of these utterly different men had for one another. For Mussolini, d'Annunzio always remained the esteemed poet, the master of the word; the head of state continued to show the man of letters the outward forms of this fervour, even when our hero exasperated him. Admittedly, it would have been clumsy of him not to have d'Annunzio on his side; but, sentimentally, a rupture would have grieved Mussolini who, to the very end, respected the master even when he had become a dotard and a nuisance. A feminine streak in d'Annunzio caused him to be drawn towards strength. This man who lived so much on his nerves could not help but be impressed by the monument of muscle. Furthermore, like the majority of Italians, and especially those of the class which he regarded as his own, the aristocracy, d'Annunzio looked on Mussolini first as a lesser evil, then as a saviour. But he was soon divided between the satisfaction of observing what the triumphant régime owed him and the chagrin of seeing another wearing the laurels that he had planted. Berenson, who had not the slightest desire to renew his acquaintance with his 'megalomaniac' neighbour of *La Capponcina*, referred to d'Annunzio as the Garibaldi of words, making his conquests with slogans and cymbals, words which, according to Berenson, Mussolini literally took from the poet's mouth to feed his partisans.

Mussolini came to see d'Annunzio at Gardone on 5 April 1921. Nothing transpired of this meeting, except that it took place in an atmosphere of the utmost cordiality. As soon as the greatness of Italy was at stake, the two men spoke the same language. Their enemies had ample opportunity to talk of complicity when they saw publicity pictures and twin effigies of the poet and the future dictator being distributed. Those close to the two men did everything they could to separate them. Mussolini's uncouth associates regarded this poet as a useless luxury in a party which they considered should stand for austerity. They even resorted to harassing tactics which, in d'Annunzio's ready imagination, made him a Napoleon at St. Helena, a Prometheus on his rock. On their side, the Comandante's romantic legionaries and his democratic mentors, such as De Ambris, sometimes managed to convince him that he should initiate an era of social justice. These men still exercised an influence on d'Annunzio, and were beginning to use his villa as a kind of hermitage; as the months passed, they had many an opportunity to remind him how badly Mussolini had behaved towards him: accepting the Treaty of Rapallo, offering only verbal support to the combatants of Fiume, making deals with the Rome government, which remained d'Annunzio's *bête noire*. Not wishing to have any contact with the official world, d'Annunzio had indignantly repudiated the offer made by the people of Trieste, who wanted to elect him as their deputy. Then, when Fiume had fallen into the hands of the Fascists, he forbade his legionaries to support that movement. Although this step did not lead to a rupture between the two men, it made

Mussolini realize that d'Annunzio was still capable of putting a spoke in the wheel.

Meanwhile, Italy was passing through an economic crisis aggravated by demands for social reform. Was Rome about to see a wave of Communism, like Berlin and Budapest? In the spring of 1922, d'Annunzio leaned towards the democratic movement; hc met Gino Baldesi, of the General Federation of Labour. Thirteen years later, at the time of the Ethiopian war, M. de Montherlant made this note about some opportunist verse composed by d'Annunzio and quickly forgotten: 'I should very much like someone to find me a Bolshevist poem by d'Annunzio (with a lyrical use of the word "red"), probably dating from 1922, the year when in Italy officers had their decorations torn off in the street. Gabriele indulging in poetic exercises on the dictatorship of the proletariat —destiny cannot be forgiven for having cheated us of such a spectacle! Unfortunately, the wind changed, and the old monkey with it. The red turned to black [that of the black-shirts]. But long live d'Annunzio all the same! Long live the old monkey!' (*Notebooks*, August 1935).

Was the visit made on 10 June by Chicherin, the People's Commissar representing Russia at the Geneva Conference, also a monkey trick? It certainly did not make d'Annunzio lean towards Russia, although shortly beforehand Lenin had declared: 'D'Annunzio is the only true Italian revolutionary', and although the poet, fascinated by the Russian experience, was thinking of writing a book on Peter the Great. D'Annunzio recounted this interview as a piece of clowning. When the commissar arrived at the villa, he said to his host: 'Thank you. You show greater courage by receiving me than I do by coming to visit you.' But, amazed by d'Annunzio's gaiety and his slightly impertinent volubility, Chicherin thought that the poet had been utterly spoiled by flattery. All this lyrical effusion seemed extraordinarily outmoded to the Russian, who at one point in the conversation said: 'In no text of my government are the words "soul" and "spirit" to be found.' To which d'Annunzio retorted: 'Do you take me for an aesthete!' In short, this was a dialogue between deaf men, summed up by d'Annunzio himself in these words written below a photo-graph of himself and the Russian: 'You think you have fooled me, but you are mistaken.'

The situation in Italy was deteriorating; strikes were paralysing the country and the government, by its weakness, was delegating responsibility for restoring order to the Fascists. All over the country there were clashes between the Socialists and Mussolini's men, but it was in Milan that the real *coup d'état* took place. On 3 August 1922 the Fascists took possession of the city hall, drove out the Socialist municipal council and declared martial law. D'Annunzio was in Milan at the time; no sooner had the city hall been occupied than a band of young Fascists ran to fetch the Comandante from his hotel, carrying him shoulder high to the balcony of the city hall. The crowd thronged round the statue of Leonardo da Vinci and clung to the lamp-posts of La Scala. An ovation erupted as soon as d'Annunzio appeared, an ovation that continued long after the end of the speech, which had been inaudible to three-quarters of the crowd (there were no microphones in those days). It was a strange speech, and Mussolini's men rubbed their hands when the enthusiasm of the crowd drowned the words. D'Annunzio spoke of goodness, an old discovery of the Tolstoyan era refurbished in his encounters with the ideologists who had come to Fiume. Admittedly, it was a d'Annunzian concept of goodness, but even so what curious language for a revolution! 'I see burning in you an efficacious, militant goodness, the goodness that asserts itself and builds fighters! a victorious goodness! ! !' Mussolini's staff officers, who were also on the balcony, caught every word of this call to fraternity and of d'Annunzio's teasing of the crowd: every time they shouted 'Long live Fascism!' he retorted 'Long live Italy!'

Mussolini, who was in regular contact with d'Annunzio during these days, drew him into a scheme that would have horrified him a few weeks earlier: it was proposed to overthrow the government by legal methods and replace it with a triumvirate consisting of d'Annunzio, Mussolini and De Nitti—De Nitti, the most despised of all the parliamentarians, the arch-enemy of

Fiume whom they had called 'Cagoia'. Together the legionaries and the black-shirts would restore the country to order. The presence of De Nitti would cover everything with a veneer of legality. A secret meeting in a Tuscan villa was arranged for 15 August. Antongini was to settle the practical details. De Nitti, no less than d'Annunzio, sincerely wanted a union of all Italians so that social peace might be restored. Had this project succeeded, these old enemies would certainly have realized soon enough that they had merely provided Mussolini with a stepping-stone, and would have returned to the shadows just as the junior consuls had faded away before the star of Bonaparte. But a curious incident thwarted these designs and left Mussolini as sole arbiter.

AN ACCIDENT?

The accident of 13 August 1922, which nearly cost the poet his life, is shrouded in a haze of contradictory explanations and reticence, on the part both of the victim and of the witnesses. It gained no place in the d'Annunzian legend, although very soon there was talk of an attempted assassination. There are two political versions of the accident. According to the anti-Fascists, the legionaries and liberals, Mussolini had sought to rid himself of a man who had become an encumbrance; according to the Fascists, it was the legionaries who, furious at a pact between Mussolini and d'Annunzio, had sentenced their leader to death. There is also a sentimental version which claims that La Bàccara, exasperated by the attentions her lover was showing to her young sister, pushed him through the window in a fit of jealousy. In the face of so many conflicting accounts, one can only relate the facts as far as they are known and try to establish a connection between the date of the accident and that of the meeting with De Nitti and Mussolini, arranged for two days later and which obviously had to be cancelled.

The scene was a large drawing-room cluttered with furniture and casts; on the walls, dark portraits of Wagner and hangings. Liszt's grand piano faced away from the window. D'Annunzio stood leaning against the low iron bars of the window, listening to the music, in a state of reverie as always. Some six feet below the window was a paved drive; the room was therefore on a raised ground floor rather than a first floor, for the leaves of the shrubbery reached up to the window. The light was fading and Luisa Bàccara had been playing for about half an hour for some friends (their number and names have never been known precisely, for the villa was open to all whom d'Annunzio had at one time or another considered his close friends, his comrades-in-arms and boon companions, and also to the new acquaintances whom celebrity had brought him). Among the guests was one of the shadiest characters of Fascism, Aldo Finzi, who a year later was to be involved in the assassination of the Socialist deputy Matteotti; Finzi was a friend of La Bàccara. At the end of the piece everyone turned towards the window, as if waiting for permission to applaud—but the shadowy figure of the master had vanished. La Bàccara rushed to the window and saw the gardeners carrying away her lover's body. The doctors, who had appeared rapidly on the scene, diagnosed a fracture of the skull and an effusion of the cerebro-spinal fluid. For two days the poet was in a coma; it was feared that his brain had been damaged. But, with an astonishing vitality, d'Annunzio regained consciousness, his intellect intact; for such a serious accident the convalescence was quite short.

Among the piles of telegrams and letters that accumulated at the poet's bedside was this cryptic message from Paul Valéry: *'Elle sait ce qu'elle fait celle qui vise à la tête'* ('She knows what she is doing who aims at the head'). Valéry must, of course, have been alluding to Death and not to the pianist, who would have had some difficulty in leaving her piano to push her lover out of the window. The temperamental Bàccara, who had been humiliated in her passion and believed she was sacrificing a great career to d'Annunzio, was not loved. Consequently, she was the first to be accused; no one at the time was prepared to call it an accident. The most severe towards Luisa Bàccara was 'Sirenetta', Renata d'Annunzio, who came to look after her father, as she had come to Venice in the war. The blundering Antigone was banished from the house as soon as she uttered one word against the musician. It must be added that most of those who were in the room, and who detested Luisa Bàccara, affirmed the pianist's innocence. Later, d'Annunzio hinted in a rather ambiguous fashion that he had tried to commit suicide. Perhaps the longing for death which always haunted him had suddenly become more urgent for a man who felt burnt out; perhaps he had let himself be carried away by an attack of dizziness, so that he would not have to face up to the great decisions expected of him at the three-man meeting which, in so many respects, must have been odious to him. Even if that meeting had assured him the position of First Consul, would he have had the strength to hold it? Perhaps a sudden vision of the responsibilities of power, of which he had suffered so many bitter experiences in Fiume, overwhelmed him with an immense weariness to which only death could bring an end. This lassitude is evident in the letter to Mussolini written on 1 December 1922: 'I cannot believe that you would hesitate to observe faithfully our first pact of brotherly peace: *iuratae foedus amicitiae*. You must free yourself from contrary advice, nearly all impure. The observance of the pact and the granting of the amnesty shall be the foundations of our common civic edifice. For myself I ask nothing and want nothing. Do you hear? Nothing. If you cannot tear me from this sadness and this spiritual unrest by a brotherly solicitude, I shall go once again into exile, as in 1912. I prefer exile to a daily torment. *"Non veder non udir . . ."* My child, good and pure, will tell you of my anguished expectation. Be true and courageous towards the man who, in war and in peace, has been the truest and the most courageous of companions. *Deorsum nunquam*. Accept the accolade of a comrade of Carso. Make sure that this is not the last.'

The date 13 August 1922 marks a breaking-point in the life of the poet. Thereafter, he was to grow old without dignity in a sort of Escorial, a combination of opium-den, sacristy and museum of plaster casts. If Donna Maria's fall from the window of the apartment in Rome remains a mystery which discretion has prevented from being unveiled, Gabriele's fall from the window of the Vittoriale has long remained a political mystery which many persons have not wanted to see solved. A keen collector of d'Annunzian souvenirs, Baron Rapizzardi, knew that another collector, Signor Cappelletti, possessed a copy of the report of the accident drawn up by Mussolini's chief of police. On the death of Signor Cappelletti, the baron immediately asked for this document. It had already disappeared.

THE FIFTH WHEEL

In the Fascist machine that was advancing towards power, d'Annunzio was merely the fifth wheel, but a gilt wheel which could be seen from afar and which sometimes creaked. Mussolini is supposed to have made this comment about the man to whom he was to show such generosity: 'When a decayed tooth cannot be pulled out, it is capped with gold.' What more natural than that Italy should allow its greatest citizen to live the 'inimitable life', to build, to plant, to take baths of *eau de Cologne,* and to keep the superb mistresses with whom he became briefly involved? But d'Annunzio was a prodigal spender and the money sent to him from Rome, as well as what he received from his publishers, vanished so quickly that he could in good faith sign his letters 'the poor in Christ', in the manner of his dear St. Francis, an improbable choice of patron who, he believed, had checked his fall from the window. As a votive offering the disciple erected, under the fateful window, a statue of the saint with arms outstretched to welcome him.

Until the Fascist march on Rome of 28 October 1922, d'Annunzio retained a few illusions about the role that he might still play. When Mussolini expressed a wish to meet him at the beginning of October, he replied to the 'Duce' (calling him by this title for the first time) that he was not well enough to receive him. He was, in fact, revising his wartime speeches for a collection entitled *Per l'Italia degli Italiani.* Torn between his legionaries and the black-shirts, the Comandante hesitated, offering fine

words to both and at the same time maintaining contact with
the trade-union elements. Meanwhile, Mussolini, attributing to
the Comandante an importance which he no longer enjoyed, informed him in advance, through Antongini, of the March on
Rome and even suggested that d'Annunzio should lead it himself, since he had organized the March on Fiume so successfully.
In his reply to this invitation of 25 October d'Annunzio would
not commit himself. On the 28th, he received this letter from
Mussolini: 'We have had to mobilize our forces to put an end
to a wretched situation. We are complete masters of a large part
of Italy, and in other parts we have occupied the nerve-centres
of the Nation. I do not ask you to march at our side, which
would have given us infinite joy; but we are sure that you would
not oppose this wonderful youth which is fighting for your and
our Italy. Read the proclamation! At another time you will assuredly have much to say.'

In fact, d'Annunzio was dismayed when, on 29 October, Antongini told him that the Fascists were in Rome and that Mussolini
was the head of government appointed by the king. Immediately
he sent his secretary to the capital to represent him and every
day would send him notes like this one: 'You know how, everywhere, my name and my ideas are misused. Put friends and
enemies on their guard. My thoughts are always clearly expressed
by myself and signed boldly by myself . . . This is what you
must repeat to the Duce: Organize victory, show severity, austerity, an indefatigable energy. A beautiful pediment must be built
again on the Italian temple, despite the profaners both within
and without . . . Draw Benito's attention to the third zone
where foreigners are infiltrating.' Other advice of this kind showed
that senility was clouding d'Annunzio's judgement in a frenzy
of words. Was it really necessary, in the very first of these messages, to enjoin the dictator to restore the Oriental Institute of
Assisi to the Franciscans, build airfields, and beware of Austrian
propaganda at Trent? The faithful Antongini had this message
copied and distributed among Mussolini's entourage—but Mussolini had other fish to fry. On 5 November d'Annunzio sent

another significant letter: 'So far we can say with Shakespeare "Words, words, words" . . . Yesterday I sent a cordial telegram to Mussolini and he has not yet replied.'

D'Annunzio was soon disenchanted. The local Fascists jeered at the poet; his aristocratic poses irritated the new masters of power, still in a puritan phase like all who have known few pleasures during a time of long struggle. He discovered that Farinacci, the chief of the Fascio of Cremona, loathed him. On 22 November he wrote: 'I want to be alone and keep my thoughts to myself.' Realizing that Gardone was already a backwater, he resolved to make it a prison; in just the same way he had called his stay in France an 'exile'. This fiction would be a clever ploy to annoy Mussolini and attract pity. However, if d'Annunzio was a prisoner, it was of his own habits—especially drugs—and vanity: he never wanted to return to Paris an outmoded old man, or to Rome where he would have felt just as out of date in the materialist world of the Fascists, who were parodying his ideas and his vocabulary.

On 16 December 1922 he wrote to Mussolini a melancholy letter, in which he implored the dictator to remove pernicious advisers and threatened in mournful tones to return to the path of exile rather than suffer a daily torment.

'Your letter reaches me at a time of lonely grief which lacks only the "stigmata of blood". I lift up my head to carry an ever heavier and more secret burden. I have decided—today, the 16th of December—to withdraw into my silence and once again devote myself wholly to my art, which will perhaps console me. The best of myself, offered to my country during so many years of zealous effort, is today deformed, denied or even denigrated. The protestations of love and fidelity do not deceive me. Italy today does not love me and does not believe in me. Exile will be the punishment for my long and whole-hearted devotion. I know this. I accept destiny with submission. In a few days it will be the second anniversary of the Christmas of blood. I shall be beside my dead. But my God commands me not to spill more blood as yet. I must endure; I must wait; my grief I must transform into goodness and courage . . . Return to the task; return to meditation; return to the profound religion. The new cry will resound, the new sign will rise up . . . "Make of yourself an island", says a sage of Asia. That is what I have done for myself, and I await interment without a tear. Take this "viaticum" for yourself.'

D'Annunzio's exile would have struck a terrible blow at the prestige of Fascism; he knew this and the letter may have been merely blackmail. Mussolini, rapidly hardened by power, was suspicious of poetry, fearing some impulsive act, some ill-timed speech, from this troublesome old man. When the deputy Matteotti was assassinated in June 1924, what remained of the opposition press quoted these words of d'Annunzio: 'I am saddened by this foul affair', a comment highly disagreeable to the dictator. As if in an attempt to silence the poet, Mussolini bought the manuscript of *La Gloria* for two hundred thousand lire, and promised a national edition of his works and a national theatre company that would perform only his plays. D'Annunzio retired once more to his gilded shell. The opposition movement, which at one time had hoped to see him at its head, collapsed; it consisted mainly of intellectuals for whom d'Annunzio had little esteem. Marinetti also had nothing but contempt for his literary colleagues and led a section of Futurists over to Mussolini's side. As far as is known, d'Annunzio never intervened on behalf of writers oppressed by Fascism.

On the other hand, he continued to support the demands of the sailors against the shipowners backed by Mussolini. He arranged a meeting with Giulietti, the president of the Federation of Sailors. As always with d'Annunzio, gravity and farce went hand in hand: when he saw the bearded figure approaching the villa he muttered: '*Troppo pelo per un coglione solo*' ('Too much hair for one fat-head'); but Giulietti, who had heard the remark, muttered in his turn: '*Troppo coglione per così poco pelo*' ('Too great a fat-head for so little hair'); whereupon the two men embraced each other like brothers! In another melancholy letter to the Duce, d'Annunzio wrote: 'How sad, for a loyal and ardent heart such as mine, is this hesitation in giving the name of companion to one who used to seem proud of it. I do not know what name to give you in these difficult circumstances. I thought of not writing to you any more. I need a reply from you; one year of uncertainty has already passed, another must not pass.' On 7 January 1923 Mussolini sent a long telegram to soothe the old man, who was interfering in things that did not concern him. In his reply of 9 January, a curious letter urging Mussolini to move towards the workers, d'Annunzio wrote: 'Your telegram has that strange tone which is, perhaps, fundamental to "Fascism", but which remains totally foreign to my interior life. You, too, do not realize how keen is my perspicacity, what summits my freedom of mind can attain. You speak to me of "categories" that would be best left as fodder for the gossip-writers or for certain forgotten heroes whom vanity turns into babblers . . . Try to free yourself from the partisans who falsify you and lead you astray. Remove from you those who, for instance, are conducting a most sinister "reaction" in the Marches against the men of the trenches, and who in Puglia are using police methods to repress all forms of "d'Annunzian" spirituality. In the movement which calls itself "Fascist", has not the best been engendered by my spirit? Was not the present national upheaval heralded by me forty years ago and set in motion by the *condottiere* of Ronchi? . . . I wish you the strength and the perspicacity necessary to push the tiller "to the left", if indeed you are prepared to use this old method which has now become ignoble. For my part, I will help the workers to gain redemption, in the spirit of some vigorous pages which you will find in my "Message to common labourers". '

D'Annunzio was, admittedly, behaving in an irritating manner. Why did he persist in asking for an airfield near his villa? So that he might escape, when necessary, from his dark thoughts, so that he could receive visitors of distinction in royal style, or, who knows, so that he might himself lead a squadron on some desperate expedition against the ruling power? Mussolini very firmly refused him his airfield. Around this time the Comandante, replying to someone who wanted him to write a book about the Duce, said: 'It has already been done', and showed his *Cola di Rienzo*, opened at these prophetic lines: 'The populace hanged him by the feet from a post and stoned him. For two days and a night he was the target of these games.'

When, on 15 March 1924, Fiume was annexed to Italy, Mussolini proposed to the king that d'Annunzio be created prince of Monte-Nevoso. This snow-capped mountain is a peak of the Carso range, around which much of d'Annunzio's war had been fought. The glowing telegrams exchanged on the occasion of his elevation to the nobility might have suggested that harmony reigned between King, Dictator and Poet. In fact, the poet's bitterness and his predilection for lost causes now made way for a haughty aloofness, interrupted by an occasional effusion. D'Annunzio had to admit that, in the mediocre Europe of the post-war years, Mussolini had given Italy a certain authority and that he enjoyed great prestige in the eyes of all aristocrats. If the king bore no love for Mussolini, the queen mother admired him and the Duchess of Aosta positively swore by him: at the wedding of her son in Florence Cathedral had she not scandalized all the royal guests by making the Fascist salute before the altar? And we know what great prestige this princess had for d'Annunzio.

In 1926 the poet gathered together, under the title *Libro ascetico della Giovane Italia* ('Ascetic Book of Young Italy'), some prose works of the years 1895–1922, but in a much revised form. This collection puts one in mind of the lanes of the Pincio, overcrowded with statues of heroes, but at the end of which one discovers the most beautiful views in the world. As always, *patria* and *bellezza* rank equally; St. Francis, Leonardo and Dante are constantly evoked by the author, who felt that he had relived those almost divine lives. Everywhere aestheticism adorns the patriotism, even in the titles: 'To our mother Italy, To our mistress, intelligence . . . Sacred spring of winged Italy . . . Three prayers at disused altars . . . Seven documents of love.' And in these concluding words: 'The fate of Italy is inseparable from that of Beauty, whose mother she is eternally.'

In 1925 d'Annunzio went to Milan to salute the Duce; he invited Mussolini to come to see him, but in this invitation one discerns a warning which was to pass unheeded: 'You came once with a proud simplicity, before the March. I should like the same simplicity to guide you to a place where all is silence and labour. A visit to your companion-in-arms, without retinue, without acclamations, without the throng, without speeches, will assuredly be supremely elegant.' But elegance was not Mussolini's chief concern and the visit took place amid great pomp, on 25–27 May, to celebrate the presentation of the villa to the State; an Augustan inscription commemorates the occasion. Some years later, d'Annunzio, feeling himself forgotten, begged for another visit in a letter reminiscent of the most touching passages of *King Lear*. On 12 November 1932 his request was fulfilled, an occasion to which the photographs bear painful witness: d'Annunzio, shrivelled up in a sort of uniform trimmed with fur, looks like the dwarf guarding the Rhinegold; Mussolini, in bowler hat and raincoat, casts a stony eye over the marvels that were costing so much to maintain and embellish. The visits to the old master had become an irksome obligation to be discharged as quickly as possible. The Duce had surely done enough for the Comandante. The national edition, a typographic monument, had cost millions and had brought trouble from the Vatican, which took this opportunity to reaffirm that the poet was on the Index. Yet homage continued to be rendered to the Comandante from time to time. D'Annunzio, for his part, continued to offer advice which Mussolini would have done well to follow. In a letter dated 9 October 1933 he wrote: 'This night, I know that your hesitation and uncertainty of that sweet day are giving place to your watchful perspicacity, and that you are preparing to repulse proudly the yokel Adolf Hitler, that ignoble face spattered with the whitewash and glue in which he soaked his long brushes, the pole which he transformed into the sceptre of a ferocious clown, and with the tuft of hair stuck at the base of his "Nazi" nose . . . France must not disarm. I have learnt by heart for her some passages from the *Song of Roland*. Italy must not disarm; on the contrary, she must—whatever the sacrifice—multiply her armaments. Make a realistic assessment of our air force and hasten to put it in order, as is your habit.' In 1935, Mussolini believed that d'Annunzio could help him to establish a *rapprochement* with France. D'Annunzio invited President Barthou, an old bibliophile friend, to his villa, but the assassination in Marseilles, in which Barthou and King Alexander of Yugoslavia were killed, shattered this last hope of having a part to play. Politics, however, finally provided the opportunity for a swan-song, but one which, to Frenchmen, has a particularly false ring.

THE LAST FANFARE

It is difficult for a Frenchman, who cannot forget Claudel and Maurras, to be entirely critical, when he considers d'Annunzio's view of Mussolini, a man who was surely not his ideal, but was the enemy of everything Gabriele had always hated, the last if crude representative of the grand tradition, or because he praised Fascist power in language which a change of régime has made ridiculous or indeed criminal. These eulogies were the product of senility, despite the quality of the style. One ought not to forget either that many non-Italians approved of the politicians who provoked the final flourishes of Gabriele's great but, alas, cracked voice. The Ethiopian war was the culmination of a long nationalist policy that had begun with the humiliation of Aduwa. France and Britain, which had voted for sanctions against Italy, were hardly in a position to decry such ventures. D'Annunzio told them so in fine phrases to which nobody listened. Had his style become so outdated in the world of *Realpolitik* that he was heeded only in Italy? M. de Montherlant heard the voice and delivered a severe judgement: 'The scarlet and the black. D'Annunzio's sinister appeal with regard to the Ethiopian war, where, in soft-witted words devoid of both thought and art, he calls, probably under threat from Mussolini, for support for this same man, whom he hates and who is strangling him, support for the most unjust and odious of wars. The Quarto speech was already bottom-of-the-drawer. These are the scrapings of Quarto.'

Yet, in *Contra Barbaros*, written in French in 1935, d'Annunzio recaptured some of his old verve in invective. The League of Nations seemed to him the emanation of Anglo-Saxon capitalism: 'It is these great phantom leaders who today are the object of the base rancour of the fraudulent banker-politicians and the vexation of the miserable arbiters whose authority is constantly draining away through their lower passage . . .'

To Mussolini, who had asked him to compose this 'message', d'Annunzio wrote: 'You cannot imagine the cruel effort it has cost me . . . How could I have addressed to the people of France any kind of peremptory exhortation? How could I have attributed to myself an infallible gift of persuasion? Instead, I have had to demonstrate that my long love for the land of France, my mighty knowledge of its language and my true power as a French writer, give me the right to decide hazardous destinies.' The text is full of charming anachronisms which date from the time when d'Annunzio was writing *Le Martyre de saint Sébastien* and reading the French authors of the Middle Ages. It aroused no response in France. Mussolini, thinking that his national poet could still command a wide audience, had encouraged him to address this epistle to President Lebrun, in a binding of crimson silk embroidered with a Gallic cockerel, with golden clasps and tassels like a Golden Bull sent by a Byzantine prince to a Frankish chieftain. At the Vittoriale a reply from the Élysée was awaited anxiously and impatiently, but nothing came: 'This man must not like poetry', the Comandante eventually declared. On the same day he had sent a copy of the 'message' to his king, with a commentary emphasizing that France had seized possession of so many countries overseas that she had no right to say anything about the Abyssinian question; he signed this letter 'Gabriele d'Annunzio, Duke of Ragusa', as much to pour scorn on the Italian fiefs which Napoleon had given to his officers as to suggest an appropriation of the Dalmatian port. Other 'messages' were published concerning the imposition of sanctions, but they are of little interest; it is sad to see d'Annunzio stoop so low as to mock the defeated Emperor of Austria-Hungary, whom he dubbed 'a vulgar colour-print from a provincial café'. Alas, in remarks of this kind the vulgarity of the petty-bourgeois from Pescara reasserts itself.

The imposition of sanctions threw Mussolini into the arms of Hitler, whom d'Annunzio nicknamed 'the Charlie Chaplin of the Nibelungen' and whom he liked to lampoon. Learning that Mussolini would be stopping at Verona on 30 September 1937, on his return from a triumphant journey to Germany, the poet decided to go and wait for him on the station platform. A newsreel shows d'Annunzio, on the arm of the architect Maroni, shuffling along the red carpet up to the carriage window, through which the Duce is leaning. With the smile of an ogre, Mussolini takes the poet's hands in his and then, followed by his staff-officers, makes his way to a balcony to harangue the crowd. The little old man toddles after him, chattering away and waving his withered hands in the air; Mussolini, without slowing down, smiles at him from time to time, but the ovations of the crowd prevent him from hearing a word of what d'Annunzio is saying. Then the Duce walks on ahead, not inviting d'Annunzio to follow him on to the balcony, and leaving him, supported by his disciple, to push his way through the crowd towards his enormous yellow car. No one had heard a word of the 'conversation' between the two men; according to Mussolini's men, the poet had said to the Duce: 'I admire you more than ever for what you are doing.' According to Maroni, the old man, utterly overwhelmed as they returned to the Vittoriale, said: 'This is the end.' Both versions may be true. D'Annunzio, sensitive to Mussolini's magnetism, would never have opposed him in anything; once he was far away and the magnetism had been dispelled, the poet probably had a very clear vision of the fate awaiting Italy. He was never again to see Mussolini. From time to time he would remind the Duce of his existence in letters written in heroic language. Mussolini offered him the presidency of the Italian Academy on the death of

Marconi. In spite of his contempt for Italian literary life, the poet accepted, but did not go to Rome for his reception. He remained at the Vittoriale, a little principality with a mysterious protocol, where the echoes of public life reached him only through the chitchat of his court.

20

The Vittoriale

A HAUNTED VILLA

To those who believe that ghosts are souls to whom death has brought no peace, and who return either to demand justice, or to expiate some heinous crime at the place where it was committed, d'Annunzio's villa on Lake Garda must indeed seem haunted. The spirit of the writer who was so unappreciated in his old age, the reluctant mouthpiece of a brutal political creed, hovers in these dark and cluttered rooms, in the damp, overgrown gardens, with the spirits of those whom he carried with him along the paths of error and pleasure, who suffered so many jealousies and humiliations. To those unimpressed by the world of the imagination, this necropolis of a recent glory, dingy rather than imposing, teeming with evidence of d'Annunzio's affectation and metaphysical pretensions, suggests a Trianon designed by de Chirico. The useless arches, the poles from which no flags flutter, the grandiose inscriptions which are already crumbling, the coats of arms fixed on the walls like the decorations on an old general's tunic, the theatrical steps leading nowhere, the fragments of ancient sculpture, the boundary-posts linked by chains, the grotesque Medusa masks, all this suggests megalomania rather than grandeur. The Vittoriale is more a model for a vast monument worthy of the Palatine, than a monument in itself; it is stage architecture constructed round a charming villa. Discovered by Antongini shortly after the return from Fiume, the villa, like the holy-of-holies forbidden to visitors, is hidden behind the huge and gloomy rooms filled with plaster casts, relics and heroic mementoes (an aeroplane, two automobiles, machine-guns), rooms in which the rites of some outmoded patriotic cult should be performed, a flamboyant palace which the poet built during the seventeen years that he lived here, to protect his secret abode and to assert his yearning for power.

The Vittoriale is a dream-palace like the castles of Ludwig II of Bavaria, designed to keep out those who might have disturbed the dream. Never since the Pharaohs has a man left such a concrete testimony of his ideas, his desires and his daily life. D'Annunzio is present in the Vittoriale as Tutankhamen was present in his tomb in the Valley of Kings, when it was entered by the archaeologists: a similar desire to achieve self-preservation by magic means creates the same overpowering atmosphere in the villa. In both, symbols abound; many of d'Annunzio's symbols escape us, but others are immediately familiar as we pass from the square of the comic-opera village to the gardens of the poet-prince. There is a religious symbol, the Annunciation painted on the entrance porch and the motto 'I have only what I have given'; a symbol of the Italian resistance on the river Piave in 1917, the pile of a bridge crowned by a Victory; further on, a truly d'Annunzian symbol, a motto in cement covered with cracks, which means 'Remain calm in face of danger'; to the right is the Greek theatre, completed in 1935, and beyond, through the cypresses, the lake can be seen. Between two ochre walls on which roses grow is a rotunda consisting of alternate niches and pilasters. In one of the niches is the poet's tomb, against a green marble ground with the bronze crown of the Italian Royal Academy (in which d'Annunzio showed so little interest), the Lancers' pennon and the flag from Fiume. There are two bronze vases, one containing soil from the cemetery at Fiume, the other soil from the cemetery at Pescara. So many precautions against oblivion, such a clutter of mementoes! The centre of this architectural complex is the severe, paved *Piazza di Dalmazia*, in the middle of which stands a flagstaff embossed at the base with heroic masks; opposite the flagstaff is a loggia from which to harangue the crowd—a stage crowd of well-drilled extras who would disperse through the porticoes and along the walls. A tall umbrella-pine and some laurels give this court as much dignity as all the high-flown allusions. Beneath an arch stands the vehicle used in the advance on Fiume, a V-type Fiat; under another arch, the enormous yellow limousine of the last years. On one side of the court stands the two-storey d'Annunzio museum with its huge rooms. On the ground floor is the room where the poet's body lay in state between casts of Michelangelo, then galleries full of bronzes, plaster casts, weapons and banners. On the first floor the showcases contain yellowed photographs, letters, prize-books and uniforms, some dried-up pomegranates and a bouquet of roses gathered half a century ago which again remind one of the cups of wheat or lotus-leaves found in the tombs of the Pharaohs. The rooms of the museum, designed by the architect Maroni, are panelled with polished wood and lit by stained-glass windows in the shape of port-holes. The most curious part is the auditorium, a vast rotunda containing the aeroplane used in the flight over Vienna.

In the house proper, sometimes known as the *Prioria* or 'Priory', the dark claustrophobic atmosphere, still pervaded with stale perfumes, gives one the feeling of entering one of those Italian cabinets with multiple compartments, hiding-places, and inlaid work that produces perspective effects. The rooms, hung with silk brocades or decorated with rich book-bindings, the worked ceilings, the narrow windows darkened by the stained glass, are just like a set of drawers, one for trinkets, another for books, a third for portraits, but more often than not containing a jumbled assortment of all the tokens of a long life the latter years of which appear to have been devoted to preserving its every memory, however trivial. One can imagine secret passages behind the panelling, an alcove behind a tapestry. Everything is padded, smothered, cluttered, rather like a seraglio. In fact, d'Annunzio's life, as secret as that of the sultan in his palace, had become the web of intrigues and rivalries already apparent on the occasion of the 'accident'. A sort of harem, supervised by an official sultana, provided the insatiable old man with a variety of pleasures.

But the seraglio is also a library, for there are books everywhere. The vast 'Map of the World Room' was the library proper, lined with handsome bindings; a refectory table is cluttered with documents and albums, but why the Austrian machine-gun? There are also masses of books in the 'Lily Room', whose principal ornament is an organ, and in the 'Dalmatian Oratory', a narrow room where a pious humanist might meditate among folio volumes in parchment bindings. Here the master held brief audiences, sometimes in a monkish robe. In the 'Leda Room' or bedroom, Shakespeare, Dante, Verlaine and Stendhal were within easy reach. In a passage one finds Parisian novels, Willy and other spicy authors side by side with Jean Lorrain and Gide; in a little office lined with old editions from *La Capponcina,* unanswered letters accumulated; a severed hand painted in red above the door underlines the ironical significance of the name, 'the writing-room of the one-handed man'. Here are to be found the most famous editions of the sixteenth century, for d'Annunzio possessed a much sounder judgement of books than of works of art. Finally, in the 'Officina' or study, the only light room in the whole building, there are encyclopaedias, dictionaries and volumes of the classics.

The visitor must stoop as he enters the low doorway leading into this huge room, the walls of which are covered with plaster casts of the Parthenon frieze, photos of the Sistine Chapel and of the frescoes of Mantegna. Three tables are littered with boxes full of papers, bizarre mementoes and masses of photographs (mistresses past and present, the Duchess of Aosta in a Byzantine ceremonial costume); a bronze plaque bears the handsome face of the beloved pilot Natale Palli. A doleful mask of La Duse, below the wing of the Victory of Samothrace, dominates this agglomeration of objects; when the poet sat down to work, he would cover the face of the muse with a veil.

Around the magician all was ritual and mystery. Professor Praz, for whom the Vittoriale evokes joss-sticks and the music of *Tristan*, has made two important observations about the décor of the house: in the poems of the *Laudi*, d'Annunzio regarded Nature as a sublime furniture-store, *Magnalia Naturae*, whose mountains, waves and trees were objects which he arranged to suit his own fancy; then, as he declined, his pantheism was restricted to furniture, and hence the strange arrangements of columns in the middle of a drawing-room, the gilded casts, the bewildering juxtaposition of Chinese curios and the Renaissance. Professor Praz also stresses 'a devout profanation that approaches surrealism', exemplified by the broken steering-wheel of a motor-boat placed beside a ciborium in front of a predella. In the 'Room of Relics', which is devoted to juxtapositions of this kind, an accumulation of statues reaching from the floor to the ceiling represents the 'ladder of religions': at the bottom are Chinese dragons, in the middle Buddhas, at the top the Holy Virgin. The house is littered with cushions of every possible fabric, made according to the poet's precise instructions and placed here and there to soften an amorous tumble or to sleep on, for the seraglio was also an opium-den.

If this oriental-bazaar atmosphere is reminiscent of Pierre Loti's house at Rochefort, the music room, which was draped with black or red silk to suit the mood of the piece being performed, belongs fifty years later with its bronzes in the style of 1925, the décor that Huysmans had invented for Des Esseintes. The bathroom is that of a call-girl with Levantine admirers: a dark blue bath and bidet, walls covered with Persian tiles and dishes from Rhodes. An enormous sacristy cupboard contains dozens of cravats, gaudy dressing-gowns and uniforms. The dining-room, also lined with books, is like a chest lacquered in red and gold, with black seats and a brocade table-cloth; the centre-piece is a tortoise with a richly gilded shell, originally given to the poet by Ida Rubinstein, which had died after browsing among the tuberoses. There is a 'Leper's Room' to which the poet, also touched by the finger of God and accursed in the eyes of the world, used to withdraw, like an inquisitor to his sanctum. During the first few years of his retirement, when the master still entertained lavishly, guests were received in the vast music room, which had been the scene of the accident; here, until the end of his life, films were also shown, but these occasions were usually attended only by the household staff. In his old age d'Annunzio had a special fondness for *The Bengal Lancers* and the UFA *Siegfried*.

Everywhere inscriptions, on the beams and above the doors, recall the rules of the 'inimitable life', or those of the Franciscans. There are, perhaps, a few genuine works of art that have strayed among the two thousand five hundred objects, but these are eclipsed by the false glitter of the rest. In the architect Maroni the poet had found a disciple skilful enough to satisfy all his decorative fancies; indeed, in some of his extravagances Maroni was able to anticipate his master's tastes. The idea of draping the casts of Michelangelo's slaves in purple figured velvet and giving them necklaces was a discovery for which the architect was commended; like so many homosexuals, Maroni sought to reconcile his aspiration toward the sublime with his passion for frills.

How beautiful the gardens seem when one emerges from this necropolis! The roses hide the grandiloquent inscriptions, the wistaria softens the soaring effect of the Victories, and the moss gives a patina to the cement. The gardens lie on a green hillside with waterfalls, pools, a bridge incongruously decorated with artillery shells and, under the magnolias, a field-gun in front of which German tourists like to be photographed. The huge circular cenotaph of Istrian stone, dedicated to d'Annunzio's comrades-in-arms, stands on a spur; begun in 1941, the monument was never finished and soon will be no more than a splendid ruin. Below the cenotaph, between tall cypresses, lies the prow of a cruiser with masts rising above the tree-tops; stone steps lead down to the deck. Standing on the poop, one has a feeling of sailing towards the lake over a sea of olive- and orange-trees. D'Annunzio had obtained this ship, the *Puglia*, from the admiralty when it was taken out of commission; once, disobeying orders, it had brought him reinforcements in Fiume. With Nature's assistance, this freak of fancy, worthy of the gardens of Nero, has become the strangest example of Surrealist architecture—again rather like a vast de Chirico to which the dark greenery adds the mystery of a Böcklin.

When the poet settled in the villa, confiscated from the German Professor Thode, the Wagnerian relics had helped him to feel at home. With a great concern for his own glory, and in one of those gestures that have the semblance of generosity, he made sure that he would be able to enlarge his villa without cost to himself: in 1923 he handed it over to the government, which assumed responsibility for the expenditure in which he had already begun to involve himself; then, in 1930, the much-enlarged villa and grounds were made a National Foundation.

THE SHRINE

As soon as he had settled himself in the villa, d'Annunzio was as active on his domain as Napoleon on the island of Elba. He built, planted, accumulated furniture and books, and surrounded himself with a personal court. Until the end of his life the favourite remained the pianist Luisa Bàccara, whose supremacy was constantly challenged and who found herself hated by all. Although he insulted her constantly, the poet would from time to time pay Luisa a dazzling compliment. But how frequently he resorted to perfidy to avenge himself on his sullen mistress! To a visitor who expressed surprise that such a fine artist did not go on tour, he replied: 'People would see that she has no talent.' In the jargon of structuralism, d'Annunzio had 'reified' the pianist. She was no longer a woman, but a music-box; she was placed at the piano or the organ according to the mood of the moment, and as often as not to prepare a rival for seduction. The regular frequenters of the villa thought she had the face of an owl; they mocked her silver dresses with Romanesque embroideries and frowned on her friendship with Finzi, the most sinister of the Fascists' agents, but the woman clung on, assuming complete control of the household. More amenable and complaisant was 'Aelis', Amélie Mazoyer, the French housemaid. Naturally, the two women hated each other. La Bàccara's worst enemy, however, was the architect

Maroni; this young man, who had such a gift for pastiche and was also very musical, worshipped the poet to the exclusion of all others.

As the years passed, the faithful disciples dwindled; the disillusioned Arditi and those who were turning to Mussolini no longer came knocking at the door. The 'court', on the other hand, grew in number. There was Professor Bruers, an archivist and distinguished d'Annunzian, who classified the manuscripts and prepared the new editions. The lawyer Barduzzi supervised the contracts, supplanting Antongini, who had become an important figure in the world of the official Italian cinema. The painter Guido Cadorin also spent many hours at the Vittoriale, decorating the rooms in accordance with d'Annunzio's instructions; for the 'Leper's Room', an American girl who was a brief visitor to the villa posed in the nude for 'Brother Guidotto', as he came to be known. A doctor, indispensable during the periods of depression, prescribed stimulants and possibly even procured the daily cocaine. A nurse and three chambermaids were known as the 'Poor Clares' by this Priapus posing as St. Francis; a cook and his assistants and some gardeners completed the domestic staff. An upholsterer was engaged to make the cushions and fix the hangings; a variety of craftsmen, working under the master's supervision, made elaborate but perfectly useless articles of copper, glass, embossed leather and fabric, which were presented to visitors. The mechanic of the Buccari raid looked after the motor-boats that ploughed to and fro across the lake; sailors kept guard over the *Puglia*.

The most important person in this entourage was the police superintendent of Gardone. Giovanni Rizzo, the representative of authority, was shrewd enough to humour the comic antics of the capricious old man: a spy and, at the same time, a useful accomplice when it was necessary to get rid of intruders, ready to become d'Annunzio's Hudson Lowe whenever the poet chose to look on the Vittoriale as his St. Helena, Rizzo showed great indulgence in the matter of morals, for he himself had the most eclectic tastes. D'Annunzio and Rizzo played a game in which each constantly tried to outwit the other, but really the two men understood each other perfectly. Nevertheless, Mussolini was regularly informed of the poet's activities and the visitors whom he received. Since he was by now one of the most famous writers in the world, d'Annunzio was besieged by visitors; most of the curious found the door of the Vittoriale firmly closed to them. Some proved stubborn, like the Lutheran pastor who had sworn to lead the poet back to God and spent six months in prayer at a hotel in Gardone. All those who, at one time or another, had been d'Annunzio's close friends thought that they had only to present themselves to be welcomed with open arms. They were mistaken. The most favoured stayed in hotels, at d'Annunzio's expense, waiting to be granted an interview. In 1936 André Germain, who had been welcomed to Gardone in a telegram of some two hundred words, waited three weeks with no other result than this quite remarkable letter: 'I would have derived a melancholy pleasure from seeing you again after so many years and discovering in your look of steel the dim glimmer of a dangerous impudence. But I am now an infirm and incredibly virtuous old man.'

Ten years earlier, d'Annunzio would not have written such a disillusioned letter. At that time he had not abandoned the idea of making the Vittoriale a sort of Latin Bayreuth, one of the great shrines of the Western world. But he had not been able to sustain the effort necessary to dazzle visitors. One of the most remarkable of these visitors, M. Jacques Benoist-Méchin, then twenty-five years old, in his memoirs describes this precarious balance between comedy and poetry, the conjuring-tricks which at times achieved the miraculous. The young Frenchman arrived on a torrid summer's day, 14 July 1925, to discuss an important American contract with the poet; he was accompanied by Karl Vollmoller, the German translator of the poems, famous at the time for his part in Reinhardt's productions of *The Miracle*. The visitors had found the approaches to the villa strictly guarded by Alpine soldiers; but d'Annunzio's wife, Donna Maria, entertained her guests with a good grace, for nothing surprised her any longer. Since the 'Princess of Monte-Nevoso' was staying for a while at the villa, La Bàccara had been sent away. The third son, Gabriellino, a drab creature, was also present. D'Annunzio, very pale but still full of energy, immediately began to talk about France: 'It is scandalous that the Americans should dare to claim war reparations. But the world has lost all sense of the sacred . . . Your poor country is in a bad situation. Your young writers are lamentably inadequate; in my French works I have used an infinitely richer vocabulary; only Montherlant gives me the impression of a poet of a great race . . . Come and see my relics. Now I live only through my dead . . .'

He led them to an oratory lit by an oil-lamp. Gilded boxes contained splinters of shells and fragments of torn uniforms. A hank of silk intrigued the visitors: 'The Duchess of Aosta needed silk for her hospital, so I had the idea of converting the trenches in which my company was under fire from the Austrians into a cocoonery. In this way I conquered something more powerful than death: boredom. When a shell burst, the soldiers would rush to save the worms, regardless of the danger. But who thinks of the dead in this rotten world?' As they passed from room to room, d'Annunzio told of the 'three deaths' that followed his accident: 'When I was injured, I saw a large black spider surrounded by sparks . . .' The visitors were amazed at the number of mottoes painted on the beams and engraved above the doors: 'The motto is an exercise in brevity of speech; I make a rule of finding eight or ten each day.' When they came to Michelangelo's slaves, draped in velvet, the poet commented: 'Their legs are too short, so I asked Poiret for some dressing-gowns.' He assured another visitor that Michelangelo had come to kiss him on the forehead, and since then there had been an empty triangle in his head which he had to fill with thoughts of genius. By claiming this familiarity with the artist, d'Annunzio could justify the liberties he took with the latter's masterpieces. In front of the window from which he had fallen, there stood a bronze statue of St. Francis of Assisi with arms outstretched. The saint had also received an incongruous attribute, a belt with a pistol fixed to it: 'St. Francis is the first Fascist and I am the last Franciscan.'

After the magnificent tributes to his dead comrades, a paradox of this kind jarred on the ear. 'Then he reminded me of De Max' (the French tragic actor), recalls M. Benoist-Méchin; 'the lapse of taste followed immediately after the most soul-stirring accents.'

After passing through a boudoir with old gloves hanging on the walls, 'the gloves forgotten by all those ladies who lost their heads', they returned to the drawing-room. D'Annunzio presented some books to his visitors and gave the Frenchman a dagger inscribed with these words: *Si spiritus pro nobis quis contra nos* ('If the spirit is for us who is against us'). 'And now, on this blade from Fiume, you are going to swear to devote your life to struggling against American barbarity.' There was an awkward moment, for the visitor was representing an American publisher. Donna Maria tactfully turned the conversation to music. The poet talked of the *Tenth Symphony* which Beethoven is supposed to have left unwritten because his inspiration was exhausted, and which, according to d'Annunzio, should have been dedicated to the tenth muse, Energeia, the muse of the modern world. This lyrical explosion, perfectly timed, lasted until the visit to the gardens. As the group passed through a circular thicket surrounded by marble benches, d'Annunzio said: 'It was here that I had Debussy's Quartet played on the day that Claude de France died, and also on another occasion in homage to Anatole France, to erase the memory of his ignoble political funeral!' (D'Annunzio was alluding to the display of red flags at the funeral.)

Finally, they came to the *Puglia*. A dozen sailors in impeccable white uniforms and a very handsome petty officer presented arms. 'They are very gifted', said the poet. 'What would you prefer, a little ancient music or a few cannon salvoes?'—'The cannon', replied the German. From the prow of the ship the Comandante, bent with age, ordered three salvoes: 'To Europe and to our mother, Intelligence. Fire!' The echo of the cannonade could long be heard reverberating from mountain to mountain. 'To the new Germany, to the Germany of the Tenth Symphony. Fire!' Then, laying his hand on the Frenchman's shoulder: 'To France, sweet and heroic. To the France without which all other peoples would be alone. And to the horn of Roland, which has never ceased to sound for new victories. Fire!' By an extraordinary chance, the smoke from this third salvo formed a perfect circle which rose slowly through the torrid air, bathed in the golden tint of the sun like a halo against which the figure of the poet was outlined. D'Annunzio, in a kind of ecstasy, cried: 'And now, go tell the dreadful world what you have seen.'

There had been no question of the contract being signed. When M. Benoist-Méchin took the dagger from its scabbard he saw, stamped on the hilt, 'Made in Michigan, USA'. The dagger was a piece of American surplus, one of the stage-properties of the daily theatrical performance which life at the Vittoriale involved in the early days. A comparison with Salvador Dali, whose commercial- ized extravagances certainly do not possess the same breadth, might nevertheless help us to understand the d'Annunzio who found himself growing old in a world that was turning its back on poetry. The Spaniard, following in the tradition of the Italian, but with less real talent, plays on the ambiguity between hoax and genius. He has assumed the role of magician invented by Wagner and so cherished by the Symbolists.

ADMIRERS OLD AND NEW

The women had more success. D'Annunzio was still eager to make new female acquaintances and to see what the years had done to the old ones. However, of the mistresses of his early years he saw only 'Febea' (Olga Ossani); the others did not show themselves, although Mme. de Goloubeff pestered the poet for money in long and plaintive telegrams, receiving equally long telegrams in reply. His female visitors rarely stayed at the Vittoriale; they, too, waited at the Palace Hotel until the poet's fancy prompted him to write an enigmatic note, like this one sent in January 1925 to Georgette Leblanc, the singer who had lived for many years with Maeterlinck: 'I suggest you come to have the evening meal (nine o'clock) with the Prior in the Room of the Bleeding Relics, tomorrow the 29th (2 + 9 = 11).' The next day he sent another: 'I shall send the car to collect you at 8.30 at the hotel. We shall eat yellow and red beans from the leper's bowl, at 9 o'clock. Remember that you are coming to the severe and silent hermitage. I shall be in the jersey of an old sailor condemned to fresh water, or in the dirty tunic of a Capuchin. We shall be *à trois yeux*. Avoid finery. Brother Ariel. The 29th (2 + 9 = 11).'

Romaine Brooks came occasionally from Florence, where she was the centre of a lesbian colony; usually she was accompanied by her women-friends, such as Nathalie Barney or the Duchess de Clermont-Tonnerre, both of whom had a style at the same time outrageous and elegant, and the culture which made brilliant conversations possible. In June 1935, two Englishmen arrived for lunch. The older of the two, with a long face, bare forehead and thin mouth, seemed very respectable. The younger, with a fringe, monocle, cigarette-holder and basset hound, was quite the contrary. The two visitors were, in fact, Miss Radclyffe Hall, the author of *The Well of Loneliness*, and her friend Una, Lady Troubridge, 'John' to the ladies. They captivated d'Annunzio, who wrote frequently to Miss Hall to ask for news of 'John'. He sent the novelist a copy of his *Libro segreto* with this dedication: 'To the great and pure writer I offer this bold book, which seems to me to seal our friendship.' He also received Mariette Lydis, whose equivocal drawings of beggar-women appealed to him.

Even the most respectable visitors were entitled to intoxicating dedications, like this one accorded to Mme. de Saint-Victor, whose salon d'Annunzio had frequented in Paris: 'In memory of your smile, noble goldsmith, mystical chain-maker of the Vittoriale . . . *Pax et Bonum, Bonum et Pax.*' A great name borne by a pretty woman opened the doors immediately; the Countess Borromeo d'Adda, *née* Doria, liked to walk along the avenues of the park with her small boy; the son remembers his astonishment when the poet would tear off some roses, bite deeply into them, and then throw the petals to the wind. Mme. Olga Lévy and Signora Lombardi also used to come from Venice.

The widowed Duchess de Gramont, who at the time was travelling with a Chilean diplomat, Don Antonio de Gandarillas, stopped several times at Gardone. Don Antonio, accustomed to luxury and extravagance (he had been the guest of Felix Yussupov in St. Petersburg), was stunned by the style of life at the Vittoriale—the wonderful meals served at the most unexpected times, a semi-regal protocol to which even the most intimate friendships were subordinated, the evenings prolonged until dawn and during which cocaine bolstered the euphoria of the guests and the eloquence of the host. D'Annunzio was intrigued by Mlle. Chanel, who was just beginning to become famous, and asked the Duchess de Gramont all manner of questions about the couturière.

Ida Rubinstein came quite often, at first for professional reasons; she appeared in a film of one of d'Annunzio's works and produced *Le Martyre* at Milan in 1925. On this latter occasion, according to Mr. Wilm, who was playing the part of a young warrior, d'Annunzio appeared on stage at the end of the last act and made a speech to the audience, quite heedless of the fact that St. Sebastian, bound tightly to his tree, was waiting impatiently for his bonds to be untied. As a true priestess of the great master of Beauty, Rubinstein was always generous in her productions of d'Annunzio's dramas. And she still loved him. This telegram sent in 1927 suggests that her admiration had not, after all, been platonic: 'I was truly afraid, brother, that you no longer loved me, but I can come on 11 May to see you for a few hours. I have so much to tell you and also something to ask of you. Then I should like to make myself cherished once more.'

The Marchesa Casati sent aphrodisiac telegrams and marvellous photographs of herself as Scheherazade at St. Moritz or Salammbô at the Lido, inviting the poet to weird balls. For all these women, still beautiful, intelligent and sure of themselves, d'Annunzio remained the hero, albeit one ravaged by the years. All, with bitterness or pride, saw their photographs on the poet's table or at his bedside—all except Romaine Brooks, who seemed surprised and was told: 'But you are not a woman!'

The most remarkable account of a visit to the Vittoriale is given by a woman who played little part in the poet's life, but who lived the 'inimitable life' with panache and perfect content-

ment: Cécile Sorel. In 1925 the actress made the journey to the
shores of Lake Garda and, of course, the doors of the Vittoriale
were flung wide open for her. D'Annunzio showed her his
treasures: 'His jewels, his bindings of old missals, his works, his
life, his soul—all these he gives you with his fine white hands. He
is a god who spreads around him the treasures of his heaven . . .'
In the gardens he bombarded her with roses and swore that he
would take an aeroplane to drop more roses on the Théâtre-
Français when she created one of his plays there: 'Cecilia, such
an ardour pours from you that today I feel as young as man must
have been on the first day of the world's existence.' Alas, the
actress had to dine with Mussolini: 'That mason has taken my
place? Swear by the Madonna that you will come back.' Unfortunately for the Duce, Cécile Sorel did return, in a dress of
gold and cloak of purple. D'Annunzio received her in his monkish
robe, dispatched La Bàccara to the organ and, to the strains of a
Bach fugue, there followed a scene which, as related by Sorel,
might seem extravagant but is by no means impossible. The poet
devoured the actress with kisses and then beat his chest in
penitence: 'Cecilia, is this one of your miracles? Faith has shot
through me like a thunderbolt. Do not leave me again!' Luisa
Bàccara had been watching them, and the thundering of the
organ grew menacing: 'In my gold dress I seemed like a torch; I
covered my nakedness and fled into the park. Wreaths of incense
pursued me . . .' Eventually, they sat down to eat from a table
covered with rose-petals, to the sounds of a hidden orchestra and
the nightingales in the garden; there was an elevated conversation
about the nature of the Trinity. D'Annunzio said that he felt
he was becoming a saint, one of God's poor, and that Cécile's
rebuffs had been the path of his conversion: 'Through you I have
suffered all that I have made other women suffer. O Duse, my
most beautiful victim, I have crucified you on myself, O Duse! I
bring you more than love, I bring you the punishment of God!'
The poet told Sorel how he was able to commune with the soul
of Eleonora Duse by biting into a pomegranate in front of a
Buddha. Then, late at night, leading the actress to her car, he

broke a briar branch and made it into a crown which he placed on her head, causing the forehead to bleed. His last words were: 'To d'Annunzio, Sorel and France are one!' These follies are recounted in a book entitled, appropriately enough, *Les belles heures de ma vie* ('The happy hours of my life').

La Duse never came to the Vittoriale; she was back on the boards, at the age of sixty-three, as much through necessity as from a desire to escape from loneliness. She died in April 1924, in a drab hotel in Pittsburgh. D'Annunzio demanded that Mussolini order a state funeral at St. Mary of the Angels in Rome. According to a young friend of the poet, d'Annunzio went to Rome in his huge car, in which he could sleep and eat, just to catch a glimpse of the ceremony; he left immediately afterwards, without making himself known to anyone apart from this young man whose poetic sensibility and beauty engaged his attention at this time. Two years earlier, when d'Annunzio happened to be in Milan, in the same hotel as the actress whom he had not seen for sixteen years, he had knocked on her door and talked to her about *La Città morta*, which La Duse wanted to produce. As he left her he knelt and said: 'How you loved me!' The next day La Duse confided to her friend, Signora Signorelli: 'What an illusion . . . If I had loved him as much as he thinks, I would have died after our separation, but I have been able to continue living.' Learning that the actress owed the hotel a considerable sum, d'Annunzio settled the bill immediately. Although La Duse never came to the villa, her memory was present in every room. When d'Annunzio discovered that the actress's daughter, prompted by filial piety, had burnt all the letters he had sent to her mother, he protested: 'What a crime against the spirit!' One cannot help thinking of Mme. Gide burning her fiancé's letters.

The last important visit that d'Annunzio received was also the most flattering: that the beautiful and intelligent Princess of Piedmont (wife of the heir to the Italian throne) should wish to meet him brought temporary consolation to one who knew that he was sinking into oblivion. This was a difficult meeting to arrange, for there was no point of contact between the royal court and the Vittoriale; the princess happened to express her admiration for the poet in the presence of her husband's aide-de-camp, who had been in d'Annunzio's squadron during the war; this officer then arranged the meeting from Turin, where the young couple lived, without informing Rome. On 4 October 1932 the visitors left the train at a station near the lake. D'Annunzio ushered them aboard a motor-boat, which he drove himself. But the weather was so bad that they were forced to turn back across the stormy water and take an open car. The poet wore a check cap which offered little protection. At the Vittoriale, the royal couple and their host sat down at a table covered with a lamé cloth and provided with unmanageable napkins of the same material; their attendants were served separately; a quartet played in muted tones. For the siesta the princess was shown into a bedroom decorated with bluish masks, but the oppressive atmosphere of the house prevented her from sleeping a wink. After tea, at which Luisa Bàccara and her sister were present, the pianist played César Franck's *Symphonic Variations*. Music had been the chief subject of conversation with the princess, a relative of Ludwig II of Bavaria. D'Annunzio insisted that she should have Monteverdi played at the concerts which she organized at the palace in Turin. He talked also about himself, how he had just passed through a period of mysticism but realized that he was about to fall back into drugs and vice. The princess was a little surprised that he should have said 'vice' and not 'women'. Her Highness had another surprise in store for her: d'Annunzio begged her to put on a monk's robe and knelt in front of her to attach the cord round her waist. Although the visit was secret, cannon-shots were fired from the *Puglia* as the guests, in a covered automobile this time, left for the station. After this visit, the princess received not only books inscribed with heroic dedications, but also fabrics printed in the workshops of the Vittoriale, rather like those made by Fortuny.

21

The Tomb
beneath the Laurels

HOMAGE

Although Anna de Noailles never came to the Vittoriale, there was an exchange of letters, after a long silence; they are written in a style which is perhaps a little too exalted for two people apparently reluctant to meet again. When, in 1929, the 'great Castalian sister' received a letter worthy of her, she replied: 'Sublime and consoling friend, since your great mind came to dwell with me, encompassing me and penetrating my whole being, I have accepted life (and in preference death) by the miracle of your rediscovered presence, your light, your eternal youth.' D'Annunzio sent a magnificent bouquet of flowers to the poetess's funeral in 1933, and about this same time he read one of her novels, *La Damnation*, underlining this passage: 'I know what is meant by the past, by decline, and what the cold shadows mean . . . I know those moments in life when, wearily seating himself between his destiny and his death, man in stupor contemplates his inert and dark soul.'

The French writers who had been dazzled by d'Annunzio in their youth remained faithful to the poet, even if, like Paul

Valéry, they were of a temperament far removed from his own. Valéry came to the Vittoriale in 1924, fascinated by the figure of the poet-prince of whom the Symbolists had dreamed and to whom d'Annunzio had given life. In a letter to the poet he refers to himself in the third person: 'He still has the feeling that you gave him of having known the absolute personality of the Poet— the Being who is against Time. You are the last. Your name will mark the completion of an age in the profound history of the earth.' While one can laugh at the exchanges with Cécile Sorel, one cannot help regretting that so little of the conversations with Valéry has been preserved, conversations about Leonardo and the 'Third Place', the state between life and death. D'Annunzio told the Frenchman that he would like to write a book entitled 'Aspects of the Unknown.' Valéry admitted: 'We were a little intoxicated by our meeting.' Then, for himself, he wrote: 'I have the feeling of always being clumsy and awkward in his presence.' For a man as unsusceptible to magic as Valéry, the wizardries of d'Annunzio proved surprisingly effective: 'He is an alchemist; gold is his combustible. What one sees and knows of life has no importance; the important he was unable to express.' On his return to Paris, Valéry wittily summed up life at the Vittoriale: 'I was dying of thirst, for to ask for a glass of water was out of the question. One had to implore "my sister water" and that was quite beyond me.' The correspondence between the two men became less frequent. Valéry, preoccupied with his new role of official poet, contented himself with insisting that d'Annunzio should come to Paris when the Comédie-Française produced *La Fiaccola sotto il Moggio*. But d'Annunzio did not go; instead, he sent five hundred francs for the academician's sword.

Critics have discerned d'Annunzio's influence in the works of Apollinaire and Valéry Larbaud, and on the Surrealists. The greatest influence is to be found in the works of M. Henri de Montherlant, who has acknowledged this debt, writing on the centenary of the poet's birth that 'reading *Le Feu* at the age of sixteen brought me a style of life and a style of writing'. He admits that from 1915 to 1925 he was possessed by the life of d'Annunzio, and that as a writer he was under his influence up to the age of forty-five, in other words up to and including *Le Solstice de juin*. D'Annunzio may also have influenced Ezra Pound, and possibly Lawrence Durrell; but Pound, who lived in Italy, had a political rather than a poetic affinity with d'Annunzio.

Nothing could prevent the poet from feeling that he was slowly sinking into oblivion. Owing to his lack of interest in contemporary art, he had no cause for excitement when Honegger wrote the music of *Phèdre* for the Paris Opéra, or when de Chirico designed the scenery for *La Figlia di Iorio* in 1934. D'Annunzio, for his part, remained loyal to the France that had been consecrated for him in the ordeals of war or in the imaginations of Barrès and Anna de Noailles, at a time when political France was moving in a direction of which he totally disapproved. In 1936, between two pamphlets, the poet wrote *Le Dit du sourd et muet qui fut miraculé en l'an de grâce 1266* ('The tale of the deaf-mute who was miraculously cured in 1266'), a sort of miracle story in old French which made philologists wince. In 1933 he had begun a study of the French language, *Enfantosmé ou La farce des philologastres* ('Enfantosmé or the farce of the philologizers'), which he promised would be flavoured with examples '*moult judicieux et plaisants*'. D'Annunzio did not, thank heaven, persevere in this deplorable 'olde worlde' style, imitated from Balzac's *Contes drolatiques*. Meanwhile, his links with Fascism won him admirers from the French Right. Pierre Pascal, a fervent disciple of Maurras, often stayed at the Vittoriale, as did a teacher from the university of Poitiers who wrote a study entitled *D'Annunzio, saint Jean Baptiste du fascisme* ('D'Annunzio, St. John the Baptist of Fascism'). But such gestures were of hardly more significance than the palms laid on the tomb of a hero.

A DECREPIT PRIAPUS

During these last fifteen years of his life, d'Annunzio was no longer a Don Juan, but merely a prey to a senile erotomania which sometimes, in a few last efforts to re-create the 'inimitable life', managed to pass for passion, but which more often than not showed itself in fleeting fancies and in those bizarre or even disgusting pleasures which jaded voluptuaries need to revive their senses. Although there is no point in trying to establish, as is the tradition in Italy, whether or not d'Annunzio was a coprophile, this admission to Donna Maria, who had come to spend a few days with the poet, says enough about his habits: 'I am a monster', he said to his wife. However, once these horrors were over, the way was clear for poetry. On 2 February 1925 he noted: 'After a succession of orgies, days and nights of pleasure, of carnal oblivion, I am undergoing a kind of convalescence. The germs of my spirit penetrate the thick flesh like the young shoots of a timid spring. Amid my works of art, the jewelled peacocks and the chased silver, the process of the imagination diminishes. The fresh bloom enhances the value of a work of art . . . The coming of spring. The safeguard of the spirit, the image of my life cannot be changed. The solidity of my carved effigy . . .' D'Annunzio was trying to reassure himself; he sought to console himself again, in a passage a little farther on, just before an extremely morbid meditation on fading flowers: 'The weakness of the flesh corrupted by abuse, exposed to melancholy by the scents of flowers.' He was reverting to the style of his youth; this line might have been taken from Georges Rodenbach or Albert Samain.

The entire life of the Vittoriale revolved round the pleasures of the master, who was served by the comely 'Poor Clares', immediately answerable to Aelis but supervised by Luisa Bàccara, a situation that caused endless friction between the two women. However, these servant-girls were only rarely the objects of the poet's attentions. People were sent into the villages, and even to Venice or Milan, to look for women whose novelty would stimulate his fancy. A whole network of procuresses and policemen lived off this traffic. The old man entered into this sexual game just as he had entered into the political game, without illusions and finding, perhaps, greater satisfaction in the contempt which these proceedings inspired in him than in their accomplishment. These prostitutes had to go through all the different stages of seduction that the master devised for his society women: tea in semi-darkness, flirting on the cushions, elevated conversation until the dawn and finally, at the end of their tether, practising their art to draw from the old man cries of pleasure that shook the whole house. These women were hardly ever kept for more than a day or two; they would leave handsomely rewarded, their arms full of flowers and books with dedications evoking the youth which they had momentarily revived.

There were also a number of genuinely passionate affairs, with women who remained shut up with the poet for weeks on end without seeing daylight. One of these was the very beautiful actress Elena Sangro. There was a Milanese countess and the widow of a Spanish journalist, Consuelo Gomez Carillo, who later married Saint-Exupéry: 'born of a ferocious Mexican tribe, with her wolf's teeth, she puts all my precious objects in jeopardy'. There was a young Englishwoman and the lady-companion of a Frenchwoman, Mme. d'Espagne, who owned a villa at Gardone. This woman inspired such keen feelings in the poet that he offered her a villa in the park and masses of dresses and jewellery; but La Bàccara took alarm and the girl was sent back to France. The last two favourites were a girl from the neighbouring village whom he nicknamed 'the Venus of Cargnacco', and who inspired a few fine phrases, and the woman whom he called 'Sthènele', 'Manah', 'Maya', 'Tormentilla', but mostly 'Titti', the recipient of letters of which Signor Gatti has written: 'One is stupefied by the contrast between the audacity of the propositions and the trembling handwriting.' These women, some of whom were charming, others mad, and some simply adventuresses, contributed nothing to his literary output, which had ceased a long time since; they occasionally provided a pretext for bitter thoughts: 'With what savage lust, what perverted pleasure, what impure imaginings have I fed myself during these recent times? How has my body retained no trace of them, like a vessel that has been washed and washed again so that it preserves neither the colour of a wine, nor the scent of an oil, nor the sweetness of an elixir?'

Of more interest than these adventures were a number of

pederastic experiences with which d'Annunzio satisfied an inclination that had long been repressed and then, during the war, kept secret or hidden under the mask of comradeship. That the man who had written such fine pages on the Greek statues and the nudes of Michelangelo should have been susceptible to the beauty of boys is in no way surprising, but only once did d'Annunzio refer in his writings to the agitation aroused in him by such beauty: 'I had not seen a forge in action for a long time. A virgin stupor was born within me, like a primitive spirit. The iron became red and twisted, resisting and giving off sparks. I watched the one who seized it with the tongs, holding it firmly and taming it. It was a young boy with long hair and covered with soot. The coloured sweat stuck to his body like blood. The whites of the eyes drew me, like those of a wild beast in a menagerie. He struck me like a thunderbolt. I turned away and left, pulling Nerissa by the hand' (*Libro segreto*).

The Comandante had yielded to temptations of this kind in Fiume and then in Venice. It was in Venice that a M. Paul L. met him in the company of a handsome sailor. 'Ah! Beauty!' d'Annunzio commented; 'I like to caress, but nothing more . . .' The sailor, whom M. Paul L. happened to meet on another occasion, was less discreet.

Like the seraglio at Constantinople, the seraglio at Gardone had its page-boys as well as its dancing-girls. While the study and the bedroom are cluttered with female images, strewn over every article of furniture, in the rest of the house most of the drawings, bronzes and reproductions are of young men, not to mention the casts with gilded lips and pearls, for which Maroni had been responsible but which the master tolerated. The suspicions aroused in the mind of even the least prejudiced visitor to the Vittoriale are confirmed by the reports of a man whose memory of his former good looks and success on the stage has not, as so often happens, become distorted or embittered over the years. The person in question, who came to the Vittoriale as a youth in 1924, the apprentice to a stage-designer who had been commissioned to produce a play in the original open-air theatre, tells us that d'An-

nunzio, who was extremely short-sighted, was at first attracted by
his voice and attached himself to him so that, like a page-boy, he
could guide the poet round the gardens and tell him everything he
saw. A friendship blossomed between the old man and the youth,
who was invited to stay at the Vittoriale on this and several sub-
sequent occasions. D'Annunzio confided to his companion everything that passed through his head: 'The visitors are tiresome, but,
like the flies in the evening, they are part of my life . . . Happiness is for imbeciles, for us perfection exists only in our imagination . . . The majority of people need only to excrete, nothing
else matters [to them].' On more than one occasion d'Annunzio
quoted this sentence from Nietzsche: 'A virtuous man (one could
say a "normal" man) is a being of an inferior species for the very
reason that he is not a "person", and that his merit consists of
conforming to a type of man that is fixed once and for all.' Yet
d'Annunzio did not encourage familiarity: 'Call me Poet and
not Master, but do not call me by my name, which is a tear in
my soul.' In the course of a walk during which he had talked at
length of the beauty of the Greek statues, the poet ordered his
companion to take off his clothes: 'But . . . the gardeners . . .'
—'The gardeners will not see what I see, only I matter. Look
me in the face. The sin is to look to see if we are being watched,
for then you associate yourself with the stupidity of the others.
Raise your arms . . . *che bellezza!!* [what beauty].'

When the young man decided to leave for Paris, the poet gave
him a mandragora which he had carved and also three letters.
One of the letters was for Maurice Rostand, another for
Émilienne d'Alençon, 'the greatest of sodomites and the greatest
of whores, so you can be sure of finding what you want.' D'Annunzio told the young man not to open the third envelope until
he was in Paris. It contained the then considerable sum of forty
thousand lire in new banknotes. Of course, this little adventure
gives no grounds for pronouncing d'Annunzio a pederast; but the
hero, like Jupiter, after so many Ledas, Danaës and Europas, had
his Ganymedes. 'He was not just a man who loved women, he
was a man who loved', Miss Nathalie Barney once said.

LAST LINES

These are the aberrations of a man for whom old age and oblivion were terrible ordeals, and it is perhaps unkind to think of them ironically. To one who sought to turn his thoughts away from these calamities and to forget that he looked like 'a tortoise without its shell', everything was justifiable, from the most vilified pleasures to the most extravagant building projects. It should be remembered also that the official bard, the worn-out polemicist, was still capable, when left alone with himself, of writing a few more fine pages between sexual crises or between doses of cocaine. These pages, together with a great many passages copied from the notebooks, were published in 1935 in a bizarre book made up of bits and pieces and entitled *Cento e Cento e Cento e Cento Pagine del Libro segreto di Gabriele d'Annunzio tentato di morire* ('Hundreds . . . of Pages of the Secret Book of Gabriele d'Annunzio Tempted by Death'). This work may not be on the level of Montaigne's *Essais*, which d'Annunzio knew well, but a similarly desultory manner is to be found in the meditations and the quotations. It is not directly comparable with the *Memoirs* of Casanova, but the memory of a night with La Casati, a kiss stolen in a museum in Florence at the age of sixteen, or the skin of Elena Sangro, could still set the old man dreaming. Nor is it comparable with the *Mémorial de sainte-Hélène*, but how beautiful are the insights into past greatness and power. The *Libro segreto*, which we have so frequently quoted, is superior both to *La Contemplazione della Morte* and to the *Notturno*, to which it forms a sequel. As in the other two books, the best passages are meditations on death and the vanity of glory, by a man who had had everything: 'I no longer accept anything that comes from outside. I can no longer tolerate anything foreign. I do not believe that anybody or anything is capable of enriching my life.'— 'I am like a shadow across the bronze door, neither living nor dead, incapable of destiny, neither earthly nor subterranean, between the days which are to come and those which have been. Everything lives and everything perishes through form.' The book ends with four lines of verse written in 1902: 'The whole of life is unchanging. Melancholy has but one face. The summit of all thought is folly. And love is inseparable from treachery.' This is the disenchantment of an ascetic raised in the mould of Christianity, but who, despite little comedies with neighbouring monks, was to remain faithful to his pagan ideal: 'It is better to believe in the body than in the soul, in the limits of the body than in the excesses of the soul. Too often the soul is merely a lie of the flesh.'

With all its contradictions, its moments of enthusiasm and of disgust, its childishness and its superstitions, this book gives the most complete picture of d'Annunzio at the different stages of his life, for many of the 'hundreds' of pages date from the years in Florence and even Naples. It was ill received. The Church again showed its indignation and the critics were not interested, finding the book indecent and outmoded; it was bought only by scandal-seekers.

During these latter years, d'Annunzio dreamed of success in another art-form, the cinema. He owed it to himself, he would say, 'to lead the seventh art, this mysterious mode of illuminating the depths of human life, to a greater strength'. He conceived a number of vague projects, the *Metamorphoses* of Ovid, a life of Marco Polo, a heroic St. Francis of Assisi fighting at Damietta, but never embarked on a single scenario. An Hungarian actress who intended to play La Duse in a film of *Il Fuoco* was indignantly shown the door: 'Your scenario is a tissue of lies, calumnies and sadistic obscenities, "ô *Marquise de Sade embêtie et imprudente*" ["stupid and rash Marquise de Sade"], disguised as St. Elizabeth of the lepers!'

In his constant preoccupation with death, d'Annunzio became increasingly absorbed with spiritualism. Maroni, a passionate devotee of the world beyond, put him in contact with La Duse, 'the gentle dead one', who was supposed to come to visit him at night. 'Aelis' Mazoyer was to recall the gloomy winter evenings in the music room where, in the candle-light, La Bàccara, her sister, the poet and herself would put questions to an incoherent pedestal-table. This charming woman, utterly without pretensions, was very close to the poet in this final stage of his life. When sanctions were imposed against Italy, he would pour forth to her his hatred of Léon Blum, in earlier days an enthusiastic and perceptive critic of his works and a great friend of Mme. Romain Rolland. The *Message to enslaved France* exhausted d'Annunzio (Mussolini, in reply to the 'Carnival Caesar' gibe, had called France the 'bastard sister'). Aelis could not help being amused by the poet's visits to a neighbouring monastery and by the air of piety, if not contrition, with which he received the priests to whom the death-struggle of a famous sinner presented an irresistible challenge. Yet on more than one occasion he asked her to make the sign of the cross on his forehead. Nothing could banish the idea of a death without hope; after a séance, d'Annunzio declared: 'The *néant!* It is the *néant* [nothingness] that draws me. How much more awesome than *nulla* or *niente* is this French word.' In a letter to a friend he quoted the words of St. Catherine of Siena: '*Muoio di non morire*' ('I am dying of not dying').

D'Annunzio had always regarded March as a sinister month; in anguish he awaited the arrival of March 1938. On the 'Barbanera', a popular calendar that predicted the weather and important events, and which he always kept close at hand, he had underlined: '1 March, death of a famous man'. On the evening of 1 March, as he was about to go down to the dining-room from his study, he had an attack of dizziness; he asked for an injection and died of a stroke a minute later. Maroni took matters in hand immediately, sending Luisa Bàccara away, informing the authorities and the family, and having the body moved into the lying-in-state room, between the casts of Michelangelo's slaves. The telephonist in Gardone who transmitted Rizzo's message to the Palazzo Venezia heard a voice exclaim: 'At last!' Mussolini did not waste a moment; he arrived by car with Ciano in the middle of the following night. After devoting an appropriate time to meditation, he asked to be shown to the archives, where he stayed the rest of the night. With his infallible sense of the theatrical, the dictator ordered that the vigil over the poet's body be held in torchlight aboard the *Puglia*. He remained until the day of the funeral, leading the mourners beside the Princess of Monte-Nevoso. People had come from all over Italy—the legionaries of Fiume, innumerable admirers and veiled women carrying armfuls of flowers. Luisa Bàccara, in the back row of mourners, stumbled and was helped to her feet by one of the men who had plotted to murder her in Fiume. No one had come from France. Maurice Rostand had asked Monzie, the minister of education, to send an official delegation, but in vain. The body was laid in a temporary chapel until the tomb was completed. That evening, when Aelis had fallen asleep, worn out and feeling that her life also was finished, her master appeared to her and said: 'There is nothing! There was nothing!'

GHOSTS

That d'Annunzio should have 'appeared' from time to time at the Vittoriale after his death is hardly surprising; the magician had created too powerful an impact, had succeeded too well in building up the atmosphere of a necropolis, not to manifest himself to anyone endowed with a little imagination. The architect Maroni, who became the keeper of the Vittoriale, induced these visitations by playing the organ and burning incense. There is a book in which the poet's 'messages' are recorded, but they are of little interest. Did d'Annunzio appear to Mussolini when the dictator came to see Clara Petacci at the Vittoriale, in the autumn of 1943, at the time of the short-lived Republic of Salo when the Fascists regrouped themselves round Lake Garda? The Germans had assigned the villa to the Duce's mistress, who took up residence in the public rooms (the private apartments were never touched). It was here that she received the brief visits of her harassed lover, and then was subjected to a terrifying scene by Donna Rachele. Clara Petacci left the Vittoriale a month later, to be executed in Milan.

The Vittoriale, with its awe-inspiring and yet stifling atmosphere, the trees that have grown too high and the stones which retain the dampness of the hillside, might almost serve as a setting for an exotic *Huis clos* in which the poet could be confronted, one by one, with the women who loved him. Without indulging in such a sombre fantasy, one cannot help thinking, when one sees the countless photographs that clutter the tables, of the fate of the women who, whether for a year or for only a few days, lived the 'inimitable life'. Was it from weakness or kindness that the poet took pleasure in maintaining nostalgic contact with the women he had abandoned? Once the danger of reconciliation had been averted, he led his victims to believe that he had suffered more than they, and that he cherished the exquisite memory of the wounds they had inflicted. To all of them he would send, from time to time, a little certificate of immortality, even to his very first victim, Giselda Zucconi, who lived for a long period in Florence in her family's villa, after marrying an obscure art teacher; all her life 'Elda', who died in a rest-home in 1942, never lost the faraway look of one who has gazed at the sun.

No one was better able than Donna Maria di Gallese, Princess of Monte-Nevoso, to give feeling to such a look, too sensitive to be wasted on a trivial world. Donna Maria died only in 1954, at the age of eighty-nine, and was buried beneath a terrace of the Vittoriale, rather like a faithful dog. Every year since the poet's death she had spent a few weeks in one of the villas on the estate, *La Mirabella*, which Mussolini had placed at her disposal. The Italian government continued to pay her the allowance which she had secured from her husband, not without some difficulty, a few years before his death. But on the collapse of Fascism this pension was so severely curtailed that Donna Maria was compelled to sell the finest pieces of furniture in her apartment in Paris. The death of her second and favourite son, Veniero, and the dispersal of her circle of faithful aesthctes cast an even greater gloom over her last years. To the end of her life the princess kept her elegant figure, her melancholy tone and a certain disillusioned irony, though she had been the first to believe in the d'Annunzian legend.

Barbara Leoni died in poverty after the last war. The widow of an Austrian painter named Fuchs, whom she had married two years after the break with d'Annunzio, Barbara lived in Rome surrounded by a coterie of poetry-lovers. She had been obliged to sell d'Annunzio's letters, most of which are unprintable. So that Barbarella's remains should not be laid in a pauper's grave, a group of d'Annunzian enthusiasts clubbed together to buy a plot in a cemetery in Rome.

According to André Germain, Maria Gravina ended her days running a second-rate boarding-house in Monte Carlo, after a turbulent life of court cases and love-affairs. Her daughter Renata, who was quite unlike her, the only one of his children whom the poet had ever loved, never laid claim to this paternity, marrying a naval officer. The son Dante-Gabriele, on the other hand, made the most of his father's name in the course of an undistinguished theatrical career.

Eleonora Duse was truly mourned, as has already been seen; her effigies always remained at the poet's side, honoured with the devotion which d'Annunzio owed to the greatest saint of his church. The memory of her suffering has helped to preserve the memory of her genius. Her devotees still visit her house at Asolo, now a museum, in the hills above Venice.

The most distinguished *grande dame* among the poet's mistresses knew, when she had been abandoned, that only one Master was worthy of her. In her distress the Marchesa Rudinì had gone to Lourdes in 1910, out of curiosity; there she had a mystical experience so shattering that she became a Carmelite nun shortly afterwards, leaving the two sons born during the years of her passion. She died as Mother Superior of a convent in Savoy, after founding three other communities. Merciless towards herself, she was adored by the nuns: 'The woman who had been Nike, and who now was only Mother Mary of Jesus, saw in its terrible nakedness, with its virtues and its frailties, the soul whose mirages she had once admired, which she now knew in its tragic reality, and for which, with a supreme effort, she implored God . . .' (André Germain).

The Countess Mancini ended her days unobtrusively, as one

might have expected of this charming person. It was soon realized that she was not mad, but had simply suffered terrible periods of depression; her persecutors, her husband and father, died quite suddenly, leaving her a modest fortune, and she was able to devote herself to the poet's memory. Up to the last war she was often seen, quietly dressed, attending the literary lectures at the Liceo in Florence.

Mme. de Goloubeff had a very different end. The Russian revolution, which deprived her of resources, had left her in a difficult position. Unlike Mancini, she was almost mad, though she was never shut away; however, in the arms of various ladies she found temporary consolation for being deserted by d'Annunzio. To preserve her 'Caucasian Diana' appearance, she took up riding and became as slim as a jockey; but one day she had a terrible fall which disfigured her. She managed to keep the kennels at the *Dame Rose* and two greyhounds until 1932. Thereafter, she found herself destitute in the most miserable of suburbs, living in the Hôtel de la Gare at Meudon, where she died in November 1941. The poet Pierre Pascal helped to support her and published her correspondence; the copies of these letters (the originals had been sold long since) were bound in a sort of studded missal-cover, with the title *Le Livre d'amour*. D'Annunzio had sent her small sums from time to time, but had firmly forbidden her access to the Vittoriale.

The Marchesa Casati would have been horrified at the thought of being an object of pity, even when she too found herself plunged into poverty. A disturbing figure, extravagant to the very last penny extracted from the last of her creditors, Luisa Casati survived in London until 1951, a ghostly echo of the d'Annunzian heroine. In 1936, disguised as Cagliostro for a Magicians' Ball, she tempted the devil one last time, but a dreadful storm scattered the guests and even the hostess had to flee from her Palais Rose, at Le Vésinet. The marchesa was a link between the Medusa-woman of the Decadents and the 'vamp' of the silent films; fifty or more artists, from Boldini to Van Dongen, painted the face of 'Corè'.

Romaine Brooks cannot be placed among the victims; she was much too sensible. The artist died only a year ago, having spent the latter part of her life in Nice, in chosen solitude and not even seeing Miss Nathalie Barney, who had counted for much more than d'Annunzio in her life. In a villa at Fiesole, Romaine Brooks had for many years practised the rites of an austere aestheticism far removed from the flamboyant taste of Casati. She spoke of the poet with a detachment tinged with compassion: 'Romaine is the only one who ever found that he had a sense of humour', Miss Barney has said.

Among the actresses of the Parisian period, the tall and elegant figure of Ida Rubinstein towers above the rest; with an unlimited expenditure of energy, if not of personal fortune, she continued to produce poetic dramas, but, alas, Gide and Valéry were not as rewarding as d'Annunzio. She died shortly after the war, in her hotel on the Place des États-Unis. Isadora Duncan suffered her well-known fate: her death in a fast car, strangled by a silk scarf, is indeed worthy of *Forse che sì forse che no*. Cécile Sorel, a little too d'Annunzian in her politics, found in the pomp of religion the consolations which the theatre had refused her. Of the two ladies of Chantilly, Mme. Boulenger is now dead, but Mme. Hubin, 'Nontivoglio', still lives in a beautiful house on the fringe of the park. The Duchess de Gramont, a widow at thirty, married a great-grandson of Victor Hugo, managed a picture gallery in New York, and now lives in Aix-en-Provence. Mme. Romain Rolland, after marrying the pianist Alfred Cortot, who made her very unhappy, died in 1946. Mme. Simone, on the other hand, far from fading into the shadows, still recalls, with a verve almost devoid of tenderness, the great man who was one of the many that she charmed. The Duchess of Aosta, with a morganatic husband thirty years younger than herself, watched proudly from her palace in Naples as the war passed and the monarchy vanished.

In Venice there lives a woman who was loved by d'Annunzio during the first war, and who is today regarded with a kind of baffled respect; she occupies a floor of the Morosini palace, furnished with reliquaries and embroidered hangings, and questions the future by every means at her disposal; each evening she goes up to the *altana* to hail the setting sun, as it gilds the lagoon, with these words: '*Ciao Veronese*'. In a more forbidding palace lived Mme. Olga Lévy, whose beautiful dark eyes still held sublime and incommunicable images even in her last years. Luisa Bàccara is still living, alone and impenetrable, and has never, in spite of hard times, sold a single letter or souvenir. One is reminded of the story that Henry James set in Venice, *The Aspern Papers*, and one wonders if, like James's hero, some young writer will arrive one day to force the secrets from the poet's last companion. It is said that at Viareggio, in winter, a very thin woman with grey veils fluttering in the wind can be seen wandering along the beach, thinking of the poet who is supposed to have spent a week of love with her there. And in Capri, some twelve years ago, a princess dressed in black and surrounded by a dubious court used to talk of d'Annunzio in language reminiscent of Tacitus describing the old age of Tiberius. But whoever approached these heroines soon realized that they were echoing a myth rather than recalling their own past experience. Certain places also smack of d'Annunzio, so that even today one can glimpse the kind of atmosphere that the poet loved. In France, the visitor will still find two types of dwelling of which the poet was especially fond: one bordering the park at Chantilly, where 'Nontivoglio' still lives; the other at Caresse in Béarn, with gardens which Mme. Combes-Saint-Macary arranged in imitation of the Vittoriale, and with an eminently d'Annunzian name, *Le Bijou*.

It would be indiscreet, and in any case futile, to attempt to trace d'Annunzio's illegitimate descendants; in such matters one can never be too cautious. There is, nonetheless, good reason to believe that the poet's blood flows in the veins of two persons who bear historic names. None of his three sons achieved anything out of the ordinary. The eldest died without posterity, and so there is no longer a Prince of Monte-Nevoso. The second, Veniero, enjoyed a measure of success in the cinema and left a fairly bad reputation behind him. The third, Gabriellino, was an agent for

Fiat cars in the United States. The sons inherited very little, as the Vittoriale Foundation included lands, works of art and author's royalties. The d'Annunzio family, moreover, behaved with discretion, showing no inclination to assume greater prominence after the death of its head than it had enjoyed during his lifetime.

It is not only the shades of his mistresses who haunt the Vittoriale. Mussolini and his spies, the comrades of Fiume, still bitter as they gather round the unfinished mausoleum, the witnesses of the mysterious accident, the admirers who had to leave without seeing the master and those who were disappointed at seeing him in his troubled old age, all lie in wait for the magician who was caught in his own snares, a prisoner of the setting which he had created to protect his dreams from the outside world. There is another ghost, one impatient to see reappear the glory which he so quickly betrayed: like a hyena attacking this mighty corpse, Malaparte, who in some respects recalls the more disagreeable traits of our hero, took the liberty of writing, eight days after the poet's death, that he was the greatest *cafone* (a word suggesting both 'charlatan' and 'boor') in the whole of Italian literature. Better minds, writers such as Ungaretti, Benedetto Croce and, with less ill humour, Mario Praz, have said that d'Annunzio's glory was merely a fashion. Indeed, it is thanks to the fashion for decadent oddities and aristocratic extravagances that the glory of d'Annunzio is beginning to shine again for all who are bored by a mediocre democracy and by the conformism born of prosperity. If the May 1969 number of American *Vogue* ever reached the shades of the Vittoriale, the ghost of the Comandante must have felt a little warmer. How d'Annunzian are the Roman or Tuscan beauties photographed in eccentric but always luxurious garments! And how fascinating is the article by Alberto Arbosino, who explains why the great ladies of Italy still live like the poet's heroines, in defiance of the wave of vulgarity which has been raised by the prosperity of the multitude. For all who have a taste for the luxurious and the bizarre, d'Annunzio, who belonged to the same world as these great ladies, will always remain a *chic* hero, a *chic* genius—not a very serious thought, perhaps, but more agreeable than the judgement of E. M. Forster: 'poet, hero and cad'. (There was a last example of the close association of the bizarre with the sublime in d'Annunzio's life when in 1956 Jean Cocteau caused the Italian Radio acute embarrassment by stating in the middle of a glowing account of his late friend: 'Every day I go to talk about him with the boys in the Piazza di Spagna'; had Cocteau forgotten that the 'boys' were male prostitutes?)

Although Italy has no square, avenue or monument (apart from the Vittoriale) named after its greatest modern writer, the poet's centenary was celebrated with a certain splendour. Perhaps the most moving tribute to be found among the faded wreaths heaped on the tombstone of the Vittoriale is that left by a writer who also attained great fame and who is much less likely to return to favour, a man who adored and despised d'Annunzio in turn, Romain Rolland: 'He was, in the dull, vapid Italy of the closing nineteenth century, an unforgettable apparition. He reawakened the land of Beauty.'

Bibliography
Index

Bibliography

Antongini, Tom, *Vita segreta di Gabriele d'Annunzio.*
————, *Quaranta anni con d'Annunzio.*
Barrès, M., *Mes cahiers.*
Barzini, L., *The Italians.*
Bedarida, *Mélanges offerts à* . . .
Bini, W., *La poetica dell' decadentismo.*
Borghese, G. A., *Gabriele d'Annunzio.*
Boulenger, M., *Écrit le soir.*
Bourget, P., *Cosmopolis.*
————, *Sensations d'Italie.*
Bruers, A., *Nuovi saggi dannunziani.*
Carraccio, *D'Annunzio drammaturgo.*
Cimmini, *Poesia e poetica in Gabriele d'Annunzio.*
Colette, *L'Étoile Vesper.*
D'Annunzio e Venezia (Catalogue, Exhibition 1963).
Dietschy, M., *Le Cas d'André Suarès.*
Doderet, A., *Vingt ans d'amitié.*
Dollot, R., *D'Annunzio et Valéry.*
Falqui, E., *Bibliografia dannunziana.*
Fatini, G., *Il Cigno e la Cicogna.*
Faure, G., *Au pays de d'Annunzio.*
Gatti, G., *Le donne nella vita e nell'arte di Gabriele d'Annunzio.*
————, *Vita di Gabriele d'Annunzio.*
Germain, A., *Vie amoureuse de d'Annunzio.*
————, *La Bourgeoisie qui brûle.*
Gide, A., *Cahiers.*
Gramont, E. de, *Souvenirs.*
Guabello, M., *Raccolta dannunziana.*
Jullian, P., *Prince of Aesthetes.*
————, *Dreamers of Decadence.*
Leblanc, Georgette, *D'Annunzio au Vittoriale.*
Lefèvre, Raymonde, *Un prince de l'esprit.*
Le Lièvre, *Théâtre italien en France.*
Mariano, E., *Itinerario poetico di Gabriele d'Annunzio.*

————, *Il Vittoriale degli Italiani*.
Mazoyer, Amélie, *Avec d'Annunzio–Carrefour* 1950.
Mazzarotto, B., *Arti figurative nell' arte di d'Annunzio*.
Michelis, *D'Annunzio a Contraggenio*.
Mirandolh, *D'Annunzio e Proust*.
Montera, P. de, *Gabriele d'Annunzio*.
Montesquiou, R. de, *Les Pas effacés*.
Montherlant, H. de, *Carnets*.
Nicolson, Harold, *Some People*.
Ojctti, U., *D'Annunzio Maestro e Soldato*.
Orsay, Countess d', *Ce que je peux écrire*.
Pascal, P., *Le Livre secret*.
Passerini, G. L., *Il vocabolario dannunziano*.
Pecci, G., *D'Annunzio e il Mistero*.
Pierrefeux, G. de, *Le Surhomme de la Côte d'Argent*.
Praz, Mario, *The Romantic Agony*.
Pringue, G.-L., *Trente ans de dîners en ville*.
Quaderni dannunziani, 20 volumes.
Quinton, R., *Maximes sur la guerre*.
Régnier, H. de, *L'Altana*.
Rhodes, A., *The Poet as Superman*.
Rostand, M., *Souvenirs*.
Sermonetta, Duchess di, *Memories*.
Signorelli, O., *Eleonora Duse*.
Simone, Mme., *Sous de nouveaux soleils*.
Sitwell, Osbert, *Noble Essences*.
Sodini, A., *Ariel armato*.
Sommaruga, A., *Cronaca Bizantina*.
Sorel, C., *Les Belles Heures de ma vie*.
Suarès, A., *Présences* 1925.
Tosi, Guy, *Lettres à Hérelle*.
————, *D'Annunzio et la France au début de la guerre*.
————, *D'Annunzio et Anna de Noailles*.
————, *D'Annunzio et Romain Rolland*.
————, *D'Annunzio et Anatole France*.
————, *D'Annunzio en Grèce*.
————, *D'Annunzio et la société florentine*.
————, *D'Annunzio et Debussy*.
————, *Barrès regarde d'Annunzio*.
Valeri, N., *D'Annunzio davanti il Fascismo*.
Vassili, Count, *La Société de Rome*.
Winwar, F., *Wingless Victory*.
Zola, E., *Rome*.

Index